OOPS!

TALES

FROM A

SEXPERT

To Catherine,

With my best wishes, and
with thanks for positive energy,

Vivian Peters V.

10/18/18

OOPS! TALES FROM A SEXPERT
BY VIVIAN PETERS

DEDICATION

With deepest gratitude, this book is dedicated to the six people who welcomed me into the world on the day I was born: my grandmother, my parents, and my three sisters. They loved me; they were prepared. From day one, I felt treasured. Later, I realized how important that was. It gave me a solid foundation on which I could build a full life. That realization is what inspires me to work towards a world in which all parents are prepared to parent and all babies are wanted and loved.

And to Paul, my husband, who still leaves me feeling wanted and loved every day.

And it is dedicated to you, the reader, and to the hope that the time you spend with this book will help lead us to a day when *every* baby conceived in this world will be wanted, loved, and nurtured at least as much as I was.

PRIVACY, AUTHENTICITY AND RESPONSIBILITY

When people request education and medical services related to sexuality and reproductive health, it is critical that their identity and experiences are kept private. The author's goal in writing about people who confided in her is to reach the general public while simultaneously protecting the privacy of the individuals involved. She believes that there is a lot of misinformation and misunderstanding about the vital issues raised in this book and that having accurate information presented in an accessible format benefits everyone: the people she served and society in general.

Thus, all the stories in this book are originally based on true stories; nothing has been made up. But names have been changed, and many key identifying details that could connect an individual to their stories have been omitted. Also, details from peoples' lives, such as descriptions of their homes, towns, appearances, habits, personalities and relationships have been compiled and redistributed; they've been paired in new ways with the sole purpose of protecting individuals' identities. Similarly, the names of the towns, community organizations, and professionals (including the author) have been changed. And while all the stories are told in the first person, the story about Pam and Jesse in Father Knows Best??? *was actually experienced by a colleague, as were some of the* Snapshots.

The U.S. Department of Health and Human Services' Office of Population Affairs (OPA) oversees the Title X program. OPA funds a network of over 4,200 family planning centers;[1] the local Planned Parenthood affiliate that the author worked for was one of them. Yet this book solely reflects the experiences, views and opinions of the author, not those of any organization, supporter, funder, individual, or program.

Nothing in this book is intended as a substitute for the medical advice of physicians. The reader should consult a physician in matters relating to his/her health.

The views expressed in this book are solely those of the author and not those of Planned Parenthood.

Table of Contents

FOREWORD

Paul's hugs are always comforting, but that one was even more comforting than most. He just stood there, holding me, letting me cry; treasuring me. He didn't speak; he didn't need to. Amanda had called, and I was heartbroken. There was nothing he could say; I just needed to be held.

But more about Amanda later; this, dear reader, is not yet the time for the whole story, about why a busy professional who's pushing forty finds herself weeping over someone else's teenage daughter. For now, suffice it to say simply that I had invested years with her as a volunteer, that I loved her, and that the phone call and all that led up to it had everything to do with her sex life and my attempts to talk with her about it; my attempts to learn how to be helpful to a struggling teen.

And for now, I want you to know that it motivated me to change careers, to become an educator at my local Planned Parenthood, working with teens and adults in the northern tip of Appalachia, where I found myself a social misfit; where I wanted to serve.

I knew before I started that people in this community have basic assumptions about life that are completely different from my own. Assumptions about what it means to be a woman, a man, an adult. Attitudes about love, sexuality, contraception, and parenting. I was curious and *wanted* to know why they started having kids when they were so young, and why they had so many. I remember wishing that I could just knock on strangers' doors, sit down, have a cup of tea together and just chat about all that. To listen to them.

For fifteen years, I've been able to do exactly that: go into people's homes and schools and have these intimate conversations with them, to listen to the voices of people living in rural poverty. Many of them lack formal education and the skills needed to navigate the intricacies of the health care system. One by one, my clients have opened my eyes, helped me understand those puzzles a little more. One by one, they've shown me how differently they see and experience the world, how different their experiences and basic assumptions are from mine. And it's given me insight into the high unintended pregnancy rates in the U.S. today, which is something that haunts me, something I want to change.

Albert Einstein said that imagination is more important than knowledge. And he, I'm told, was a very wise man. Well, I hope Albert was right, because

I can imagine a lot. I read that around half of all pregnancies in the U.S. today are unplanned, but I can imagine that number dropping to almost zero. Why not? I invite you to imagine that with me: after all, Americans have access to birth control methods that are 99% effective. And I read that women in poverty, young women, women without formal education and women of color have much higher unintended birth rates than everyone else, despite the fact that those methods are supposed to be available to all of us.[2] And I wonder: why should that be? Sperm cells seek out egg cells to fertilize; the sperm don't know if we've got our PhD, they don't know our zip code, they don't see our skin color or our paychecks. So I can imagine all that changing; in my mind's eye, women of all races, ages, incomes, and education levels are equally successful in timing their pregnancies. And I can imagine the positive impact that would have on so many other social problems.

I imagine a little scene: all the teen girls who got pregnant in the U.S. each year get on a school bus, each along with the guy who got them pregnant. Just to go on a little picnic or something: it would take over twenty-eight thousand buses. Twenty-eight thousand: that's a lot of buses, and that isn't even making space on the bus for any of them to bring their babies. But I can *imagine* that number getting close to zero, too. I can *imagine* the benefits that would bring to our society.

So one of my hopes in writing this book is that simply sharing the experiences I've had will be helpful to other adults who find themselves in the sometimes uncomfortable, unfamiliar or unexpected role of mentoring a teen they love about sexuality, the way I struggled with Amanda when I was almost forty.

So please, dear reader, join me for some stories. Let's journey together. Hop in my car; drive with me along the beautiful country dirt roads, up the rolling hills, through the little hamlets, past the sparkling streams. Come into the homes and schools I visit and listen with me to the stories I've heard over the last fifteen years. I hope you'll weave these stories into your own life experience, bring your own wisdom to them; think about them, talk them over with your best friend, unravel the mysteries they reveal to *you*. And with me, please imagine a world in which people in poverty are as successful as everyone else in planning their families. And a world in which one of the adults in each of our teens' lives—the parents, the teachers, the doctors, the grandparents, aunts and uncles, the mentors—just one of them is effective in reaching each teen in time. Then maybe we'd need fewer buses to take those pregnant teens to a picnic, maybe a lot fewer.

And maybe if we all imagine that, we can make our vision a reality.

My Grandmother's Douche Bag

"In a gentle way you can shake the world."
—Mahatma Gandhi[3]

"Hi, my name is Vivian. I'm from Planned Parenthood. Have you ever heard of Planned Parenthood?"

"Oh yeah," Amy replied, looking like I had brought up something very annoying. "My mom's always bugging me to go there. She's *such* a pain."

"Oh, really? Do you know how come she wants you to go there?"

"Yeah, she thinks I need birth control," she said, rolling her eyes.

"Why do you think she wants you to get birth control?"

" 'Cuz she thinks I'm like immature. She acts like I'm a little kid. She doesn't realize I am growing up. She still thinks I'm like her baby. She's always buggin' me and it drives me nuts. She says if I got pregnant I couldn't handle raising a kid yet but she just doesn't see that I've grown up. She drives me nuts!"

It was easy for me to imagine why Amy's mom might have concerns. During the three minutes I had just spent walking with her from the main office of the high school to my office, I noticed that she flirted with every boy we passed. And even though the flirting was brief, each boy had responded and returned her gaze; each one seemed to walk a little taller, with a little more zip in his stride after the exchange with this pretty and confident girl. She had waited with the last three boys outside my door, enjoying their attention as long as she possibly could, until the bell rang, when she came in and flopped comfortably onto my beanbag chair. So I had sensed that she was popular, and then her rant about her mom made it even easier for me to relate to mom's reported concerns: what tenth grader is ready to raise a child? But I knew I was going to have to tread lightly if I was going to get anywhere with her.

"Do *you* think you could raise a kid yet?" I asked.

"Well," she replied slowly and more thoughtfully, "part of me does, and part of me doesn't."

"You sound split on this. This is important. I don't know you at all, but you clearly know yourself. Would you tell me about that conflict; what about the part of you that *is* ready to have a baby, what's that about?"

"I could love a baby," she fired back immediately.

Although the word "clueless" popped, uninvited, into my mind, I knew that wouldn't move anything forward, so I adopted a tone of objective curiosity instead.

"Wow," I said. "This is amazing to hear. We live in such a materialistic society; everybody always talks about what it takes to have a kid as far as stuff goes, all the stuff we need. Whenever I ask people about their desire to have a kid or not, they almost always start about money and jobs and houses and cars and stuff. And yet I believe the most fundamental thing all babies need is love. Here, when I asked you that question, your immediate first thought was that a baby needs love, and that you can provide that. If you don't mind me asking, just because I'm curious, how do you think it is that you've grown up in this society and yet maintained your focus on that?"

Sitting up taller, prouder, looking pleased that she had *finally* found an adult who respected the fact that she had something like adult insight, she eagerly told me that it was because of what she's seen with her aunt and her aunt's kids.

"She has three kids, but like, she's always dropping them off at our house for me and my mom to watch them. They miss her. They love her." She became increasingly exasperated and emphatic as she continued, "But they need more from her. They don't feel like she loves them the way she's just always dumping them off so she can go out to the bar and everything. I would never do that to my kid. I would be there for my kid!"

After she filled me in a little more, I sat back thoughtfully, and brought closure to that part of our conversation.

"You're only fifteen, but you've seen a lot. And you've really thought about what you've seen. And you're ready to apply it to your own adult life. Before we move on, I just have to say that I wish *every* baby born in this world was born to a mother who had said to herself: 'I am ready to love this baby. I've thought about what it takes, about the compromises it'll involve, and I'm ready to make those sacrifices and love a baby.' I have so much respect for the way that you've figured out how important it is for babies to feel loved."

I paused a bit before changing directions.

"So, you mentioned in the beginning that you're split on the whole "readiness" question. If you're so certain that you could love a baby, and that it's that love which is the most important thing, which part of you feels like you're *not* ready?"

Her reply was quite realistic. She's only in tenth grade; she hasn't graduated from high school or college. She went on describing very reasonable goals she'd like to reach: college education, a career, money saved, her own place to live, a partner who will be there for her and the kids, a license, a car, and independence from her mom in every way; living independently, financially independent, able to completely take care of herself. I gave her time and space and bits of prompting to examine each of these goals, to think each one through.

Then I asked, "Do you believe all the goals you just listed are goals you could ever reach?"

"Absolutely."

"So realistically, if you waited to reach all those goals, how long do you think that might take?"

She quickly did the arithmetic and concluded that by her mid or late twenties she'd be ready; she'd have accomplished most, if not all, of these goals. Around ten years.

"So in around ten years you'll be around twenty-five. You'd still have many years of fertility remaining, right?"

"Yeah."

"Listening to you, I can see why you're split on this. It sounds like on the one hand a baby needs love, and you're ready to provide that love *now*. But on the other hand, babies need all these other things that you *can't* provide now, but you're confident that you will be able to provide in a reasonable amount of time. So the way I see it, the question is: is there any way you could have it all? If you had a baby now, you wouldn't have all this other stuff. But what if you waited? It sounds like the big question is: if you waited, is this capacity you have now to love a baby something that you see as fleeting, something you'd lose by waiting to reach these other goals, or is it something that you feel you'll still have if you wait?"

"Oh! My! God! I will never lose that! No matter how old I am, I will love my baby!"

"Then how do you see the dilemma? What would be the advantage of having it now or waiting?"

"Actually, when I think about it like that, there's no benefit in having it now. I should definitely wait." She went on a little more, thinking it through while we chatted. Then she added, "You know what? I should really go on birth control. Can you make me an appointment?"

Before the end of the period, I had explained the parameters of my role as a Planned Parenthood educator working inside her school; that since I'm not a school employee, the school requires that I get parental consent to work with students on an ongoing basis, like they do with all outside agencies. And that I can only schedule medical appointments from school after obtaining parental consent, and that I can only meet with her during lunch or study halls. She agreed that I could ask her mom for consent to meet in school and she gladly signed the release allowing me to confirm the appointment date and time with her mom. "My mom's gonna be sooo happy!"

The bell rang; forty-three minutes had passed. She returned to the drama of the hallway; the same three boys were eagerly waiting for her outside my door, and together they walked down the hall to their next class, flirting all the way.

Clearly, she and her mom had been butting heads on this issue for some time. Forty-three minutes ago, she had entered my office thinking that her mom was an annoying adult for not seeing that she's "ready" to have a baby. Now, she was concerned that she couldn't get an appointment for birth control fast enough. I felt like her priorities had shifted 180 degrees in 43 minutes. All by simply taking her seriously, accepting her exactly where she was, having a positive regard for her right to set her own goals. Her mom had apparently been *telling* her that she's not ready to have a baby, but no adult had been *listening* to her, letting her examine what "being ready" means; letting her think out loud and hear herself.

Parents underestimate their influence in general, and often miss these opportunities to be a real support to their kids. There's a tendency to focus on "what to say" instead of "how to listen." Many parents could be much more effective if they learned to improve their listening and conversation skills, to help their teens learn to think these things through.

In the days that followed, Amy got her consent form signed, we scheduled her initial exam, and she selected a birth control method, obtained it, started using it, and openly discussed it with her mom. She graduated from high school without becoming pregnant.

I've often thought about how much her motivation changed during those forty-three minutes, and how the foundation for her subsequent behavior regarding correct birth control use was established in that time. I think about how many teens in the U.S. have a daily study hall, and I wonder how many times something this pivotal transpires during that time.

> **TIP FOR PARENTS**
>
> **SHIFT THE FOCUS FROM "WHAT SHOULD I SAY?" TO "HOW SHOULD I LISTEN?"**

Ashley's face appeared in my doorway, looking panicked and completely unconcerned about interrupting the notes I was frantically trying to write before my next student arrived; three minutes for everyone to get to their next class. The tone of her voice matched the look of urgency on her face.

"Oh my God, Vee, I'm *so* glad you're here! I went to take my pill this morning and I went in my drawer and *there weren't any there!* What do I do?" She didn't have a study hall that day, so we couldn't have the meeting

I really wanted, the one where we discuss planning ahead, but somehow, I knew I'd find a way to help, and come back to the "plan ahead" lesson some other time.

After she left, I kept thinking about her *tone*. She sounded shocked, disappointed, and a bit angry; almost outraged that there were no pills in her drawer. But she had taken the last one yesterday, and she had been given three packs. So how did she *expect* more to appear? It was as if she blamed the pills, not herself, for their absence. As an adult, she left me bewildered. As an adult, I know that when prescriptions are running low, a person has to arrange for more before they run out.

"What was she thinking?" I wondered, exasperated. "That they'd magically appear? That there's some kind of a "pill fairy" that notices when you swallow the last one, and appears in the night replacing the empty pack with a full one? How do these teens *think?*" I asked myself, rhetorically.

And then I realized: it's not a rhetorical question. It's a real one. They think—she thinks—like we all do: based on our life experience. The problem, I surmised, is that in her world, today, there *is* a fairy. The fairy who watches when the last gulp of milk is swallowed, the last blob of toothpaste is squeezed from the tube, and the last bowl of cereal is poured from the box. There *is* a fairy that magically replaces it. The next day, without thought, Ashley goes through the motions; eating the cereal, brushing the teeth, not so much without being grateful for the fairy, more not realizing that the fairy exists. Ashley's fairy is probably mom. Mom probably notices all that stuff. Those secret replacements happen while Ashley is doing other things: going to school, visiting friends; living her life.

That silent, invisible process of monitoring inventory of essential supplies and replacing them when necessary is so important to all functional households, yet still so undetected by the teen mind. At least by Ashley's. If Ashley had chosen to *involve* her mom in her decision to go on the pill, mom could have helped; like so many moms I've worked with, she would have kept track of when they were running low and either had Ashley call for an appointment or called herself and then told Ashley to go. Mom would have initiated it. Mom would have helped. Mom would have been "The Fairy." Like so many teens that do choose to access contraceptives without involving a mom, Ashley hadn't yet thought about all those steps she'd need to take.

I had been working so hard with her to involve her mom in her pill use; she had still refused. We needed mom now; it's so important for a teen that's trying to learn all that to have a caring adult in their everyday life. I was so glad to be there that day for Ashley. But it left me wondering, as I've wondered so many times, about all the teens that don't have either a mom in their home, or me in their school, or someone to help them learn those skills. Girls like Ashley who don't have a mom or a Vivian or some other "Pill Fairy" to help them learn to manage all these details often get pregnant. Is that really the best we can do?

When we look at the subject of teen pregnancy, when we read the statistics and the numbers, there's one thing that's rarely mentioned; when those hundreds of thousands of girls get pregnant each year, they get pregnant one at a time. One by one, there's a girl. One by one, there's an egg. One by one, there's a story, there's sex; there's a mistake.

And one by one, there's an adult who could care about her, who could reach out to her, who could support her through the complex process of navigating her sexuality, her relationships, her ability to access and effectively utilize the medical establishment. Day by day, she's going through her life, and if someone—one person—reaches out a caring hand, more often than not she'll grab it.

"Mom, was I planned?" Beth asked her mother, looking at her with the most intense, attentive expression. I felt a bit unsettled. I didn't know how mom would feel about being asked that question so suddenly and directly, and in front of me. And while I don't consider myself a "formal" person, the absence of the little rituals like mom and I introducing ourselves to each other first, and a little meet-and-greet chitchat did seem to be missing. And before hitting her with such a question, pausing to say, "Hi, Mom," and letting her put down the two large bags of groceries as she walked in the front door would have felt more appropriate to me.

But this wasn't about me. And I knew immediately that the absence of, "Hi, I'm Vivian, I'm from Planned Parenthood," really didn't matter. She knew who I was; she had phoned me, we had had a long talk. She had requested that I come over, and had warned me she might be a little late joining us; "I have to stop for groceries on the way home from work, but I'd love it if you'd meet with Beth alone first." And she knew her daughter; she knew the way a young teen mind works.

"Yes, absolutely, you were planned," her mom replied immediately, without hesitation, looking lovingly at her daughter. And she continued, "You were planned; I knew from the time I was five that I wanted you. I couldn't wait to grow up so I could have you. You were definitely planned."

She paused slightly, placing the grocery bags on the counter, and continued. "The only thing that you surprised me a little with was the timing. I had planned to have you a little later, when I was more ready to really raise you. You just came a little earlier than I had planned. But you were definitely planned."

"Oh," Beth replied, looking like she understood and accepted her mom's loving explanation, but also like she wanted to hear more. Mom didn't miss a beat.

"We made it work, but that's why I couldn't really always give you every-thing I'd have wanted to give you. That's why I wanted you to meet Vee to-day. Now. While you're really young. So that when you have your kids, you don't just plan them, but you learn to plan the timing, too. It'll make your life so much easier."

"We were just talking about that when you got here," I added. "About how some people think ahead and plan the timing of their pregnancies; about how it can be hard, but it can be done. About how it takes knowing yourself and also knowing all about your reproductive system, and about the resources in the community that are there for you."

"Yeah, Beth, it's so important," mom said. "I didn't know about Planned Parenthood until after I had you. Nobody talked to me about this stuff when I was growing up. Nobody told me about Planned Parenthood and birth control and about setting goals and stuff. It can just make life so much easier if you wait, if you don't start a family while you're in school, while you're a teenager."

It was nice to hear the caring, affirming, helpful tone in mom's voice. And to hear the confidence with which she used so many of the words and phrases I had used with her on the phone. She had told me at the end of our conversation that it had been helpful, but it wasn't until I heard her say some of those same things herself that I understood her gratitude; it was such a contrast to how tongue-tied she had been at the beginning of the call, when she could barely articulate why she was calling. And it all sounded so appropriate; to hear a mom explaining the concept of family planning before the details of sex and contra-ception were even necessary. Beth was young; she didn't even have a boyfriend, but she had recently started menstruating and her mom really wanted Beth to navigate her way through her teen years without a baby in tow.

Many parents wait until their teens are sexually active, or close to it, to dis-cuss contraception. But dialogues like the one Beth's mom had can be so helpful setting the stage for future success.

Brenda had known that "some lady" was coming that day, and alt-hough we told her that I was an educator from Planned Parenthood, she didn't seem to give a hoot about where I was from or why I was there; all she paid attention to was the fact that her foster mom was allowing her to go for a walk, without any staff person. And without any of "those stupid little brats." A rare and welcomed treat; they keep twelve-year-olds on a pretty tight leash in foster homes. So she was delighted to get out.

"What did they tell you about who I am or why I'm here?" I asked her.

She shrugged. Not so much like she didn't remember, more like she didn't care. Finally she replied, "Cynthia told me about all these people I'd meet here. I don't remember which one you are." Cynthia was her caseworker from the local Department of Social Services (DSS).

"I'm Vivian, but you can call me Vee. I'm the educator from Planned Parenthood. Do you remember her saying anything about that?"

She looked confused. "You're the Parenthood one? Wait. I thought that's the one who talks about"—and here she interrupted herself, glanced around to make sure nobody else could hear, and whispered—"sex."

"Well, yes, that's one thing we can talk about"—but before I could finish my sentence, she looked at me, confused, and said—"That's YOU? But you're *old*. I thought you'd be *young!*"

Some people might have taken offense at that unexpected remark, but there was something about the nonjudgmental innocence that made me treasure it.

"Oh, wow, you did? Well then, that must be very confusing for you. Listen, there's nothing I can do about my age, but if my age makes you uncomfortable, I want to stress that you don't *have to* talk with me about anything"—but again, before I could finish my thought she interrupted, saying—"Oh, no, it's OK. I was just surprised. That's all."

"I know what you mean, sometimes when someone isn't what we expect, it can be confusing."

It was a beautiful, sunny, warm spring day, and she wanted to walk down the road to the old covered bridge by the river. She was thrilled that I was willing to go that far; a good twenty minutes each way. She was very bubbly and chatty and the only thing she seemed to love more than being asked questions about herself was having a grown-up willing to listen to her answers. We had fun.

A lot of the kids I've worked with, kids who are "at risk," disconnected, hurting, a lot of them don't have any "interests." I mean *none*. And it breaks my heart when I'm with a teen that completely lacks dreams. Brenda was the opposite. She had an interest: singing. She had been singing in the school choir for years and she had recently performed her first solo in the talent show, alone, on the stage, and loved it.

"You shoulda heard everyone clapping! It was soooo cool! And I told my caseworker and my foster mom and I'm gonna be able to get private singing lessons!" She was thrilled. So was I. Finally, a system was working; a foster parent and DSS noting an interest, a talent, and nurturing it. I love it when that happens.

"Good for you! That's great!"

"Yeah, and when I grow up, I'm gonna be famous, like Britney Spears!"

"Wow, famous!? That's exciting!"

We chatted a bit more about her singing and her dreams of being a star. She had it all figured out: "First I'm gonna do a few concerts to figure out which are my best songs. I'll try lots of songs, and I'll see which ones the audiences really love. Then I'll record them: just the best ones. I know it'll be a hit album. Then the concert tours."

Her young face was so sparkly; even though I was sure she had had a rough road behind her, it was inspiring to see how her eyes and face told the tales of hope. I hoped with her and for her, I really did. I had read so much about the mysteries of resilience in youth; she was the living, breathing epitome of that.

Looking at her, I easily pictured her standing alone in her room, singing in front of the full-length mirror, confident. Her skin, her hair, her pierced belly button, all looking perfect. Going over her mental checklist and concluding "I've got everything Britney's got." And on some levels that may be true.

Everything, that is, except a multi-million dollar recording contract.

Picky, picky, picky.

But in our world, in the adult world, that matters. A lot. I didn't want to shatter her dreams, but I did want to help her keep her options open. And I didn't think that becoming a young teen mom would help. This was several years before Britney and her sister made headlines about becoming teen parents, so I couldn't work that angle.

Brenda's older sister had become a mom at fifteen. Cynthia had paid attention during the training session I had recently provided, when I identified foster care placement, being the younger sibling of a teen parent, and having a parent who was a teen parent as "red flags" to watch for. I had suggested that I could work with some of these kids *before* they become sexually active. I was thankful for the referral. All Cynthia had told me was that she wanted me to meet with Brenda, "like you said at the training; just to build a relationship, so she knows about you and sees you as a resource…I don't think she's sexually active or anything, she's so young…" so I figured I'd try to get her to examine her dream of being a star relative to parenting.

"Do you think you ever want to have kids?" I asked.

"Oh, definitely!"

"Do you ever think about *when?*"

"Not really, I dunno, someday," she replied, shrugging off the question, seeming to want to get back to *important* things.

"Some people have kids when they're still teenagers, other people wait till they're older. Do you ever think about which you'd prefer?"

"Nah, I just know I wanna have kids. Two kids. I know I want one boy and then one girl, but I don't care when."

"And what about how your two kids will be with your singing. Do you think you want to have them before you get famous or after?"

"Oh, that totally doesn't matter. I know I'm gonna be famous. They'll deal with it; they'll like it! They could even come to my concerts. They could even bring their friends!" She was more focused on the delight of a now slightly larger audience than the reality of trying to launch an entrepreneurial career as a teen parent.

"What about if you have the first one before you get famous, and then you have to perform while he's still a baby? What would you do?"

"Oh, he could just stay backstage. It doesn't matter; I'd just have somebody watch him," she replied dismissively.

"What about if you heard them introducing you, and you were about to step out on stage, and he started crying? Do you think you'd still go out? What do you think that would be like?"

For the first time, she didn't fire back a quick answer. She paused. She looked up at me; she wondered. She remembered the feeling of being backstage before performing: she loved that feeling. She really thought; I could see the wheels turning.

"Actually," she paused, and then answered, very slowly, carefully. "Actually, that really would be hard. 'Cuz if he was crying, like, I'd probably wanna stay. But I couldn't stay…"

We went on some more. A bit about how kids cost a lot of money and it would be easier to afford everything after she's famous. And we talked about a lot of other things. Not about sex per se, but I did explain the concept of family planning to her. That we all make choices. That she'll get to make choices as she grows up: her own choices. That her choices will determine whether and when she becomes a parent. And I had the opportunity to explain that some people start their families right when they start having sex ("that's what my sister did") but that other people think about their futures, about their goals, and decide to wait. That for people who decide they want to have sex before they want to have children, they can get birth control. "If you ever reach a point in your life when you think you might be ready for sex but you're not ready to become a parent, you can call me, or any Planned Parenthood. That's our job: not to tell you when you should or shouldn't get pregnant, but to support you in the process of reaching your goals."

She didn't have a boyfriend yet, but she seemed to love considering the opportunities to create a future that would work for her.

I thought it was a nice chat, but didn't think much more about it until I was getting ready to leave. We had talked about a host of other things, too, and being a sexual health educator, I had figured that since she wasn't reporting anything close to sexual activity or any need for reproductive health services in the near future, I didn't think there was anything too important about our visit. Like most visits with teens that are not sexually active, I had left her my card and identified Planned Parenthood and myself as resources.

Saying goodbye, I wasn't lying when I said I had really enjoyed our visit, and she quickly added that she had, too. I said I knew it was fun, but I hoped it was also helpful.

"Oh, God, it was really helpful," she said, bug-eyed.

"Oh, good. Can you tell me how it was helpful?" The visit had been an hour, and we had talked about a million things, mostly things I haven't written about, above. I wanted to know what had stood out to her.

"The part where we were talking about Britney Spears, about how I'm gonna be a singer just like her. The part about how like if I had my kids like before that it would be different. I never thought about it like that. But it really would be different. It would be harder. A lot harder. I'm not gonna do that; I'm gonna wait. Not like my sister; I'm gonna have my kids when I'm older."

That's why I wrote about that part.

I loved the fact that at age twelve, despite all the struggles she had already faced, she still had so many dreams and she was so eager to share them with me. Girls like Brenda always give me faith in the future; as long as a kid has dreams, I feel optimistic. And the fact that she was beginning to consider her childbearing capacity within the context of those dreams made me feel like our visit had been time well spent. And it gave me hope.

She was such a contrast to the teens that concern me most. So many times when teen girls have come to me for pregnancy tests, and they're awaiting the results, I get them chatting. About how their lives would change if the test is positive, if they became a mom soon. The ones that concern me most are the older teens: 17-, 18-, and 19-year-olds; when I ask them what they'd give up if they had a baby right away and they say, "nothing." No dreams, no hopes for their future that a twenty-four hour a day job would interrupt. Those are the ones I find sobering.

Brenda wasn't like that; it was refreshing.

"The lady downstairs said I could wait upstairs. Is this where I'm supposed to go?" Andrea asked as she stood in the doorway to my office. She didn't look nervous; she looked happy and relaxed as she chewed her bubble gum.

"Sure, come on in. I'm Vivian. I'm an educator here. Do you mean you have an appointment downstairs?"

"Kinda not really. I mean I didn't have no appointment, I just came here for a pregnancy test but the lady told me they're busy but I could come up here for like twenty minutes and then they can do it." She blew a huge, pink bubble, popped it, carefully formed a long strand and twirled it around her finger repeatedly before chewing it again.

"Oh yeah, sure. You can wait up here; she'll buzz me when they're ready for you. You can just hang out and wait, or is there anything you want to talk about before your test?"

"Yeah. If it's positive, can they tell me who the father is?"

"Well, they could eventually, but not today."

For the first time, her face registered a look of emotion: fear. She blew a tiny pink bubble and snapped it quickly.

"You look concerned. Do you want to talk about it?"

"Yeah, like, if it's positive, I gotta know right away whose it is. 'Cuz like, that's like, like, everything. 'Cuz like, I know it's either Adam's or CJ's or Brian's. And I gotta know 'cuz like I gotta decide what to do!"

"What do you mean?"

"I mean, like, if it's positive, if I'm pregnant, I gotta decide if I'm gonna keep it or not. 'Cuz if it's Adam's or CJ's, they're both like such losers I'm gonna get an abortion. You can get 'em here, right?"

"No, actually, you can get the pregnancy test done here, but once you have the results of the test, we don't have the facilities here for the next steps either way; the nurse will give you a referral, whether you want to carry to term or terminate. Either way, we don't do it here in Springfield." Her face told me what I already knew; that's a pain. But her words went back to the three potential dads.

"The thing is, if I knew it was gonna be Adam's or CJ's, I'd almost hope it's negative. I mean, like, I don't want their kid. But Brian is sooo cool!"

With an overwhelming feeling like nothing I could do or say could possibly make this girl grow up as fast as I wanted her to, I couldn't resist trying. "So you think you might be ready to raise a child if it's with Brian?"

"Oh, yeah," her eyes sparkled. "That would be awesome."

"Raising a child is a huge big deal. Do you ever think about what it'll actually be like?"

"Oh yeah, but I love kids. And they love me." So in her own eyes she's all set.

"Besides love, what else does it take to be a good parent?"

"Oh, I know it takes a lota money. That's why I hope if I am that it's Brian's. He's rich. I mean really rich. I mean, really, really rich. I mean, like, with him, I'd never have to worry about nuthin'! I mean he's got like five hundred dollars!"

Sitting there, listening to Andrea, I thought about recent trainings I had attended about new research findings on adolescent brain development. In a darkened auditorium, looking at slides with diagrams contrasting the human brain during adolescence and adulthood, I listened to trainers who are comfortable using words like hypothalamus, amygdala, and prefrontal cortex in casual conversation. Their diagrams confirmed what parents and those of us who work with young people like Andrea have suspected for a long time: adolescents don't think the way adults do. But now they give us a scientific explanation.

We learned about the frontal lobe—it's the seat of judgment, reasoning, problem solving, and rational decision-making. It provides for logic and understanding of consequences. It governs impulsivity, aggression, and the ability to organize thoughts and to plan for the future. And researchers recently discovered that it is not fully developed until the mid twenties. This discovery is significant; an important part of adolescence is learning how to assess risk and consequences, but the adolescent brains are not yet wired for these tasks.

As the prefrontal cortex area of the frontal lobe matures, we learned, through experience and practice, teens can reason better, develop more impulse control, and make better judgments. There is an increased need for structure, mentoring, and guidance during these years, we were told.

"Like, duh," I had thought.

But it was when I saw the two diagrams together, confirming that the prefrontal cortex is one of the last areas of the brain to fully develop, that I was so disturbed. Comparing the adolescent and adult brains, I saw the little area the size of a pea in the teen brain where all that happens, compared with the much larger proportioned one in the adult brain.

The diagrams gave me insight into so many conversations I have had with teens and the adults who love and cannot understand them. Like the girl who had recently told me that her goal is to be appointed to the U.S. Supreme Court by age thirty; to be the youngest justice ever appointed, and yet clearly did not connect this lofty goal with the fact that she was failing both English and Global Studies. And like my friend whose son took the family car, filled it with friends, and set off for Florida over spring break, without telling anyone or considering the need for things like permission or gas money. He made it almost to the New York and Pennsylvania border before running out of gas and phoning mom. "What was he *thinking?!?!*" his mom had asked me. She needed to see this diagram, too, I thought. We all do.

Sitting there, listening to Andrea, it felt as if I could see inside her skull to the cross section of her brain; that diagram haunted me. I couldn't remember any of the names of the parts of the brain, but I sensed the presence of something the size of a pea that I needed to see grow to the size of a Ping-Pong ball. Fast, or we're all in trouble. How puzzling it is, I thought, that along the human journey, somehow we evolved to be capable of reproducing before we become capable of understanding that in America in this century, five hundred dollars is not enough to last a lifetime! And how unsettling it is, I thought, that the teens who don't get that are so often the ones who do become pregnant.

Looking at Andrea, I thought about sloths. I don't know if it's really true that they can delay implantation, but I heard somewhere that they can; that their bodies somehow know when there will or won't be enough food for the young and adjust the gestation period accordingly. If we can't make birth control easier for teens, couldn't we at least figure out a way for them to just carry that egg around longer? In ten years, Andrea will probably have what it takes to be a great mom. But now...?

The clinic buzzed my office; they were ready to see Andrea.
She left and I ate an entire sleeve of Oreos.

B illie Jo called, "Come in," when I knocked on her door, so I let myself into her trailer. I didn't blame her for not wanting to get up; Alison was seven weeks old, had just eaten, and looked so cozy sleeping in Billie Jo's arms, snuggled up together in the recliner.

The first thing I noticed was how happy Billie Jo looked holding her new baby. And next was the brand new, squeaky clean enormous flat screen TV. The trailer, and everything in it was old and worn out; the stuffing coming out of the upholstery on her chair, the worn-out cushions on the couch, the bent lampshade, the broken knobs on all the cabinets, the grime that was so well worn into the floors and walls. So the TV stood out like a sore thumb, the way it glistened. Billie Jo didn't care about the filth or all the old stuff; they finally had their own place and she was glad about that. And at sixteen, with a new baby, that's a lot to have. Alan, her boyfriend, had quit school and gotten a job and was paying the rent.

When we had scheduled my 10:00 A.M. visit, I had no way to know what a big day this would be for her; the TV had *just* been delivered that morning. No, I had deliberately scheduled the visit because she had decided she wanted to try a birth control method for the first time, and I had been meeting with her during her pregnancy and afterwards, helping her make a plan. She and Alan had agreed they didn't want any more kids for years, if ever, but had never used anything besides an occasional condom, and knew almost nothing about any of the available birth control methods when we met. She had scheduled her six-week checkup, and I was there to see if she had gone and if she had gotten her pills as planned. And if she had, I wanted to check her comprehension about when to start, how to take them, and what to do if she ever forgot one. So my focus was clear when I knocked on the door.

But I hadn't known about the TV. The giant TV. This was in the late 1990s, before many people had them. Knowing that Billie Jo and Alan were young parents with very little money, I was surprised to see something so extravagant. And I had no idea when I saw it that it would derail my entire plan for our visit.

"Is that new?" I asked.

"Yeah, they just delivered it this morning! Alan hasn't even seen it yet!" she answered with glee. Then she continued on her own with no prompting from me, "We got it from that new rent-to-own place. We only had to put $80.00 down"—here she got interrupted by the ringing phone. It was Alan calling from work, "Did it come yet?"

"Yeah, it looks great! You're gonna love it!" There was such enthusiasm in her voice, I was sure he could feel her ear to ear smile over the phone.

They kept the call short; I was thankful for that. But almost immediately the phone rang again. "Yeah, it's here…yeah, tonight…yeah, Alan'll be home by six, come anytime."

Again, I was glad she kept it short with her friend.

"So how's it going with Alison?" I asked.

"It's good. Claire came yesterday, she said she's gained three pounds two ounces since she was born and she's two inches longer; she said she's doing good." Claire was the public health nurse.

"And did you get to your six-week checkup?" I asked.

"No, I gotta reschedule it, I couldn't go 'cuz"—but here, she got interrupted again by the ringing phone. "Yeah, they just delivered it! Come over tonight…!"

More calls. Each call brought just a few questions. Apparently everyone knew the TV was scheduled to be delivered that morning. Everyone was looking forward to partying together, watching a movie; everyone was calling to check, to see if it was really going to happen.

It was.

It was Friday morning; soon it would be Friday night. There's nothing unusual about a group of teenagers excited about getting together to watch a movie on a giant TV on a Friday night with no parents around; lots of teenagers would love that. But with the continued telephone interruptions, it was clear to me this was not going to be a day on which I'd successfully get her to focus on the urgency of her postpartum visit, on starting her birth control. I kept the visit fairly short; after about the fifth call, I simply reminded her how important it was and left them a bunch of condoms.

I knew they didn't have a lot of money. I knew those rent-to-own places charge high interest, I knew those enormous TVs are very expensive, that Alan wasn't making enough to meet the monthly payments, and that even if they *were* able to make the monthly payments, they'd end up paying several times the cost of the TV by the time they actually owned it. My mom was a math teacher when I was growing up; she instilled in me a love of numbers. Even when I was sixteen, I'd have understood about the percentage of interest in the payments and I'd have been able to figure out that that was a total rip-off. But Billie Jo didn't think like that. She took a simple delight in the fact that it was there, for tonight.

Most adults agree that once you have a baby, the baby's needs come first, then your needs, then your wants; so many adult parents squirrel away any extra pennies to prepare themselves to meet their baby's future needs. Putting one's wants before one's needs is pretty typical for a teenager, as is wanting to party on a Friday night. But it isn't a great recipe for best practices in parenting.

When teens have their first baby before they've experienced all those fun times on Friday nights with their friends, someone misses out. Either the teen parent misses out on the opportunity to party, or the baby misses out on receiving that "you come first" message that enables them to thrive. Teen pregnancy prevention efforts that focus on postponing the first pregnancy are so important in that regard. Nobody should have to miss out: neither the teen nor the baby. But when that doesn't happen, the next best thing is secondary prevention: trying to postpone the *next* pregnancy. That's what I was hoping to be successful with in my work with Billie Jo.

I wasn't that day; but I was eventually. Instead of visiting, I had several short but productive phone calls with her. Fortunately, she remembered a lot of the information we had covered during the pregnancy, so the gentle nudges I provided on the phone paired well with her desire not to have another pregnancy, and those gentle nudges were enough to keep the ball rolling. She rescheduled and went to her six-week checkup, got a prescription for pills, filled her prescription, started her pills, took one daily, and even reported that she was glad to be on them; she appreciated my support. "I ain't gonna be like my sister now. She's already got three kids and she just found out she's pregnant again."

But the next time I stopped back in to see her, I wasn't surprised that the TV was gone.

"Would you call for me?" Carmen asked, pushing the phone towards me.

"I could, but I think it would be good for you to learn to do it. Why don't you try this time?"

"I'm scared, I'm shy. I don't know what to say," she replied. Her accent was thick but her words were clear.

"You know more than you give yourself credit for," I said. English was Carmen's second language, but I was certain she could make herself understood to a medical receptionist.

In the past, I had always called for her; there was so much else to do during our visits, there hadn't been time for me to help her learn to make the call. But today was different; I had scheduled an hour and we still had half an hour left.

"You know what to say. Just tell them you want to have an IUD inserted. You can really do this," I said, trying to be encouraging. "Do you have Dr. Alexander's number?"

She had the number but she said, "I like it better when *you* call."

"I tell you what. How about if you call but I'll be sitting right here, and at any point if you don't know what to say, you can just hand me the phone and I'll take over. At least you'll be doing some of it." I figured once she did it she'd realize how easy it is and do it again on her own.

"OK," she agreed, reluctantly. She dialed the number and I could hear the receptionist answer, "Good morning, Dr. Alexander's office."

"Hi, may I please speak to Dr. Alexander?" Carmen asked.

"May I ask who's calling?"

As Carmen started to give her name I held up my hand up like a stop sign to get her attention. She said, "One sec," to the receptionist and I whispered to her, "Just tell her you want to *make an appointment* to see Dr. Alexander, to get your IUD inserted. She can schedule it; you don't have to talk to him." Carmen nodded at me with gratitude.

"I mean could I make an appointment to see Dr. Alexander? I want to get an IUD."

"Oh, OK; sure. Let me see what we've got. You'll need two appointments for that."

"Yeah, I know," Carmen agreed.

The receptionist scheduled it and Carmen wrote down the date and time. It went fine. She looked a little sheepish and giggled softly when she hung up. "Sorry, I thought I had to talk to the doctor."

"Don't be sorry, you did great," I insisted. "That was the receptionist. It's her job to schedule the doctor's appointments."

"I didn't know; I thought I had to ask for the doctor. 'Cause, I mean, he's the one who's gonna do it. I sounded stupid," she said, holding a throw pillow in front of her face, hiding in shame.

"You sounded fine!" I insisted. "They do that because that way the doctor pays attention to the person who's there. Any time you call, you'll always get the receptionist."

"Yeah, *now* I know. But like, I didn't know that. That's why I wanted you to talk."

"I'm sorry I didn't think to explain that beforehand. But you did it perfectly. It's good that you did it and that I was here to help you; it's good that we did this one together. That's my job; to get you on the path so you can take care of all this. Now, if you ever have to do it again you know how."

It wasn't her lack of the English language that was a barrier for her. It was her lack of knowledge of how medical centers in her new country operate: patients call and the receptionist answers the phone and schedules appointments. Period, finished with. Now that Carmen knows that, she can use it.

Being comfortable and familiar with how medical establishments work and having the ability to navigate our way through the system to get our needs met requires a set of skills. Most of us who have those skills don't even identify them as skills; we just think of it as common sense, if we even think of it at all. But common sense isn't "common" if you've never been exposed to it. Carmen came from a subculture that hadn't prepared her with that skill set. I was so grateful to be able to have helped her learn that; as a mother of four, it's a skill she'll need.

So many of my clients since then have made comments that showed me that their definition of "common sense" is different from the mainstream when it comes to accessing medical services. Like Beverly, the woman who greeted me at her door, saying she had a doctor's appointment scheduled in fifteen minutes. I said I'd visit another day, but she wanted me to stay, saying, "Don't worry about it; I can be late. It doesn't matter."

"It *does* matter; I don't want to make you late. It's important that you get there on time," I replied.

"He's not like that, Vee. He doesn't go all by the clock and stuff. Last time I had an appointment he kept me waiting for like an hour! He won't care if I'm late." Common sense told her that that justified her being late this time, but to most doctors, they expect patients to be on time for each appointment, regardless.

Or the patients who walk in the door to the doctor's office and tell the busy receptionist a long, involved, personal health issue, instead of simply requesting an appointment to see a nurse or doctor. They lack a clear understanding of a receptionist's role, and then they wonder why the receptionist has an "attitude" with them.

"Hi, I'm Vivian, I'm looking for Barbara," I said when the woman answered her doorbell.

"Yeah, I'm Barbara," she said, and looking threatened and defensive, she added, "What's this about?"

"It's about your request for the Reproductive Life Planning Service. Do you remember filling this form out?" I asked, showing her the form, hoping the sight of her own handwriting would immediately comfort her, giving my presence legitimacy.

"Oh, yeah, that Planned Parenthood thing," she said eagerly, her expression quickly softening.

"Yeah, I'm here to tell you it's been approved. That means you're entitled to free home-based education. I'm the educator who does the visits. I hope you don't mind me just stopping off like this. Usually I call first, but you hadn't put a phone number. So I stopped by to see if you'd like to schedule a visit."

"Oh! That's great! No, no, no I didn't put the phone 'cause I have no more minutes. Oh, thank you so much for coming all the way out here—I don't believe it! Do you want to come in? Can you help me get birth control pills? I *really* need them!"

I'm not used to such a greeting. Most of the people who are so clear about what they want simply get it; they don't involve me. People who request my services generally haven't set a goal and decided on a plan for how they're going to reach it.

So she was easy. Unlike so many of the people I serve, she had excellent communication skills: she answered every one of my questions appropriately, staying on topic. No rambling, no misinformation, no major barriers. A few simple, straightforward questions and answers revealed that she had used the pill before, had liked it, had insurance, and simply needed more. She had been to Planned Parenthood as a teenager, but wasn't sure if she could go back as an adult. She wanted to; she had really positive memories of the way she was treated there. She had used the pill during her teen years, then she had her three kids, using pills that her OBGYN prescribed after the birth of her first two kids to space her pregnancies. Her son was her third child; he was three months old.

She was thrilled to learn that the nurse practitioner that had welcomed her as a teen was still at the same local Planned Parenthood, that her insurance would cover it, and that we welcome adults. We set up the appointment in what felt like the easiest home visit I had ever done. She didn't need anything else; I could leave.

Part of me was ready to go; I had clearly filled her need. I could call it done. And she'd make my statistics look artificially favorable: a reproductive goal stated, a plan made, and the first step already accomplished in one visit is a rare and significant accomplishment.

But something in me wondered, and felt that there was a "training" opportunity here for me. If she had gotten pills after her first two babies were born, why hadn't she gotten them after her third baby was born? Why had she left the hospital with a new baby and a little bag of condoms, and no pills? Something didn't add up.

So after she thanked me for helping, as I prepared to leave, I said, "You know, if you don't mind me asking, I'm simply curious: how come you didn't ask the doctor for pills when you were at the hospital?"

She paused, and the confident tone in her voice disappeared as she replied, looking at the floor, avoiding eye contact for the first time, speaking softly, "Yeah, I know, I should have. I guess it's just 'cause I'm an idiot."

Surprised, I replied with a gentle smile and a soft giggle, "Listen, I don't want to be disagreeable, and if you don't want to discuss it I'm totally fine with that. But I can't hear you say you're an idiot without at least closing by saying 'No! You're not!' In my job I listen to a lot of women talk about their goals and plans regarding family planning, and compared to what I hear, I have to say, on the contrary, that you're remarkable. Before I even knocked on your door, you had a goal, you knew what method you wanted, it was one you've had experience with; you knew your body. I don't often start working with people with that level of self-awareness. So while I've only known you for about a half hour, it's crystal clear to me that you communicate effectively: you're focused on your goal, you remain on topic, and you're perfectly intelligent and capable of getting what you need. That's why I thought it was puzzling that you had left the hospital without pills. That's all."

Sitting a bit taller, she spilled her tale.

"The nurse came in and said I was almost ready to go home, that the doctor would come in and talk to me but that first they were going to show me a video about birth control, and I watched it, and it was like, yeah, there's all this new stuff but like I just want the pill. And then the doctor came in and he said, 'Did you see the video?' and I said, 'Yeah,' and he's like, 'Do you have any questions?' and I'm like, 'No,' and he's like, 'So what method do you want?' and I'm like, 'I'll just take some condoms.' I mean: I am such an idiot! I knew I wanted pills! I'm just too proud. It's so stupid. I even told my husband: I just shoulda said 'Pills!' "

"Why didn't you?" I asked. "What stopped you?"

Speeding up her speech, getting louder and angry from the memory as she spoke, throat tightening, face turning red she went on, " 'Cause like who the hell is he! Like some big shot doctor with fancy clothes and a fancy house and a fancy-ass car and everything; just 'cause I got Medicaid, who the hell is he to think I shouldn't have kids? I mean, I may not have no big house and no fancy car and all that stuff like him, but hey, I'm a good mother! I love my kids! They may not have a lot of clothes but they're always clean when they go to school, and I give them breakfast every morning, and I take care of them…" and wow, she was off and running! She had obviously taken the doctor's "offer" of birth control not as an offer, but as a judgment; that she's poor and that it would be best if she didn't have any more kids.

The ultimate insult.

I could understand her side of the story. Yet in that one moment I felt a sudden, overwhelming awareness of the entire history that had led to the other side of the story: the side that had brought that one woman and that one doctor together in that room, theoretically programmed for success. And it pulled at my heartstrings.

Throughout the last hundred years, from the Margaret Sanger era and the overturning of the Comstock Laws to all the Supreme Court cases that brought us to where we are today, a complex system of reproductive health services has been developed. We've got computers, machinery, laws, and most importantly a network of dedicated people who have worked so hard, with hope, with the vision that individuals could take charge of their fertility. It had all led to a moment; a woman and a doctor in a hospital room, the woman wanting pills, the doctor willing to prescribe them, with a cabinet containing them, with insurance to pay for them, and a hospital ready to dispense them.

Yet the system failed that one woman on that one day: a patient hearing a doctor's words and reaching conclusions that were quite possibly not what he meant, taking offense, and declining the pills.

A chain is only as strong as its weakest link, and on that one day, the weak link was human communication. And like any chain with one broken link, it is the one broken link, not the countless other perfect ones, that ultimately defines the strength of the chain. So the final count was zero, despite all that had been done by so many well-intentioned people for so long. And despite all the things the doctor had done well: he had checked to be sure she had seen the video, which was current and accurate. He had offered the opportunity to ask questions. He had offered a choice of methods. This was not malpractice!

But I am convinced that if that doctor had added a question like, "Do you hope to have any more kids?" and she had said, "No," and then he had offered birth control as a response to her request, it would have changed the entire outcome of the interaction. I believe it was the omission of that single question that led to the problem.

Before leaving, I did take the opportunity to try to explain a little about my understanding of the doctor's words.

"One thing about doctors, they're trained to think of everything from the perspective of health. They know that mothers and babies are healthiest if there are at least two years between pregnancies, so your doctor may have simply assumed you know that, and that you'd therefore want birth control."

"That may be so," she said, sounding skeptical, "but I don't think that was what he was thinking."

I didn't push it farther; I didn't have reason to. I had opened the door to suggest that she might have misunderstood his intent, and I was also aware that she might *not* have. Without knowing the doctor, without having been there, my opinion was worthless, and definitely not worth wasting time discussing. But she had certainly gotten me thinking, and provided me with the "training" I had wanted. I've used this story at many of the professional trainings I've done; I think it's an important one.

As I drove away, I wished every doctor and nurse involved with discussing contraception at discharge in every hospital maternity ward could have a video of her rant! Even without commentary, I couldn't help think they'd all improve their communication skills. It was one of those days where I wished that this private conversation we had just had could be broadcast to thousands of people.

Maybe someday, I thought, I should write a book.

Before she left the hospital with her new baby, Brittany's doctor had said he'd give her birth control pills at her six-week checkup. And he probably would have, if she hadn't shown up pregnant at that appointment.

She was in the second trimester of that pregnancy when I visited her home. I was there to help her prepare for the challenge of preventing another pregnancy right after this baby was born. She had never used any birth control, but before even giving her an overview of the methods I started by trying to explain the importance of abstaining from intercourse right after giving birth.

"The body needs time to heal," I said. "It's important for your health. Plus, if you don't want to get pregnant again right away, it's really important to wait until you're on birth control."

Exasperated, she snapped, "Don't tell *me*, tell *him!*"

Five words. Just five words. I heard her; those five words spoke volumes: about the nature of her relationship with her partner, about her lack of assertiveness regarding something so important, about her lack of comfort or skill discussing her concerns with her doctor. She went on to elaborate about how frustrated she had been when her doctor had withheld the pills after the birth; she had known her partner wouldn't wait, but didn't have the words to advocate for help. She felt trapped but simply went home, from a doctor who insists on abstinence to a partner who wouldn't have any part of that. She had tried to tell him, "The doctor said it," but he hadn't been there at the doctor's office, and he ignored her words.

"…Last time, everybody told me, but I'm like, hey, I know. *It ain't me!* Nobody tells *him!* Maybe if you tell him…" she continued, almost pleading, with the only glimmer of hope she had, of not getting pregnant with her third child as quickly. After all, she had told him she wanted to wait last time, but he hadn't waited.

Like so many of the women I've met through this job, Brittany left me feeling as though I had stepped back in time a hundred years. These voiceless women who don't know how to communicate effectively with their partners and doctors to successfully space their pregnancies are living in our world today, but they're facing the challenges that women struggled with a hundred years ago.

It's a long drive home from Brittany's house. Driving, my eyes stay close to the road, but my mind wanders far. I drive for miles through woods and farmlands, past old Victorian homes and hundred year old barns, and only see another car occasionally. The timeless magnificence of the landscape has barely changed since those barns were built, and my mind wanders to the past when they were brand new, when horses, not tractors, plowed these pastures, probably around the time my own loving grandmother, "Bubbe" was born, and I think about how different her life was back then from mine today.

She had come to America from Poland in the early 1900s, eleven years old, the oldest of many siblings, and did grueling work in factories before child labor laws, to help put food on the table. When she married, her husband refused to wear condoms, not liking how they felt, and insisted she have abortions each time she became pregnant. His refusal to wear condoms left her with little alternative back then. She hated that; she wanted to prevent pregnancy.

It wasn't until long after Bubbe died that my mother told me about all the abortions. Mom didn't know the precise number, but they were numerous. Apparently the mixture of Lysol and water that she used faithfully in her douche bag after sex wasn't as effective as the rumors that inspired it.

I think about how Bubbe finally got the courage to tell him, "I don't care what you say: I'm keeping this one!" and about how that led to the birth of my mother, my grandmother's only child, and eventually to me. We were born from her strength, from her newfound assertiveness; life goes on. My mother, my sisters, me; all born from that strength.

Thinking about my grandmother, desperately douching with Lysol, trying to prevent pregnancy, with no effective alternatives, is chilling. But it also fills me with gratitude for the important work that's been done, work that has led to progress that's given me countless opportunities that Bubbe would never have even imagined. And it inspires me, and motivates me to broaden the reach of that progress.

A lot has happened in those hundred years. For me, yes. And for society, yes. But not for Brittany. Granted, she doesn't douche with Lysol; some progress has been made. But when I think of a continuum with my grandmother at one end and me at the other, Brittany, like so many of the people I serve, falls much closer to Bubbe. Our progress hasn't spread to these pockets of poverty in the back woods yet: to the flimsy trailers where the pipes freeze; where the dishes have to be stored in the lower cabinets in winter because the weight from the snow on the roof prevents the upper cabinet doors from swinging open; where phones and cars often don't work, intensifying the isolation; where the men dominate; where the women *react* to their circumstances.

It hasn't spread to Brittany's house yet. But each time I help a woman like Brittany learn to use her voice and each time I see one successfully prevent a subsequent pregnancy, I feel it spreading.

FORTY-THREE MINUTES

✔ **FACT**: The U.S. has the highest teen pregnancy
rate in the industrialized world.[4]

"Hi Vee, could I talk to you this period?" Crystal asked, appearing unexpectedly in my doorway.

"Do you have study hall now?"

"Yeah."

"Great! Sure, come it. What a nice surprise; I haven't seen you in so long. How have you been?"

"Great, actually. I've been thinking I really wanted to talk to you. So much has happened!"

"You know, I'm here every Friday, but I don't think I've talked with you this whole year."

"I know, last semester I didn't have any study halls, but now I do."

"Are you a junior now?"

"Yeah."

"Wow, you're really growing up. How's it going as a junior?"

"It's really good. Like, sooo much has changed. I mean, I can't believe I haven't talked to you since I been with Dave! It's like I'm a totally different person. I mean, everything: it's so different! It's the most amazing relationship. I've never been in a relationship like this before. I always thought it was a good relationship with Charlie when I was with him. But it's so different now with Dave. He's so kind to me, and so gentle and affectionate. And we can talk about everything. It's so different from Charlie. I mean, like, with Charlie, my friends always used to say I'm better off without him. I never used to get it, why they'd say all that stuff. I just thought they were being mean or something. But now that I'm with Dave, it's like: I totally get it. I mean, everything. Even just the way he talks to me. He's sooo respectful! And I mean it makes me feel different about everything!"

She kept talking, fast and almost non-stop for half an hour. She went on in great detail about the relationship and the introspection, self-questioning and personal growth she was experiencing. It brought back lots of memories of her sophomore year; we had spent so many study halls together. She and Charlie had been a steady couple and were sexually active when we met, and although she clearly stated the goal of graduating without a pregnancy, all they were using was condoms. Their use had been sporadic at best, and she knew almost nothing about birth control methods. Yet she was unconcerned. After all, she knew girls that had much more frequent sex than she had, and they hadn't gotten pregnant, so compared to them, she felt safe.

Over the course of our weekly visits I had helped her realize she was placing herself at risk and helped her talk to both her mom and Charlie about sex. She had gotten her first pelvic exam and effective birth control methods. And even once she started on a method. There had been so many times when she had misunderstood basic instructions: the time she switched to the NuvaRing and thought she had to wait for the end of her period to insert a new one, leaving herself unknowingly at high risk; all the times she was due for follow-up appointments and didn't realize it; those gentle appointment reminders I had given her right after school, all the times I had advocated for her at the clinic, when the schedule was already full during the evening hours and she had neglected to call ahead of time to schedule an appointment. She had been so needy, had consumed so much of my time; but she never did get pregnant. So she had been a textbook case of successful intervention, and it felt good.

By the fall of her junior year she was using her method correctly, and since she didn't have any study halls, we had barely had more than a "hello" in months. So I just sat and listened, and let her talk, uninterrupted. It seemed to be what she wanted.

Finally, it was almost time for the bell to ring, so before she was going to have to leave, I looked for a bit of closure, saying, "Well, it's been good to finally catch up with you today. I'm listening to you, and it sounds like you're becoming so much more self aware; from what you're saying, it sounds like being with Dave is genuinely making you take a long, hard look at yourself. And it makes me realize how much you and I had lost touch; I didn't even know that you and Charlie had broken up." But realizing I had barely seen her since the end of last spring semester, I figured it had been months; a lot can happen. So I closed by asking, "How long have you and Dave been together?"

"Since Tuesday."

The bell rang. It was Friday; she went to Earth Science, leaving me alone with three minutes to ponder how different a teen's sense of the significance of time is from my own. The way she spoke, it sounded to my adult ears like this was a long-term relationship; yet everything she reported had happened in three days. I forced myself to switch gears as my next student, Carly, arrived.

"Hi, how ya doin'?" I asked.

"Good. I have an appointment after school today."

Good, I thought. I knew she had the appointment scheduled; that's why I had paged her. I wasn't going to bring it up, hoping she would remember without my involvement. She did.

"Good for you, taking care of your health. Do you want to talk about what it's for?"

"I wanna get tested."

"What for?"

"STDs."

"Good for you, that's so important. You've been tested before, haven't you?"

"Yeah, but not for a really long time."

"Well, that's a very important part of taking care of yourself. In addition to getting tested, are you protecting yourself from STDs?"

"Well…kinda…sorta," and after a pause she added, "not really, I guess."

"What do you mean?" I remembered she had told me many times that she always uses condoms, every time, and she had come to my weekly teen drop-in at the clinic to pick up condoms so many times that I believed her. But I hadn't seen her in a long time. "Do you still use condoms every time?"

"Well, I always did, but lately, not anymore."

"How come?"

"Since I been with Dale. He don't wear 'em. I wish he would!" she said, sheepishly.

"Oh, wow," I replied. "I remember when you and Ethan were together you told me you used them every time. What happened? How come you don't use them with Dale?"

"I dunno. He just doesn't put 'em on," she said, sounding completely detached from the decision making process; sounding like a victim. And she continued, sounding increasingly frustrated, "Ethan wore 'em; every guy I been with wore 'em. I don't know why Dale doesn't."

"It sounds like you want him to."

"I do! I don't wanna get nuthin'!"

"Have you asked him to? Have you talked about it?"

She looked at me like I was nuts and said in a rhetorical tone, "I mean…like…what are you supposed to say?" And continuing like she was an actress in a play delivering a ludicrous line, "Hey, would you please put on a condom?"

I thought to myself, "that's exactly what you could say," but it was clear from her tone that those were words she couldn't even imagine herself saying to someone she was about to have sex with. So I said, "Well, that might work but it sounds like you can't imagine yourself saying that. Is that right?"

"I mean, do people actually say stuff like that? I mean, like, who talks like that! That's not something you talk about! That would feel so weird!"

"Well, different people have different comfort levels. Some people are comfortable talking about condoms, some people aren't. It sounds like you're not comfortable imagining talking about it."

"Oh, God, no! That seems totally weird!"

"But it also sounds like you definitely *want* him to wear one."

"I do. But it's like, all the other guys I was with, I never talked about it. I just got the bag from you and gave them the bag and it was like, they just wore them."

"And what happened with Dale?"

"I dunno. I just gave him the bag, but he just looked in it and tossed it on the chair and didn't say nuthin'. He made, like, a weird face. That was it."

It had never occurred to me, all the times that I had given her condoms, all the times she had told me that her partner always wore them, that she had never talked about it with her partner. We had never discussed that before. But now that she had a partner who just took the bag and tossed it aside, rejected, she had a new challenge to face. I never had realized she was unprepared.

We discussed it some more. It became apparent that while she couldn't imagine discussing condom use within a sexual context, it was easier for her to imagine herself bringing it up with him in a non-sexual setting. With a little prompting from me, she figured out that her visit to the clinic for STD testing provided the opening she was searching for, and before the bell rang, she had a plan: after her appointment, regardless of the outcome of her testing, she was going to tell him, "Ya know, Dale, I got tested for STDs today, and I got thinking, I really want you to wear a condom from now on." She could imagine herself saying that. She guessed he might comply, but even if he didn't want to for some reason, she figured he'd at least answer her, and a dialogue might ensue. She was fine with that.

She looked relieved when she left.

"Last time we spoke, you said it was super important to you to graduate without a pregnancy. Is that still your goal?" I asked Candy after a little chat.

"Oh yeah, definitely."

"And I remember you went on the pill, right?"

"Yeah."

"Are you still on it?"

"Kinda, yeah."

"What do you mean 'kinda'?"

"I mean, like, I'm still sorta on it, but I have to wait 'till Wednesday to start them again. I mean, I wanna be on it; I really don't want to be pregnant. But I'll be on it again Wednesday. After Wednesday everything'll be OK; I can't wait!"

"How come you have to wait 'till Wednesday? Don't you take one every day?" I suspected some comprehension problems so I wanted to hear more.

"Well, yeah, usually I do. But I can't take another one this week, till next Wednesday."

I was completely confused.

"What do you mean, why do you have to wait?"

" 'Cuz the next pill in the pack says 'W-E-D.' The nurse said to always check the day when I take the pill; they have these tiny little letters right on the package. She said it's so you always take them on the right day. She said to always make sure before I swallow it that it's the right day."

"It's great that you're so careful; you're right, that they're packaged so you always know what day you're on. But there's one for every day; you shouldn't ever have days where you wait, where you don't take a pill. Did you skip a day?"

"I don't know what happened. I don't *think* I skipped any. But I went to take it yesterday and it said 'W-E-D.' That means Wednesday, and yesterday was Thursday so I was like, damn, now I gotta wait a whole week; I sure hope I don't get pregnant before I can take the next one!"

She had skipped a pill. Wednesday's pill. She had listened to the nurse's instructions; I've listened to those instructions so many times I could probably recite them in my sleep. But it's a lot of information to absorb quickly, especially if it's all new, like it was to Candy. She had totally latched onto the part about making sure that the little letters are the correct day. But she had completely missed the entire part about what to do if you miss one day. And she had filled it in with her own "common sense": wait until Wednesday and restart. That would have left her restarting in the middle of a cycle, which is the worst thing to do. She had also completely missed the part when the nurse explains that if you have any questions you can call the clinic, or read the instructions.

Fortunately, she wasn't pregnant, and we called the clinic together and she spoke with a nurse. By the end of the class period she repeated what she heard and it all sounded right. She understood that she had made a mistake that left her vulnerable to pregnancy; she'd try to abstain and use condoms if she did have sex, and she knew which pills to take and when. I started to write myself a note to keep a close eye on her over the next few months; I couldn't have known at that moment that with ongoing support she'd do fine, but she did.

It often happens like that; as teens learn to listen to a medical provider, they sometimes hear certain parts of the important information but miss other important parts. Then they cling to one part they remember hearing and simply fill in the blanks, on their own, without even realizing it. A little handholding by an experienced adult goes a long way during that developmental stage.

Fourth period: page Donna. Always. If I try every week, I might actually get to meet with her once or twice a month. She loves to talk with me; it's her favorite way to pass the time during study hall. If she sees me in the hall beforehand, and we have a chance to confirm that I'll page her, she always shows up. But by fourth period there's always something she's done wrong that she's feeling guilty about. And rather than own up to it, when she hears her name paged to the office she assumes someone has "caught" her and hides. She simply finds a discreet place to spend her study hall: a bathroom stall, a stairwell far from the office. Anywhere.

Frequently, when I page students to the main office, they arrive looking nervous, but upon seeing me their faces light up with new hope. "Is that why I was paged; did you page me?! Thank God!" It wasn't that class skipped, that cigarette smoked, that enemy punched, that baggie of weed in their locker discovered. No, it was just me offering a visit that resulted in their name being broadcast over the loudspeaker. "Whew!" I'm used to that look of relief, but Donna was the queen in that department, looking more relieved than anyone that she wasn't "in trouble." Probably because she had more to hide.

Donna had become sexually active a few months ago. She told me that she and her boyfriend were "really careful," and she had no interest in hormonal birth control; she was completely confident that she wouldn't end up pregnant, but I had my concerns. The behavior she referred to as "really careful" was using condoms, but not every time. So I knew she was putting herself at risk. My first goal with Donna was to change her perception of her own risk; people change behavior based on perceived risk, not actual risk.

Although they had just started having sex fairly recently, they had taken to it like ducks to water. Some people find their first sexual encounters to be awkward, even painful, or embarrassing, or scary, especially when they're so young. Not Donna. Oh, maybe the first or second time: I don't know. But she told me she loved having sex, and I believed her. And I felt like I had my work cut out when I found myself, early on, fielding questions like "Is it true that if you're having sex for like four hours you're supposed to use a new condom like every hour? That's what my friend told me but it's hard to take it off."

I figured I'd try to get her thinking about how easy it is to become pregnant, and that while condoms are a great start, couples that are serious about preventing pregnancy find more long-term success by using two methods: using a "backup method." I was trying to stress that it only takes one sperm cell to start a pregnancy. And if I wasn't going to have any success getting her to consider hormonal protection, or spermicides, or any other method, I at least wanted to get her to realize how important correct, consistent condom use is.

"The condom has to be on before foreplay; before there's any genital to genital contact."

"Yeah, I know. But like, I get it about that when you're like doin' it. But, like, what about when he just like picks me up or something and it just like slips in? I mean, like, just for a second. Could you get pregnant from that!?" She posed the question with a tone of disbelief and wonder, implying that while she could imagine using a condom every time they "do it," it would be impossible for her partner to have a condom on every time it "just slips in."

Pondering their young bodies, all I could think about was hormonal protection.

"Yes, any time his penis is…" I paused; her face turned beet red and she covered it with her hands, saying, "Oh my God, I was trying not to use that word!"

"Listen, Donna," I said softly, "I know that a lot of people are uncomfortable hearing some of the words I use. Please understand that I don't use these words because I want you to feel uncomfortable; I use them to make sure you understand everything clearly, because this is so important. Your whole future rests on this. I need to be certain we're on the same page, that you know everything you need to know to stay safe."

"It's OK," she added, with the red almost completely going away, returning quickly to normal.

"Anytime his penis is even touching your genitals, you're at risk of pregnancy. No matter how long the encounter lasts. That's why a lot of people use two methods of protection. If you were on a hormonal method, it would protect you 24/7. That's why a lot of teens choose them: they're so effective, and they even provide protection during spontaneous, unplanned sex. Even during very brief encounters."

It was taking me time to convince her that she was leaving herself genuinely vulnerable to pregnancy, and it was time I felt I didn't have. So I shifted the focus and found that she was pretty aware of HIV and willing to get tested; she knew her boyfriend had had other partners. When she learned that the test was just a blood test, that she wouldn't have to get undressed and that I'd be willing to meet her at the clinic and sit with her during the blood draw, she agreed to schedule an appointment to get tested.

"Here's the clinic number," I said, handing her a card. She looked terrified.

"Would you call?" she begged.

"Well, I could, but it would be good for you to learn. Would you like to try? I could tell you everything you need to say, and everything they're going to ask you on the phone."

"I don't wanna. Would you?"

"Well, OK, for your first one, but it's good for you to start to practice. Would you do part of it? Would you dial?" I asked, figuring I'd pull her into the process a little.

"Yeah, I mean, I'm not scared to dial, I just don't want to talk."

"OK, how about this: you dial, then I'll talk, and then in the end, once it's all scheduled, I'll have the receptionist repeat the time and date and you can just listen. OK?"

She agreed. She dialed the phone and I held the receiver so we could both hear. We got the recording, saying they were busy helping other patients, putting us on hold. I figured it was good practice for her, and I let her listen to the recording until the receptionist picked up. I scheduled the appointment and then said to the receptionist, "OK, thanks. I'm with Donna right now. I'd like to put her on. Would you please just confirm the date and time with her?" I handed Donna the phone and the receptionist gave her the details. She wrote the date and time on the card I had given her. It's happened like that for me with so many teens that are afraid to call. Usually once I have them dial and listen once or twice, I can gradually get them to do more and more of the call until they're doing it themselves.

The day of her appointment she was nervous, but she showed up. That was before there were rapid tests that give results in twenty minutes. Back then the nurse had to draw a vial of blood and send it to the lab for results, which took around two weeks. The nurse was required by law to talk with the patient alone first, but then, before they used the needle, Donna asked her if I could join them. So I went in and simply held her other hand as the nurse drew her blood.

Afterwards, the nurse quickly, routinely peeled the identical identifying labels from the strip and placed one on the blood sample, and one on each of the many forms. She easily did it without interrupting the friendly, comforting chatter she had started with Donna. It clearly helped Donna relax. But Donna didn't take her eyes off the nurse's hands the whole time. It was peculiar; amidst this light-hearted chat they were having, Donna's gaze spoke volumes. I could feel her thinking, "Wow, that's *my* blood, mine alone; it'll go to a lab and it'll tell a story. It'll tell if everything I've been doing has led to HIV or not." Previously, it never seemed like Donna connected information about risks with her behavior, her health. It had frustrated me that she didn't perceive herself to be "at risk" of anything, despite her risky behavior and despite my best efforts.

I've read so much about the benefits of sexually active individuals getting tested for HIV, but watching Donna's gaze glued to the nurse's hands suggested another benefit I have never read about: for some people, like Donna, being alone in a medical setting with a trained professional taking a blood sample and preparing it for testing gives them a unique, important opportunity to ponder some of the potential health risks of their behavior, of the choices they've been making. I felt that she got more "education" from watching the nurse handle her blood sample and her labels than from all the "education" I had provided; I felt genuine learning happening. The kind of learning that might actually lead to behavior change.

When it came to accessing effective contraception, there were other challenges. Like many people who had been sexually abused as children, Donna was extremely reluctant to get a pelvic exam. She finally agreed to consider it after I explained that if she changed her mind at any point, the practitioner would stop. But she was afraid she'd be too tense to speak, to say anything to the practitioner. So we made a deal. I agreed to come into the exam room once she was covered up in her gown and sit by her side holding her hand. If she squeezed my hand hard I'd tell the practitioner that Donna had had enough for one day and we'd stop the exam mid-way.

She would be in total control, yet she wouldn't have to speak; I would be her voice.

The practitioner was fine with that arrangement.

When the practitioner said she was ready to insert the speculum, Donna nodded. As it entered Donna's vagina she gave my hand a firm squeeze but then immediately released it.

"That was it," the practitioner said, pausing. "Are you OK?"

Donna nodded, "Yes."

"You're doing great. It'll just be a minute. Keep breathing…"

Donna did fine. It was over quickly. She survived her first pelvic exam. She got and used an effective method of birth control.

Our plan worked. It often works like that: breaking the process down into tiny steps, finding out which one is the obstacle, and putting our heads together to overcome it. As soon as she believed she could *try* the pelvic exam and be in control of ending it if it was intolerable, she was willing.

The next morning, I called my boss, Eileen. She knew that Donna had been so important to me; I think it was because I believed that despite what a troublemaker she was, there was hidden a smart girl with a lot of potential. To me, she epitomized my belief that targeted intervention can be effective and life altering, even with the most high-risk teens. Without intervention, I felt like she was on the fast track to becoming another inept teen parent. With intervention? I had been optimistic enough to believe I could make a difference, and determined to try, and it felt like there had just been a giant step in the right direction on the road to success.

I could feel a quiet peace come over Eileen as I told her about Donna's appointment. "Vee, this is amazing," she said softly, slowly. "And it's so strange. This is so important; when I think of the significance of this, it's like there should be a parade or a celebration or something. You and she should be given some kind of a medal. But it's weird; because of how private it is, that can't happen. With other professions, it's so different; if the band wins a competition, or the football team wins the tournament, people in the community gather and everyone celebrates the success. But we can't with this, even though in reality it matters so much more. This work you are doing is so important, and when you're successful, the odd thing is: *it looks like nothing happened!* If this keeps moving forward in the new direction it's now heading, Donna will graduate with a flat tummy like everyone else, and you won't even be acknowledged." And after a pause she asked, "Are you OK about how the community doesn't see the results of how hard you work? About the lack of fanfare?"

"Are you kidding?" I asked. "When something like this happens, it's so far beyond my community for me; I feel the entire universe giving me a big hug." And I meant it.

Very soon afterwards, we even got Donna to involve her mother in her birth control use, and for the rest of Donna's high school career, mom, Donna and I partnered effectively. Those were turbulent years for Donna. From smoking pot in a car in the school parking lot to giving blowjobs to her boyfriend and some of his buddies under the stairwell, Donna's behavior when she skipped class frequently got her suspended. And I'll never know if the rumors were true, when people were whispering that Donna and her boyfriend had sex under the bleachers during a basketball game. But I'm sure mom got tired of the school calling in the daytime and the cops calling in the middle of the night. Despite it all, mom never lost her focus on the significance of pregnancy prevention.

Donna graduated without experiencing her first pregnancy.

Years later, when she was twenty-four, she came to our clinic for her annual checkup. Afterwards she brought her 18-month-old baby up to show me: her first child. And she thanked me, and filled me in a bit. It was going really well, she loved her son and was enjoying being a mom, she was glad she had waited so long and thankful to me for having helped her protect herself earlier. "I mean, even though I waited till I was twenty-two, it's still hard. But I mean, if I had been like fifteen or something…" and I don't remember exactly how she finished that sentence, but I do remember how she rolled her eyes in disbelief even at the thought that that could have happened. It often happens to the girls like Donna, the girls who are the troublemakers, the "at risk" girls, but it hadn't happened to Donna. I felt a gentle peace from having been a part of that chapter of her life; for having helped her pivot in a workable direction at a critical time.

I was trying to quickly write my notes during the three minutes between classes when a girl appeared in my office doorway saying, "Hi Vee. I have a question." I recognized her, but I couldn't place where or when I had met her.

"Refresh my memory; what's your name again?"

"Carla Armstrong."

"Thanks. Do you have class now, or study hall?" I asked.

"Class. But it's a really quick question."

"OK, let's hear it. But you can't be late for class."

"OK. What happens if someone has sex and the guy has a condom on and it doesn't break or anything and he doesn't like *go* inside, I mean, like, he pulls out like long before he goes and like none of it goes inside: is there still a chance?"

"Do you mean is there a chance of pregnancy?"

"Yeah."

"Let me make sure I get it. The guy put the condom on before there was any genital touching, then the penis went inside the vagina, but then he pulled out before he ejaculated. Is that right?"

"Yeah, like long before he went."

"And afterwards there was no more genital contact?"

"Yeah. Like, is there still a risk?"

"Well, I can't say there's *no* risk, but if he really did that, the risk is very low." She looked very relieved as I continued, "But if the girl is concerned, and if this happened in the last five days, she could come to Planned Parenthood after school and get Plan B. I don't know if it's you or a friend but if—"

"It's me," she said, interrupting,

"So listen, if it's you, there's also the issue of what's going to happen next. Am I right that you don't want to be pregnant?"

"Definitely I don't! Not for a long time." And pulling up her sweatshirt, tapping her flat belly, she continued, "I wanna keep it this way!"

"Then we need to talk! Do you have any study halls today?"

"Yeah. Seventh."

"Can I page you then?"

"Yeah."

"OK Carla, I'll page you seventh period. This is extremely important."

"Yeah, I know. I even talked to my mom about it!"

"Good for you! I definitely want to hear more about this. I'm glad you're free seventh period."

"Good."

"Now get to class!" I said, smiling. Then I added, "And I just have to tell you, I'm so glad you stopped in. I'm really looking forward to 7th period; you just made my day."

I was serious and I could tell she knew it but she looked surprised and puzzled. She tilted her head to the side and asked, "For real? How come?" I guessed that she expected me to only be disappointed that she was putting herself at risk.

But I looked at it differently.

"Because I come to this school to try to reduce teen pregnancy. My goal is that every student graduates without a pregnancy. If you're not pregnant now, and you're willing to talk with me during 7th period, and you're willing to be so open and honest—with yourself, your mom and with me, I feel like you're giving me this amazing opportunity to support you: I can see you in my mind's eye accepting your diploma with your tummy still so nice and flat. It's gonna happen. *Now* is the time to take charge; you're gonna make it."

The bell rang and she dashed off to class; it was right down the hall from my office, and I could see her turn and enter the classroom exactly as the bell finished ringing. Not even late. Pretty good, I thought.

And right away my next student, Debbie, appeared in my doorway.

"You have study hall now, right?" I checked as I always do when I've paged a student.

She came in, sat down, and stared at the floor. No eye contact.

"Yeah," she replied, not looking up.

"Would you like to meet with me?" I offered.

Shrugging her shoulders she said, "I dunno."

"Well, it's completely up to you. You don't have to stay, you can go back to study hall if you'd rather," I said, wanting to make it clear that she's in charge, that talking with me was voluntary.

"Hell no! I don't want to go there!" she said, finally making a sentence, but still not looking up.

I had known her for years; as the younger sibling to a teen mom, I had visited her home to help her older sister prevent subsequent pregnancy. Now, their mom had requested that I build a relationship with Debbie, to help her navigate her way through her teen years without becoming a mom herself.

Mom was sharp; having an older sister who is a teen parent put Debbie at statistically higher risk for earlier parenting, as did having a much older boyfriend, Carl. Mom didn't know the statistics; she didn't need to. She saw all the attention given to the baby and to the older sister, and was aware of the impact that her own exhaustion might have on Debbie's teen years.

Debbie had been all bubbly and excited telling me all about Carl a few weeks ago. Why was she so withdrawn now?

"Well, is there anything you want to talk with me about?" I asked.

"Not really."

"How've you been?"

"OK."

"How's school going?"

"OK."

"You still with Carl?"

A nod.

"How's it going?"

"OK."

"How are things going at home?"

"OK."

"How's your mom?"

"She's a pain in the butt."

"How so?"

"She treats me like I'm a little kid. She doesn't realize I'm growing up! She still thinks I'm like twelve years old or something."

"What do you mean? What does she do?"

Finally looking up, seeming to find delight and energy at the prospect of finding ears willing to listen to her complain about her mother, she eagerly continued with passion.

"Like with Carl. She likes him. I *know* she likes him. She lets him come over; she even lets him stay for dinner. My dad likes him. He works on my dad's car with him. But if I ever just want to go up to his apartment to watch a movie or something, it's 'No, no, no! ' " She wagged her finger in a scolding "no" motion, making fun of her mom, mimicking a mother correcting a toddler.

"Why do you think she lets him come to your house but she won't let you go to his apartment?"

Disgusted: "I don't know."

"There must be a reason, don't you think? Have you asked her why?"

"She says 'cuz he has his own apartment. She doesn't trust me. She thinks I'm stupid. It's just to watch a frickin' movie! I don't know what her problem is. She says I'm 'too young,' " she said, scrunching her face, again mimicking a mother inappropriately over-disciplining a young child. "She's nuts. She thinks I don't know what I'm doing. She thinks I'm gonna have sex or get raped or something. I dunno. She's just stupid. She makes me so mad! I am not a little kid!"

"So what do you do?"

"I lie," she sang, cocking her head back and forth, looking very pleased with herself. "I tell her I'm going to Eva's house and then I go over to Carl's."

"Oh, wow. So you do have time alone with him. How's that working out?"

"Fine, I guess."

"You guys are getting along well?"

"Yeah."

"Do I need to worry about you?" I asked, speaking softly, confident that she knew me well enough to know that I worry about teens that are putting themselves at risk of pregnancy.

"Nah," she replied, but only half-heartedly.

"Do you mind if I ask if you're still on the patch?" I knew mom had gotten her started on them and had been making sure that she was using them correctly for a few months.

"Yeah, I am."

"Do you mind if I ask if you and Carl have had sex?"

"Yeah. Just a few times."

"Did you like it?" I asked, sensing from her expression that there was a problem.

"Not really."

"Then how come you did it?"

"I dunno, it just kind of happened. Like the first time, I wanted to. Definitely. I remember that. I don't know why, I just like really felt like it. I mean, it was like, first his hands started getting a little happy, and like, I liked it; I liked how it felt and stuff. But then afterwards I got thinking I really don't wanna get pregnant, and I kinda wanna wait."

"You know, there are a lot of important reasons to wait. I'm glad you're thinking about that. Have you told him that that's how you feel, that that's what you want?"

"Yeah."

"What did he say?"

"He said that's fine, we don't have to do it till I'm ready."

"Well, good for you for bringing it up! That's so important, and it takes a lot of self-awareness. I'm so glad you're actually using your voice; you *are* growing up. Then what happened?"

"It's like weird."

"What do you mean?"

"Like, I told him, and he says, 'OK,' but then it just happens again."

"When you say 'it happens,' what do you mean?"

"I mean, like, we'll be sitting there just watching a movie, and like he puts his arm around me and like I'm fine with that. But then he puts his hand on my thigh, and the next thing I know, we're doin' it."

"Do you say anything? Do you remind him that you don't want to? That he agreed?"

"No, I just do it."

"How come?"

"I think 'cuz by that time he's like all into it and everything and I guess it kinda feels like, well, like, uh, if I don't like just do it then he'll like hold me down or something, and, like, that would hurt!"

"It would hurt. Do you know what it's called if you tell a guy 'no' and he does it anyway?"

"Rape. But this wasn't rape 'cuz I didn't say nothing."

"I'm glad you shared this with me. This is really important. I'm very concerned about you. I want you to be safe. I'm listening to you, and it sounds like you've really decided that you don't want to have sex with him anymore. Is that right?"

"Yes."

"Well, let's put our heads together and figure out a way to make sure that happens, OK? You must have thought about this. Right? What are you thinking of doing?"

"I think I'm gonna call him again and tell him I don't wanna do it no more."

"I'm glad you're so clear on what you want. And I can't stress enough that is your right! Do you think that plan will work?"

"I dunno, maybe."

"To be perfectly honest, 'maybe' isn't good enough; I need to know you're going to be safe. Which part of you thinks it might not work?"

" 'Cuz like I told him that before, and then, like, we'll get together and it's really good again like it used to be, and I figure, 'he gets it,' and we get together a few times and it's like everything is great and we like do stuff and play video games and hang out and watch movies and it'll be a bunch of times, and like, I really think like he gets it and then, bam, all of a sudden, there he is, like I never said nuthin'!"

"Hmm, so he listens for a while, but then at random, he starts touching you again?"

"Yeah."

"Can you tell why it's some times and not others?"

"Not really."

"Does it ever happen when other people are around?"

"No."

"Where does it usually happen?"

"In his apartment."

"Where else?"

A pause; a long pause. "Nowhere. It's always when we're in his apartment actually."

"So you mean he comes to your house, or you go out, and you get along well, and there's no sex, and he seems fine with that?"

"Yeah."

"But then when you go to his apartment, sometimes he starts touching you and you don't say anything, and the next thing you know you're having sex?"

"Yeah," and after a slight pause she added, "but not sometimes, more like every time."

"Well, that might narrow it down a bit. What do *you* think you could do?"

"Ya know what? That's really true. Now that I think about it like that, it only ever happens when I go over there. I'm just not gonna go up there anymore! That's it, I've had it. Next time he tells me to come over I'm just gonna say 'no' and if he doesn't like it he can stuff it."

"Do you think that'll work?"

"Oh, I know it'll work."

"But it sounds like you're scared to say, 'no' to him. Do you think you can actually do this?"

"Oh, I know I can. I'm just scared to say it when I'm there 'cuzza what he could do. You ain't never seen him but he's big. I mean really big. He's like over two hundred pounds and he's taller than Mr. Benjamin. I'll tell him on the phone. I ain't scared of him on the phone! If I just don't go up there he'll never try that no place else."

"What about when he comes to your house?"

With her eyes sparkling, almost laughing at the thought, she answered without hesitation "Are you kidding? With my dad there? And my *mom*! Hah! He'd never do nuthin' like that with them right downstairs!"

I was glad that Debbie took her parents' presence so seriously as a "red light" to sexual activity; not all teens do. She sounded confident that sex wouldn't be an issue under her parents' roof.

We chatted a bit more. I agreed that standing less than five feet tall and being so petite puts her in jeopardy when she's alone with someone more than twice her size, but stressed that her rights aren't based on her size. I emphasized that her safety is critical, that she has the right to say "No" every day, even if she's said "Yes" before. And I underscored that it *is* rape if she says "No." I congratulated her on coming up with a plan to stay safe. She declined my offer to connect her with a woman I know from the local Safe Against Violence program; she felt confident she could prevent any potential violence on her own.

Teens often try hard to "grow up" quickly. They desperately want to make their own rules, and they deeply resent when their parents "impose" them, even in a case like this, when it was the same "rule" that she herself eventually identified as being what she wanted and needed. By asking her the important questions and allowing her to think hard, she was able to lead herself to the exact behavior plan that her mother was unsuccessfully trying to demand.

But now it was going to work.

"Are you still on the pill?" I asked Erica.

"Yeah," she replied.

"How's that working out for you?"

"Fine."

"Are you taking one every day?"

"Yeah."

"Good for you. Do you have plenty more?"

> **TIP FOR PARENTS**
>
> **TRY TO GET YOUR TEEN TALKING; LISTEN MORE THAN YOU TALK.**

"Actually, I'm gonna go to Planned Parenthood today; I need more."

I was glad she said that; according to my notes, she should have been running out, and my attempts to find her over the last several weeks, to offer to schedule the appointment she'd need, had failed. So she was on my "high priority" list today.

"Do you have an appointment?" I suspected that she didn't, as I had checked the schedule that morning and her name wasn't on it.

"No, I'm just gonna get more pills, I'm gonna go down today after school."

I knew that the clinic was booked solid from the time school gets out until 8 p.m. when it closes. But still, I knew they'd bend over backwards for a teen running out of pills, but a "heads-up" would help. Plus, I wanted her to start learning how to correctly access medical services on her own.

"When you need more pills, it's very important to call first, for an appointment."

"Oh no, I don't need to: they're expecting me," she said with a dismissive tone.

"What do you mean?"

"She gave me three months' worth of pills, and told me to come back when I need more."

"But it takes time; you need to schedule the appointment so they reserve time for the nurse to talk with you and take your blood pressure and make sure everything's OK and to see what pills you're on and to give you more."

"Oh no, she didn't say that. She just said, 'Come back in three months.' She doesn't need to look it up; she *gave me* the pills. She put them in my hand! She knows which ones I'm on." Her dismissive tone was turning into a tone of annoyance; she was frustrated with me.

"But she gives lots of people pills; she needs to look up which ones are for you."

"No she doesn't! She made a whole big thing about why she picked that pill for me, about the headaches I used to get. She knows! Don't worry!"

Like many teens, Erica had been terrified before her initial appointment at Planned Parenthood. The thought of that exam table, nurse practitioner, and speculum had been enormous obstacles beforehand. But after I helped her go, once she experienced our supportive and friendly medical staff, she felt so comfortable, so welcomed, that she felt like family.

But that created a new set of obstacles. When the practitioner had said, "Come back in three months," Erica took it literally, unaware of the implicit, "Wait two months and then call to make an appointment." She had no idea that now that she had broken the "fear barrier" there were still professional expectations that need to be met at a medical facility. She was as frustrated with me for not understanding the "new level" she and the practitioner had reached as I was with her.

Once again, I had to teach a teen how to "be a patient"; that's often a big part of my job. Sometimes, like with Candy, it means learning to listen to instructions. Other times, like with Erica, it involves teaching them the basics about how medical establishments operate. Building those skills helps teens succeed. Teens who choose to access medical services without involving their parents often haven't mastered those essential skills yet; formerly, mom or dad always took charge.

"So how do you know you're not pregnant?" I asked Darcy. I was confused, because she had clearly said she didn't want to be pregnant, but appeared unconcerned about the unprotected sex she had just told me about.

"I can't get pregnant."

"What do you mean?"

"Like in class, the way you said it happens. I can't get pregnant."

I was puzzled. I had been a guest in her health class a few weeks ago, and I had shown them a large diagram of the female reproductive organs and explained how pregnancy happens. And we had gone over the basics of pregnancy prevention, including the fact that a person can get pregnant the first time they have sex, that abstinence is the only 100% effective protection, and a quick overview of methods, including several that are over 95% effective. So her lack of concern didn't make sense. I wanted to know more about what she was thinking.

"Do you remember how I said pregnancy happens?"

"Yeah, but it's like, it's not like that in me."

"What do you mean?"

"Like the way you said in class, that the sperm has to swim up to reach the egg. Every time I have sex, then afterwards, when I get up it's like it all drips out, I mean like *all* of it. I mean like a whole little puddle. You said it goes up. Mine never goes up, it goes down. It just all drips out."

I explained that that is normal, and added, "Do you remember that I said that when a guy ejaculates there are millions of sperm cells in that fluid?"

"Yeah."

"Do you remember how many have to reach the egg to start a pregnancy?"

"One?"

"That's exactly right. Just one. Even if it seems like they're all dripping out, if you don't want to get pregnant it's important to realize that just one of those sperm cells has to swim up. It's totally normal to have that dripping after sex. Everyone does. It doesn't mean anything is "wrong" with you! You are at very high risk for pregnancy, even when the fluid drips out."

She appeared totally relaxed and comfortable discussing it with me in private. Yet she hadn't brought it up in class. I don't think most teens would be comfortable asking questions like that in front of all their peers.

But for Darcy, it was essential that it be addressed.

"How have you been?" I asked Ellen. "Pretty good I guess. Just tired." We hadn't seen each other too much since her son was born; she had missed so much school, and when she was there, she needed her study hall periods to get extra help with all the schoolwork she had missed.

"How's everything at home?"

"OK, I guess."

"Are you guys still living at your grandparents'?" A bumpy road had gotten her there. First, the breakup with a boyfriend had prompted her to place herself in the middle of a road facing a fast-moving, oncoming truck. Her sister saved her. While teen dating drama is common, her reaction was not, and it landed her in a psych ward. She was released to a foster home, the third one that year. But then, when she got pregnant, her grandparents agreed to take her in, so the father of the baby could be with her. So here she was in Springfield.

"Yeah," she said, not sounding too thrilled.

We chatted a bit more, and then I asked, "Have you guys thought about how many kids you want to have eventually?"

"Yeah, but I dunno. I always wanted one boy and one girl, but Fritz don't want no more."

"Ever?"

"Well, that's what he says, but I dunno," she said, looking hopeful.

"Do you think he'll come 'round?"

"I dunno. Maybe."

"Do you ever think about *when* you'd like another?"

"Yeah, I think about it, but I dunno. I always thought I wanted my kids close together so they could play 'n stuff, but now I dunno."

"Sounds like you're thinking about waiting?"

"Yeah, I guess. I mean, like, I know I gotta wait."

"How come?"

"I gotta finish high school first."

"How come?"

" 'Cause, like, it's just so hard goin' to school and taking care of Daryl. If I had another, I mean, like, forget it! " Her look of exasperation spoke much more powerfully than her words. I don't know why it's so difficult for her to read or learn, but I do know that it's a struggle, so I was being completely honest when I told her that I had enormous respect for the fact that she's so determined to graduate; that despite the exhaustion she often feels after being awake during the night with her son, she comes to school and tries so hard.

"So are you still on the pill?" I asked.

"Yeah."

"How's that working out?"

"Fine."

"Any problems?"

"No."

"Do you have plenty?"

"Yeah."

"Do you take one every day?"

"Yeah."

"Good for you! What time do you take them?"

"Like around 10:00 at night."

"How do you remember?"

" 'Cause I just leave them on the little table next to the lamp so I see them right when I go to bed and I just take it."

"Sounds like you're doing very well. You're really taking charge. Good for you."

With many girls I've worked with, I'd have left it at that. But I knew Ellen too well. It all sounded too good to be true. I simply couldn't quite believe that she was actually swallowing one pill daily. I figured if I could just keep her talking about it, she'd eventually reveal if there was a problem. So I persisted; she didn't seem to mind at all.

"Well, you've chosen a highly effective method. If you swallow a pill within an hour of the same time every day, they're very effective. The problem is, if you're late, or you skip it, you'd be at risk of pregnancy. Do you guys use condoms, too, just in case?"

"Uh-uh," she shook her head. "No. He don't like 'em."

"So you're just relying on the pill?"

"Yeah."

"Do you feel like they're giving you enough protection?"

"Yeah."

"Have you ever missed one?"

"I've been late a couple of times."

"Like around how late?"

"Like maybe a half-hour or so. Maybe like an hour," she said, dismissively.

"That sounds like you're doing great." I still had trouble believing it, as much as I wanted to. "Did you ever, like, totally forget? Like, did you ever go to take your pill and see that the one from the day before was still in the package?"

"Yeah."

"And whadja do?"

"I just threw it out."

Bingo! I *knew* it was too good to be true!

"How come?"

"I dunno. I didn't know what to do. That's what everyone said."

"Who's 'everyone'?"

"Felicia. She said if it's just been an hour, take it, but if it was all day, throw it out 'cause you're not supposed to take two the same day. She said you're *always* supposed to take one, and that you have to take the one that says the right day."

I explained that that's incorrect, and stressed that what appeared to her to be a minor mishap could in fact leave her at high risk for pregnancy. It was frustrating, trying to get her to see what to do when she's stuck; trying to tip the balance *away from* asking an uninformed friend who is right there, willing to comfortably give misinformation and *towards* accessing a health care system that uses forms with big words, runs by a schedule, and isn't in her living room. I encouraged her to always feel free to call the nurse if she has a question (she won't), or to flag me down in school to ask questions (she won't). Then I redirected the conversation, offering her information about methods that don't involve daily action on her part.

In my training, I had read a lot about teen moms; that they're at high risk for becoming pregnant again. It had surprised me when I first read the statistics about that; I knew that one of the factors that contributed to teen pregnancy is that invincible feeling, "It won't happen to me." Logic had me figuring, if it had already happened to a teen, that would be her wake up call, and she'd be more careful in the future; she'd need little support from me.

But my boss Eileen had explained to me that it isn't just that invincible attitude that leads girls to get pregnant in the first place: successfully obtaining and consistently, correctly using effective methods of contraception takes a specific mindset and a specific set of skills. And there is nothing in the experience of being pregnant or even giving birth that teaches a person those skills. The same skills that were missing in the beginning are still often missing. Ellen epitomized that.

Eventually I helped her get on the shot, so she wouldn't have to remember a pill every day, but then we lost touch; she moved to the next county. I still don't know how she fared with the baby, or with the twins I heard she had two years later.

A minute after I heard Diane's name paged to the office, a girl appeared in my doorway; I figured she was Diane.

"Hi, I'm Vivian; are—"

"Yeah, I know who you are. Mrs. Bishop told me you were going to page me."

"Oh, good. Come on in. I don't know—"

"Yeah, she said I should talk to you 'cause of this essay I wrote," she said, and continued talking at lightning speed. "We had to write something about a conflict and I wrote this whole thing about my boyfriend and about how I broke up with him and stuff and like how I really like him and stuff but like how he went to kiss me and it was just like kinda like nothing, I mean, I like him, but like when he kissed me I really didn't feel anything, I mean like anything really special, and then, like, when we were all changing for gym and it was just girls, like, I feel a lot more feelings for girls and like I don't know but like maybe I just like girls better I mean like I *liked* my boyfriend but more just like as a friend and that's what I told him and like I kinda broke up with him I guess but like I didn't want to *hurt* him but I was thinking maybe guys just aren't for me. And that's what I wrote the essay about, like, about how I felt confused 'cause I like him and everything and then when Mrs. Bishop read it she said maybe I should talk to you about it."

"I'm glad she—"

"I mean, yeah, as a friend, but ya know not like *everything*," she added, clearly not noticing she was interrupting me. I was glad she opened right up about the essay; Mrs. Bishop had told me about it, and had said she had gotten Diane's permission to tell me about the content, but still, it was better to hear it straight from Diane. "And like when I'm with my girlfriends like sometimes it's just like we're really good friends but honestly like when it comes to physical, like attraction, honestly, like guys really I think maybe just don't do it for me."

She went on and on, talking non-stop, with seemingly no interest in listening, so I simply let her. I was glad she was so comfortable, and while I was prepared to offer her some support, each time I tried to speak she cut me off. Several times during her forty-three minute monologue I felt like I wasn't "doing my job" if all I did was listen. And the next week, when Mrs. Bishop thanked me so profusely saying, "I don't know what you did or said with Diane, but she seems so much better. She's so much more engaged in class, so much more confident and positive," I felt like I was getting credit for something I hadn't done. I shared my confusion with Eileen, "I mean, the girl just talked a mile a minute. All I really got to do was sit there and nod. I mean I didn't *do anything*. I tried, but each time I started to talk she cut me off. So I let her. I didn't even get to say any of the basics: that some people are clear about their sexual orientation from early childhood but others take years to truly know themselves. That it's not a race; that there's nothing wrong with giving yourself time to figure out who you are and what you want. Or websites she could use to read more. I mean, honestly, at the end of the period I just thanked her for coming down and being so open, and I told her she could come back and talk again any Friday, but really, I barely said, 'boo.' So when Mrs. Bishop was thanking me, I felt kind of like she's crediting me for something I didn't do."

"No Vee, she's not. Don't worry about it. You did exactly what you needed to do: you gave her a safe place to talk. It sounds like that's exactly what she needed, and like that's *all* she needed right now. She knows you're there; if she needs support or resources she'll come back. She knows you're safe; that's so important. I mean, think of how you told me about the day Mrs. Bishop told you about the essay, how awkward you said she sounded; how uncomfortable she seemed even just explaining second hand what was going on for this girl. You need to realize, that's the kind of reaction a kid's going to get from so many adults. Even if you think you didn't *do* anything, trust me: she was checking you out every second. The way you described her as being so intense, so tightly wound: she's been needing a safe place to talk, and I'll guarantee she was watching you every second. Just the way you sit and listen and nod, or a gentle smile that says, 'It's ok to say what you're saying.' If she had picked up the slightest clue that you weren't comfortable with what she was saying—a simple gesture, a subtle change in your expression—she'd have shut right down. And she didn't. Believe me, she was looking for signs from you that say 'continue' or 'shut down.' It's subtle, but it's powerful stuff. You let her explore herself, and that's what she needed."

Listening to Eileen, her logic sounded right. But it saddened me to think about how many young people lack anyone to turn to with their simple need to be heard as they question their sexual orientation.

As requested by the school nurse, principal, guidance counselor, and two teachers, I paged Gayle and met with her during her study hall. I figured it must be important since five people had flagged me down when I entered the school that morning, literally before I could unlock my office door and take off my coat. Gayle was new to the district and everyone wanted to be sure she met me. The nurse explained that nothing had *happened*, "She's just getting a lot of attention; we don't know anything about her history, we just want to be sure she knows about you."

It made sense: two weeks prior to her arrival, a colleague and I had spent two days going into every high school physical education class like we do each year. We spent a class period facilitating activities that taught about teen pregnancy, pregnancy prevention, and STDs, and we outlined our education services and how to access them. By the end of a half-hour of interactive activities we had left each class with important messages:

- "Your futures are important. Becoming a parent while you're in high school can throw your life dreams off track."
- "We know that most teens that do become pregnant get pregnant by mistake. It doesn't have to be like that; you deserve better!"
- "Abstinence is the only 100% safe way to get through high school without a pregnancy. But for any of you who do have sex while you're still in high school, there are methods of protection available to you that are 99% effective."
- "Our vision is that every single one of you graduates from high school without being involved in a pregnancy and without contracting an STD; that goes for the male and female students."
- "Sexuality is a very real and important part of life, and it's very private; your sex lives are none of my business. But if there's ever anything I can do that would be more helpful than minding my own business and respecting your privacy, please flag me down and let me know how I can help. We know that many of you will graduate without a pregnancy or STD with no support from us; we encourage you, and that's fine. But some of you may benefit from some extra support, and that's why we're here: every single one of you deserves a bright future."

And I explained that I could help them talk with their parents or their partners; that I could help them learn about and access the various birth control methods, or talk with them about anything they wanted. Gayle had missed the class by two weeks so I agreed to go over it all with her.

We all may have different ideas of beauty, but according to the "popular culture" definition of beauty, Gayle was gorgeous. Her blond hair bounced gently as she walked. Her flawless skin was radiant, her make-up sparingly but perfectly applied, and her Barbie-doll body flowed with confidence down the hall, leaving a stream of boys with twisted necks, straining for a slightly longer glimpse of this stunning new creature that had appeared, unexpectedly, on a random Wednesday, to call Springfield home. Most of the other students had known each other longer than they could remember, often having stories of best friends from kindergarten who were still best friends in high school.

But Gayle was new.

New! Therefore: mysterious.

Gorgeous and mysterious; no wonder all the school officials were concerned.

"Hi, I'm Vivian," I began. "I'm from ABC Springfield, and I understand you're new to the district. Am I correct that you have study hall now?"

"Yeah."

"Well, thank you for coming down. The school likes me to introduce myself and explain my role to new students. But first: welcome! How's it going for you here so far?"

"Oh, it's great. I really like it. Everyone is so friendly. All my teachers seem so nice, and the kids are great. I was so scared to move. In my old school, new kids were always treated like crap. Usually people just ignored them and it looked like it was so hard to make friends. I was dreading it. I never moved before. But it isn't what I pictured at all. I mean, like, kids sat with me at lunch the first day!"

"I'm glad to hear that it's going so well!"

"Yeah, I love it, and I'm even going to the basketball game tonight."

We chatted a bit more, and then I directed our conversation. "So like I said, I'm with ABC Springfield. Have you heard of ABC Springfield yet?"

"No."

"OK, well, the ABC stands for A Better Community. It's a local teen pregnancy prevention program. The main goals of the project are to reduce teen pregnancy and STDs here in Springfield. We know that most of the teens that do get pregnant don't mean to; it happens by accident. I'm an educator from Planned Parenthood, and as part of the project I'm here in school one day a week to meet with any students who want to talk with me in private. Many students reach the goal of graduating without a pregnancy without any problems along the way, but for some students there can be some bumps in the road. So that's why I'm here, to help students set goals and reach them. Tell me, do you ever think about whether you want to have kids someday?"

"Oh, yes, someday, definitely."

"Have you ever thought about *when* you'd like to become a parent?"

"Not 'till I'm a lot older."

"What's, 'a lot'?"

"Like not 'till I finish college and have a good job and money and everything."

"Good for you! Those are great goals. That's the kind of thing I try to get students to focus on: setting and reaching goals like that. That's what I'm here to support. So if students are having a hard time in relationships, or having trouble talking to their partners or parents about sexuality, they can come to me. Lots of students wait to have sex, and that's great, and if it ever gets hard to communicate those boundaries in relationships, I'm here to help. Or if teens want birth control, I can either help them talk with their parents or help them figure out how to get it on their own, so they don't put themselves in harm's way. Does that make sense?"

"Oh yeah," she said, "But you won't have to worry about *me* with any of that stuff. I'm definitely not going to have sex 'till I'm married."

"Well, that's a super healthy choice; there are lots of great reasons to wait.

And I have to say, I like your confidence, and I really respect your decisiveness! Do you mind if I ask you where you get it from?"

"Oh, sure, I *know* I won't have sex. 'Cause in my old school like they showed us this movie about kids who have sex, and like, they are so stupid, like, I'd never do that! Some of the kids did it and got pregnant, and, like it ruined their lives. And then these other ones thought they could use protection so they got condoms but like what they didn't know was that they can break and they showed us this one girl and"—distorting her face, scrunching up her nose, she explained—"it like broke inside her and like she got like all infected and everything and I am not kidding you it was so gross!" Continuing with emphatic momentum, "And then there were these girls who went on the pill and they got like cancer and they had to get chemo and they lost all their hair and like I would never do that!"

I became concerned. Very concerned. For while I respect that there are numerous valid reasons for a young person to choose to remain abstinent until marriage, her reasons, to me, weren't based on reality, personal goals, or faith. They were based on fear and misinformation.

I had read and heard so much about then President Bush's $175 million dollars a year that was earmarked to, "Abstinence-Only-Until-Marriage Education," and as a Planned Parenthood educator I had read and heard accusations regarding the misinformation that many of these programs were allegedly passing off as "education" in public schools with federal money; like most of my colleagues, I was unaware of any other example of the federal government funding misinformation and forbidding accurate information from being taught in public schools, and we were all kind of shell-shocked about it. I knew that the data was clear, that comprehensive sexuality education which includes both abstinence and contraception was more effective than abstinence-only education, and that it's what most Americans support. Yet it was eye-opening to me, sitting there with this beautiful young woman, listening to her recite with confidence one piece of misinformation after the next, misinformation she had been taught in school, from a program funded by federal money.

> ✔**FACT**
>
> THE AVERAGE AMERICAN WOMAN SPENDS ABOUT THREE DECADES—MORE THAN THREE-QUARTERS OF HER REPRODUCTIVE LIFE— TRYING TO AVOID AN UNINTENDED PREGNANCY.

I certainly didn't want to talk her out of postponing sexual involvement! By then, I had seen so many teens that had become sexually active long before they had the maturity to deal with the consequences.

But I couldn't help wonder; here's this beautiful young woman. Someday she will have sex. There could be times in her life, even when she's a fully mature adult, when she wants to have sex with a male partner but doesn't want a pregnancy. During these impressionable young years, some film had scared her off the possibility of effective contraception, and I was guessing that that would influence her decision making for years.

I had the next period free; I didn't have any students to page, so I figured I'd have a little time to get caught up on my paperwork. Plus, after Gayle, I thought a few minutes alone would be nice.

But then Fran appeared unexpectedly in my doorway. I barely knew her.

"Hi Vee," she said, looking happy and relaxed.

"Hi Fran," I replied.

She stood there, with the body language that says, "Can I stay and talk?"

So I asked, "Do you have study hall now?"

"Yeah."

"Would you like to come in?"

She did. She was very chatty, going on and on and on, filling me in as though she'd known me for years, known me well. She told me about how she had been out of school for over a month with what sounded like some very complicated medical problems; endometriosis and a few other diagnoses I'm familiar with, but also lots of other problems I'd never heard of, including stories about things attacking various organs. It sounded serious. I questioned whether there was an underlying diagnosis that connected all these problems, and that's when she told me that a lot of it might be from when she was addicted to heroin; she recently got out of rehab. She'd been using for two years, tried it first at age eleven.

Most of us probably have a mental image when we picture a heroin addict; Fran certainly didn't match it. Lately, there's been a lot of press about young teens using heroin, but this was several years before those stories were so common. She was fourteen; that's young. And she looked even younger. There was a gentle innocence to her face, a simplicity to her haircut, a softness to her smile: a little country girl.

We discussed so many things, about her health, her relationship with her mom, her heroin use, how it led to the stealing, the cops, the dealers. I wanted to let her talk all day, as she seemed to want to, but as she told me how the urge to use comes and goes, I needed to ensure that she'd have an adult she could talk with the way she talked with me, when I'm not in her school. Starting that contact immediately felt urgent.

I had two primary concerns. First, she could need important support on days I'm not around; I wanted to ensure that she always had an adult to talk with. Second, the fact is that even though she blurted all this out to me, I am not a specialist in drug rehab or substance abuse. And she had said some things that deeply concerned me that I knew needed follow-up attention by someone with more specific training than I have.

So I explored my concerns. "Is there any adult here in school you're comfortable talking with about this stuff, the way you talk with me?"

"No."

That concerned and truly surprised me, as I was certain she had only spoken with me once or twice, long ago, and yet she was so open, so comfortable, so chatty. It seemed like she'd be able to talk with almost anyone.

So I asked if she's ever tried talking with the school psychologist, thinking I could bring her down there immediately, or at least get a release to talk with him. She got bug eyed and a look of horror came over her face: "No!"

"How come?" I asked.

"I wouldn't wanna talk to anyone who's like got a *title* and stuff. The thing about you: you're *just Vee!* Like today, when I came upstairs, my friends said, 'Where ya goin'?' and I said, 'I'm goin' to talk to Vee,' and they were just like, 'Oh, right.' Like it's no big deal. Anyone could talk to you; it doesn't mean anything. But like if I said, 'I'm goin' ta talk ta the psychologist,' they'd all be, 'like…wooooooah!' "

She loved to talk; she spoke so easily and openly, yet she was so aware of how she would feel and how her friends would feel if she talked with someone with "a title." The stigma of the title created a huge barrier, despite her obvious need for services.

I did finally get a release to talk with the school nurse, and the nurse turned out to already be aware from Fran's mom of all that was going on. It left me feeling so puzzled: aware that I have the opportunity to build this comfort simply by the *lack* of a title.

It seemed so ironic to me that adults work and study for years for PhD's and yet it is the very title and formality that alienates so many of the people they could be serving. Strange. I felt so thankful for the fact that I'm allowed to let kids call me by my first name in school, even by my nickname; that I have opportunities to create such comfort with them. I had never before felt so thankful for the *lack* of a title.

It reminded me of another girl who had poured her heart out to me numerous times, and then told me she loved talking with me, saying, "It's like counseling, but without all the baggage."

It made me love my new name: "Just Vee."

At the day's end, driving home, I reflect on the vast range of topics I discussed with teens during the consecutive forty-three minute conversations. The common theme that unites them all is that I'm trying to support each one in the pursuit of graduating from high school without a pregnancy or an STD. But on any given day, the issues I address from one student to the next are so varied. And over the course of a high school career, the issues I address with any particular student can be equally varied. In addition, the way each issue can effectively be addressed with each teen keeps changing; the girl who responds to my question, "Why do you think you failed your global studies exam?" by saying, "Because my mom forgot to remind me to study," is showing me her developmental stage. She still expects and needs a lot of support; she's not ready to go it alone. Neither is the girl who stopped me between classes and told me she had forgotten to take her pill for three days, "But I remembered and took them all today." She also admitted to having had unprotected sex with an IV drug user, and when I offered to meet with her during her study hall she asked, "Why? I already know everything I need to know." Addressing these issues with teens needs to be customized to the issue and to the teen at the stage they're at when they're facing them.

The thing about teens' needs is that they are so very time specific. Their needs must be met *when they present themselves as needs.* The same student who sat through a health class in which correct condom use was discussed might have been lost in thought about one of a million other things if that student wasn't sexually active or concerned about it at the time. The same teen that uses condoms consistently for two years but finds herself tongue-tied with a new partner needs the support when that happens. Once these concerns become concerns, they need to be addressed in a timely fashion; "timely" in the teens' perception of the world, where an entire sense of self can be overhauled from Tuesday to Friday. And often, they need to be addressed in private.

That's why I believe that having knowledgeable, supportive adults available to teens upon request *when they need them* is essential. As is letting the teen set the agenda; putting out the message, "I'm here to support you; it's up to you to let me know if and how I can be helpful," and then following their lead. Once they feel safe, their stories and their questions enable the adult to figure out where they are and how to be helpful.

There are lots of excellent classroom curricula that provide roadmaps for teaching students important information about sexual health. They are generally created to answer the question, "What's the most important information that teens need to know?" But despite the importance of that question, to truly help many teens, the real question that needs to be addressed is, "What does the teen that is struggling *today* need to learn *today,* and how can we identify and help that teen *today?*" It's not just about information: it's about *timely* information. It's not one-size-fits-all, and it frequently is too private to be discussed in a classroom.

High school study halls provide such a rich opportunity to put time that is otherwise often wasted to such important use. The kids are there; they have the needs and they have the time. And they love to have these conversations, opportunities to relate their sexual experiences to their life goals, to consider how the timing of becoming a parent impacts their future. They love to discuss their sexual health within the context of their relationships, and within the context of their unfolding everyday lives in a non-clinical setting. They quickly build comfort on the unfamiliar soil of discussing something as intimate as sexuality with a total stranger when they don't feel they're being preached to or judged: when they're listened to, when they feel safe and affirmed. Age doesn't have to be a barrier; I'm older than almost any of these kids' moms, yet they love to talk about these issues with me.

And it results in measurable behavior change; they end up talking to their parents, their partners, their medical providers. They think more seriously about their goals, their intimate relationships, about whether and when to have sex. And when they do have sex, they get contraceptive methods and use them more correctly and consistently.

Walk through the halls of any high school in America today, during those three minutes between bells when the students are changing classes. Tell me you don't feel the sexual energy and tension that is ever present. Tell me I'm the only one who sees it. Tell me I'm crazy. And please think for a moment about what I think about: Fallopian tubes. Half the students have them: all the girls. On any given day, about a third of those girls might have an egg in her tubes; around half the girls will have had sex before graduation. You do the math; that's a lot of opportunities for unintended pregnancy. They're going through those halls, switching from class to class, to do their science labs, to learn about world history, to learn computer skills, to read Shakespeare; to learn what high school students learn. About almost everything except sex. Silently, they wonder about all the issues I've discussed here and a thousand others related to sexuality and sexual health.

And yet the adult communities in most schools largely ignore it. It's our collective silence, our collective denial of the power of teen sexual energy, our collective neglect of the fact that the adolescent brain isn't yet up to the complex task of safely navigating their own way through all this; it's our collective unwillingness to deal in a supportive way with our teens that is contributing to our shamefully high teen pregnancy rates.

It doesn't have to be that way.

CLUELESS

"**A**re you a virgin?" Gloria asked me.

She was sixteen.

The question seemed to come out of the blue, when she was telling me some long story about her ex-boyfriend, and it seemed odd since she knew I was married. I had been taught how to respond when teens ask me personal questions: "Find out where the question is coming from. What teens really want to talk about is themselves..."

So I replied, "Wow, that's an unusual question. Do you mind if I ask why you want to know?"

" 'Cause I want to know if you know how I *feel*. 'Cause like, before, when I was a virgin, I was, like, a little horny like some of the time. But now that I'm not a virgin anymore, it's like, I'm really horny, like, all the time."

"Oh. That's why you're asking. Now I get it; now it makes sense. You're wondering if I can understand what you're going through."

"Yes!"

"Well, I want to say, yes, you're explaining yourself extremely well. I definitely feel like I get what you mean."

She went on with her story, about her conflicting feelings about the temptation to go to bed with her "ex" even though he had cheated on her, and how torn she was.

And she never noticed or cared about the fact that I hadn't answered her question.

SNAPSHOT

"THIS IS JUSTINE, THIS IS LACEY. SHE'S A VIRGIN, SHE'S NOT."

–TEEN GIRL, INTRODUCING ME TO HER FRIENDS

One by one, teens like Gloria have shown me how teens think and communicate.

"I gotta go on the pill fast!" Frances said with a sense of urgency as she plopped down on the beanbag chair in our drop-in center. She's another one that showed me that teens don't communicate the way adults do. "I am like sooo horny all the time, if I don't go on the pill, I know I'll end up pregnant, and I am so not ready to have no kid!"

"You can say that again!" said her friend Eve, rolling her eyes as she plopped down on the other beanbag. Eve had never been to my drop-in before; I'm always glad to see a new face. And it's nice when a teen I know like Frances models that kind of comfort.

"I remember you said you were going to talk to your mom about going on the pill. Did you?" I asked.

"Ugh, yeah, I mean, I tried."

"What happened?"

"She said I'm too young to have sex. She said I have to wait 'till I'm sixteen."

"How old are you?"

"Fifteen and two months."

"Hmmm, so your mom wants you to wait ten more months?"

"Yeah; I mean, like, I was trying to wait. She told me when I'm sixteen long ago. I been waiting. Like, I mean, I'd have sex every day if I wasn't so scared of getting pregnant. I mean, I waited a lot, but then, I had sex, and like the last couple of weeks I like did it a lot and I mean I loved it and finally I said, 'Mom, look, you said I could go on the pill when I turn sixteen but I'm so horny, I'm the horniest person you'll ever meet. And I don't wanna get pregnant. I really want to go on the pill now!' but she said I have to wait till I'm sixteen."

"Wow, you were really honest with your mom. What was it like for you to be so open with her, to tell her all that? Was it hard?"

She paused only slightly and shrugged.

"Not really. I tell everyone."

"Eleven partners? That's a lot considering you're only fifteen. Do you mind if I ask you how old you were the first time?" I asked Gina.

"I was thirteen."

I knew her parents were very strict; that she was rarely allowed out of their sight, so I was a little surprised that she had even found the necessary privacy, especially when she was thirteen.

"Where were you?"

"At Christian Camp: that was so fun!"

She wasn't the only one who reminded me that teens' sexual behavior often happens in places adults wouldn't consider to be appropriate or private enough.

My husband had just reminded me of that over the weekend.

"You should have come with me today if you really want to be successful in your job," he said on Saturday when he got home from fishing in the rain. There's nothing he loves doing more than strolling down the middle of little trout streams in his waders, fishing for hours, covering miles of pristine waters. And he lives by the old fisherman's adage, "The two best times to go fishing are when it's raining and when it isn't."

"What are you talking about?" I had asked him.

"I went for about two miles down the creek and I came to where this little road goes over the stream—and I didn't think about it but I'm really quiet when I'm fishing—and I'm just casting away, when I hear all this rustling under the bridge, and I turned and looked and there's these two kids running away and the guy is putting his shirt on while he's running and the girl already took off like a rocket and I realized they were a couple, hiding out under the bridge. I mean it's probably the only dry, private place in the county. They must have been so bummed out that I showed up. I mean, if you saw that little creek and that little bridge, the last thing anyone would expect is for a person to appear from up the creek: it's in the middle of nowhere." And after a pause, he added, "Maybe next time I go fishing you should give me some condoms to leave these kids under the bridges."

And then there was Greta; she showed up wanting a pregnancy test a week after I had given her a bunch of condoms. On that day, she had said she was certain that condoms were enough; she didn't need birth control. She insisted they used condoms every time: no problem.

"You sounded so confident that you'd always use condoms; do you mind if I ask you how come you didn't use one this time?"

"We would have, but we didn't have them with us."

"I remember you said you always have them with you; what happened?"

"We left half of them at his house and half of them at mine. That always worked before, 'cuz we were always either at his house or at mine when we did it."

"Where were you this time?"

"In the back of the van; my dad was driving him home."

"You mean you had sex in the back of the van while your father was right in the drivers' seat, while he was driving?" I must have looked puzzled. She explained.

"Oh, Vee, you don't know my dad: he'd never take his eyes off the road!"

And another girl once told me, "We were on the couch watching this movie and my boyfriend was fingering me and I mean it felt really good but I was worried his mom would see."

"Where was his mom?" I asked.

"Right there in the kitchen, and there's no door! I mean I could see her perfectly!"

"Was *he* concerned that she'd see?"

Her explanation was simple: shrugging her shoulders she said, "We had a blanket over us."

"I just ain't gonna have sex no more! The minute you have sex with a guy, he turns into a jerk!" Heather said. "Or if I ever do, it's gonna be exactly the way I want."

"How's that?" I asked.

"Like, it's gonna be completely different. I mean, it'll be with someone really special, someone I've been with like a long time. And it ain't gonna just be like we have sex. It's gonna be a whole thing. Romantic. I've got it all figured out; I know exactly what I want and I'm not gonna settle for nothing less."

"It sounds like you have a clear image in your head."

"I do. It'll be when I'm older, when I really know the guy. And we'll go someplace really special, like on a honeymoon. And first we'll go out to dinner in a really nice restaurant. And we'll be someplace really beautiful, like at the beach, in a beautiful hotel. And we'll go for a nice, long, romantic walk on the beach. And then when we get back to the room we'll have a whole bunch of those little, tiny tea lite candles, and we'll make a circle out of them, a big, giant circle in the room. And we'll make love inside the circle, surrounded by that soft light from every direction. And it'll be really special, y'know, the way soft candle light is so relaxing and beautiful."

Heather had had numerous sexual partners, but the encounters often left her feeling unhappy. We'd had several conversations about building trust over time, not just rushing into a sexual relationship as a way to get to know someone. So I was glad she was finally thinking about what she wanted, and admitting that spending time getting to know the person first would be a plus. I hoped that hearing herself articulate some goals would help her stick to them. Still, I had concerns when she told me about quitting her birth control.

It's always tricky when girls like Heather plan abstinence. It's the only 100% effective method of avoiding pregnancy, and it certainly bypasses both the STDs and the heartaches. But it leaves them so vulnerable to pregnancy if the plan fails. So I always ask them to consider remaining on their methods just in case, but if they choose not to, I try to monitor them closely.

"How's it going?" I simply asked a few weeks later. She looked down at the floor and shrugged her shoulders.

"Do I need to worry about you?" I asked playfully, trying to make her comfortable enough to talk. She was usually so chatty and bubbly that I knew something was wrong, and since she connected me so much with Planned Parenthood I figured whatever was bothering her was about sex.

"I dunno," she said, and after a long pause she added, "maybe kinda sorta."

"What's going on?"

"Well, ya know that plan I had? About how I was gonna wait?"

"Yeah?"

"Well, like, it didn't really work."

"Do you want to tell me what happened?"

"Well, I went over to Greg's again, just to watch a movie. We weren't gonna do nothing."

"And?"

"Well, like, stuff happened. I mean, I wasn't gonna have sex, but then we did."

"What's your thought about that now?"

"I shouldn't'a done it! I mean, after we did it I went home, and he called me like a half hour later and said we ain't goin' out: he's goin' out with my cousin again. He's a jerk just like all the others."

"Oh, wow. That must've been hard to hear."

"It was. But now…well, like…I just really hope I'm not pregnant. 'Cuz like, remember how I quit my birth control when I decided to stop having sex? So I didn't have nuthin'?"

"Yeah, I remember. But I thought you were going to wait; I remember your whole story, you had it all planned out with the walk on the beach and the circle of candles and everything, and that it'd be with someone you've been with for so long. What happened?"

"Well, I kinda waited for some of it."

"What do you mean?"

"Well, 'cuz like I've known Greg since like second grade. And, I mean, it wasn't a beach, but like we went to the mini-mart for some chips 'cuz we were really hungry, and then we walked back to his trailer. And like, I mean, it wasn't the whole thing I pictured, but like, he had these two candles, one by the bed and one on the dresser."

So there we were: the fantasy downgraded. The love of a life had been reduced to an old friend, the dinner in the restaurant had been replaced with a bag of chips, the walk on the beach had been demoted to the walk home from the mini-mart, and the circle of candles was reduced to two.

Hope would have been one of the last people I'd expect to appear in the clinic for a pregnancy test. But there she was. Afterwards, she came upstairs and plopped down on my couch looking exhausted and defeated, so I was a bit surprised to hear that the test was negative.

I had worked with her for years and the only time she had ever been putting herself at high risk for pregnancy was when she had first started having sex. She was still living with her mom then, but once she was placed in a foster home she took charge of her fertility, got to the clinic, and thrived with the supervision that the foster home provided. And even when she got out of foster care at eighteen she was consistently getting to her appointments and using reliable methods.

Like many teens in unsupervised homes she had numerous sexual partners before age sixteen, yet she was always comfortable and assertive about both condom use and hormonal contraception. So it truly surprised me that she thought she was pregnant; I wondered why she had quit using effective methods if she didn't want a pregnancy. I asked.

Sounding frustrated and fed up, she replied. "It's like, I went on the shot and in the beginning it was fine and stuff but I was bleeding a lot and they said that would probably stop and it kind of like maybe stopped a little but like I was still bleeding and then I started gaining weight and I just got to where I was like, like, sick of the whole thing and I told Ed, 'I'm so sick of this shot but I don't wanna get pregnant,' and he agreed and he was like, 'I want you to be happy; if you don't like it you should just quit it,' and like, I really like the way he was so respectful and everything, and like I had that brochure that you gave me and we sat down with it like sooo many times to decide what to use and like he hates those condoms and that spermicide is such a mess and a pain in the butt and every time we talked about it we'd decide, 'That does it, we're just gonna use abstinence 'cause that is all such a pain.' And it always works for a little while but then, like, it gets so hard and we end up doin' it and then it's like: uh-oh, we ain't got nooo protection 'cause we were using abstinence. And now it's happened like four times and I mean I've been lucky but honestly I don't know what I'm gonna do!"

She finally paused and took a breath. After talking a mile a minute she sat back, looking exhausted. It was "my turn" so I decided to start with the positive and then try to build on that.

"Wow, it sounds like it's been rough. But I'm glad you came in, and that you know what you want and that you talk with him about it. And you're aware of the risks and it's great that you're looking to do better. I don't know if I can help but I'm certainly willing to give it a try. Let's look at where you are right now; you said you've been using abstinence and that it does work for a while, but then it stops working. Let's build on that; when you have talked with him and decided to abstain, how long does it usually work?"

She tilted her head and scrunched up her nose and eyes in thought, looking back and trying to remember, and replied, "Um, usually around twenty minutes."

"Vee, you should go into the middle school classes and talk to all those kids!" Grace demanded.

I knew that she had no idea of how politically charged the idea of having a Planned Parenthood educator in middle school classes is, but I was curious to learn what motivated her to suggest it.

"Why?" I asked.

"Because some of them are having sex, and they aren't ready. I mean, maybe a few are, and you could help them get birth control. But honestly, most of the ones who are having sex really aren't ready; they need help. You could help all of them the way you helped me."

"What do you mean?"

"Don't you remember? When I was having sex with Frank, and he was older, you got me to stop?"

I got her to stop? I had no idea what she was referring to.

"I don't remember; what happened?"

"How could you not remember that?! I used to come talk to you all the time!"

"I remember you used to come up all the time when you were in middle school, but please forgive my memory. I talk with so many people, and it was over five years ago; I don't remember the specific conversation you're talking about."

"When I first started coming up here, me and Frank were having sex, and you asked me if I wanted to; you said I was so young. And I told you I wanted to the first time, but then I didn't want to anymore."

"Oh, yeah."

"You were the one who said that every time the sun comes up it's a new day, and that I always have the right to say 'no' even if I've said 'yes' before. Don't you remember? You told me that I have a voice, and that I could talk to him; that I had to tell him if I didn't want to have sex. Those other kids need to hear that; I think some of them are having sex and they really aren't ready." Her words were so emotionally charged, her face turned red and her voice cracked as she spoke.

"Wow, you've got a great memory. I do remember you used to come up here every week and tell me about Frank, but I didn't remember all the details. I'm glad it was helpful." She had come in to talk to me so many times over those years; while there was no way I could remember every conversation, it certainly sounded like words I had said to dozens of young teens, so I didn't question it.

"Lots of grown-ups tell them, 'Don't do it,' but it just sounds stupid. You were the only one who really helped me figure out *how*, like, what to say. Like, you never said it's bad or anything, you never shut me down like that; you just let me talk and talk and talk and then you helped me figure out what I wanted, and what I needed to do. Remember? Like, we practiced: you told me to look at you and pretend you were Frank and I got to practice what I'd say. That's the only reason why I could say all that stuff to him. Those kids need that."

Holly slinked into my office at Planned Parenthood, sat quietly on my couch, and started sobbing into her hands. I said hello softly and pushed the box of tissues a little closer to her. She didn't take one, she didn't look up, she didn't say hello, she didn't say anything; she just kept sobbing.

Finally, she spoke. Fast. "Oh, my God, Vee. I'm so ashamed of myself. And I'm sooo scared! I feel so stupid. I mean, last night Glen came over and like we weren't planning anything and then like we started just kinda foolin' around and like I didn't think nothin' about it, I mean, it was just, like, fun. But then my mom went out to the store and like the next thing you know we were like, alone in the house, and we started like doin' it, and like we hadn't like planned it or nothing and like I mean I even kinda thought about it and stuff and like I even said to him, 'I have condoms but they're upstairs,' and like we were just kinda foolin' around and it just kinda like slipped in and I said like, 'Just for a second,' and he said, 'OK,' and stuff but oh my God, Vee, I mean like it just all happened so fast and the next thing you know he like did it inside me and like then we stopped but like I said, 'Did you come?' and he was like, 'Yeah, I'm sorry,' and I was like, 'Oh my God,' and he was like, like, he just kept saying, 'I'm so sorry,' and then we got all dressed and stuff and I was just so upset 'cause like I mean I had those condoms you gave me, I mean, they were right upstairs. And I told him I was gonna come here today to see if I could get those pills you told me about for after. Oh, my God, I can't even believe I'm telling you this. I mean, you were the one who told me that condoms alone aren't enough; I feel sooo stupid. And then he just said maybe I should go on one of those birth control things you told us about last time, after all. I mean, if I'm not pregnant. Just, ya know, to be more careful."

Finally she came up for air, took a tissue, wiped her face, and for the first time looked at me.

"Wow," I said. "This sounds really intense. You look and sound so concerned, and I can understand why. And yes, I can definitely help you get the EC pills downstairs in the clinic, and then we can talk about what to do next."

"Oh, my God, thank you so much. You must hate me now. You told me to be careful; you must think I'm so stupid."

"Actually, no," I said, speaking softly and slowly. "To tell you the truth, as I sit here listening to you, I can understand how upset you are, but I'm thinking exactly the opposite. I'm sitting here wondering how I could clone you, wondering how I could find a way to make every teenager in the country more like you."

"What are you talking about? I just did, like, the stupidest thing in the world!"

"You mean the thing about having sex that wasn't planned, without protection?"

"Yeah."

"Well, yes, you did that; that's not the part I want to clone. And I can understand why that's the part that you're focused on. But that's not the part I'm focused on."

"What are you talking about; what other part is there?"

"The part about the fact that you're sitting her telling me this! I mean, I don't want to downplay your concern, I really don't. But from my perspective, it's like this: I know that lots of teenagers have unprotected sex. It happens lots of times, for zillions of reasons. And you're right: that's a big part of why I have my job, to try to help teenagers prevent unwanted pregnancy. But the fact is, not all teens protect themselves every single time they have sex: I know that. So as I listen to you, I'm wondering: of all the teens who had unprotected sex this week, how many of them had the courage to do something about it. You came here. To me, that's huge. Not just that you admitted it to yourself, but that you admitted it to me. Especially knowing how ashamed you felt; I can only imagine how hard it was for you to walk alone up those stairs, sit here crying, and then tell me everything you just said. That is not easy! So many teens that have unprotected sex either can't or won't deal with it; they just stay home and pray they're not pregnant. So I wonder how we could make it so every teen in this country who ever had unprotected sex was as quickly responsible as you afterwards. We'd have a fraction of the teen pregnancy rate we have today!"

"Oh, man. I never thought of it like that. Actually it was hard, but I knew I had to do it."

"Yeah, you did, and that's a big part of what makes you so special in my eyes."

Gradually, she stopped crying, sat taller, and I think she understood and appreciated what I meant. She did get the EC, she wasn't pregnant, and with ongoing support she got and used effective methods for the rest of her high school years. She graduated without a pregnancy.

"Could we get some condoms?" Hannah asked, standing in the doorway of my Planned Parenthood office. It looked like the question took all the nerve she could muster. I'm used to that with teens I've never met, like her and her friend Ginger. Clearly someone had told them the drill.

"Certainly," I replied, and as I tossed some condoms into bags I added, "You came to the right place. And you can come back for more any

Thursday. If you just wanna pick up condoms and split, that's fine, or if you ever wanna stay and hang out that's fine, or if either of you wants an appointment downstairs I can help you set that up, too. Do you know about the clinic downstairs?"

"Uh-huh."

"Good. And listen, condoms are a great start, but if either of you are sexually active, it's important to know that condoms alone aren't the most effective protection. There are a lot of birth control methods available that you could use with condoms for a lot more protection. If that's something either of you ever wants, I can help you get it."

Their eyes had quickly scanned my office: our teen drop-in center. And while the posters about abstinence and birth control and preventing STDs had briefly caught their eyes, their gazes came to rest on the "birth control mobile" that hangs, almost playfully, in the corner. They were silently looking at the different pills, patches, condoms, spermicides and other miscellaneous items a colleague and I had made into a colorful mobile; they handled a few items, making the rest bounce around from their long, colorful ribbons. That mobile has been my favorite way of wordlessly encouraging people to ask questions; it's so inviting, so unthreatening, so intriguing. And all the ribbons hang from a coat hanger; 95% of the people who see it don't get the metaphor, usually because they're too young to know that back-alley abortionists used to use coat hangers before abortion was legalized in the U.S. But it's there, and I like it.

The mobile intrigued them, and they sat and stayed a while. We chatted a bit. They pointed to a lot of things on the mobile asking what they were. They were especially interested in the various hormonal methods of birth control.

"Which one is the most accurate?" Hannah asked. I often hear teens use the word "accurate" for what the medical establishment refers to as "effective." I explained how the effectiveness of all the hormonal methods varies; emphasizing that correct use is critical for maximizing effectiveness.

There was some interest, but also resistance. They both said that they didn't want to get pregnant, but that they were just using condoms.

"Do you feel like the condoms alone are giving you enough protection?" I asked.

"I dunno, kinda, sorta." Not a ringing endorsement, but at least they were thinking.

"Well, if you ever decide you want more protection, this is a place you can come to."

"Yeah, but I heard you have to get like that thing if you want birth control."

"You'd need an appointment, and it's generally recommended you get a pelvic exam. Is that what you mean?" Today, teens requesting hormonal birth control don't always need a pelvic exam first, but back then it was almost always required.

"Yeah, I guess. I would never do that! That is sooo disgusting! I mean, I can't believe anyone would do that," Ginger replied, writhing in her seat as she spoke.

"Do you know anyone who's done it? What have you heard?" I asked.

"Oh," Hannah eagerly piped in. "I heard they clamp you with this thing and then they like cut you!"

"Wow!" I exclaimed. "No wonder you don't wanna do it! I wouldn't either if that's what I had heard; that sounds painful!" And they willingly examined my sample speculum and listened to my explanation of what it is and how a pelvic exam is performed. Their favorite part was that it only actually takes a few minutes. Their least favorite part was that someone would be looking at their genitals, naked, and touching them.

"I mean, you can go if ya wanna," Ginger said to Hannah. "But not me. I would never do somethin' like that. That is like sooo gross! I am like a very private person. I would never let nobody look at me like…there!"

"Well, it might help you to think about why the person is doing that. It's not to invade your privacy; it's for your health."

"Ugh! That is just too weird! I would never go to no gynecologist. The idea that some doctor would wanna look at *that* all day; what a pervert!"

"Would it help you to know that if you come to Planned Parenthood for your care, it would be a woman who does your exam?"

"Especially not no lesbian!" she insisted.

Ugh, I thought. Where do I go with this one? Do I address the homophobia first, or the fear of the exam? Ouch.

"One thing I think you may not realize is that whether a gynecologist is male or female, and regardless of the doctor's sexual orientation, doing a pelvic exam is not a sexual experience. Yes, it involves our sex organs, but the little bit of touching that happens isn't sexual touching; it's not about sex, it's about health. Our practitioners don't do the exams because they want to look at your private parts, they do them because they want you to be healthy and reach your goals. And they know how important it is that teens have someone they can go to and trust, someone who will be respectful, someone who won't judge them. Does that make sense to you?"

It made sense to Hannah, but Ginger was still fixated on how disgusting she thought the whole thing was. I continued, as Hannah gave me a look that said she wanted to know more about what to expect.

"Have either of you ever used tampons?" I asked. They both had. So I added, "Does it hurt to put one in?" They both looked at me like I was nuts, which was just what I wanted.

"OK, imagine this. Imagine that you go to a doctor's office, and you get undressed, and you're wearing one of those weird paper gowns, and you lie back on the exam table and open your legs, and the doctor puts in a tampon, or pulls one out. Would that hurt?"

They couldn't even find words. I didn't really need them to. Their expressions answered my question.

"That would be the weirdest thing going, right?" I asked.

Still communicating silently, they confirmed: vigorous head nodding, "Yes."

"But it wouldn't hurt. It would be weird, but that's all it would be. Having a speculum put in is about like that. It may feel awkward; we're not used to having a stranger look at the private parts of our body. But it doesn't hurt. And if we accept that there's an important reason, that there's something more important than the awkwardness of the moment—like the rest of our lives!—and if we realize that it's just a minute of awkwardness, it makes it much easier to deal with. Does that make sense, what I'm saying?"

Hannah was pushing herself, opening up to the idea. Ginger was still disgusted.

I paused a bit; we shared some necessary silence. They were pushing themselves a lot and I was thankful for that. Sometimes it's hard to strike a balance; Hannah was just about ready to agree to a much-needed pelvic exam. Ginger needed time to process all this; I was clearly trying to get her to think outside her comfort zone.

"Listen," I said, "I know this is a lot to think about. Having your first pelvic exam is a big step. I don't know you; you know yourselves. Only you really know if you're ready or not. I don't want to push you or rush you, you need to grow up at your own pace, but I do want to stress that if you're having sex and you're not ready to sacrifice a couple of minutes of comfort for the sake of the exam, then you're really jeopardizing a lot. And strange as this might sound, the more you don't want a stranger looking at your genitals, the more important it is to have the exam."

"What do you mean?" Hannah asked.

"If you schedule an appointment now, for prevention, and you get in there and you don't like the practitioner, at any point you can say, 'Stop,' and you can choose to end the appointment, get dressed, and leave. Then you can go find a different provider, someone you like; you have total control. But if you get pregnant, and if you have the baby, you lose most of that control. Not all of it: you can choose your obstetrician, but if you go into labor and have some kind of emergency and rush to the hospital, you may have a lot of strangers looking at your private parts, and you may have no say about it. So I really want to encourage you to consider this: if you're not ready to have a pelvic exam, you may really not be ready to be having sex. You're playing with fire."

"I really want to do this; I'm ready," Hannah said.

"You're probably smart," Ginger conceded, finally encouraging her friend, instead of sounding condescending. "I'll wait to hear how yours goes before I decide."

I helped Hannah schedule her initial appointment. I was glad to be able to get her on Lila's schedule. Lila was an older nurse practitioner. She had once told me about how nervous she was during her own first pelvic exam; she was in college in the 60s when it was still illegal for doctors to prescribe contraception to unmarried women. Everyone in her college dorm shared one wedding band to wear to the gynecologist. "Just wear the band and say you're married; they don't check," her friends had said. But she's very petite and her fingers were so tiny and the band was enormous. So all she could think about as she laid on the exam table with her feet in the stirrups was that the doctor might notice the huge wad of tape she had wound around the inside of the band in a pathetic attempt to make it look like it fit. Fortunately, the doctor either didn't notice or didn't care. But the thought of that possibility had terrified her. Now she loved helping nervous people relax. I knew she'd love working with Hannah.

"Vee, she's nineteen and she's still a virgin!" Jenn said shortly after introducing me to her friend Helen. "I told her to come talk to you 'cause she's nineteen. Nineteen!" And looking exasperated, she turned to Helen and asked, "How could you still be a virgin at nineteen?" in a tone of disbelief.

I knew that Jenn had started having sex early, when they were in middle school, so I could see where it seemed "long" to her, but still, her words stung; her entire demeanor seemed so disrespectful.

"Wait a minute, Jenn," I said, and turning to Helen I added, "I hope you don't mind that Jenn shared something so personal. But I just want to add that whether or not you're a virgin, I want you to feel welcome to come here anytime. And I hope you'll always feel safe here, and not like you're being judged, no matter what your situation is." And turning back to Jenn I asked, "Why are you concerned about that; you make it sound like it's a problem?"

" 'Cause she's nineteen! I mean, I told her: I don't want her to die a virgin!"

"Whoa!" I said. "Jenn, nineteen isn't that old! I mean, yes, sex is part of life, but there are many years ahead; actually, I have to say, there are a lot of benefits to waiting."

"Well, yeah, waiting is fine and all," she said dismissively. "I mean, yeah, like when we were in middle school and stuff I could see it. But now? Nineteen?!"

"Jenn, we're all different. What seems like a long wait to some people might feel just right to others. I really want to encourage you not to pressure

Helen or any of your friends into doing anything they don't want to do; no-body likes to be pressured. And nobody likes to be judged." Turning to Helen I said, "I hope you're comfortable with yourself exactly as you are; I hope you aren't feeling pressured to do anything you don't want to do."

"I'm OK," Helen replied.

From "hello" it had been clear to me that Helen was developmentally much slower than her friend. In fact, she seemed so limited that I was truly glad that Jenn was her friend. I just wanted her to be more accepting, so it was a little tricky. We talked it over and gradually she seemed more respectful, more accepting.

But then Jenn said, "Vee, you gotta get Helen on birth control. Fast."

"Why?" I asked.

Since Helen had expressed no interest in boys, it seemed premature to me.

" 'Cause she's nineteen! And even if she hasn't had sex, she will someday. And remember how long it took when you helped me get on it? It was like, weeks. Remember? And you explained all that stuff to me about condoms and pills and shots and everything? It was so much to do and to learn and everything. And I mean: that was me." And turning to her friend, she added, "Even if you aren't having sex, you gotta be ready before! Even if you don't have a boyfriend, you gotta be ready." Turning back to me she said, "Vee, once she has a boyfriend, it's gonna be too late." She went on, elaborating: her concern was that once Helen did have a boyfriend, she might lack the communication skills necessary to postpone sexual involvement until protecting herself with a birth control method, and she might lack the skills and support to make and carry out a reproductive life plan.

Once I got Jenn to back down from trying to encourage Helen to have sex, we were able to have a productive conversation about Helen's life goals. The more she spoke, the clearer it became to me that she was quite limited. She didn't know if she'd ever want kids, but, "Definitely not for a long time," until she was fully ready. While I had been put off by Jenn's approach in the beginning, I had to admit that some of her concerns were right on target, and I appreciated that she was putting such caring energy into helping her friend.

Faye, a nurse, joined part of our next visit, to help Helen build comfort with our medical staff and with the concept of a reproductive life plan, with a pregnancy prevention plan that she could have "on hold."

"Have you ever kissed anyone?" Faye asked Helen after a brief introductory chat, and after Helen had confirmed that she doesn't want kids for a long time.

Helen shook her head, "No."

"OK then, you're cool for now. But here's the thing. Someday you probably will; it may not be for a really long time, but it'll probably happen someday. So here's what you need to know: if you're ever with someone, like if you're alone together, and you start holding hands or kissing or hugging or something, you might start to get a kind of tingly feeling all over."

"Yeah!" Jenn said, with a look of understanding. "That's it: it's a tingly feeling!"

"Have you ever felt like that when you're with someone?" Faye asked Helen. She shook her head again, "No."

"OK then, it's all good. So here's the thing: as long as you don't have that tingly feeling you're fine. But it's important to realize that sometimes things can happen fast. If you're ever with a guy and you start to get that special feeling all over, you need to come back here right away and see Vivian. Then she can go over everything you need to know. Can you do that?"

A nod, "Yes."

"So Jenn, since you're so concerned about Helen, since you care so much about her, maybe you can help. Do you two see each other often?" I asked.

"Yeah, we see each other every day. In school."

"Perfect. So Helen, would you be comfortable either coming up here to see me on a Thursday or telling Jenn if you ever get that feeling that Faye is talking about?"

"Sure," Helen said, looking fine with the plan.

"And also, Faye mentioned kissing and holding hands; feeling special with someone. If you get those feelings, we need to talk. Quickly. When it's just kissing or being close. We need to talk before you ever let a guy touch any of the parts of your body that are usually covered by your underwear. Even if you have all your clothes on. OK?"

"OK"

"Perfect. So we're all set?"

We were.

Several months passed, and one day in school Jenn approached me with a sense of urgency. "Vee, I talked to Helen. She's had a boyfriend for a while, but yesterday she said for the first time she got that tingly feeling. Like what Faye was talking about."

"I'm so glad you're there for her. Do you think she wants to come see the nurse again?"

"Yeah; I asked her if she wanted to and she said yes. I said I'd bring her down after school today. Is that OK?"

"Yes. Good for you! I'll be there. We'll talk, and we'll go from there."

Together, we got Helen to bring her mom with her, and the door that Jenn had so awkwardly opened led to Helen's mom, the Planned Parenthood medical staff, Jenn and me working together as a team to help this challenging girl graduate without a pregnancy.

The doorbell rang, and there stood Jamie, with a big smile, happy to see me.

"Hi! What brings you here today?" I asked. I had been alone in the Planned Parenthood building, doing some paperwork, when I heard the doorbell. Since our clinic is only open two days a week, I can usually get some uninterrupted, quiet time to do office work during the days we're closed. But sometimes people drop in to see me, and other times patients come, confused by the locked door, not realizing that some rural clinics are only open part time; not reading the sign with our clinic hours.

"I came for my appointment! Remember?" She looked confused: how could I not remember? After all, we had just met together yesterday, when we had scheduled it, to get birth control.

Working with her had been quite a challenge. It's always harder with girls like Jamie who can't read, girls who have trouble understanding actions and consequences, girls whose older sisters had all become teen moms. But she had responded to my question with certainty; that she didn't want to have a baby by age fifteen. We had spent so many weekly meetings going over one aspect at a time: making a plan for graduating without a pregnancy and dividing it into manageable steps. I had tried hard to make each step as clear as possible while still keeping an eye on the big picture. I had piled on the praise when she agreed to take charge.

"You mean you came here today for the appointment we scheduled together yesterday?" I asked.

"Yeah! Don't you remember? You said that's the next step: go to Planned Parenthood for birth control."

"I remember saying that, yeah, but do you have the little appointment card I gave you?"

She reached into her bag and proudly pulled it out immediately; she knew exactly where she had placed it. She handed it to me and I held it out for her to see, pointing as I spoke.

"See? It says here that your appointment date is November 15: see where I wrote that? And that the time is 3:30. That means that that's when your appointment is. Remember? That's what I told you when we called the clinic yesterday; that that was the earliest appointment they had for after school."

She looked puzzled and saddened. "You mean I can't have my appointment today? Now?"

"Right. There's no clinic today. I'm the only one here; there are no nurses or anyone else."

"Oh......man....?" Her voice trailed off, disappointed.

I told her how sorry I was for the misunderstanding. I praised her for her motivation, for remembering that coming for her appointment was the next step, and for saving the appointment card and knowing where she had put it.

But she had that look on her face that made me feel like the stereotype of a sleazy used car salesman who uses the "bait and switch" method of getting customers to come through the door by giving misleading information. I certainly hadn't intended for her to walk all the way to the clinic for her appointment on the wrong day. With all the things I had emphasized, I simply hadn't realized that she also needed more support figuring out a way to remember the date and time of the appointment, so that she'd show up when the appointment was scheduled. With most patients, simply stating the date and time and writing it on an appointment card is enough, but for Jamie, she needed more. I invited her up to visit in my office for a little while and she gladly came up. Together we made a plan for how she'd remember the date of her appointment, and she did.

Jamie wasn't the only teen who took my words literally and then left me feeling like I had inadvertently made things sound simpler than they are.

Emily showed up one Thursday after school and said, "I only have a few minutes, I have to go to practice at 4:30: I need birth control fast!"

"I'm Vivian, I'm an educator here: you came to the right place."

"Yeah, I know who you are, don't you remember me? You came to my class, you said Planned Parenthood is open Thursdays and teens can get birth control and that we should come *before* we have sex. That's why I came today, I remember you said it's open Thursdays."

Honestly, I didn't remember her; I had said that to every class, over a hundred students.

"Wow, I'm so glad you remembered that we're open Thursdays, and that you're here! Am I understanding you right, that you haven't ever had sex yet?"

"Yeah, I mean not like *sex* sex. Like, on Tuesday, me and my boyfriend were like, y'know, like he was eatin' me out and stuff and like we almost did it but I told him, I gotta go on birth control first."

"Good for you, for using your head at a time like that! This is really important. I can give you condoms quickly right now, but to go on birth control it'll take a little time. You'll need an appointment, and they'll explain when you can start your pills, and it takes the first few weeks before they're fully effective." She looked heartbroken and betrayed.

"But I told him what you said, that Planned Parenthood is open Thursdays; that they have birth control here. I promised him I'd come get it today, and that we'd do it on Friday night." After a pause, she added, "I promised him!" to underscore the urgency; she was not a person who would break a promise, and she didn't want to put herself at risk of pregnancy. And she looked like she was stuck in an ethical dilemma that was entirely my fault.

She had heard me correctly. But she had missed the whole part about the fact that it takes time; you need an appointment, and that most birth control methods take time to start. A person often has to wait for their period, and during the first month on some methods they aren't fully effective. Hearing "Planned Parenthood is open on Thursdays and you can get birth control there," and "It's important to get birth control before you have sex," had left her with the mistaken notion that she could simply walk in on Thursday, get birth control, have sex on Friday and be totally protected. And this was before EC was available.

While I was able to schedule her an appointment for the following Thursday and send her off with a bag of condoms and spermicides, she, like Jamie, was unfamiliar with the complex process of navigating one's way through the health care system, and became easily frustrated and disappointed as she began to realize that birth control is not a fast food item.

"I need more pills," Megan said.

"When?" I asked.

"I think by Monday. I think I take my last one on Sunday."

"Well, good for you for coming to me before you run out. That's definitely something I can help you with. But I'm confused: I remember you got three packs when you started. You should still have a whole pack left, shouldn't you?" I had just looked at my notes that morning, to prepare for the day, and she wasn't on my "urgent" list; I had seen her name on next month's list.

"Well, yeah, I have some. But it's not a whole pack: it's missing a few. I don't wanna screw it up and use that weird pack; I want to get a whole pack."

"What do you mean, missing a few?"

"I mean, like, I have it, but like, I wouldn't know what to do when I get to the ones that are missing."

"I don't get it, have you been taking one every day?"

"Yeah."

"So why are some missing from next month's pack?"

Looking just a tiny bit guilty she said, " 'Cuz I gave some to Jennifer. Please don't be mad at me, Vee! She really needed them and she's too scared to go herself. And, I mean, Vee, she really doesn't wanna get pregnant! I mean, she asked me for them and I just couldn't say 'No.' She's my best friend! And it was Friday!"

"So what do you mean; what did you give her?"

"I just gave her the three pills that said, 'Friday,' 'Saturday,' and 'Sunday.' Just to get her through the weekend. That's all she needed. She saw her boyfriend over the weekend, but he went home; she won't see him again during the week. So that's why I don't want to use my last package: I wouldn't know what to do when I get to those three days."

The word "clueless" might have just popped into your mind, too, dear reader. You're probably an adult, like me, so it's likely you know that birth control pills don't work like that, and perhaps you never thought about teens sharing prescription drugs. But I probably wasn't as shocked as you might be. By then I had heard other teens doing the same thing; it happens. And while it bothers me, everything is relative; it didn't bother me as much as the girl who ground up and snorted her friend's antidepressants in an attempt to get high. At least this time the motive was admirable.

"Listen Megan, I'm really glad that you care about your friend and that you want to help her avoid pregnancy; it's so important! But I have to tell you at the same time, I'm very concerned. It's not the fact that you're trying to help her that worries me. It's the way you're trying to help her. It's not 'helping.' There're two reasons. First, just taking 3 pills for sex over the weekend doesn't protect her: she'd need to be on it, to take it every day, for the pills to work, even just to work on those 3 days. Like the way you take them every day. She'd need to do that. Does that make sense to you?"

"Well, kinda, but I mean, she really wanted them and I figured it's better than nothing."

"Well, it sounds like what she 'really wanted' was the protection they offer, and as a friend, you can help her get that. You could help her get them from the nurse herself. That's my second concern: those pills were prescribed for you. Just for you. You went through that whole appointment: all that information they got; all those boxes you had to check off on the health form; all those questions the practitioner asked you about your health; and the whole physical exam you had, taking your blood pressure and everything. That was all to see if the pills would be safe for you. It may not have seemed important to you, but it is: it's very individual; methods that are safe for one person might not be safe for everyone. Does that make sense to you?"

"I mean, kinda, but see, I wouldn't just give them to anyone. I mean, it's hard to explain, but like: Jennifer?! You don't know her that well, but I mean, like, I've known her since 4th grade, and I am not kidding you: we are *exactly* the same. I mean, I know she'd get the same ones…"

We went on; it was tricky, and it took time. Success happened in stages: first helping her get Jennifer condoms, next bringing Jennifer in to work with me, and finally getting Jennifer to get her own appointment and her own prescription.

It took time, but it happened.

"There's a lot of talk about STDs and HIV these days. Is that something that concerns you?" I asked Jolene. She had just told me that she's slept with five guys, and while I was glad she was thinking about birth control, I wanted to figure out if she was also aware of the risks of STDs.

"Oh, no," she said in a dismissive tone.

Just as I suspected. So I wanted to give her a reality check.

"How come?" I asked.

" 'Cuz I only sleep with people I know really well."

"So are you saying you believe that knowing someone well protects you from STDs?"

"I mean, I know there are STDs, but it's like, people who sleep around get them."

"Well, you're right that the more partners people have, the more they're increasing the chance that they'll get one. But when you say you know your partners well, I'm not sure what you mean about feeling protected."

She was clearly becoming exasperated by my inability to see that she was safe; in her eyes, she was very safe. She continued, "Vee, I mean, I don't just know them. I mean I know them really well. Really, really, really well. Like Gary: I don't just know him, I've known him since fifth grade. I mean, Vee, I even know his mother; I ate dinner at their house!"

So I spent quite a bit of time with her. I knew that eating dinner at someone's mother's house isn't protection from STDs, but I also understood that that was a lot for her to take in. Eventually, I did get her to start using condoms and get tested for STDs, but that day, I didn't even try. All I tried to do that day was to get her to change her perception of her own risk.

So many teens are like Jolene; they perceive themselves to be safe when their behavior is high risk. Not just their risk regarding STDs, but about pregnancy, too.

Girls like Jan.

I've worked with enough sixteen-year-olds that go on the pill to know that after a "pill start" appointment is where important conversations begin, not where they end. So after some well deserved praise, congratulating Jan for moving forward, I asked her, "So you started your pills?"

"Yeah."

"How's it going with them?"

"Fine."

"Do you take one every day?"

"Yeah, usually."

"You've taken a really big step, taking charge of your fertility. Are you proud of yourself?" I hoped she was. She had a lot to be proud of. Despite how rocky the year had started, her school year had ended up well. She was thriving in the foster home. The little kids there loved her, and she liked the way she felt safe and the way they all had dinner together most nights as a family. She had gotten a summer job working for a local family in their small furniture building company.

And when it came to her reproductive health, she had made a lot of progress. Before we met she was having unprotected sex. In the months we had worked together she had set life goals, considered how her reproductive capacity could impact those goals, made a reproductive life plan, picked a method, talked to her partner and foster mom about it, made and kept an appointment, gotten a method, and started using it. Even though she never would have used that language to describe what we had done together, it didn't matter. She was on track.

"Yeah, I guess," she said, shrugging her shoulders.

"Do you feel like they're giving you the protection you need?"

"Oh, yeah. Definitely."

"Good for you. But let me ask you something. You said you 'usually' take one every day. What's 'usually'?"

"Well, most days I take them; sometimes I forget, but the thing is, like—" her voice softened to a whisper and she added, "On the days I have sex, then like I always take them. Then I'm really careful. I mean, like, really careful. Like, I am not kidding, Vee, I'll sit and look at the clock, and take it exactly on time. The nurse said within the hour, but I do it within the minute!" Her eyes twinkled as she referred to the days when she had sex, and she appeared confident and proud when she spoke about the focused care she used on those "risky" days.

My heart sank. Like so many teens, her "actual risk" and her "perceived risk" were not in synch. She thought she was protected because she took the pills carefully on the days she had sex, but she frequently forgot the pills on days she didn't have sex, thinking there was no problem. She completely misunderstood the basics of how the pills work despite the fact that I thought I had explained it to her so clearly. And so had the nurse. Ouch.

Normally, under circumstances like these, I'd have simply pulled my plastic model of a vagina and the mysterious organs that lie behind it out of the bag I always carry with me. It's a bright purple bag that looks like it would have gym clothes in it, but mine has three-dimensional models of the male and female reproductive systems and samples of all the birth control methods, for education. I've learned that even if a client requests a visit to discuss how to talk to her pre-teen about puberty, it might lead to questions about her own birth control, or the vasectomy she's wishing her partner would get. So I just always bring everything; that way I'm never unprepared.

Today was the one day when it wasn't handy. I had arrived at Jan's home to find all the younger kids in the living room, so her foster parents had suggested that we just walk downtown to the park. I had left my bag in my car because it was 90 degrees out and the bag seemed too heavy to haul. Plus, I thought it might be a bit more than the Clifton Village Park is ready for since anyone could have seen us on the park bench. We had the necessary sound privacy for conversation, but not visual privacy.

But now I needed my model, desperately. I needed to show her the ovaries, fallopian tubes and uterus again, and explain how pregnancy happens and how pills prevent it. I sensed there was so much misunderstood, that it would be hard to explain even with the model. How could I possibly explain it without the model? No way, I thought. But I had to. Had to! Sitting in the park, I didn't even have a pen and piece of paper, to draw a makeshift ovary.

So I just had to wing it. How, I wondered, could I possibly make that complicated journey of egg and sperm understandable, quickly and efficiently? I needed her to understand that ovulation is essential, and that pills prevent ovulation, but that if she skips pills, she could ovulate and become pregnant, even several days later. And it popped in my head: *just the essentials!*

"Look," I began. "This is really important. I don't think you understand how the pills protect people from pregnancy. I don't think you're using them right; it sounds to me like you might not be protected. I don't want anything bad to happen to you; I want to explain it so you get it."

She looked concerned. I clearly had her attention, so I continued. "Think of it like this." And holding up three fingers I said, "There are three things that have to happen in order to get pregnant." Pointing to the first finger, I continued, "The first is that an egg has to be released from the ovary. That's called ovulation. If our ovaries never released an egg, we could never get pregnant. Are you with me?"

"Yeah."

Pointing to the next finger I said, "Then the second thing that has to happen in order to get pregnant is that the egg has to meet up with a sperm cell. That's called fertilization. Any genital-to-genital contact with a male partner can lead to that. And the sperm cells can live for days in our body once they're there. So if there was an egg already released, or if one is released a few days later, either way, it can meet a sperm cell and get fertilized. Do you get that?"

"Yeah."

"Then the third thing that has to happen is that that fertilized egg has to go the rest of the way through our Fallopian tube and go into the uterus and attach itself to the inside of the uterus. That's called implantation. Do you get that?" I asked, pointing to the third and final finger.

"Yeah."

"Does this make sense to you, what I'm saying?"

"Yeah. Totally."

"OK. The other thing to understand is the way the pills work. They give a chemical message to our ovaries saying, 'Don't release an egg.' Think of it as a message that our ovaries need to get every day. Do you see why I'm concerned?"

"Well, yeah, 'cause like, if the pill tells the ovaries not to release an egg, but I don't take it, then, like, ya mean, like, there could be an egg there?"

"Exactly. So even on a day when you don't have sex, if you skip the pill, your ovary can release an egg. You won't feel it; you won't even know it's there.

But it'll be in your Fallopian tube, and then if you have sex, even several days later, you'd be at risk of pregnancy because of the egg that's already there."

"Oh, wow." She looked concerned. "Good," I thought.

"Does this help you understand? Does this make it clearer?"

"Yeah. A lot. I mean, like, I sorta got it before, but now, like, now I really get it. I mean, I got that they prevent pregnancy, but I didn't get it about the whole days thing." And after a thoughtful pause she added, "That means I really have to take it every day."

Sometimes time is forgiving. It was with her. She wasn't pregnant, and started taking her pills much more carefully after our visit. She didn't get pregnant.

The more I thought about that "One, two, three," explanation of how pregnancy happens, the more I loved it. It started out as just a desperate attempt to improvise. I shared it with the team of Planned Parenthood educators from four local counties at our next monthly meeting. By then, I was old enough to be a mother to most of them, and I felt like I needed a reality check. But they agreed: most explanations any of us had read or heard about how to teach how pregnancy happens are centered on sex. "Vee, it's like, when we talk about the sexual stuff, it's such a distraction. And when we try to explain about all the internal organs, it's so complicated. So much of what's important is the ovulation piece. The girls don't even think about it; it just happens."

They all agreed that this was the most useful way to quickly and effectively teach how pregnancy happens, and together we created a classroom activity around it, to use as an introduction before discussing birth control. And after sharing it at a regional educators' conference, its use quickly spread. I love the success it enjoyed; it amuses me to imagine all these teens in health classes "getting it" better than they would have, and realizing it all happened because I didn't have the strength to carry my gym bag to the park on a 90 degree day.

Necessity really is the mother of invention.

"She's beautiful, Karen; congratulations!" I said, seeing her four-week-old daughter for the first time. I had known her for several years, but I hadn't seen her since she graduated from high school, so I hadn't even known she was pregnant. Being a single nineteen-year-old mom is never easy, so I figured she'd have a tough time, but still, I was so thankful she had made it that long. After all, she had been sexually active when I first met her in eighth grade, and I could remember what a daunting task it felt like at that time, contemplating seeing her through middle school and high school without a pregnancy.

I had spent so much time with her during those years; we had so many meetings at school, in her home, and in my office. Sometimes we had visited with her mom, but since mom worked two jobs, she really appreciated that I was willing to visit with Karen even when she wasn't there. And Karen had been happy to sign the necessary consent forms for mom and me to talk openly about her birth control methods and Planned Parenthood appointments.

Getting Karen to graduate without a pregnancy had been such an ongoing challenge; we had gotten her to learn the relationship between sex and pregnancy, and the concept of birth control, first. Then I had taught her about the specific methods. She had tried several hormonal methods: the pill, the shot, and the patch. My file with her case notes was one of the fattest in my load; she had so much trouble reading, and her critical thinking skills were so rudimentary, but she listened well, liked the attention, set goals, and really did try to learn. With mom's and my help, we had kept her protected by hormonal methods and she had graduated; it had been a real success story. I couldn't even count the times mom and I had phoned each other, taking turns reaching out to the other for help each time Karen hit a bump in the road.

Mom would call me when Karen complained about side effects and I'd talk with her and get her to the clinic to talk with a nurse and switch methods when necessary. Similarly, I'd call mom when I couldn't find Karen in school, to remind her about upcoming appointments, to get mom's assessment on the likelihood of Karen showing up. Together, somehow, we got her to graduation. I think mom was surprised that Karen was her first daughter to graduate; her two older sisters had dropped out when they got pregnant despite the fact that they were both relatively good students. Academics were a huge struggle for Karen, but with all the curriculum modifications, she did, in fact, graduate.

Mom would probably have been able to continue to oversee Karen's hormonal methods, but Karen moved out and lived with her boyfriend shortly after graduating. She did continue her birth control for a while, but without the daily support, she quit, unbeknownst to me.

So when she came in with her baby we did a little catching up and then I asked, "Have you thought about how many kids you want total?"

"Oh, I don't know, not really. I mean, maybe someday I might want more, I dunno. All I know is that right now I don't want no more: she's a handful."

"Yeah, I think I know what you mean. She looks so perfect, but do you mean you don't have the energy for another right away?"

"Definitely."

"Have you thought about how to avoid another pregnancy right away?"

"I dunno, kinda. I mean, like, I think about it, but I don't know what to do."

"Well, I know you know a lot. I mean I remember you used a lot of methods while you were in school. Are there any you used before that you'd consider, or are there any you haven't used that you want to learn more about?"

"Nah, not really."

"How come?"

"I dunno, I don't think I want none: I'm just not really a birth control type person."

Since she had used several methods without a complaint or a pregnancy for over five years when we had worked together, I was surprised to hear her say that; I didn't know what she meant, so I asked.

"What do you mean: you're 'not a birth control type person'?"

"I mean, I don't wanna get pregnant, but birth control? I dunno. I just don't think it works for me; I heard everyone's different, that it works different for different people. I guess I'm just one of those people it doesn't work for." She sounded defeated.

"What do you mean?"

"I mean, look," she said, nodding to the infant in her arms, continuing, "I tried everything. I tried the pill, the shot, the patch, we even used condoms. But look: I still got pregnant. I just don't think birth control works for me."

"What do you mean? Were you on birth control when you got pregnant?"

"I mean, not right when," she said in a dismissive tone.

"What do you mean; what were you using?"

"I mean: I used everything."

"But when you got pregnant: were you using anything right then?"

"Well, not right then."

"What was the last thing you used?"

"The pill. I was on it when I moved outa my mom's."

"And what happened with that? Did you stay on it when you moved in with George?"

"Like for awhile."

"Like how long?"

"Like a couple of months."

"And then what happened."

"I ran out. My mom used to take me to get them."

"So you were on your own about them when you went to George's?"

"Yeah, I guess."

"Did you want to get pregnant?"

"Not really, but I ran out of pills."

"Is that when you got pregnant? After you ran out of pills?"

"Yeah, like, I stayed on them 'till they ran out."

"And then you weren't on anything?"

"Like, I was gonna stay on them. But I had to go to work and everything, and then I'd always forget to call."

"Yeah, it's so hard. So you weren't taking them anymore?"

"Yeah."

"For about how long?"

"I'm not sure."

"Can you remember?"

"Let's see; I moved in with George in August, and I know I had pills then. Actually, I remember, I had two more packs, so I took all of those. So I guess like September and October I was on them."

"And then after October you weren't on anything?"

"Right." She paused to think for a minute and added, "Yeah, that's right."

"And when did you get pregnant?"

"Um, like, lemme see: after I quit the pills, I remember I had my period in November and December, but then when it was supposed to come in January it didn't come."

"And is that when you got pregnant you think, in December or January?"

"Yeah."

"Well, it sounds to me like birth control really did work for you. The thing about birth control methods is that they only protect you when you use them. It sounds like all those years in school, and the months afterwards, whenever you used them, they worked. It sounds, actually, like they all worked really well. From what you're telling me, it sounds like you got pregnant about two months after you quit using any kind of birth control. Is that what it sounds like to you?"

"I dunno, maybe; I just got so frustrated, 'cuz it was like I tried everything. All those stupid appointments I went to, and all those stupid shots and pills and everything: for what?!" she asked, looking at her baby, like her baby was a sign that she's not a "birth control type person."

We went on a bit. It was frustrating, her insistence that birth control doesn't work for her despite the fact that five years of consistent use had prevented pregnancy, and then she became pregnant two months after quitting any method.

> "Get a Aborshin"
> —TEEN GIRL'S RESPONSE ON HER PREGNANCY TEST FORM, WHEN ASKED WHAT SHE'D DO IF SHE WAS PREGNANT

Today, IUDs would be an option for girls like Karen; back then she wouldn't have been able to get one.

And once again, she left me pondering both the necessity of support for girls with limitations like hers and the need for continued support even after they graduate and move out.

So many teens haven't developed the critical thinking skills and maturity they'll have in their adulthood. Like the girl who told her friend she wasn't worried about pregnancy because even during unprotected sex, she always wore the gold crucifix her dying grandfather had lovingly placed around her neck, assuring her it would always protect her. Or the sexually active girl who wasn't on a method, who had punched her locker so hard that she required medical attention, but was ambivalent about pregnancy: "If it happens, it happens." She didn't see her inability to manage her anger as any reason to doubt her readiness to become a mom; "Oh, I ain't worried about that. I'd never hurt my kid!" Or the girl who had finished a pack of pills and said, "And I went to open my next pack and there weren't any more there! And I figured it must be a sign from God that it's time for me to get pregnant."

Teens frequently don't explain themselves using the same language as adults, like the girl who wondered if her partner was "old enough to sperm me." And they don't present themselves like adults. The lively teen couple sporting neon blue, orange, green and pink hair, with everything pierced and a T-shirt that boasted, "I put the FUN in dysFUNctional," just asked for condoms, but I sensed they'd also benefit from some time to grow up.

Time will give so many of these teens a chance to build the skills they'll need to become effective parents. But if they become sexually active, they can get pregnant in the blink of an eye. The urgency of that reality is underscored when we consider the teen that thinks that "using abstinence" becomes challenging after "twenty minutes."

Teens are, in fact, our future adults. And most of them are also future parents. Just because they often don't speak or behave according to the script adults would like to write for them doesn't mean they don't deserve the best we have to offer. During those turbulent times, having a supportive adult who is flexible and willing to accept them exactly as they are and address their individual needs can often get them through those years without pregnancy; it can help lead to the future success they each deserve.

SHE WANTED MIRACLES

"You know your children are growing up when they stop asking you where they came from and refuse to tell you where they're going."

–P.J. O'Rourke[6]

"**M**ommy, can I ask you a question? What's giving head?" Freddie asked from the back seat. He was ten.

A scary question for a lot of parents to hear, but hearing it while driving 65 on an interstate added unique challenges for Sandra.

"Wow, Freddie, I'm glad you feel comfortable asking me questions like that, but I think we should wait till you're older to talk about this."

"OK, mommy, there's no rush. I was just wondering if it was anything like oral sex."

For lots of parents, talking to their kids and teens about sexuality is one of the most challenging aspects of being a parent. And the conversations often take place long before the parent has realized they need to be addressing the subject.

It happens suddenly.

People have babies; they become parents: they're often thrilled, but also overwhelmed. Everything changes. New joys, new challenges. Should I pick her up when she's crying, or just let her cry? Finally, eventually, one way or the other, they figure it out and come to peace. But then the time flies. To some parents, it feels like they just got that one down, when suddenly there's somebody like me knocking at the door to talk about birth control. It can be unsettling, jolting. Parents often figure they'll have these conversations when their kid needs it: "soon."

But "soon" is sometimes yesterday.

"Soon" might have been yesterday for Jackie's mom; that's what she was concerned about. It was springtime. As Jackie was having her first pelvic exam her mom waited in my office and explained, "I mean, she's only fourteen and she says she's not having sex and I believe her, but she's in a very serious relationship and it's like: summer's coming. Who knows what's gonna happen? I mean, I told her I believe her, ya know, that she's not having sex and stuff. But I told her we gotta be looking ahead; we gotta be thinking about your future. The thing about sex, especially when you're young, is that it's not always planned: you don't say, 'on July 14th I'm gonna have sex for the first time.' But within moments, everything can change. I mean, I told her I hope she'll wait for a long time. But I said, 'It won't hurt to go on some kind of birth control even if you don't have sex; it'll be good for you to get used to it *before* you need it. And you're better off being on it and not needing it than needing it and not being on it.' She got that. I mean, at first she didn't want to come here, but I kinda talked her into it. I'm so glad. 'Cause I can watch over her; I can try. But I mean, realistically, I can't be there 24/7. If she sneaks out or something, I mean, over summer vacation," she paused mid-sentence, clearly a thought had interrupted her, and she continued slowly, with a look of deep concern, "I mean, Vivian, there are so many places they could disappear to, I mean, with summer right around the corner, I mean, there are bushes everywhere!"

Although Jackie's mom was looking ahead for "soon" on her own, not all parents do. And they often find that nothing has actually prepared them for knowing how to handle their teens' sexual development, even though they want to. It can be unsettling; I try to be sensitive to that as I knock on peoples' doors.

I tried to be sensitive to that when I met Kayla's mom.

The funky, dingy stairwell with the wobbly, busted banister and peeling paint was about what I expected, going up to Kayla's apartment. The steep, narrow steps were so shallow that I had to walk up sideways. The loose, dim, bare light bulb dangling from its fixture and the frayed wires hanging from the exposed electric box made me glad I wasn't a building inspector.

Hillary, Kayla's caseworker, had asked me to visit and had given me just a bit of background. At fifteen, Kayla was sexually active, and her mom, whom she lived with, was worried about her. Mom had gotten pregnant with Kayla at fourteen, and now, seeing her beautiful daughter permanently glued to her boyfriend's side triggered fears. Mom had left school shortly after Kayla's birth, unsuccessfully tried for her GED a few times, and was somehow barely scraping by. Cleaning the local Laundromat and the bank at night, when it was closed, weren't the best jobs in the world but they were better than nothing and she was thankful she could at least pay the rent. So I didn't expect a palace. Hillary had warned me: mom is eager to meet you; Kayla is ambivalent but willing.

Mom welcomed me into their home; Kayla would be home from school to join us soon. Mom was much younger than me, but her face told some hard stories. A few teeth, a hard past, but she had one thing that kept her focused:

hopes for her daughter. Lots of hopes. Kayla was bright. Beautiful. Lively. And not yet pregnant. And healthy: especially healthy. Mom had lost a friend to AIDS, and she didn't know if she was more concerned about her daughter's sexual involvement or her lack of concern about HIV. Mom was terrified. About pregnancy, yes, but more about HIV. Unlike many parents, she really "got it," that the virus is here, in our community, hard to detect. And that the teen mind doesn't comprehend the reality of risks.

We chatted a bit; we bonded. I couldn't promise miracles; she wanted miracles. But she'd accept anything I could offer.

"Are you and Kayla generally close?" I asked.

"Well, yeah, we are. I mean it's always been just the two of us. Yeah, I'd say we're close. She talks to me and stuff. I mean, when she was little we were super close, but now mostly she just likes to hang out with her friends."

"I know what you mean, when kids become teens they often choose their friends if given a choice."

"I'll say."

"But still, even if it seems like she's always with her friends, your influence is super important. Studies have actually shown that teens that are generally close to their parents make healthier choices about their sexual involvement; even if you're not talking about sex, just having a close relationship is so important."[7]

"Oh, we're close alright, but she really just listens to her friends now."

"It sounds frustrating."

"It is. It scares the heck outta me."

"Yeah, I can see that. You know, the other thing I want to point out is that parents often think that peers have the most influence on their teens, but really, when it comes to decisions about love, sex, and relationships teens say their parents have a bigger influence than their friends or the media or popular culture or anything.[8] They just don't always show it."

She seemed only mildly encouraged, which I could understand; I just didn't want her to feel helpless. We agreed it's hard to get teens to really think things through, to be realistic, and to understand that actions have consequences…and then Kayla came home.

She smiled and gave me a friendly greeting, and immediately plunked herself down at the kitchen table with us. She seemed surprised and appreciative that I started by saying, "Wow, you just got home from school. Do you want to take a few minutes for yourself before we visit?" A snack, a bathroom break, and then a little chat.

"How was your day so far?"

"Good. I finally passed that damn global test."

"Congratulations! What do you usually do after school?"

"Just hang out with my friends."

"Sounds like fun. Thanks for coming right home today. Will you get to hang out with them later?"

"Yeah."

"So listen, what do you know about who I am and why Hillary asked me to visit today?"

"She said you're from Planned Parenthood."

"That's right. I'm an educator there. Do you know anything about Planned Parenthood?"

"Yeah, my friend went there 'cuz she thought she was pregnant," she said with a naughty giggle and a twinkle in her eye.

"Did she wanna be?"

"Hell, no!"

"What about you; do you think you ever wanna have any kids?"

"Ever? Well, yeah, of course. Like: someday, but not for a looong time."

"When you say not for a long time, like, what do you think? Is it a certain age, or is it stuff you wanna do first, or what?"

"No, I dunno. I just don't want no kid now. I like to party and stuff and I don't wanna have to stay home with no kid."

"I don't blame you. I mean, you're fifteen; you've got a lot of time ahead of you. There's no rush to become a parent. Besides hanging out with your friends, are there other things you think about that you'd wanna do before becoming a mom?"

"Shit, there's a lot. I mean, like, everything. Like, I mean a ton."

"Like what else?"

"Oh, God, I dunno." It definitely sounded like something she never thinks about. "Like finish school and have my own place and everything. And a car. Definitely; I'm gonna have my own car someday."

Her eyes sparkled as she contemplated the car. So I pursued it.

"What kind of car do you want?"

"A Mustang. A red Mustang. A convertible. Brand new: I already picked it out!"

"Oh wow: you've got expensive taste. Have you thought about how you'll pay for it?"

"I dunno. I'll get a job I guess," she said dismissively.

"You better finish school and get some fancy-ass job if you want a Mustang," mom chimed in. Mom had had jobs as long as Kayla had been alive and still couldn't afford a car, let alone a brand new Mustang.

We went on a bit more; gradually Kayla listed some goals. Clearly, she hadn't thought too much about goals in general, other than the goal of spending as much time as possible hanging out with her friends, partying. And the car.

"Listen, it sounds to me like you've got it figured out: you want kids someday, but not for a really long time. It sounds like you want to spend most of your free time with your friends, not with a kid, for now. And like you eventually want to have a job and that car and your own place before you have your first pregnancy. Is that right?"

She agreed.

"So I just want to say, I think those are all perfectly reasonable goals. And reachable ones. There's no reason why you can't do all that; lots of women do. But here's the thing. You're growing up; you've got a boyfriend. It's important to realize that your bodies are ready to make a baby any time. And the teen years can be really challenging as far as that goes. Here's the deal: we all start out the same. We're not having sex and we don't want a baby, so there's no problem. Some people decide to wait to have sex until they want to be a parent, so for them, once they're having sex, if they want a baby, there's no problem. But some people reach a point in their lives in between, when they do want to have sex but they don't want to be a parent. That can be a huge problem, 'cause our bodies are really well designed to make babies. That's when birth control can become really important. If couples do want sex, and they have sex, they can make the choice. If they use birth control, there's still a risk of pregnancy, but there are methods that are around 98-99% effective at preventing pregnancy. Does that all make sense?"

She nodded and looked interested, so I continued.

"Now, I want to be really clear: your sex life is absolutely none of my business. I don't want to intrude. But I do want to say this: if I can ever be helpful to you in reaching your goals, let me know. If you ever decide you're ready to have sex before you want to be a mom, birth control can be really helpful, and I can help you learn about the different methods and get one if you want."

"Oh, we use condoms," she offered, opening the door to some frank talk about the need for consistent condom use, the challenges that brings, and an entire overview of sexually transmitted diseases, HIV, AIDS, and all the methods of contraception. Throughout the visit, mom took full advantage of opportunities to express her concern about HIV and the importance of prevention, and we had a lively and productive visit.

As I prepared to leave, mom got all choked up. "Oh, thank you so much! This was so helpful. I love the way you talk with her." And struggling to find the right words, hesitating and pausing as she spoke, sounding astonished, she continued, "I never would have known how to do that. Like when I grew up, nobody told me nuthin'. It was just, like, 'Don't do it.' That's it. And man, that didn't work: I got pregnant when I was fourteen. I always swore it'd be different when I had a kid. And, I mean, like, when Tony died of AIDS, Kayla was only eight, but like I swore, it's gonna be different: we're gonna talk about it. But I never knew what to say. I just kept sayin', 'You gotta use a condom, you gotta use a condom, every time.' But like, the way you talk about it, it's like, like it's a subject. Like it's something you can think about, and plan for."

I loved that: "Like it's a subject."

It *is* a subject: an important subject. And I was honored to have the opportunity to introduce that concept to them.

Kayla's mom's gratitude left her not just willing, but eager to sign the permission slip for me to meet with Kayla during her study halls at school. In the weeks that followed, we met regularly. We discussed the various birth control methods; how you get them, how you use them, side effects, effectiveness, and what happens at a pelvic exam. Eventually, Kayla decided to make a medical appointment at Planned Parenthood. We scheduled it together and I reminded her the day of the appointment. But she didn't show up.

"Oh, I forgot," she later explained. I offered another try; she accepted. Same thing: we scheduled it, I reminded her, but she didn't show. Each time, she insisted she forgot, but that she still wanted the appointment.

Finally, I enlisted Hillary's help. Kayla happily signed a release, and when Hillary paged her to the main office at the end of the school day, she gladly accepted the ride to the clinic in the DSS car. She got her initial exam without incident and started on a method: first the pill, later the shot. But the shot has to be injected at the clinic every twelve weeks, and she'd always flake out and miss appointments unless we had Hillary drive her.

So we did.

As Hillary put it, "I'd rather transport her to Planned Parenthood four times a year then see her get pregnant. Hey, if that's what it takes..." I'm not allowed to transport patients in my personal car, so I was thankful that Hillary was so willing and available.

Our meetings became less frequent, less necessary. She eventually started not just showing up for her appointments, but scheduling them on her own. During her senior year, I ran into her in the hall one day and she wanted to visit during study hall; she was eager to get me up to date. With no prompting, she proudly shared lots of news. She was doing really well in school. Her sights were set on college. She was hanging out with a new group of friends. And she appreciated that I noted how much more grown-up she seemed.

"I remember when you first wanted birth control, we'd schedule those appointments but you wouldn't show up. Now, it's not just that you show up, you even schedule them yourself. You've completely taken on all the 'adult' responsibility. You're so different. What do you think changed?"

"Oh, that's when I was getting high all the time. Like, back then, I mean, I'd plan to go, but like if my appointment was at 3:30 or 4:00 or something, I figured I'd just stop at Jenny's house for a little while, 'cuz I had time, and like it's right there on the way, and then we'd end up getting high, and then, like, next thing I knew it'd be like 7:00 and I'd be like, 'Shit, I missed my appointment!' "

Well, that explained a lot. I was so thankful that Hillary, Mom, the clinic, and I had all been there for her during those months. Like many teens, Kayla went through a period during her teen years when she was engaging in what adults like to refer to as "risky behaviors" but what Kayla would have referred to as "having fun with my friends." And like many teens, she eventually grew out of it. She graduated without a pregnancy. So many teens go through periods of months or years when their behavior is spontaneous, without direction, without thought: impulsive.

And then they grow up.

I think about how many of them go through those times without an adult support system, without adults specifically guiding them away from becoming a teen parent. I don't know what finally became of Kayla, but I do know this: whatever she did become, she never became a teen mom.

Personally, I think every teen who spends some months or years partying and getting high and having sex without thought deserves to be surrounded by a small handful of caring adults, guiding them away from unintended pregnancy as we guided Kayla, until they outgrow it. Because the thing is, the partying doesn't usually last forever.

But the kid does.

And the way I see it, the kid, the mom, the dad, and the society all deserve more.

Young people benefit from support and guidance as they navigate their way through their teen years. But sometimes, talking about sexuality can be difficult and uncomfortable. Many parents feel that they are inadequate if they're uncomfortable discussing sex with their children and teens, like my friend who confided in me about her feelings during a TV show she was watching with her teenage son and daughter.

"I mean, Vee, my parents never talked to me about sex. The messages I grew up with, it was all about guilt and shame. I swore I wouldn't be like that with my kids. But we were watching this movie on TV, and I didn't realize what it was, and we were all really into it, and then this scene comes on where this couple is in bed and it got pretty heated and my kids were right there and I couldn't believe how uncomfortable I got." She was punishing herself; feeling like her silent squirming gave her kids a message that sex is bad.

But I reminded her that there are valid reasons why we keep some conversations about sexuality private: boundaries are often appropriate and important; there are reasons families don't talk about the private aspects of sex. The uncomfortable feeling might not have anything to do with guilt and shame: it's about privacy. That's not necessarily a bad thing; I worry about the teen girl who was so comfortable telling me about her clit ring in front of her father, and about the mother who taught her daughter how to flirt in a bar.

So many parents try to help their teens prevent pregnancy by trying to talk about sex; indeed, parents are encouraged to. But many people find it awkward. There's often a persistent silence within families.

It starts early, during infancy. As a baby's fingers begin to wander around it's face and body, parents create celebratory games.

"That's your nose! Where's mommy's nose? Where's daddy's nose? Good!"

But when those same young fingers wander towards the child's own genitals, the game ends. Some parents may teach the child the names of their body parts; "That's your penis," but silence frequently prevails. The same child who is encouraged to explore their own nose, mouth and ear is not generally encouraged to explore their own genitals.

And that silence speaks volumes: from the start, it sends kids a message, "We don't talk about that," despite the unique sensations that touching one's own genitals elicits.

And then we wonder why teens won't talk to adults about sex?

I was so impressed recently as I watched a friend changing her daughter's diaper. At first, mom appropriately kept her daughter's hands away from the messy poop, "Your diaper's dirty; I need to clean you." But when she finished cleaning up the mess, as her daughter's hands returned to her genitals, mom simply said, "Yes, OK, now you're clean." Her daughter ran a finger along the fold and mom said, "That's your vagina. Check it out: it's complicated." Her daughter explored it exactly the way she explored every other aspect of her new body, and when she was done mom put on the clean diaper.

Bravo, I thought; I bet that kid will grow up with a healthy attitude about her body and her sexuality.

For parents who have concerns about talking with their teens about sex, I think it's important to remember that sex isn't a single subject; there are different components to human sexuality. It is an enormous realm of human life, filled with mystery; it's complicated. But to focus a conversation on one or two aspects of sexuality is not to deny the existence of the others; it is simply a way to be helpful to young people about some very important aspects of their lives.

By keeping that in mind, parents can more easily figure out which aspects to discuss and which not to; not everything needs to be discussed. Many parent/teen conversations could be more helpful to the teens if the parents would center the dialogue on life goals: shifting from the private nature of sexual feelings to the context of sexuality, and to sexual health. Talking about reaching life goals without an unwanted pregnancy or STD can be comfortable and easy, and it is essential. Giving teens opportunities to "think out loud" about their futures; articulating goals, and considering how becoming a parent might impact those goals can be much more comfortable for some families to discuss. Parents can take advantage of their relationships with their teens by providing them with opportunities to discuss all that: focusing on being a supportive listener; encouraging the teens they love to be thoughtful in the relationships they build and in their behavior. Then, when appropriate, sometimes the conversations can flow naturally into conversations about the decisions the teens face about sexual involvement, and always into ensuring that the teens know how to access any related medical services they need.

And parents don't always have to go it alone. If they don't feel confident there's help available that can make such a difference opening helpful dialogues, like the help I provided to Kayla's mom. It's funny; in some ways, parents are so used to asking for professional help. If a kid's tooth hurts, a parent calls the dentist. If a kid flunks math, parents call tutors. If a kid can't see the blackboard, here they go to the eye doctor. Yet when those same kids become teens, when she comes home in a tight, low-cut top, or when mom finds condoms in his pocket while preparing laundry, it's different. When there's a concern that sexual behavior may be on the not-too-distant horizon, that same parent expects to be able to handle it themselves, and thinks, "There's something wrong with me; I'm inadequate," if they find themselves tongue-tied. They wouldn't think, "Something's wrong with me," if they didn't know how to fill a cavity in their child's tooth, but they expect so much of themselves on the often equally unfamiliar territory of reproductive life planning.

> **TIP FOR PARENTS**
>
> REMEMBER, THERE ARE MANY COMPONENTS TO HUMAN SEXUALITY. TO FOCUS A CONVERSATION ON ONE OR TWO OF THEM IS NOT TO DENY THE EXISTENCE OF THE OTHERS; IT IS SIMPLY A WAY TO BE HELPFUL TO THE YOUNG PEOPLE WE LOVE.

Julie wasn't following her mom's rules, and their caseworker warned me she'd probably be removed from the home soon. Every time mom tried to talk with her they just ended up in a shouting match. Mom had recently learned that Julie was sexually active, and her fears about that topped everything. The tension in the air was thick the day I first went to their home.

I kept the introductory chat short and went right into an activity that I like to use with teens alone or with their families. Handing Julie the little stack of cards I had made, I explained that I call them "Milestone Cards." She knew what a milestone is, so I asked her to go through the stack and arrange them on the table in the order she hoped to experience them in her life, with permission to create a discard pile for any she doesn't want to include. And most important, I asked mom to watch without comment; I assured them both that mom would get to discuss it in the end, but asked her to hold her thoughts until Julie was done.

Julie quickly, easily, and gleefully put the first few colorful cards in order: it was fun for her to imagine buying her first car, graduating, having her first apartment, traveling around the world and then getting married and having kids, and she enjoyed the little illustrations on each card as she handled them. Then she got to the second half of the deck, where the cards were about sexuality and sexual health. It was a little more challenging, but she stuck with it to the end.

Once all the cards were on the table I invited mom to comment, as promised, and mom shared Julie's hopes for the exciting future the cards implied. Then I isolated the two cards that said "Go on birth control," and "Have sex for the first time" and moved them together, in that order, towards the beginning, middle, and end of the sequence of life milestones, asking, "What would happen if these two stayed in this order but if they were moved to here? Or to here? Would it affect the other milestones?"

"Not really," they agreed.

Then I set the "Birth control" one in the discarded pile and kept the one that said "Have sex for the first time" and asked, "And if we discarded this one and moved this one to here or to here or to here, which ones would it affect?"

Julie easily grabbed the "Have first baby" card and moved it next to the "Have sex for the first time" card, saying, "This one would probably move up, closer to here."

"It could," mom and I agreed.

"And which other ones could that affect?" I asked.

"All these!" she replied, tapping lots of the exciting cards she had placed further down the line.

"How so?" I asked.

She named valid reasons why she wouldn't get to do a lot of the things she had looked forward to if she had a kid before being independent. Mom agreed with all of Julie's assessments about the impact that simply discarding that one card and moving the other one would cause. The cards enabled them to both quickly see that Julie's entire future—all her dreams and goals—could be altered suddenly if she had sex without birth control.

After the activity, I easily and quickly got Julie to schedule her first gynecological appointment, and I agreed to return for another home visit about birth control methods a few days before the appointment.

"That was so helpful; that was actually the first time we sat and had a serious, civilized conversation for an hour about something this important. It actually felt really good to talk, to talk seriously, and to listen, and not to scream," mom said as I prepared to leave. The look of gratitude went deep.

Like so many parents, Julie's and Kayla's moms really wanted their daughters to have a bright future; as bright a future as possible. And like most parents, their image of a bright future did not include becoming a teen mom. The only model Kayla's mom had for talking to her daughter about sex was to tell her, "Don't do it." She had added on her own, "But if you do: use a condom." But still, she felt that that wasn't enough; she welcomed my involvement. And Julie's mom hadn't been able to calm herself in weeks; the shouting matches she and Julie had been having had been completely unproductive.

> **TIP FOR PARENTS**
>
> **TALK WITH YOUR TEEN ABOUT LIFE GOALS, AND ENCOURAGE THEM TO TALK ABOUT TO HOW THE TIMING OF BECOMING A PARENT WOULD IMPACT THOSE GOALS.**

I've seen that same look of deep gratitude on so many parents' faces; parents who were tearing their hair out worrying about the teen they love, feeling alone, with no one to help.

It's strange; so often when I tell people I'm an educator at Planned Parenthood, and that I work with teens, they assume that the parents would be angry. When a parent *is* angry, when people do protest, it makes the news and everyone talks about it. The media thrives on angry people; it sells newspapers and it keeps viewers glued to their televisions. But in real life, what I experience with parents day to day, all the time, is gratitude. I realize that gratitude doesn't make headlines or boost advertising, but it concerns me that so many people expect that parents would be angry when a professional tries to help ensure healthy life outcomes as their teen navigates their way through the onset of sexual activity.

They aren't.

"I think I better go on birth control. Could you make me an appointment?" Joy asked. She was fiifteen and had just had sex for the first time. So we scheduled her appointment to start on birth control quickly, and then I asked her, "And what about telling your mom, what's your thought on that?"

She squirmed and twisted in her seat, trying unsuccessfully to find words. "I dunno," she finally said.

"Do you want to tell her?" I asked.

"I dunno, like part of me does. I mean: I don't want to lie to her."

"Good for you. So what's holding you back?" I asked. Joy and her mom were very close.

"I mean, I dunno," she said, squirming again.

"Hasn't your mom tried to talk to you about this stuff?"

"Oh, yeah."

"What did she say?"

"Well, she said…," and although she squirmed nervously and hid her face in a throw pillow as she spoke, her words were clear: "She said she got pregnant when she was sixteen, and that it was really hard, and that she really hopes I'll wait 'till I'm older to have sex, but that however old I am she'd want me to come to her and she'd help me get birth control 'cause she doesn't want my life to be so hard."

"Wow, your mom said that?"

"Yeah, like when I was thirteen," she said, giggling, setting the pillow down, making eye contact again, and then, looking totally relaxed, she added, "Or maybe twelve! She says that all the time."

"Do you think she means it?"

"Oh, yeah."

"So how come you're so reluctant to tell her."

"I mean, I mean, I can't tell her…that!" She said, squirming, again twisting her body in a knot around the pillow she was clutching, as her face turned red.

"What's the holdup?"

"I dunno."

"How do you think she'd react if you told her?"

"I dunno."

"Do you think she'd really follow through?"

"Oh, yeah."

"What would she be like?"

"She'd just be so…disappointed."

"Why?"

" 'Cause I'm only fifteen. She wanted me to wait longer."

"Well, yeah, but you told me she said however old you are, she doesn't want you to become a teen mom. You want birth control now, and you say it's what your mom wants you to do; wouldn't she be proud of you? For taking care of yourself? For doing what she asked you to do?"

More squirming, clutching the pillow, face red. But no words. I paused a little longer, but she still didn't speak, so I continued.

"Joy, why do you think your mom said that to you?"

" 'Cause she thought she had to."

"What does that mean?"

"Like, 'cause she thought she has to be there for me. Ya know: 'cause she's my mom."

"Joy, she's your mom, but not all moms say that to their daughters. It sounds to me like your mom chose her words very carefully, telling you exactly what her hopes are for you, and it sounds like you're planning to do exactly what she'd want you to do. I can't help wonder: maybe if you told her that you want to go on a method now, maybe she'd be proud of you."

"I dunno."

We chatted a bit more. Finally, I closed by saying, "Joy, I want you to know that I really respect that you made this appointment, that you're going to go on birth control right away, that you're taking charge of preventing pregnancy. You're being so mature about that; I work with so many teens that aren't so careful and thoughtful. The most important thing is that you're protecting yourself, and I'm really proud of you for that. And as far as telling your mom goes, it's totally your decision. But I just want to ask you to consider one thing: maybe your mom told you all that because she really means it. Maybe she'd be relieved, not disappointed, if you tell her you're going on a method. Maybe she knows that when a girl first goes on birth control, there are a lot of questions, and maybe she wants to be there for you, so you're not alone. If you tell her, maybe she'd see it as a gift, as a thank you for being such a caring, open mom. And maybe it would make your life a lot easier, not having to lie, not having to hide your method. Maybe she could handle it; maybe it would bring you closer. I'm not saying it would; you know your mom better than I do. I'm just saying, based on what you told me, I want you to really think about it, and whatever you decide, I'm here for you."

A week later, she showed up for her appointment with her mom at her side. I said, "I'm so glad you came together."

"I guess I'm glad, too," mom replied, looking as dazed as her daughter had looked anticipating the conversation they might have; looking like she'd like to squirm and hide behind a pillow like her daughter did, and then she added, "Just a bit shocked."

"When did Joy tell you about this appointment?" I asked.

"This morning, while I was driving her to school. I was just about two blocks from school and she said, 'Mom, I have a 3:30 appointment at Planned Parenthood today if you wanna come,' and I was just so shocked, and like normally I work 'till five so it's just been kinda a crazy day. I had to figure out how to get out of work early; it would've been nice to have like a day's notice, but anyway, I'm here. I made it. Just a little crazy."

Looking at Joy I asked in an incredulous but playful tone, "You told your mom this while she was driving?" and shifting my gaze back to mom I added in the same tone, "Oh! My word: did the car stay on the road?!"

They both laughed, surprised. They clearly needed permission to relax and I was glad to be able to provide it.

"Yes, it did, but please don't ask me how!" mom replied, visibly thankful that I understood how overwhelming it all was for her.

We chatted a little more, and as much as mom was in shock, she could see the big picture: the talks she had had over the years with her daughter had worked. Joy was taking charge of her fertility and was, in all likelihood, never going to be a teen mom.

I was so glad that Joy involved her mom, and that mom had been so clear with her daughter about what her own hopes were. But it really got me thinking; here was a mom who had said everything "right." She had opened the dialogue; she had acknowledged that Joy might have sex earlier than mom would want, and had stressed that she'd want her protected no matter how young she was. And yet, even with that, when the time came, it was so hard for Joy to take her up on it.

Like so many teens I've listened to, when there's a hesitation about telling a parent about the decision to use effective contraception, the fear of disappointing a parent is a bigger and more common obstacle than the fear of an angry parent. I usually find it easier to help teens overcome the fear of an angry parent.

Teens like Kimberly; after telling me she's sexually active and that she definitely didn't want to get pregnant, she said, "I'd love to go on the shot, but my mom would kill me if she found out."

"I'm glad you're thinking about protecting yourself; it's so important. But you sound really scared of your mom," I replied.

"Oh yeah, I totally am. I mean, I know I could get it without telling her, but I'm not kidding, if she found out somehow, I mean, I mean, it totally wouldn't be worth it."

"Really? What would happen if your mom found out?"

"Are you kidding? My mom?"

"Seriously: what would happen?"

"Seriously? She would totally kill me."

"Really? I mean, honestly: is your mom a violent woman? Are you seriously scared for your physical safety if she found out?"

"Oh, I mean, no, not that. She'd never hit me."

"You sure?"

"Oh, I'm sure."

"Well, I'm glad to hear that. I mean, some people do become very violent when they're angry; I'm glad you'd be physically safe. So if that's not it, what is it?"

"I mean…she'd be so angry, and so upset."

"I believe you: definitely. I think for a lot of parents, it's really hard to accept when their little kids grow up into adults, even though that's what they ultimately want. I listen to a lot of parents; when they learn their teen is having sex, it's often the most jolting thing for them. They have such trouble accepting it. Especially right when they first find out. That's part of why I'm so glad your mom isn't violent. But you've seen your mom get angry?"

"Oh yeah, she gets really angry."

"Can you remember the angriest you ever saw her about something you had done? Don't tell me what you had done: it's none of my business. But can you picture it?"

After a little pause she replied, "Yeah." She looked thoughtful.

"But she didn't hit you, right? She just got angry: maybe yelling or freaking out or something. Right?"

"Yeah."

"OK. Now let me ask you this: what happened afterwards?"

She paused again; this time she looked even more thoughtful.

"Actually, afterwards," and she paused even longer. "Actually, afterwards we were even closer."

"Hmmm."

"You know, really, we were. That's weird. I mean, she gets really angry, but actually, when I picture it like that, yeah, that's weird."

"Well, I can understand that it seems strange. But actually, when you think of it, it kind of makes sense. When people hear something that's startling and that's not what they want to hear, they can feel anger, and they can act out quickly on that anger. But afterwards, once some time passes, when whatever they heard sinks in, their thoughts and emotions can change."

We discussed it a little more, and I was able to successfully get her to realize that preventing a pregnancy while she was still a teen was more important than avoiding a potentially uncomfortable conversation with her mom; one that might be hard to get through, but that would, in fact, end, and things would be better afterwards. That's happened to me many times with teens that fear their parents. Sometimes, getting them to imagine the conversations they'll have with their parents beforehand helps them prepare. Sometimes strategies like being in a public space to tell them something that'll be hard to hear helps; they're more confident their parent won't scream in a booth in a fast food restaurant than in the living room.

Some teens truly want to talk with their parents about these issues.

And some don't.

And lots of teens are somewhere in the middle, not even knowing what they want.

Facilitating a lively conversation among a small group of young teen girls underscored that for me. They had such varying answers to so many of the questions I had put out, and they were all so eager to talk about everything from their experiences to their values and attitudes about sexuality. By the end, each of them had shared so much and appeared to value the opportunity to seriously discuss these issues, to be taken seriously, so I wanted to help them open similar communication doors at home, to keep the support coming about these important aspects of growing up.

"You all seem to really enjoy talking about this stuff," I said before closing the group, adding, "Do any of you have conversations like this with your parents?"

Eyes darted back and forth from girl to girl, with most heads shaking, "No."

"You all have so much to say! I wonder if your parents would want to hear about how you're thinking. Do any of your parents ever try to talk with you like this?"

Most shook their heads "No," again. One girl said, "Sometimes my mom tries to talk to me about sex 'n stuff. I pretend not to listen; I kind of moan and roll my eyes and stuff. But actually"—she continued with a naughty gleam in her eyes—"really, I listen to every word."

"Same with me." said another.

"But you seem to love to talk about this stuff; doesn't acting like that shut them down?"

"Yeah."

"So how come you do that?" I asked.

"I dunno," and after a pause she added, "It's embarrassing."

Embarrassing, I thought to myself. Embarrassing. That was their best reason? Embarrassment prevented those important conversations at home; I was glad that at least we were having them together.

Katelyn appeared at the door to my office, and although I had never met her, she immediately started speaking so quickly that I could barely follow her.

"I went to the dentist and he has to do this whole thing and he said first he had to ask if there's any chance I could be pregnant and I said I didn't think so but he said is there even a chance, so I didn't know what to say 'cuz like I have a boyfriend and we're like, um, like, *interactive* and everything but we always use a condom. And like I didn't know what to say and my mom was in the waiting room and he said I have to come back with a letter from a doctor saying I'm not pregnant and I started crying 'cuz I told him, 'I'm NOT!' and I begged him, 'Pleeeze don't tell my mom!' and he said he wouldn't if I bring the letter but I don't even know where to get it. Can I get it at Planned Parenthood?"

Finally, she paused, came up for air, ready to listen.

"Wow, it sounds like this was really challenging. I'm glad you thought to come to me; hopefully I can help you. Yes, you can get a pregnancy test at

Planned Parenthood and you'll get a written documentation saying whether the test is positive or negative."

"I don't need the test; I'm sure I'm not pregnant. I just need the letter."

"Are you asking me if we'd give you a letter saying you're not pregnant without first running a test?" I asked in disbelief. I was so surprised by the question, and the medical incompetence that it implied we might offer.

"I dunno; that's why I'm asking." The innocence of her reply made me quickly realize that I was dealing with a frightened and clueless ninth grader, not an adult accusing my organization of negligence.

"Boy, did you come to the right place; that's a really important question and I'm the person who can answer it. The only way Planned Parenthood could give you the letter saying you're not pregnant is by running a pregnancy test first. Then they'd give you the written result. And it's really easy and fast; you just pee in a little cup and then wait about five minutes."

"But would I need to get my mother's permission? Would she have to know?"

"No, that's entirely up to you; you don't need anyone's permission, and you can share the letter with anyone you choose, like the dentist, but you don't have to share it with anyone. We won't tell anyone the results of your test without your written consent."

We went on to discuss the benefits of using more protection than just condoms, and the possible benefits of involving one or both parents in the decision, so she doesn't have to hide it.

She was so resistant to hormonal contraception; she clearly understood that she'd have more protection from unwanted pregnancy, and she was completely open to the idea of protecting herself, but the choice of either telling her parents about it or hiding it stopped her. She was so afraid of the conversation with a parent that involved content indicating, "I'm having sex, I don't want to get pregnant, I want to protect myself with more than just condoms and I don't want to live a lie, hiding a birth control method and/or related medical appointments from you, so I want your support in this." It was the fact that she, like so many girls I've listened to, couldn't find words to communicate the message that was leading her to have sex with less protection than she wanted.

Girls like Jean. She didn't want to hide birth control from her mom, and she was scared to talk to her about it.

"I understand that you don't want to tell your mom you want birth control, but if you keep having sex without birth control, you may very well end up pregnant, and soon. Have you considered that?"

"Yeah, I think about that a lot, that's what I'm scared of."

"And have you thought about telling your mom *that*?" I asked, expecting and hoping to get her to see that that conversation would be much worse.

Wow, was I wrong!

She fired back almost immediately, "Oh, I could tell her that. That wouldn't be so bad."

"What do you mean? What do you think she would say if you told her you were pregnant?"

"Oh, I know what she'd say. She'd say I haveta get an abortion. She already told me, 'If you get pregnant you're getting an abortion,' " she said, pointing her finger, mocking a livid parent.

"And what would that be like for you?"

"Oh, that'd be OK, I mean, I don't wanna have no kid."

"So, you're saying it would be easier to tell your mom you're pregnant than that you want birth control?"

"Oh, definitely, yes."

"How's that?"

" 'Cuz like, if I told her I was pregnant, she'd be like really upset, and she might cry, but like, it would only be for a minute. Then she'd be like all lovey-dovey and she'd say, 'I'm here for you' and stuff. She'd forgive me. I do stupid stuff all the time. She's used to it. But she always forgives me."

I had no trouble believing the part about that she does stupid stuff all the time. As much as I try not to judge, she presents herself, almost proudly, as an airhead.

"But if I told her I wanna go on birth control, that would be like I'm *planning* to do something stupid. That would make her really mad."

I've listened to so many teens who face that same concern; the fear of a conversation with a parent about their desire to use effective contraception, and of the dozens—if not hundreds—of times a girl has told me she's scared to tell her parent she wants birth control, all except one has told me that she's having sex anyway, and while they don't use direct phrases like, "I'm putting myself at higher risk for unwanted pregnancy," or, "I'm compromising my health due to fear of parental conversation," that's what the behavior they report tells me.

The only exception I can remember is one girl who was really close with her mom. Her mom had made an enormous effort to keep that communication door open, telling her daughter repeatedly, "If you ever want birth control, please come to me. I promise I'll be there for you. I'll take you to get it: please don't lie or feel like you can't come to me. I want to be there for you."

The girl sat trembling on my couch, "When I'm with my boyfriend, I really feel like I'm ready. But I told him we can't 'do it' until I get on birth control, and that I'm gonna tell my mom. But whenever I try to tell my mom, I chicken out. But I know that means I'm not ready. I love my mom—we're so close. If I'm not ready to tell her, it means I'm not ready to do it." She's literally the only girl who ever reported to me that she waited for sex until she could find the words to share with her mom. Shortly after our talk, she addressed it with mom, and went on a birth control method with mom's knowledge before having sex.

There was one other girl who would have waited for sex until she spoke with mom; she wanted to tell her mom. She came up to my office at Planned Parenthood to talk with me, right after school, an hour before her initial appointment. Although we had never met, she had seen me in school and knew who I was.

"Can I come in and just talk to you?" she asked in a hesitant voice at my doorway.

"Of course. Welcome, have a seat. What's up?"

Sitting comfortably on my sofa, she kicked off her shoes and put her feet up and started in.

"I have an appointment downstairs at 4:00 to go on birth control. I'm gonna do it. I really think it's the right thing. I just want to talk to someone first. I remember you came into our class and said we could talk to you about this stuff; that's why I came up here early. I just always thought that when this day came I'd have my mom here. When you said that we could come here with our parents or without them, I thought that that was for kids who couldn't talk to their moms. I didn't think it was for me, so I feel a little funny."

"Have you talked with your mom about this?"

"Oh yeah, lots of times. Just not this week, since I made the appointment."

"What's up with you and your mom?"

"Well, like, I live with her; it's always been just the two of us. We're so close; I'm the center of her whole world. She had me when she was seventeen. She's always told me that she has no regrets in the world; that even though she was young and didn't really have anyone to help her, she loves me so much that having me was the best thing that ever happened to her. I know she means it; she really does. But she tells me it was so hard, and that she really wants me to be older and to finish high school and go to college before I have kids. She begged me to tell her when I start having sex and she told me since I was like thirteen or something that she'd be there for me no matter what, that she'd help me get birth control, that I shouldn't sneak. Nobody helped her, and she told me she doesn't want it to be like that for me."

"Do you believe her?"

"Oh, absolutely."

"Then how come she's not here with you today, how come you didn't tell her?"

"See, that's the thing. I really want to. I talked to my boyfriend about it, too. He's great. He really understands that I don't want to lie to my mom or to hide anything from her. He said he'd wait as long as I want. But the thing is: I don't want to wait anymore to have sex."

She paused for a while before continuing.

"See, my grandfather is dying; he's got cancer and he's staying with us and hospice comes in and everything, but it's my mom's dad. And it's just been so hard for her. He could go anytime, that's what they tell us. But they've been saying that, and I told my boyfriend, and like, we've been waiting. But I don't want to wait, and really, y'know, it's my life. I wanna live my life. The only reason to wait right now is to tell my mom. So like I was gonna tell her last night that I had the appointment today, but I went in, and she was just crying and crying and crying and it's all so hard for her with my grandpa and all. I just didn't have the heart to give her one more thing to think about. But I really wish she were here. This is such a big step for me, I wish I could have her here, but I know I can't; I have to think about what she needs, too. She totally doesn't need to be thinking about this!"

As I listened, I felt the deepest respect for this young woman, for her mother, for her boyfriend. I was disturbed that she and her mom couldn't share this important day, but I agreed with her assessment: that it was too much for her mom today. As she left to go down to the clinic for her appointment, she comforted herself out loud by telling me, "After my grandfather dies, we'll have the funeral. I'll wait a little while 'till I think she can handle it. Then I'll tell her I came here today. I'm gonna save the papers and everything to show her the date. I know she'll understand why I didn't tell her. She'll be a little upset at first; ya know...that she wasn't here, but then I know she'll come 'round. Then we'll probably like go out to dinner or something. She'll be so relieved that I took care of this myself; that I'm not gonna get pregnant. That's so important to her. And to me! I know in the end she'll tell me I did the right thing."

It was truly a gift she was giving her mom; taking care of her own needs, sacrificing what would have been the comfort of her mom's presence for something more important—her mom's peace of mind. Allowing her mom to focus on her own dying father instead of her newly sexually active daughter.

Mom had helped her get to this point; mom would be proud.

Parents can help their teens in so many other ways, too. Sometimes, being helpful has to do with the "big things"; the messages the parents give their teens about setting life goals, about sexual values, about communicating effectively about boundaries, and about reasons for waiting for sexual involvement. And sometimes, teens benefit from their parents' helping them with some of the technical details of preventing pregnancy; using specific methods correctly, setting the stage for success. Parents who really know their teens know which details are likely to cause barriers, and they can help ensure that their teen masters the skills they're going to need. I've seen that countless times with parents of teen girls who help them remember to take their pills correctly, reminding them to pack them before leaving for sleepovers, reminding them to call for refills before running out, or keeping count of precisely twelve weeks on the calendar for Depo shots.

And moms like Judith, Harry's mom, can help their sons overcome barriers. Being a professional in human services, Judith worked with lots of teen parents, and each time she heard teens admit they had had unprotected sex because of their fears of buying condoms, she thought of her own son, and she worried. Harry is smart, but he's shy. And living in a small town like Springfield, buying condoms will almost always involve being seen by someone who knows you. For some teens—male and female—that's not a problem. But for others it is.

So the first time he asked her for the car to take his date out she was nervous. He had used her car alone a few times, but the presence of a girlfriend and the absence of a parent were going to make this car a new place, and Judith felt justified in her concern. She was driving him home from work when he asked her for it.

She hesitated.

"Mom, what's the problem? You know I can drive!" he exclaimed defensively.

"I know."

"So?"

"It's not that. It's about you being alone in the car with Lori. I'm just not sure you're ready for this."

"Maaa," he whined, "We're just going to the dance. It's no big deal."

"I know. I want you to go; I'm glad you're going. That's not the problem. It's the car."

"I'm just going to drive to her house, pick her up, drive her to the dance, and then drive her home. You know I can do that."

"I know. It's the part about you two being alone in the car. I know you're growing up; I'm just not sure you're ready for this. It's a new kind of freedom; this is all just so new with you driving."

"Oh, God, mom: don't you trust me?" he asked, outraged.

"I do trust you. That's why this is hard for me." She was nervous, she was stammering a bit; she was on new ground.

"So if you trust me, why is it hard? Why is it any different than when you let me take the car to Lexington that time? This is easier; this is like four miles; that was twenty."

"I know," and after a pause she added, "But there wasn't a girl in the car that time. A girl you really like. It's different."

"Mom, I've told you: we're not going to have sex!"

"I know; that's great."

They had had numerous frank talks about sex before. But now she was looking at him, imagining him with the car, with his girlfriend, and she was afraid that all those talks might not be enough to keep her son safe.

"I'm glad you're going to wait for that; I really am," she continued. "But here's the thing: we both need to face the fact that you're growing up. I guess this car thing really makes me think about it differently. I mean it's not that I don't trust you or don't believe you. And I'm not saying I think you're going to have sex the first time you take the car out: I don't. It's just that someday, you *will* be ready to have sex, and I need to know that you'll be able to protect yourself when the time comes. I guess it's just that I see the car as sort of a milestone. I mean, as a mother, I have to ask myself, 'What mother would give her son a car and the keys knowing he was going to be alone with his girlfriend; what's that mother's job in protecting her son when he is ready?"

"Maaa," he whined again, "You've done your job; you don't need to worry about me."

"Well, I hope I have." she replied, and after a thoughtful pause she added, "So if I've done my job so well, when the time does come, once you are ready for sex, what would you do to protect yourself?"

"I'd make sure my girlfriend went on birth control, and I'd wear a condom."

"Good for you. And where would you get it?"

"Maaa," he whined again, rolling his eyes in frustration. "This isn't like the old days; they sell them everywhere now."

"I know that. But I'm asking, where would *you* get them?"

"Anywhere. They sell them in the grocery store, in Wal-Mart, they give them away at Planned Parenthood."

"I know. But here in Springfield, Planned Parenthood is only open two days a week, and they're not open on the weekend, at night. I'm asking: if you were in a situation where you needed a condom right away, and you didn't have one, and you had the car, where would *you* get them?"

"Oh, my God, mom," he said, exasperated, "I mean, look, they sell them right there," he said, pointing to the convenience store they happened to be approaching.

Judith quickly pulled off the road into the convenience store parking lot.

"Yes, they sell them in there. Are you telling me that's where you'd get them?"

"I mean, if I needed them, I could. "

"You're telling me you could walk right in there and buy condoms?"

"Why not?" he demanded.

"OK," she said, and fumbling through her purse for a twenty-dollar bill, she handed it to him saying, "Walk in there with this, and come out with a bag of condoms."

"Are you kidding me?"

"Why would I be kidding?"

"I don't need them. I'm not going to have sex."

"I'm not saying you are. I'm saying that I need to know that when you're ready to have sex, that I know that you could get condoms." Noting his look of terror she added, "It's not a question of where they sell them. It's that this is a small town and everywhere you go, people know you. It takes a lot of maturity to go into a store and buy condoms and not be scared of who sees you. I need to know you can do that before you ever drive the car alone with a girl."

"Are you saying if I go in there and buy condoms, you'll let me use the car?"

"Yes. Do you want me to drive you somewhere else, or is this where you'd go?"

Taking the money, he shrugged and said this store was fine. He bought a bag of condoms and slinked back to the car.

"Good for you," she said. "It's not easy; I know that. But you can do it. I just needed to see that with my own eyes. I won't always be with you, but you always need to remember that you can do that. It's just not worth having a kid that you're not ready for, throwing your whole future off because it's hard to buy condoms. You might think I'm crazy, but I've seen so many guys who got their girlfriends pregnant; I just needed to see that you could do that," and after a pause she repeated, "Good for you."

It's because of how well she knew her son that she was able to identify that obtaining condoms could be a barrier for him, and she was able to use his desire to take the car as an opportunity to ensure that it was a barrier he'd overcome.

Most of my referrals in the high school were for teens, but Ms. Carter, the school nurse, asked if I'd be able to meet with Lauren's parents. "They're coming in to see me at noon; I was wondering if I could maybe introduce them to you. They came in last week; they have so many concerns about Lauren. She's a senior, but she really has a lot of special needs. Academically, emotionally, socially she's about like a second grader. She's the sweetest thing; she's really a nice girl. At the end of our meeting last week they told me that Lauren has a boyfriend now for the first time. He's maybe a little ahead of her but not much. They're really worried. After they left last week I thought of you; maybe you could help them."

I agreed to try.

Mom did almost all the talking, for almost an hour. It was so clear to me that she had a powerful need to be heard. She went all over the map about Lauren and their relationship, which was close and loving, and her concerns that Lauren will never be able to live independently and take care of herself. She needs help with even the most basic life skills. But she's sweet, caring, warm and friendly. "That's why it scares me sometimes, like seeing her with a boyfriend. She's always loved to please people. He's a nice boy; I really like him. He came over for dinner, it was good. I mean, she's never had a lot of friends, and he's really good to her, and it makes her happy and everything. But"—now mom lost her bubbly demeanor, stopped looking me in the eye, turned her gaze towards the floor, and continued speaking a little more slowly, sounding almost guilty—"it isn't like I don't want her to have someone who cares about her, but it *scares* me."

"Can you explain what it is that scares you?"

"Well, like, just, uh, um, like, what could happen."

"With the boyfriend?"

"Yeah."

"About them getting so close?"

"Yeah."

"Well, yeah, there's a lot at stake. And it sounds like there's a lot that Lauren might not understand; there are a lot of skills we need to build healthy, intimate relationships. It gets complicated; there are the emotional parts, the physical parts, the timing of how to build a relationship over time, how to pace—"

Here she interrupted me, "Oh my God, yes, Vivian; all of that. I mean she's so young in some ways. She doesn't have *any* of those skills." We discussed her friendship skills at some length.

Then I shifted gears. "Every now and then there are stories about girls who get pregnant and they're shocked; they didn't even know how pregnancy happens or what they did that led to it. I don't know Lauren, but you do. From what you've told me so far, I'm wondering, do you think she's at risk of that kind of thing? Do you think she understands how pregnancy happens?"

Here even dad chimed in. They both clearly stated that that was a huge concern of theirs. That even though they had explained to her how pregnancy happens, and what sex is, it was all way too complicated for Lauren to understand. They were concerned that one of these days, Lauren's period would be late, and some doctor would tell them she's pregnant. "And I mean, Vivian, there's no way she could raise a kid. It would be us. There's nobody else; it would be our kid." They were realistic, and they knew that they didn't have what it takes to raise another child. And they were scared: very scared. They could keep a close eye on their daughter, but they knew they couldn't watch her 24/7, and it was in contemplating those brief unsupervised moments that their fears were triggered.

"Well, have you considered helping Lauren go on a reliable birth control method, so that if she did have sex she'd be less likely to get pregnant?" I asked.

"Oh, absolutely. Yes," mom said, and continued with a naughty, almost apologetic look. "Part of me can't wait 'till she has sex so I can take her to my doctor and get her on the pill. I mean, not like I want her to have sex—I don't. But I mean, I know we'll sleep better at night once I can get her on the pill," mom said.

Dad nodded vigorously in approval.

"Why do you want to wait 'till she has sex to help her get started on the pill?" I asked.

"What do you mean?"

"I mean, if you're concerned that she might have sex in the somewhat near future, and that she might become pregnant, why do you want to wait?"

Mom looked baffled. She asked again, "What do you mean?" and elaborated this time by adding, "Are you allowed to go on birth control before you have sex?" Dad looked equally puzzled.

"What do you mean allowed?" I asked.

"I mean, you have to get birth control from a doctor, right?"

"Yes."

"But like, would a doctor give her birth control even if she hasn't had sex?" she asked in an incredulous tone.

"Well, I can't speak for her doctor, or for any individual doctor, about what specific prescription they'd write for any specific patient, but I can say with certainty that not having had sex wouldn't stop most doctors from prescribing a method."

"But it's to prevent pregnancy; how could they do that if the girl hasn't had sex? Like, at Planned Parenthood would they be allowed to do that?"

"Oh, absolutely: yes. It's to prevent pregnancy, but ideally, patients who don't want pregnancy would all go on a reliable method *before* their first sexual encounter."

Mom heard my words; so did dad, but they were having a difficult time absorbing the meaning. To them, it clearly sounded too good to be true. "You mean, I could just take her to a doctor and tell the doctor we want birth control and get her on it? Like, now?"

Again, I was careful not to speak for any doctor about what prescriptions they would or wouldn't write, but I was clear with mom and dad that if that's what they want, there's no reason to delay asking.

It took me quite awhile to get them to fully comprehend that if they wanted to help Lauren get on a birth control method, we could most likely make that happen quickly. But it was time well spent; by the time they left that first visit, we had scheduled a medical appointment for Lauren and I had helped them plan the conversation they'd have with her.

As I left the building after school, the nurse saw me and called me into her office. "I don't know what you did with them, but boy, if your ears were ringing afterwards, you should have heard them talking about you. They came back in to thank me for introducing them to you. They went on and on about it. They looked so much more relaxed and happy. Whatever you did: thank you."

I thanked her in turn; "I thought it went really well." I said, adding, "I'm so glad you introduced us. I think it was a really important meeting, and without you making that connection it never would have happened." We exchanged that look of mutual gratitude that we exchange so often, and each left to enjoy the weekend.

Lauren did go on the pill before she ever had sex, and mom monitored all the necessary behind-the-scenes work with my continued support.

Sometimes being helpful to families is very complicated; in their case it was pretty simple and straightforward. These parents were missing one vital piece of information: the fact that effective contraceptive methods are available by prescription before a person has had sex.

When it comes to helping parents help their kids navigate their way through their teen years without an unwanted pregnancy, the challenges are not the same for every family I've worked with. But frequently, one or two visits have brought up something as straightforward and helpful as this one did. It isn't rocket science, it's simply being available to be present to people with the information and support they need when they need it. Mostly, it's simply creating comfort, creating a time and space that allows them to feel safe, and then a lot of listening. Listening to their concerns, listening to the information they have, listening for the barrier, and filling the holes.

I stepped in the door and immediately began to remove my snow-covered boots. The linoleum floor was glistening, like it had just been waxed. The entire kitchen sparkled. I'm so used to going into messy, sometimes filthy homes that the contrast was striking. Joan said, "Oh, you don't have to do that." I thanked her as I continued to untie my boots, making casual chit-chat about her kitchen being one of the cleanest ones I had ever seen. She said she was thankful that I noticed, and confided her frustration about caseworkers that just waltz in right after she cleans and leave mud all over and don't even notice. And she stood a bit taller as though it was the first time any professional had ever come into her home or her life and opened with a compliment.

We went into the dining room and sat around the table with her daughter Kelly, who was fifteen and had recently returned home from foster care.

"Do you ever think about having a family of your own someday?" I asked Kelly after a little introductory chat, and after briefly explaining my role.

"Yes," she replied without hesitation, "Definitely someday, but not for a looong time."

"And Joan, do you ever want to be a grandmother?"

Her response was equally quick and certain.

"Definitely. But not for a looong time."

So I told them I was glad they both agreed, and the conversation remained calm and civil as they answered my questions, confirming that they could both think of a lot of benefits of postponing parenting until Kelly graduated from high school, went to college, had a good job, her own home, and a man who would stay with her and help raise a family.

Then I began to navigate the trickier territory of Kelly's sexual development, explaining that my role is to be sure that Kelly has the information and support she needs to successfully get through her teen years without an unintended pregnancy. As they each began to contemplate and discuss this, their voices got louder and angrier, and their conversation quickly transformed from taking turns speaking and listening, to non-stop interrupting each other.

Joan was complaining that she can't trust her daughter and pointing to lies Kelly had told regarding her whereabouts, making Joan concerned about what is actually happening in her daughter's life, specifically her sex life, and Kelly took those words of doubt as personal put-downs, responding with defensive accusations of her own about how her mother had role-modeled lies, that her whole life was a lie, that she had no business "dissing" her daughter, "Just 'cuz you married a freakin' crack head..." and denying—vehemently denying—the implication that when she snuck out while she was grounded it had been for sex.

"You're just jealous 'cuz I have friends and a life, something you wouldn't know anything about," she screamed.

Knowing this wasn't going to be productive, and knowing I couldn't out-scream either or both of them, I let it go on just long enough to get the gist of where they were, and then put my hands up in a "stop" position and began to whisper.

It always amazes me how effective whispering is at stopping shouting. They immediately silenced themselves to hear my soft, slow words.

"It's clear to me that there's a lot of anger here, that these are issues that bring up a lot of feelings, a lot of history, a lot of important concerns for both of you. But I'm not a therapist and I'm not a magician. To be honest, I have about an hour to spend with you today. As I listen to you, I'm thinking to myself, 'This is complicated. And there's nothing in these heated words that I—or probably anyone—can fix in an hour.' So I'm asking myself, 'Does that mean I can't be helpful?' and honestly, I don't know."

"But here's one thing I'm thinking," I continued. "I go in a lot of homes where teens and parents are having trouble communicating about sexuality. You're not the first. From my perspective, here's what's striking to me about *this* home."

Their gazes were fixed on me with anticipation.

"Remember when I came in and said how clean your kitchen looked?"

Joan nodded, "yes."

"One thing I noticed, that I'm sitting here thinking about right now, is the fact that as I walked through your kitchen, I wasn't tripping over pacifiers or baby toys. It was clear to me the minute I opened the door that there's no infant living in this home. A lot of the homes I go in with a daughter your age already have an infant living there. So here's my thought. There's obviously a lot you two don't agree on, and a lot you can argue about. But from what you each said in the beginning, it sounds like if I or anyone were to visit again a year from today, you both agree you would want that to still be the case: that Kelly's not pregnant and hasn't got a baby yet. That in a year, there wouldn't be any baby toys or pacifiers scattered on that clean floor. Am I right that you both agree that that's an important goal? Yes or no?"

They both emphatically agreed and immediately started with the "Buts."

"But she just lies all the time!"

"But she won't let me out of her sight, how am I supposed to…" and I cut them both off again.

"Listen. If we just focus on that, I think we might get somewhere. It sounds like we're not going to reach agreement on what has happened for you, Kelly, regarding sex. And honestly, Kelly, your sex life is none of my business. But we can look at the pregnancy prevention piece separately. Kelly, if your mom would agree to take you to go on a birth control method, is that something you'd want to do?"

She would.

"Joan, it's clear to me that you have a lot of unanswered concerns—important concerns—about Kelly's sexual experience. But can I ask you to just put them aside for a minute and focus on this: you admit that you don't know if Kelly is going to have sex or not in the coming year. But you both sound certain that if she does have sex, you don't want it to result in a pregnancy. So would you be willing to take her to the clinic to get a method?"

She tried to go back to reporting lies her daughter had told, boys she'd been with.

I cut her off and insisted, "Please, for right now, just answer this one thing: if Kelly wants to go on birth control, would you drive her to the clinic?"

"Well, hell, yeah; I'll drive her—that's easy. That's nothing."

"Well, it may sound like it's 'easy' or 'nothing' to you, but to a fifteen-year-old living almost an hour from a clinic that provides birth control to teens, it can be the difference between Kelly reaching the goal you both set or not."

I set a pamphlet on the table outlining the different birth control methods, saying, "There's no way I can sit here and know with certainty if or when Kelly will have sex, but I do know that if she gets to the clinic, gets on an effective method, and uses it correctly under your supervision, there's about a 99% chance that if I show up in a year you won't be needing either of these other pamphlets I carry." And I put two pamphlets out titled, "Naming your baby" and "What to expect when you're expecting."

"Oh my God I can't even imagine that." Joan said from her heart.

"Well, right now you have the opportunity to be 99% confident that that won't happen simply by taking her to the clinic. A lot of fifteen-year-olds I've worked with tell me that their mothers are nuts; that they want to have a baby and their mothers don't see how grown up and ready they are. Your daughter isn't saying that. She's saying she agrees with you, that she's not ready to be a mom. But she can't drive yet. If you'll drive her, with the motivation I'm hearing from both of you to prevent a pregnancy, the odds are really in your favor."

Joan had to excuse herself and go into the living room so Kelly and I wouldn't see her tears. We didn't need to. She had agreed to drive; that was big. Huge, actually. I scheduled Kelly's first pelvic exam, left an appointment card, and discussed birth control choices with Kelly. She was already pretty well informed for her age, and easily picked a method to start with. I left her more information to read, discussed the benefits of abstinence *and* hormonal protection, and congratulated her on taking charge of her fertility.

Before leaving, I went into the living room and gave Joan the appointment card with the date and time and double-checked that she's available to drive.

"Oh, God yes. Driving? That's so nothing."

"And so everything," I added.

I said that I really respected the effort she's making, and underlined that simply being on an effective method doesn't take away anything from mom's insistence on age-appropriate monitoring of her daughter's whereabouts, on curfew, on rules. The only thing it changes is that if her daughter does break any of the rules, the chances of it resulting in a pregnancy are much lower. And I underscored how important all those concerns were. She thanked me with a soft, sincere voice and walked me to the door, where I tied my boots back on.

As I backed out of the driveway, the digital clock in my car told me I had been there for an hour. I drove a few miles before pulling over to write my case notes while it was fresh in my mind. In an hour, Kelly had "set a reproductive goal" (postpone pregnancy until college graduation), "made a plan," (go on a hormonal method immediately), and taken the first three "measurable action steps," (scheduled appointment for initial pelvic exam, arranged transportation, and selected a birth control method) towards reaching the goal.

My subsequent visits and phone calls confirmed that she showed up for the appointment, started her method, and used it correctly with mom's support. Kelly's pills and the condoms that I provided on follow-up visits protected her for several years, and even after I closed the case I verified that Kelly never did become a teen mom. I've often thought back to that pivotal first meeting. In an hour, they went from angry, unproductive screaming to scheduling a pelvic exam and birth control method start. They had been fighting for years before I knocked on their door, and they're probably still fighting today, but no infant heard their screams; no infant had been conceived.

Studies show that 75% of teens that become pregnant in America didn't desire pregnancy when it happened.[9] I wonder how many of them would have changed their path if someone had spent a similar hour with them beforehand.

Although Joan's battles with her daughter were extreme, and not representative of "typical" teen/parent communication, the fact that she hit a wall in her attempts to communicate with her daughter is not that uncommon. Many parents try to discuss dating, relationships, and sexuality with their teens and hit a wall.

I ponder that wall; something puzzles me about it.

It seems pretty universal that when a parent sees their baby take its first step, it's a milestone that is always celebrated. The mega-message is, "You're growing up; you're not the same baby you were before, and I'm here to support you in your continuing development."

And when that baby grows into a young child the encouragement continues. The solo sung onstage may be completely off key, the softball pitched may go nowhere near home plate, but parents don't put the child down for what they can't yet do well. No: the effort is praised.

Yet when that same child grows a little more, goes through puberty, and begins to show signs of taking delight in their newfound sexual energy, parental responses shift.

While many parents would agree that intimately loving another person can be one of the most fulfilling, joyous aspects of being an adult, when they see their child reaching in that direction, showing early signs of learning to do that, they don't encourage their potential ability to someday do it well. The effort isn't praised.

Why isn't the mega-message, "You're growing up; you're starting to think about love and relationships, to explore a new part of yourself, a new part of life. I am here to encourage healthy, thoughtful, safe, fulfilling relationships; to support you in this process as you learn and grow." More often, the mega-message is a condescending, "You don't even know what love is. You may think you're growing up but you're not as grown up as you think." Insulting phrases like "puppy love" prevail.

The kid becomes defensive and the adult, adamant that he or she knows more than the teen, becomes exasperated.

A downward spiral ensues.

Why the difference? No parent would ever look at the baby who had just taken its first step and insult her, saying mockingly, "You think you know how to walk? Ha. You don't know what walking is. Look! You can't even stay up; you fell already." A parent wouldn't even dream of insulting that effort. It's assumed the kid can't walk yet. Of course he can't: he's a baby.

Why isn't the teen celebrated or supported? While Kelly and Joan's relationship had been damaged years before I knocked on their door, many parent/teen relationships have a more solid foundation, and many teens could grow up forming healthier intimate relationships if they had some support, instead of criticism and put-downs from the adults who love and care about them.

Some parents find it easy to provide that support, others struggle, others ignore it, and some, like Kim's mom, ask for help.

Kim's mom called me; her daughter was growing up, they're very religious, and there had been a sermon in church which included talking about how sinful sex is outside of marriage.

"I'm thinking about what she heard, and on the one hand it's good; I mean: I really hope she'll wait. But Vivian, one of my really good friends died of AIDS, and I think about Kim growing up, and I mean, I don't want to rush her or anything, but I know how teenagers are. I'm not naïve. I mean, what if she does have sex? I mean, like, they told her it's a sin and everything, but still, um, I just get so scared when I think about what could happen."

"This must be really hard for you."

"It is. Because I really worry about her growing up. I mean, when I was growing up, they said that same stuff in church, but back then there was no AIDS. All we had to worry about was getting pregnant."

"I know what you mean; the stakes are higher now. It sounds like you're concerned that the message might not have been enough; that you want her to wait, but that you'd also want her to know how to protect herself from AIDS if she does have sex. Is that right?"

"Yes, that's it, exactly. But like, I'm scared to talk to her about condoms or anything after what they said. I mean…I don't want to contradict it, to give her permission. It's not like I want to encourage her to be a sinner!"

> "LATEX CONDOMS, WHEN USED CONSISTENTLY AND CORRECTLY, ARE HIGHLY EFFECTIVE IN PREVENTING THE SEXUAL TRANSMISSION OF HIV, THE VIRUS THAT CAUSES AIDS"
> —*STATEMENT FROM THE CENTERS FOR DISEASE CONTROL AND PREVENTION*

"No, I'm sure you don't. But it also sounds like, as a parent, you don't want to leave her in the dark about how to protect herself from AIDS."

"Absolutely. I definitely want her to know that."

"Well, it sounds like she's heard the first part; abstinence is definitely the most effective protection."

"I know."

"But it sounds like she hasn't heard the second part, that latex condoms, when used consistently and correctly, are highly effective in preventing the sexual transmission of HIV. I mean, medically, that is accurate. Am I hearing you right: that's a message you DO want her to hear?"

"Yes, absolutely."

"And it sounds like you're not sure if she's heard it yet. Is that correct?"

"I don't know; I'm afraid maybe she hasn't."

"Well, even if she's heard it, you're her mom. Has she heard it from you?"

"I guess not. Actually, I guess that's why I called. I'm just so nervous."

"I can really understand; I'm so glad you called. I can hear how important this is to you. So are you concerned that if you tell her that, she'll hear it as a contradiction to what she heard in church?"

"Oh…hmm…um…well, kind of, I guess."

"Well, I can see where this must be hard for you. But a couple of thoughts I have might be helpful. First of all, it's great that you're thinking of talking about this with her; studies clearly show that teens that talk with their parents make healthier choices. And also, while parents sometimes feel like they're sending conflicting messages, if they talk about both abstinence and protection, teens don't perceive it that way. It's not contradictory messages; it's a complete message. Think of other things teens hear about staying safe. They hear, 'Don't drink,' but they also hear, 'But if you or any of your friends do drink, don't drive.' And they hear, 'And wear your seatbelt.' They're used to hearing messages that honor the fact that they don't always follow the first instruction; messages that acknowledge that there are different degrees of safety."

"Yes, that's it."

"It's what we call risk reduction. And I agree with you that she probably hasn't heard enough yet to know how to protect herself, unless she's heard it someplace else."

"Yeah, that's right."

"Teens get information from lots of places. But honestly, lots of teens get information from their friends, and it isn't always accurate. Here we supposedly live in the age of technology, but it amazes me how much misinformation there is out there about sexual health. So many teens are uninformed."

"Yeah, that's what I'm worried about."

She agreed that she wanted her daughter to hear a more complete message, including how to protect herself from pregnancy, STDs and HIV/AIDS, and invited me over for a home visit. I was to discuss the objective health information, including the condom demonstration that she requested, and I was to leave them condoms.

I'm used to clutter on kitchen tables and I'm used to moms quickly brushing it aside; the used coffee cups, the ashtrays, the piles of junk mail, the half empty bags of chips. But this was the first time I was greeted by a table that featured a tall, cement statue of the Virgin Mary in her classic pose, arms open, seeming to be watching over all that took place at the table. Mom saw me notice it as she brushed the clutter aside and said, "Oh, don't worry about her. She wants Kim to be safe; she doesn't want her to die!"

"I don't, either!"

I've used my wooden penis to teach correct condom use at so many kitchen tables, but never before or since in the shadow of a sculpture of the Virgin Mary. I truly appreciated how mom replied; like it wasn't a conflict, like the statue was still there as intended, to ensure the best possible life for the family, and I was thankful that mom was open to seeing it that way; nobody wants their daughter to die.

> "IN THE FIGHT AGAINST AIDS, CONDOMS SAVE LIVES. IF YOU OPPOSE THE DISTRIBUTION OF CONDOMS, SOMETHING IS MORE IMPORTANT TO YOU THAN SAVING LIVES."
> –*MELINDA GATES*

Kim's mom wanted Kim to be safe and to have accurate information. She was concerned about the possibility of Kim getting misinformation from friends. And she understood that in some ways the stakes are higher than they used to be. Those are such basic concerns, and they're common for many parents.

She was right that the stakes are higher in some ways; STDs are more prevalent now, and when Kim's mom was growing up there was no HIV/AIDS. But there are also more opportunities now. Today, there are more effective methods of contraception than there used to be, like LARCs (long-acting reversible contraception), and they're becoming increasingly available to more teens. It is a combination of more effective use of contraception and more effective methods that are responsible for the recent dramatic reductions in teen pregnancy rates.

The internet paradoxically gives parents help and reasons to be concerned.

One reason they may be concerned is the fear of images their kids might see. An internet search for "naked people having sex" provided over ten million results in less than one second. Today's parents need to be aware of the changing world in which their kids are growing up. And they need to be able to address it. It's not simply a matter of computer software or other technical aspects, it's about communication: it's important to give kids a clear message that they may see things on the internet that trouble, scare, or puzzle them, but that they can always tell their parents and they can talk about it. And even parents who don't have computers at home need to realize their kids have internet access in many places; your teen is likely to be much more internet savvy than you might realize.

In addition to the images kids might see online, there's also the information they might get. Anyone can post just about anything online, and teenagers have taken cameras in hand and posted their own voices on YouTube: teens talking to teens about sex. The fact that there's no adult editor is both freeing and concerning. One concern is the ability of people to post inaccurate information.

But to concerned parents, I'd like to remind you: it didn't take the internet to provide teens with quick, easy access to inaccurate information. Teens have had that for ages. From friends, from acquaintances, from siblings. What's changed is not the fact that teens can quickly access inaccurate information. What's changed is the context of this information; inaccurate information is now readily available from many computers, side by side with accurate information.

Parents' roles are changed by this new context. Parents need to prepare their teens to deal with the internet; they now have the added responsibility of ensuring that their teens learn how to differentiate between accurate and inaccurate information, and that is no small task for teens or for adults. But it's an important one. At the very least, parents can find websites that have accurate information and tell their teens to question anything they read or hear that isn't consistent with them. And for parents who have trouble keeping up with the ever-changing world of accurate information, the internet can serve as an excellent tool.

DRUNK ENOUGH

"Whatever affects one directly, affects all indirectly. I can never be what I ought to be until you are what you ought to be. This is the interrelated structure of reality."
–Dr. Martin Luther King, Jr.[10]

The waitress tossed a handful of wet-naps on our table; our barbecue chicken and ribs were almost ready. That pile of wet-naps in the center of the table, right next to the ever-present plastic bucket for discarding bones, is a tradition at our "famous" local barbecue joint, where everyone delights in the way they slobber on the sauce; where everyone eats with their fingers.

"How come they give you condoms here?!" Nikki exclaimed, examining one of the foil packets.

She was seven.

Every adult head in the place suddenly turned to our table, looking shocked, with a horrified hush. My husband and I ignored their stares as we explained to Nikki what a wet-nap is.

She was visiting us from New York City. We were her volunteer "host" family through a program that sends kids to the country; kids from the inner city who would otherwise never get to play outside in the summer. We knew when we volunteered that the kids came from a different subculture: urban poverty. They had never seen cows in fields or the big dipper in the night sky. But we hadn't anticipated so many small realities that they'd find new. It was years before I started working for Planned Parenthood. I simply hadn't considered how a seven-year-old growing up in a neighborhood with one of the highest AIDS rates in the country, in a family that couldn't afford to eat in restaurants, would know about condoms but not about wet-naps.

It was such a contrast to a month before, when I travelled for four hours to one of New York City's finest steakhouses to celebrate the sixtieth wedding anniversary of a childhood friend's parents. Without any help, my friend's fourteen-year-old daughter asked the waiter to butterfly-cut her steak, and the five-year-old niece successfully hailed a cab in the rain when the party ended.

Contemporary American society is composed of a rich, diverse tapestry of people from all over the world, all living together. Many Americans get to appreciate diversity in terms of ethnicity, national origin and race; we treasure dining in restaurants where we get to savor the aromas and flavors of a vast array of ethnic cuisines. We learn to work and live side by side with people from around the world, with different beliefs, values, holidays and traditions. And it makes life more interesting.

Yet when it comes to diversity of income, we generally *don't* live or work side-by-side, or even enter each other's worlds. We tend to be a self-segregating society money-wise; most people living with financial means never see the inside of a home where the families are living below the federal poverty level. Some among us, like me, look in our checkbooks or in our computers when we're wondering how much money we have; others look in their pockets. It's different. It's that segregation, that separation within our society that leads to a prevalent lack of awareness of what its like to live in poverty in America today.

That lack of awareness was underscored for me when I read Nickel And Dimed, in which the author Barbara Ehrenreich went "under cover," taking minimum wage jobs, living on the wage, and writing about the experience. Her stories all sounded just like the way the people lived in the homes I routinely visited. The only thing that surprised me in the entire book was in the "Afterword," where the author said that when the book first came out, she had gotten so many comments from readers who were shocked by how difficult life was among the working poor.[11]

Shocked?

More people need to see that.

I fantasize about how that could change; I imagine judges sentencing white-collar criminals to "time" with minimum wage jobs instead of time in jails. After all, they're a financial threat to society, but they don't threaten our physical safety the way armed robbers or murderers do. And in jail, taxpayers are financially supporting these crooks, yet nobody is learning anything and nothing is being accomplished or improved. If these guys had to live next door to the homes I visit, if they had to work the jobs my clients work, if they had to drive those cars, live on those wages, and have the same health insurance word would get out. And it needs to; maybe then, the "rules" would change.

Our economically segregated society doesn't have the blatant "rules" of the racially segregated society we had during the Jim Crow era. We aren't forced to separate ourselves by income today in the same way people were forced to separate by race a few generations ago: by law; with the "whites only" and "colored only" signs on public doors. Yet we are now opening and closing different doors for different people in another way: by income. Children born into poverty in America today are far behind the starting line for chasing after the American Dream. Since we don't tend to intermingle, many among us don't see that. But it's what's happening. And until we can break the cycles of teen pregnancy and unintended pregnancy that are so prevalent among people in poverty, and that make it so much harder to escape from poverty, I doubt that injustice will change.

> **"THE OPPOSITE OF POVERTY IS NOT WEALTH... THE OPPOSITE OF POVERTY IS JUSTICE".**
> *–BRYAN STEVENSON*

Culture shapes each of us, and just as the seven-year-old who had never seen a wet-nap is being shaped differently from the five-year-old in that same city who can already hail a cab, our economic subcultures shape us differently. Those differences impact our lives in many ways. The families that have welcomed me into their homes have shown me how differently their subculture shapes them when it comes to issues related to sexual health, and in turn to unintended pregnancy.

"After this baby is born, have you thought about whether you'd ever like to have any more kids?" I asked Laura after a little introductory chitchat. She was sixteen, pregnant with her first child.

"Oh yeah, I've thought about it. I definitely don't want no more!"

"How come?"

"I didn't even want this one!" she said, pointing to her bulging midsection. "I just never really thought it would happen. One's gonna be hard enough. I ain't got no money, I wanna finish school, oh, God, I can't even imagine wantin' another."

"Ever?"

"Well, I mean, like maybe someday. But not for like *years.*"

"So you want to go a long time before another pregnancy; that's your goal." And turning to her mom I added, "As her mom, and as grandma to her baby, what's your thought about that goal?"

"Hell, I definitely don't want her to have no more. I mean, yeah, maybe someday. But not till she gets a lot older, I mean, like, when she's outta here and has her own place. I mean, we just got these two bedrooms; it's gonna be tight already. I mean we'll manage and everything, but definitely not no more." Laura's fifteen-year-old sister sat silently at their sides.

"OK, so you both agree on the goal; that's great for a start." And looking back at Laura I continued, "Now, you're very young. You have a lot of fertile years ahead of you. And if you're serious about wanting to go for years without another pregnancy, that's a tall order. Lots of women set that goal and reach it. Certainly, it can be done. But it takes a big commitment.

It's important to realize that you can get pregnant so easily. Our bodies are designed to get pregnant and have lots of babies; if we don't want that to happen, we have to seriously work at it. That's when birth control can be really helpful. Do you mind if I ask: have you ever used any kinds of birth control?"

"Ya mean like the pill?"

"That's one kind of birth control. There are other kinds, too. Have you heard of anything else?"

"I ain't never used the pill. I thought about it, but right around when I was thinking about it," she paused to giggle before adding, "That's when I found out I was pregnant."

I was new at my job, and excited about the challenge. I had done a few home visits before, but they were all to clients who had met my predecessor. Laura was the first person that had been referred to me directly. Sophie, a worker from another program who knew them well and brought me to the home, had referred her. Sophie had told them about my services and they were interested; mom wanted all the help she could get.

I had read so much about the importance of family involvement for teens. I knew it was especially important for Laura, thinking about long-term success, since their home was "out in the boonies" and there was no way she'd be able to get to doctors' appointments without mom's awareness, not to mention gas money and car. I had also read about how difficult it could be, so I went to the home armed not only with information about contraception, but with brochures featuring titles like, "Tips for Talking with your Teen about Sexuality," and "How to Talk With Your Parents About Birth Control."

I had thought that it might be hard to get them started, but it wasn't. Not at all. Being so new, I couldn't believe how easy it all seemed. Laura's goal of delaying any possible subsequent pregnancies gave me a green light to offer to show them my case of samples of all the birth control methods, which they gladly accepted. Mom and daughters were focused and we even had some relaxed giggling and laughter as they examined birth control pill packages, learned about the shot, watched me demonstrate correct condom use on a wooden penis, and saw how to apply spermicidal foam into an applicator. It was 1996; they even watched me insert a diaphragm into the vagina of my plastic model of the female reproductive system. And they had seen the episode on Seinfeld in which Elaine tries to buy contraceptive sponges before they are removed from drugstore shelves, and refers to guys being "sponge-worthy," and they had loved it. So I told them about the comedian who was puzzled about the invention of the sponge; "Do they really think women want having sex to seem more like doing the dishes?" and they roared with laughter.

We were off and running and I was beginning to feel confident in my new job.

Then I showed them an intra uterine device (IUD) and started by asking if they knew what it was. Mom didn't wait to see if her daughters knew, she replied immediately, eagerly.

"Oh, yeah! That's an IUD," and turning to Laura she added, "I had one for about a year after your brother was born. I loved it. You don't feel it or nothin', and you don't have to mess with nothin'. It's so easy. You might really like it. Ian don't want no more kids; maybe he'd be OK with it," she said hopefully.

After a long pause, her speech slowed and her tone shifted.

"Yeah, I loved it," she continued, with a far-away, nostalgic look, "I probably would have kept it a lot longer, except for your father. Every night when he'd come home from the bar drunk, he'd be like, 'Get that damn thing out,' and I'd be like, 'Hey, you don't get pregnant; I don't want no more kids!' and he'd be like, 'Get that fucking thing out!' and I'd be like, 'Just ignore it,' and finally he was like, 'If you don't get that fucking thing out I'm gonna reach in there and pull it out myself!' and I said to myself, 'Wow, one of these nights he'll get drunk enough and mad enough and he maybe really will,' and I thought: 'Wow, that would hurt!' So finally I just went to the doctor and got it taken out 'cause like that would hurt so bad. But I really liked it."

The girls simply listened matter-of-factly; they had known their dad, they had known their parents' relationship, so their mom's story didn't leave them feeling as unsettled as it left me. He had died several years before I met them, and I hadn't known anything else about him. It underscored to me that their core values, their assumptions about gender roles, intimacy, and communication between men and women were totally different from my own.

I went on to teach them quite a bit about birth control methods; I do like to think I helped them. Yet they taught me a lot more, about the subculture I'd be serving, about the new world I had gotten myself into; about what a stretch it would be for me. I was grateful to them for speaking so honestly and openly with me.

Eileen had given me an important tip when I was first hired. "Read all you can, learn all you can, take advantage of all the trainings we send you to, but your best learning will come from really listening to your clients. So much of what influences their decisions about sexual behavior and family planning has not been written about or studied. If you really pay attention to them, they'll teach you more than any books or trainings about what you need to know."

Driving home from opening my first "case," looking out at the countryside, I thought about the wisdom of her words and I knew it was already happening; I was beginning to learn both about the county and the people in it.

Like many counties in New York State, ours is about the same size as Rhode Island, but very sparsely populated. When most people picture New York State, they think of the Big Apple, its suburbs, and the other major cities, most of which are along the New York State Thruway. But the rest of the state is a vast, expansive, open area, which is relatively undeveloped; life is different here. It's quiet, it's slow paced, it's rural. In our sprawling county, even today, when I'm out doing home visits, I'm only in cell phone service range about half the time. Most of the little towns I visit have just one stoplight, if that. And outside the towns, I'm frequently on dirt roads, and a

 SNAPSHOT

URINE SAMPLE IN A WILD TURKEY BOURBON BOTTLE

–BACK WHEN PATIENTS WERE REQUIRED TO PROVIDE THE FIRST URINE SAMPLE OF THE MORNING FOR A PREGNANCY TEST, A WOMAN FORGOT TO PREPARE A CLEAN GLASS JAR WITH A TIGHT FITTING LID THE NIGHT BEFORE, AS INSTRUCTED. APPARENTLY IT WAS THE ONLY EMPTY GLASS CONTAINER WITHIN QUICK, EASY REACH IN THE MORNING. THE NURSE WAS RELIEVED THAT THE TEST WAS NEGATIVE.

number of the shortcuts I use are seasonal roads, so they're not plowed or maintained for almost half the year. Once I get off the paved road it's common to drive five or ten miles and only pass a handful of homes, usually with nobody in my rearview mirror. If you live in our county and you want to go to a Starbucks or a Wal-Mart or a hospital that delivers babies, you'll need to cross at least one county line; there are none here. There's only one place where you'd have to pay to park your car: on main street outside the County Office Building. That building even has an elevator, the only one a lot of local kids have ever seen. There is one community college, but many of the locals don't even think about it. When I started my job, less than seventeen percent of the adults had a college education.[12]

Poverty is prevalent; about half the kids in many of our local school districts qualify for free meals.[13] The area used to be mostly farms, but the small, family farms are unable to compete today, so many of them are going out of business and the population is declining. When people think of Appalachia, New York State doesn't usually pop into mind, but we're at the northern tip of it. Many people here are extremely sheltered. They've never travelled, and I don't mean "travelled" as in international travel or even the four-hour drive to New York City. I mean people who could count the times they had left the county. Women in their twenties who still talk about their sixth grade trip to Washington, D.C. for safety patrol because it's the only time they ever went anyplace. People who have never been on an escalator; kids who ask, "Is this a one-way street?" on an interstate highway, because they've never seen a divided highway with a median strip.

Looking out my car window as I drive to homes tucked away in the hills and then meeting the people who live there, I'm often struck by the contrast of the magnificent, uplifting beauty and richness of the natural environment—the fields, the streams, the lakes, the forests—with the disheartening poverty of the local people. And the more people I meet who live in poverty, the more homes I visit, the more it gets me wondering about poverty.

My dictionary tells me that poverty is, "The state of not having enough money to take care of basic needs such as food, clothing, and housing." I suppose that's true. But there's so much that that definition doesn't address. There are different kinds of poverty; different flavors. By all objective measures, my grandparents, like so many immigrants who came to America in pursuit of the American Dream, or at least enough money to put a meal on the table, were poor; they fit that definition. But they had hope; that's why they came. They believed that their poverty was a temporary state that would be transcended. And they never lost sight of the better life they envisioned for themselves, their families, and their communities. They protested for better working conditions, they organized, they pushed; they believed their actions could and would make a difference. And they were right.

Yet the families I visit who are living in poverty today are experiencing it in a whole different way. Yes, they fit the definition of not having enough money to take care of those basic needs. But the definition doesn't address the feeling of hopelessness I see: the lack of the belief that the poverty is a temporary state. It doesn't address the poverty of the spirit.

I'm a social misfit here, in this subculture of poverty, in this subculture I serve. But it's not just finances that separate us. Attitudes, assumptions, and expectations regarding the role of women in home and society and values related to parenting and careers separate us as much as dollars do. And of course the entire assumption, that teen parenting and large families with closely spaced kids are the norm.

That was quickly underscored for me the first time I had lunch in a busy small-town diner with two female colleagues; half way through lunch we realized that we had the only table in the place with three women of child-bearing age, and none of us pregnant or holding an infant. It's the opposite from my upbringing; while becoming a parent someday was expected, there was an expectation that we'd be other things, too, and that those other things mattered. Both girls and boys were encouraged to think, "What do you want to be when you grow up?" Jobs weren't just going to be jobs, they were going to be careers; unique contributions we could each make to society.

That's the mindset I grew up with. Most of the people I serve in my job grew up with completely different mindsets, and it has a huge impact on their reproductive life planning. People I met my first year on the job showed me that: like Linda, a seventeen-year-old mom.

"Do you go to school?" I asked her the first time we met. She was living with her boyfriend and their baby at his mom's house.

"No, I was going before Joey was born. I was gonna go back, but it's just too much. I ain't gonna go back. I'm just too tired all the time."

"How old is Joey?"

"He's going to be three months tomorrow."

"Have you and Isaiah talked about whether you want any more kids?" I asked.

Her look said more than her words; that look that says, "want kids" is an oxymoron. So she welcomed my offer of education about contraception, starting with taking a contraceptive history. That part was quick and easy; Linda and Isaiah had used condoms, sometimes, but that was all they had ever used.

Although she was adamant that they didn't want any more kids, she knew almost nothing about birth control methods. I eagerly rose to the challenge of opening my bag of samples in her living room and going over each method with her, one at a time, answering her questions, being non-directive and non-judgmental. I got through all the methods; still being new at my job I was proud that I was able to discuss effectiveness, side effects, and how to use each one without having to look at my notes once.

"So do any of these look like something you might want?" I asked her at the end.

"I don't know, I'll think about it. I'll talk to Isaiah."

"OK, that sounds good," and handing her some brochures I added, "You can show these to him, too."

It was winter. I packed up the sample case and took a few minutes to put on my boots and my winter coat. As I did, having "closed" our visit, she began to chitchat with me, informally.

"Do you have any kids?" she asked.

"No," I replied. I never bring that up, and I don't like when people ask me. Especially moms. I'm always concerned that they'll take it as some kind of "anti-baby" judgment.

"Really?" she snapped back, sounding stunned, "Are you married?"

"Yes."

Looking concerned, thinking maybe she had hit a sore nerve of infertility, but on some level *knowing* she hadn't, she asked, "Do you want kids?"

"No, not really."

"How long have you been married?"

"Twelve years."

"You mean you're married and you decided you don't want kids and you don't have any?!" She looked me up and down. Then glancing down at my sample bag she added in an incredulous tone, "Oh, my God, do you mean you actually use any of that stuff?!?"

And there I stood in my long black coat, with my gloves on, boots zipped, literally with one hand on her doorknob, about to leave. I was absolutely shocked. I realized that I had just spent an entire hour showing this fertile young woman all these different methods, and distracted by her polite, respectful way of engaging I had completely missed the fact that she had looked at each method thinking—or assuming—"no way!" She hadn't honestly seen anything she could imagine herself and her partner using, and I hadn't uncovered that until after we finished.

"Now what?" I wondered.

"I've probably used just about everything in here at one time or another," I answered honestly. And realizing that she had been completely put off by even the thought of using any of the methods I had shown her, I sensed that it would be helpful to validate her perception of the inconvenience of contraceptive methods. "Every one of them is kind of a pain, but I figure it's a small price to pay for not having kids I don't want."

It broke my heart at that moment to realize that the entire hour of "education" I had so proudly provided hadn't reached her at all, in a very real way. This was in the late 1990's, years before methods like the implant, patch, or NuvaRing became available. She had been too polite to say something like, "You've got to be kidding me," when I showed her how to apply spermicidal jelly to the rim of a diaphragm before inserting it into the vagina before intercourse. At seventeen, sex simply *happened*. The idea of this kind of "staged" action interrupting sex was beyond her comprehension, and I had completely missed that.

I thought about her over and over again, and about her reaction. Polite, respectfully listening for an hour, yet completely void of any actual learning that would be likely to make a difference in her behavior. I was so thankful that she spoke so genuinely after she thought the visit was "over."

That's when she educated me. It was on the heels of that visit that I asked myself, "How can I give my clients opportunities to give me honest feedback on the actual likelihood of them finding any of what I'm showing them helpful, in a way that's comforta-

> **"TURN LEFT WHERE THE BAR USED TO BE."**
>
> *—WOMAN UNSUCCESSFULLY TRYING TO GIVE ME TELEPHONE DIRECTIONS TO HER HOME, FRUSTRATED BECAUSE I DIDN'T KNOW THE LITTLE DIRT ROADS IN HER AREA.*

ble to them?" And almost immediately I figured it out, subtly adjusting my conversation and questions to get ongoing, realistic feedback throughout visits, and it has guided me ever since, both in my direct work with clients and when I'm training professionals.

"**R**ight now we're just using condoms, but I want to go back on the pill. That's why I filled out that form; can you help me get pills?" Maria asked.

"I can try, but first do you mind if I ask you a bit about your experience with birth control in the past?"

She nodded so I continued.

"You mentioned you've used the pill. When was that?"

"Oh, that was when I was a teenager, before I had my kids."

"How'd you do with the pill? Did you like it?"

"Oh yeah, it was great. I was so freaked out about getting pregnant, I was really careful about it." And she eagerly elaborated. Shortly after she got married at nineteen she quit the pill and got pregnant immediately. The first time on purpose—they were thrilled. But the second one came much faster than she'd have chosen; it was unsettling. "It just happened!" And the relationship didn't withstand the test of time, with the challenge of two babies.

"I wanted to stay with him; I really did. Even when things got really tense, and when he started slapping me around. I wanted to stay for the kids' sake; family is really important to me. I wanted my kids to have a mom and a dad. I probably would have stayed forever, but it got worse, not better. It was bad enough when he hit me. But then he screamed and cursed and hit me in front of the kids. When they saw that, I said to myself, 'My kids will see that once. Never again.' I didn't know where the hell I was going to go, or how I was going to support them. In a way I was nuts, really, I mean, I had two kids, no job, no money, no plan. I just knew I had to get them the hell outta there."

And she did.

Unlike so many victims of domestic violence, she left and never went back. The thought of being a single mom terrified her, but somehow she made it work. And from that day until about a year ago she was single and abstinent.

"Honestly, I just had so much on my mind; I just thought I'd never be with another man. And after what I had been through, I was fine with that." But then she met Jimmy and they hit it off immediately. Within two months of meeting, knowing she didn't want "casual sex," and knowing that for her it was a serious relationship or no relationship, he showed up with a diamond ring, a promise to raise her kids with her, and they were married shortly afterwards.

"I never thought this would happen to me. He's so gentle, so loving, so good with the kids…."

They had discussed the subject of kids before they married; she had been clear that she didn't want any more, and despite the fact that he wasn't a biological dad, he had been fine with that. They had used condoms consistently and hadn't had any problem with them. Until very recently.

"So what's happening now that makes you want to go on the pill?"

"I figure I better. I just know one of these days I'm gonna get pregnant if I don't. 'Cause like, he's so gentle. When he touches me, I melt; I can't resist him. But it's like, he used to just put on a condom, but lately, it's like"—she leaned forward, a little closer to me, and even though we were the only two people home, her voice softened into a whisper as she continued—"he'll start kissing me all over my body and I'll say, 'Put on a condom, put on a condom,' and he'll just like keep kissing me and whisper, 'Why? You're such a good mother!' And I'll be like, 'put on a condom!' and he's like, 'Don't you think you're a good mother? You love your kids so much!' and I'm just, like, 'Put on a condom!' and so far he has, but I just feel like one of these days he's not gonna, and I mean, like, I just melt the way he kisses me, and I just thought, like, I should probably just go on the pill."

I reflected back to her, "It sounds like being a good mother is really important to you."

Her eyes widened and she nodded vigorously as she replied, "It is! It's like the most important thing in the world to me."

"And it sounds like you feel like you're being a good mom, and like he agrees that you are."

"Oh yeah, definitely," she said, looking at me like she had found a soul mate: like someone understood her, even though I was simply repeating what I had heard.

"OK, that part is clear. But as I listen to you, the part I'm not clear about is what it means to each of you to want *more* kids, and what it means to want to use effective contraception; how those two things relate. Do you see the desire to have more kids or not have more kids as being an indication of how good a mother you are?"

"Oh, my God! When you put it that way: no! When you put it that way, it's like, actually, almost the opposite. I never thought of it that way. But actually, it's like, that's why I don't want another. I mean, like, sure, I love kids. I mean, like part of me would love to have about ten of 'em, or as many as I could. But that's absolutely it: I want to be the best mom I can be to the two I've already got. That's why I want to go on the pill; that's why I don't want any more right now. I mean, like we're making it; we're getting all our bills paid off and stuff, but it's hard…"

She elaborated a bit, and I let her. I sensed she'd benefit from "thinking out loud" a bit. Her body language and her tone changed as she spoke about using effective contraception in this new light. She perked up as she allowed herself to realize that using effective contraception does not mean anything about the kids she already has, with the possible exception of the fact that it shows how much she loves and cares about them.

She was an intelligent woman, and in the light of day, in a non-sexual situation, talking with an objective outsider about her reproductive goals and plans, it quickly became crystal clear to her. And she formulated a plan almost immediately, with very little support from me. She'd explain to him that she does think she's a great mom, that she loves the fact that he sees her as a great mom, but that she thinks that another pregnancy right away would be a setback to being the best mom possible to the kids she already has, and that that's why she's going to go on an effective, reversible method.

"Maybe I'll want another someday, but definitely not right away." She was confident that when she explained it to him in those terms he'd be OK with it, and if he wasn't, "Too bad!"

Like so many people who face their decisions about contraception when they're in bed, at the beginning of a welcomed sexual encounter, Maria wasn't bringing a clear head to the decision making process.

In general, being in bed and about to have sex doesn't inspire rational thought.

For many people, neither does being in a medical setting.

But unfortunately, those are the only times and places many people do address those decisions: in bed or in a doctor's office.

I've asked so many of the people I visit if they have a close friend or a sister or anyone that they talk with about these issues. I'm often surprised how many say "No." Attitudes about what it means to obtain and utilize effective contraception vary widely, yet they're rarely discussed. I find women who make comments suggesting that it means they don't love their kids or their partners, or that they don't respect their own life-giving potential. Many don't distinguish between "I don't want to become pregnant *now*" and "pregnancy is a bad thing." Frequently when I question it, when I give them the opportunity to consider what they've said, the process of simply examining their own words and thinking about the beliefs and values their words imply leads them to rethink their attitude about contraception in a more positive light.

Often, it's a seemingly subtle use of words, the turn of a phrase that tips me off. I hear my clients say things that I know I'd never hear from any of my old friends, from my own inner circle; it's truly a different subculture.

My old college friend called me and told me that Jacob, her husband, got a vasectomy after their second child was born. I listened to her; I think about her choice of words. She would never have said, "We really love our kids, but Jacob got a vasectomy after Hugh was born." I'd never hear that from a friend; it's assumed they love their kids. Not just because I know them, and I know how much they love their kids. It's that neither she nor I would ever think that using any means of preventing pregnancy is a judgment about past pregnancies.

Yet when I'm listening at work, women frequently start off saying, "I really love my kids, but I'm thinking about going on birth control." I always stop them and examine the "But." Invariably they reply with, "Well, when you put it that way…," when all I've done is paraphrased what they already said. In my experience, successfully helping women articulate those subtleties and examine those values and assumptions often has an enormous impact on helping them gain control of their fertility.

And it's not rocket science; I've seen so many women who don't have other opportunities to discuss these important decisions figure out solutions to their dilemmas on their own, with so little support from me, simply by hearing themselves think it through. Maria was so thankful for the opportunity to objectively examine her own motivation and make a plan in the light of day, and I was so thankful for the opportunity to have been able to provide her with that setting.

Similarly, giving women the opportunity to pause and examine how they prioritize contraception within the framework of their ongoing, busy lives can be eye-opening for them. It was for Nan.

"I remember last time I visited you were thinking about getting an IUD; have you given it any more thought?" I asked her.

"Hell no, Vee: that's the last thing on my mind!" she said dismissively, literally laughing at my question.

"Really? You sounded serious about not wanting another pregnancy last time, at least not until you get your kids back."

"Shit, I got so much goin' on, I can't even think about that!"

"What do you mean?" I asked.

"I mean, like, I got way more important things to think about than the IUD!"

Her two kids had been removed from her home and put into a foster home; her top priority was getting them back. I let her elaborate and complain about DSS and all their demands for almost a half hour before I tried to bring the conversation back to the IUD. I didn't think being pregnant would make any of it easier.

"It sounds like you feel like there's no pleasing them, like they keep making it harder."

"Exactly!"

"And if you were pregnant, do you think that would impact when you get them back?"

"No. I know it wouldn't."

"What do you mean?"

" 'Cuz I asked the judge."

"You asked the judge?"

"Yeah, 'cuz when I went there last time, I thought I might be pregnant, and he told us all this shit we gotta do and I said, 'And what if I'm pregnant?' and he said, 'That kid would have nothing to do with this case.' "

"What do you mean?"

"He said if I'm pregnant, that's a whole different kid who wasn't even born when all this shit went down so that would be completely separate. I mean, I asked him right out if DSS could come take the kid in the hospital and he said 'no.' It turned out I wasn't pregnant, but I just wanted to know."

"But I mean, even if they didn't take the next baby, do you think a pregnancy might impact when you get Mike and Lorraine back?"

"No." she said with certainty. "They're not allowed to hold the pregnancy against me."

"I don't mean that. I mean, it sounds like you've got so much to do just to get them back. I mean, just like the way you have to keep the apartment so clean and everything, and go to all these meetings. I remember when you were pregnant with Lorraine you were in bed a lot and you were so tired; if you felt that way again, do you think you'd be able to keep up with all they're demanding you to do? I mean, the way you might feel. Like tired and stuff?"

"Actually, I didn't think of it like that." She paused, for the first time she wasn't being so dismissive.

"Actually, that might make it harder."

I let her sit quietly for a while; I was glad she was thinking. Then I continued.

"And you said you have to keep your job to get the kids back. Do you think you'd be able to keep it if you get pregnant?"

"Oh yeah, the job? Definitely. They're not allowed to fire me for getting pregnant: that's discrimination."

"I know. I don't mean fire you for being pregnant. But again, if you don't feel well, if you miss a lot of work and stuff—"

"Actually, I missed so many days when we had the trial my boss did say if I miss any more days I'd be fired."

 FACT

THE RATE OF UNINTENDED PREG-NANCY AMONG POOR WOMEN IS MORE THAN FIVE TIMES THE RATE AMONG THOSE AT THE HIGHEST INCOME LEVEL.

Again, she began thinking about the obstacles another pregnancy might cause.

We continued talking about all she has to do, comparing how it would feel to do it all if she was pregnant versus if she wasn't. By the end of the conversation she had shifted her perspective 180 degrees; she had opened our meeting literally laughing at me for asking if scheduling an appointment for an IUD could be a priority worth considering, and she closed our meeting expressing a belief that it was an essential first step to ensuring that her other goals were met. In fact, before I left, we phoned her doctor's office and scheduled an appointment. She got the IUD, and over the next few months she successfully put her efforts into getting her kids back.

When Mandy got the call in the middle of the night, saying Jeremy's dad had died, they jumped out of bed and drove to Maine.

"I told Jeremy, 'We'll stay as long as we need to.' "

They ended up staying for a month.

"And I knew the day I needed to put in the new NuvaRing, but I didn't have one. I know, I know, I shoulda called and they probably coulda sent me a prescription or something, it just seemed like such a pain in the ass and honestly Jeremy was so freaked out, I mean, I never saw him cry so much. Like every night when we went to bed, he just cried; we didn't even have sex! So I figured, we'll be home soon; I'll get it then. And then all of a sudden one night, like: boom! Jeremy was like so lovey-dovey again and I kinda thought about it but like, I just didn't want to say 'no' to him, with everything that was going on..."

Here she had used birth control methods effectively for years.

The thing about preventing pregnancy over the years is that for a prevention plan to work, everything has to go right, 24/7, 365 days a year. But just one thing has to go wrong once for it to fail. Just one thing had gone wrong for Mandy and Jeremy, just once.

And similarly, for people with limited resources even seemingly small bumps in the road can become major obstacles. Like with Marge. As an unstable mother of three in her early thirties, she wanted an IUD. She was on several prescription drugs from both her doctor and her mental health doctor, and she really didn't want a hormonal method. I had helped her prepare: she had gotten all the tests she needed and her doctor had given her a green light and an appointment for the IUD insertion. Her mom had agreed to babysit and she had a free ride to the clinic. So a couple of days after she was scheduled for the appointment, I stopped by to make sure it had all worked out.

"Did you get the IUD?" I asked as we sat at her kitchen table with her toddler running in circles around us.

"Careful, Jo-Jo!" she warned him, pushing aside the chair he was about to crash into.

"Ugh, no," she said, sounding defeated. "I was all set but that morning—"

"Boo! Boo! Boo!" Jo-Jo screamed enthusiastically, as he stopped running and stood against the refrigerator, reaching up as high as he could, on his tippy toes.

"Do you want a blue popsicle?" Marge offered him, clearly understanding his words and his body language way better than I did.

"Boo! Boo! Boo!" he repeated with a sense of urgency, reaching even higher.

"OK, I'll see if we have any left," Marge said, opening the freezer and taking out a box of popsicles. "Uh-oh: you ate all the blue ones," she sang, showing him the partially empty box. "You could have a red one or a green one," she said, lovingly offering him an alternative.

"Geen! Geen!" he demanded.

"OK, you can have a green one," she said, keeping one green one out and putting the rest away. She correctly assumed that once he had his popsicle he'd settle down to enjoy it, and we'd have a couple of precious minutes to talk.

"It's such a bummer; the morning I was supposed to go, my mom had the flu. My husband was at work and there was nobody else to watch the kids, so I had to cancel. I mean, I really wanted to just get this over and done with. But there was no way I could bring all three of them to the doctor's office with me."

"Bummer!" I agreed. "Do you want to reschedule it?"

"I was thinking about that, but I remember the doctor said if I didn't do it by next Friday, he'd have to do those stupid tests again. And I have to give two weeks notice to get the free transportation." It's true; the IUD had to be inserted within a limited time from the tests for infections, and the dates wouldn't synch with the two weeks needed for the free transport. She had no other babysitter and no other ride. "Plus," she reminded me, "Even if I could get another ride, who's to say my mom's gonna be better by then. I can't have her watching the kids if she's sick."

"Well, no, but would you like to try?"

"Nah. Forget it; we'll just use condoms," she said as Jo-Jo took the last few licks of his Popsicle. She sounded defeated and I didn't blame her. "I mean, who's to say something like this won't happen again. It's just too hard, with the two appointments."

It wouldn't have been for me; I have a car that runs and I could afford a babysitter if I needed one. But for her it was. It truly was.

Eventually she did get her IUD. Shortly after that I closed her case. It was still closed two years later when I saw her name in the police blotter, when she was arrested for having sexual relations with a minor; he was only sixteen. While most people who read the report with horror were probably focused on other aspects of an unstable mother in her 30s having sex with a sixteen-year-old boy, all I could wonder about was whether or not she still had that IUD in place; the last thing she or that boy needed was a baby.

"Two days: just two frickin' days!" Lisa exclaimed, adding, "I can't believe I missed getting that tubal by two frickin' days!"

She had correctly filled out all the paperwork for Medicaid to pay for her tubal ligation; her doctor had agreed to do the procedure when she delivered her baby, but the paperwork takes thirty days to approve. So when she went into labor five weeks early, she hadn't yet gotten the approval.

With a premature baby, she had so much else to focus on; I couldn't blame her for putting birth control on the back burner. But with all her mental health issues I also knew that it would take everything she had to keep the baby in her own custody. And I knew that another pregnancy right away could be devastating. The chemotherapy treatments that had cured her leukemia five years prior had left a trail of doctors puzzled about her fertility; most had said she'd probably never be able to conceive. But once she became pregnant everything changed. Now there was a sense of urgency: her doctor recommended the tubal because of other complicated medical conditions that would make another pregnancy life-threatening. So I really wanted to help her prevent another pregnancy, and she was interested in getting an IUD to protect her until she could get the tubal.

It was always hard for me to get Lisa to engage in a serious conversation, one in which we remain on a single topic. She usually got easily distracted and changed the subject quickly, in seemingly random directions, so with the distractions of a new baby I knew the visit might be challenging. But it was so important: I arrived focused and determined.

When I showed up at her home, she was sitting outside at the picnic table, with the baby taking a nap beside her. It was a gorgeous summer day. She was going through a pile of photographs; I figured it was probably pictures of the baby.

I was so wrong.

"Hi Vee. Look at this one," she said, handing me a close-up photograph of a wooden floor with a big hole in it, right next to the leg of a table, adding, "This one's great."

With a new baby at her side that I had never seen, she wants me to examine a photo of a dirty, broken floorboard? I wondered. It seemed like an odd greeting; I was used to "odd" with Lisa. Before I could ask why she showed me the next one.

"And look at this one!"

It was a broken banister on a staircase.

"So this is Jamie?" I asked after shifting my glance from the photo to the new baby. "This is the first time I've seen him: congratulations! He's perfect!" I hoped that changing the subject to the baby would provide the segue I'd need. It didn't.

"Yeah, he's finally sleeping, so I gotta go through these pictures now! They're for the judge. He said I had to bring pictures. Look at this one," she added gleefully, showing me a close up of mold on a wall. "This one's great: you can totally see the mold. It's black mold."

After several failed attempts to change the subject, she gradually got me to see the importance of her photographs. She had a two-year lease on her apartment, and when she told her landlord she was moving out because he hadn't made the changes she needed—changes that are required by code—he refused to return her security deposit. Without that money, she couldn't afford the deposit and first month's rent on the new apartment she had found. So she was trying to get the building condemned. If she could do that, he'd be forced to return her deposit.

"I mean, Vee, I gotta do this; I can't have Jamie breathing that mold!"

I fully agreed. As I listened to her and realized all the work she had to do to simply ensure a mold-free, safe home for herself and her son, I wished so much I had a magic wand, to make her temporarily not have to even *think* about birth control and doctor appointments. Eventually, we were successful; they used the condoms I kept dropping off until she got an IUD inserted shortly after the move. I kept her case open for a while, just checking in to be sure everything was OK and that she liked the IUD. She did. Eventually, I closed her case, without another pregnancy. Success; it felt good.

"Does the dog bite?" I asked Louise as she opened the door to let me in; an enormous dog growled at me. One of his pointy side teeth grew straight out, sideways, perpendicular to all the others. And the way he was wildly jumping around made me think that training dogs wasn't a top priority here.

"Tell her," Louise demanded of her daughter Mindy.

"You tell her," Mindy insisted to her mother, avoiding eye contact with me.

"Tell her what your dog did," mom insisted.

Mindy rolled her eyes and groaned.

"Never mind, I'm not here about your dog; I just want to be safe. Is there someplace we could meet without the dog? Outside? Or could we sit in my car? I really want to give you my full attention."

I waited as Mindy reluctantly locked the dog in a bedroom, and I ignored the loud scratching and barking that persisted during the rest of our visit.

At seventeen, Mindy held her new infant and Louise held another baby. Two two-year-olds frolicked around the woodstove. It had a flimsy chicken-wire cage around it that looked like it had been put up in a feeble attempt to keep them away, so they wouldn't get burned. Fortunately, I was visiting in the summer, when there was no fire going.

To the two-year-olds, the fence served as a plaything; they took turns jumping as high as they could over it and landing hard against the stove, shrieking with great delight.

To me, it served as a metaphor; this home is almost ready for yesterday, but not quite.

"How many kids do you have?" I asked Mindy.

"She's got two," Louise replied. "The baby, and Jake is hers." Jake was the slightly smaller two-year-old. "The other two are her sister Nellie's; I mean, they're hers, but I'm raising them. DSS was gonna take them; I can't let that happen to my grandchildren! So I'm raising them. But now Nellie's pregnant again! I told her, 'You're keeping that next one! If you can't get your shit together DSS'll take it. I can't.' I raised five kids of my own already and now I got her two and I mean, with Mindy still living here with her two, I mean, this is ridiculous!"

Nellie was Mindy's nineteen-year-old sister; she was living with her new boyfriend in an apartment about five miles from the family's trailer in the hills.

"Wow, it's great for those kids that you stepped up to the plate; I hope your daughter appreciates it," I responded to Louise. Then I tried again to engage Mindy.

"Have you thought about whether you want any more kids?" I asked.

"She better not have no more; not while she's living here!" Louise replied immediately, giving her daughter a threatening look. Louise answered most of my questions, despite the fact that I was facing Mindy when I asked them.

"So, you're living at your parents', and your mom doesn't want you to have any more while you're here. She wants you to wait. Have you thought about that, about what you want?"

"Yeah, whatever," Mindy muttered, finally speaking but still detached, uninterested.

"She ain't my problem," Louise added, nodding approvingly towards Mindy. "Nellie is! She's the one who can't keep her legs closed! Not Mindy."

Mindy's boyfriend Ken was the father of her two kids. They had both quit school at fifteen, when their first child was born. According to Mindy, they hadn't had sex since the new baby was born, and they had waited several months after the first baby before having sex. She wasn't concerned about pregnancy risk; "It ain't like we do it all the time. He don't even live near here. Like, I almost never even see him," she said, as the screensaver across the room boasted a picture of the two of them smooching.

We chatted a bit and she accepted my offer of a bag of condoms "just in case," but only half listened as I explained that it only takes one time for a pregnancy and that her body is well designed to become pregnant as soon as she does have sex.

A sudden blast of rap music, the ringtone Mindy had downloaded to her cell phone interrupted us. For the first time, Mindy got a look of interest on her face as she quickly dashed across the room to answer it. The musicians only got to use the word 'fuck' about five times in front of me and all the kids before she answered and said, "I'll call you back; this lady's here," and hung up.

"Thanks for waiting to take that." And after a pause I added, "So, it sounds like your plan is to abstain from intercourse, is that right?"

"Yeah, we don't do nuffin'."

"Well, with a brand new baby, that's a really healthy choice. It's important to give your body time to heal before you have sex again. But once your body is ready, do you think about whether you want to protect yourself from pregnancy or not?"

"They're pretty good," Louise chimed in, implying that they don't have frequent sex. "She's my good one. But Nellie, she's the one who can't keep her legs closed. I swear, I know she's only nineteen, but she should frickin' get her tubes tied. That's what I did."

"Wow, so you really took charge of your fertility," I said, thankful for an opportunity to underline that taking charge is something that sexually active people can do; it's a choice we can make.

"Yeah, but I didn't do it 'till I had five kids. That was my mistake; I shoulda done it after three!"

I didn't know the birth order of her kids, but I felt a twang regardless; mom had just essentially said in front of her daughter that she shouldn't have had her last two kids. Whether that included Mindy or not, I found the message it gave Mindy unsettling.

"But mom!" Mindy fired back, for the first time sounding motivated to speak, "Then you wouldn'ta had me!"

So Mindy was either number four or five. My concern was validated.

Mom simply shrugged.

I kept the visit short, but I was thankful that they agreed to have me come back in a few weeks. Mindy had never had a pelvic exam except when she had gone to the hospital to have her babies. She hadn't had her six-week checkup after the first one and didn't sound concerned or interested in having it after the second one. The potential benefits of voluntarily involving a gynecologist in her life were clearly not on her radar, and my gut told me that she was not going to give it serious thought today. But I hoped to find her a little more open to discussion once she had gotten caught up on her sleep.

It reminded me why I always try to do postpartum contraception planning and education during the second trimester; during the first trimester, people are still adjusting to the idea that they're pregnant. By the third trimester they're appropriately preoccupied with preparing for the baby. Waiting until after the birth leaves the new mom so tired and overwhelmed with other things that it's hard to get through all the necessary work. It usually takes several visits to come up with a goal, gather information, make a plan, and discuss it with a partner and/or a doctor. Still, I figured, better late than never: I'll just do what I can.

Mindy had never used any form of birth control except the few times they had used condoms. With two kids by age seventeen, she was clearly fertile and had decades of fertility remaining. It wasn't so much her lack of information or experience with birth control that concerned me; it was more the lack of familiarity with the concept of family planning. Hearing Mindy's mother describe her other daughter as being "unable to keep her legs closed" twice, implying that the daughter on her third pregnancy is "the bad one" who has more sex than Mindy spoke volumes to me. About the attitude that sex is bad, and about the absence of the concept of spacing pregnancies or limiting family size by using anything besides abstinence until it's time for a tubal. While abstinence is in fact 100% effective, it is only effective when it's used correctly, 100% of the time. There are so many methods available for sexually active people that are over 95% effective. There are so many people using them, using them correctly, spacing their children; people setting life goals and managing their fertility accordingly.

I think about that concept, that key concept, that our fertility is something we can manage. So many people in our society get that. And use it. For so many people, consistent use of effective contraception is like the bass drum in a band; rarely mentioned, yet it holds everything together. Successful adults don't talk about how managing their fertility enables them to live their lives as sexual beings and space their pregnancies and reach their life goals; it's private. But it's that private, unmentioned force that holds everything else together for them. It's the glue, it's the drum. In their house, in my house, maybe in your house. But not in Mindy and Louise's house. Or even in their field of vision.

And certainly not in Ken and Leslie's house, either. Their house always looks completely chaotic when I visit. Unglued. Granted, they're never expecting me: they don't have a phone, so I can't call. And I can never schedule our next visit when we're together. Leslie works at the drive-thru window of a local fast-food restaurant and is assigned her schedule at the beginning of each week. It always changes, so she never knows when she'll be home.

Ken's face lit up as he answered the door and saw me. He was holding Mimi, their newest baby.

"Oh, Vee, it's you! Leslie's at work again, but you can come in anyway. I'm glad you're here; we used up almost all the condoms you left last time and Leslie missed her appointment to go on birth control again because she had to work."

I stay focused on the task at hand; to give them some condoms and help figure out how Leslie can get birth control. I try not to be judgmental, not to question the apparent chaos of their home. On the contrary, the more I sense that they are out of control of their lives, the more motivated I am to help them learn to control their fertility. With three kids still in diapers, all living on Leslie's minimum wage job and some assistance Ken gets because of his limitations, they're stretched.

There are so many questions I don't ask, things I don't even let myself wonder about until many hours later. It's as if my brain took a photograph, unbeknownst to me, to ponder when I have time. In the moment, I don't ask why there's an enormous pile of cucumber peels on the floor in the middle of the living room. I don't ask why they got a whole large pizza last night if they were only going to eat one slice, or why they didn't cover and refrigerate the leftovers, so it wouldn't have congealed like that. I don't ask anything about the piles of cigarette butts and ashes in the center of the couch and on the coffee table; the piles silently tell stories of ashtrays removed, based on the way the butts were extinguished, but it's not until later, when I'm driving home, that my mind tries unsuccessfully to understand why someone would have taken the ashtrays out from under the piles without dumping the piles in a garbage instead of in neat piles on the table and couch. No, while I'm with Ken I just try to focus on the tasks at hand and encourage him. And it's genuine: so many teen fathers leave their babies' mother, or do less than half the childcare. Ken stayed for all three and continues to be in charge of the kids all day while Leslie is at work, with almost no outside help. I respect him for that; it's not easy. And being so disorganized in their physical space doesn't make it easier.

"Do you have any more condoms you could leave us? Leslie really liked those colored ones you brought last time. I did, too; they don't break. The ones you brought before that, in the blue package, they kept breaking."

"Sure," I reply, taking off my backpack, trying to find a couple of clear inches on the floor to set it down and get out some condoms. As I bend my knees I notice the almost empty two-liter bottle of orange soda with no cap, with ashes and butts floating in it. As I hand Ken the bag of condoms, his son Jeff crawls over, picks up the soda bottle, and starts lifting it to take a drink.

Before he can get it to his lips, without a word from me, Ken calls, "NO!" puts down the infant, and scoops Jeff up in his arms. Pretty quick, I notice, impressed. It might have been a "hotline call" if he hadn't, and I certainly wasn't hoping to have to call child protective services to report that Ken was negligent about his kids' safety; they had had enough calls like that already and

I wanted so much to empower them. They were trying so hard; Ken didn't take his eyes off those kids the whole time I was there.

But it was always like that, so much harder than it has to be. Reacting to the need of the moment, to the baby about to drink the soda with the ashes and butts. Reacting quickly, but always reacting. Simply getting through the day, or the hour, he's always reacting. Not proactively providing a safe and reasonably clear space for the kids, no; reacting all day to what they're doing, touching, getting into. It's that reactive mindset that characterizes so many of the families' lives that I serve; families that go through each day living crisis to crisis.

But obtaining and successfully using effective contraception depends on having a proactive mindset. A mindset that says, "I create the life I want to lead." That is a luxurious concept that is completely alien to so many of the individuals I've worked with: people like Ken. Not just regarding family planning; regarding everything.

When I see individuals who lack that mindset, I start with introducing that concept, that potential: that we can take charge of our fertility. It's a choice we can make. And that we can then broaden out and take charge of other aspects of our lives if we want to. Without addressing that mindset first, information about effective contraceptive methods is useless.

Natalie, the new colleague who had recently done an observation of my last home visit with Ken and Leslie as part of her training, had looked like she was shell-shocked afterwards. "Vee, I really respect that you'll go into those homes, and all the effort you put into helping these families. So many people are so quick to just label them hillbillies or white trash. It's amazing the way you really get in there; the way you're really doing something to help them make their lives better. But honestly, I have to say, I don't know how you do it; it all looks so hopeless. Truthfully, if that was my job, I know I'd quit." It wasn't just the dog that kept humping her leg during our visit, or the fact that Leslie had given it a doggie treat "as a distraction" after the dog repeatedly ignored Ken's commands to "Stop!" and "Get down!" That reasoning didn't bode well for their future ability to effectively discipline their kids, but it wasn't the primary source of Natalie's feeling of hopelessness. What she saw went much deeper.

Her job was going to be doing classroom programs; a lot of them would be focused on preventing teen pregnancy. I treasured the opportunity to show her what happens when that message doesn't get out to teens.

She got it.

"I never feel like it's hopeless; actually, it's the opposite. I've gone into so many homes like that, that are on the verge of collapsing, and over time helped the parents prevent the next pregnancy. When I can help them learn to do that, it fills me with hope," I had said.

But today, seeing that home, it takes me quite awhile to remember how and why I feel hope. It's so easy to feel despair; driving gives me a few minutes to think, to talk myself off the ledge. I have so many hopes, so many wishes about them. They're struggling. I want to help, to make a difference, but I know that simply wishing will get me nowhere. I need to refocus on my plan, on where we were, where we are, where we're going, and how we'll get there.

> "IT TAKES AS MUCH ENERGY TO WISH AS IT DOES TO PLAN."
>
> *–ELEANOR ROOSEVELT*

Reflecting, desperately trying to find something positive to focus on, I realize that Ken brought up the subject of condoms and birth control immediately upon seeing my face. Six months ago that wouldn't have happened. And I realize that all the hard work I had started with them was in fact moving forward, even though it seemed so slow. He's internalized that shift from reactive to proactive. He's internalizing the benefits of family planning. He's more than willing to take action now.

Although there was no way I could have known right then that within a year of continued visits Leslie would have changed her mind about reversible methods and instead successfully gotten a tubal ligation, I could feel the wind shifting ever so slightly, and that did give me a glimmer of hope.

The people I've visited have shown me that the shift of the mindset from reactive to proactive doesn't happen overnight. Sometimes I can help bring it about, the way I did with Leslie and Ken. Other times people like Melissa show me that it happens gradually, as families communicate from one generation to the next.

It was a beautiful, sunny, summer day when I went to Melissa's house for the first time. We sat out back, in the only shade we could find, at the picnic table. The yard told stories, as yards often do. Although it was just the two of us sitting there, I could feel that that was unusual; that the yard was often used for large, multigenerational gatherings. The worn out patches of grass told of adults pushing kids on the swings. The folding chairs by the door spoke of elderly people who didn't want to walk too far but were still part of the action. The plastic toys scattered everywhere told of groups of children, playing. The random Frisbees, shovels, bikes of different sizes. And finally, the completely bare patches of lawn right near the giant barbe cue pit and around the picnic tables next to it spoke of large groups of families, frequently enjoying summer days together. It was a gorgeous spot.

I asked Melissa about her family; her parents and her two younger sisters were the only ones still living at home. But her mom's four sisters all lived nearby and came over all the time with their kids. Melissa generally liked the company, but at fifteen she said, "They're fun sometimes, but after awhile they get to be a pain. There are just so many of them."

She gave me a perfect segue into talking about her own goals regarding childbearing.

"Do you ever think about whether you want to have kids of your own someday?" I asked.

"Someday? Oh, definitely: yes!"

"Do you ever think about how many you'd like to have?"

She paused, thought for a while, scrunched up her face and tilted her head as she replied, "Um, probably just one on purpose. All the others will be by mistake."

She was dead serious. I was kind of surprised; by then I had asked that question to so many teens and gotten so many different responses, but never that one. I pondered where it came from, what her life experience was that was so different from my own, as I knew that even as a teenager, I'd never have answered that question that way.

I could imagine her mom sitting at that picnic table with her sisters, trying to have a conversation as the kids gobbled up hot dogs and burgers, but getting interrupted a thousand times during the course of a meal; alternately putting Band-Aids on boo-boos, refereeing arguments, confiding in each other that the first one or two were planned, and all the others came along by mistake. I could imagine Melissa overhearing it all; it had both established and lowered the bar for Melissa.

Her answer stayed in my mind for years. To me, it exemplified the transitional state her generation in her subculture is in, and it pinpointed on the map of her generational timeline the precise current location, like a "you are here" arrow on a map in a mall. She's advanced enough to understand that planning pregnancy, not simply letting it happen, is an option, and she's willing to consider it. She has the concept; in that regard she's a generation or two ahead of many of the adult women I've worked with.

But she didn't yet have the concept that it can actually work, in the long run, over a lifetime. It was like watching the transition, from a reactive to a proactive mindset, in progress; in slow motion. It's a process; it's not an overnight transformation.

"Hello?" said the male voice, answering the phone.

"Hi, this is Vivian. May I please speak to Olga?"

I was calling to offer the home visit she requested. She had checked the boxes, "OK to call" and, "OK to leave message" on her self-referral form. But even when people have checked those boxes, I don't offer the fact that I'm calling from Planned Parenthood to anyone else who answers. It's simply a matter of privacy; people might not have been thinking about who else might answer their phone when they checked those boxes.

Without giving me any answer, and without making any attempt to cover the receiver or prevent me from hearing, he paused and then screamed into the next room, "Hey Olga, it's Vivian. Who the fuck is Vivian?"

"She's the lady who came to our class last week, it's just about the doctor," I heard her explain to her partner as she took the phone from him. Unlike some of the controlling male partners I've encountered, he gave her the phone relatively easily, without asking more questions, without threatening her. No doubt he knew that she had just completed her class last week and now had a little free time.

I had been a guest in her class that the local Department of Social Services provided to individuals receiving public assistance, in an effort to prepare people who were going to be removed from their rolls. She had taken advantage of my offer to follow up with a home visit, for a more private conversation. I was glad his response didn't prevent her from scheduling the appointment with me, as she had told me after class that neither she nor he wanted another child anytime soon; certainly not before she got a job.

But still, just realizing that that was how he responds to a total stranger on the phone was very revealing. I could have been anyone; it was business hours. All he knew was my first name and his spontaneous, automatic response included high volume cursing.

"Oh, Lynne; she's beautiful! How old is she?" the woman asked as she held the door to the pharmacy open for Lynne and me. Lynne apparently knew her, I didn't. Most people in such a small village know each other, but I'm from out of town.

"Seven weeks," Lynne answered, smiling, enjoying the admiration her new baby brought.

"Where are the rest of the kids?" the woman continued, glancing around, surprised not to see them all together.

"They're home with their dad; I just took a second to come down for a prescription."

"Well, I won't keep you. But congratulations!" she continued, marveling over the perfect baby girl, as friendly acquaintances often do.

We headed towards the pharmacist in the back of the pharmacy. Halfway down the aisle, another smiling villager said, "Hi Lynne! Is that the new baby?"

"Yeah!"

"She's sooo cute! What's her name?"

"Olivia."

"Hi Olivia! Aren't you precious!" she said, beaming. They chatted a bit more before we walked to the back. There was a line of three people ahead of us, so we waited behind them. The body language of the other six people waiting suggested that picking up a prescription that day would be slow.

"This might take too long," Lynne said to me, softly.

"Well, yeah, it does look crowded. But once we get to the front of the line, it should be really fast, since they just have it back there. What do you think: are you up for waiting?"

"I dunno," she said, softly, her voice filled with doubt.

I was hoping she'd wait. I had considered it a stroke of good luck to run into her on Main Street moments before. Since she had actually gone a bit out of her way to greet me, I wasn't violating our confidentiality policy by talking with her in public and by offering to go into the drugstore together to pick up EC.

"Should we just maybe give it a minute and see if the line moves?"

"I guess," Lynne said.

"Hey, Lynne!" one of the guys on the side said. He had been reading the paper, waiting for his prescription, bored, and just looked up for the first time. Like the others who knew her, he took a few minutes chatting with her, congratulating her about her newest baby.

Fortunately, the line moved quickly.

When she reached the counter, Lynne leaned forward and whispered softly, "Could I pick up some EC?"

"Pick up what?" the pharmacist asked, in a loud, scolding voice, seeming annoyed that she was whispering.

"EC," Lynne repeated, softly, not wanting all her townspeople to hear.

"I can't hear you!" he snapped, sounding frustrated, and added, "What's your name; I'll look it up." And taking the ID and Medicaid card she handed him, he walked over to look for her name on one of the prescription bags that were arranged in alphabetical order in the "pick-up" bins. Lynne gave me a look of concern, knowing she hadn't called in a prescription, knowing he wouldn't find anything in those bins with her name, but not wanting to say out loud what she wanted. Not just a look of concern, a pleading look.

Fumbling quickly through my wallet, I found one of the cards that said "Plan B," and said to the pharmacist, "It's just for this; it won't be in there."

He looked at the card and said, "Oh, right," reached below the counter, pulled out a package of Plan B, bagged it discreetly, and billed it to her Medicaid card without incident.

Success: finally. It was a relief.

"Good for you; you did it!" I said to Lynne as we got back outside. "I hope you're proud of yourself!"

"Kinda, I guess. I'm just so glad you were there."

She looked shaken. It had been unsettling for her to have all those neighbors seeing her there. There had been absolutely no privacy in the only pharmacy in this small town. In addition to the people who had greeted Lynne by name before we even got to the pharmacist, several others had nodded a familiar "hi" across the store. And everyone could hear her interaction with the pharmacist. I left Lynne with a stack of the EC cards for the future, and I learned an important lesson that day. Ever since then, any time I've told people about EC being available in drugstores, I've offered them a little stack of the cards. And months later I saw a stack of cards in that same pharmacy, in the family planning aisle, that said EC in big letters and said, "If you want EC, show this card to the pharmacist with proof of your age." Progress.

We had all been so delighted at Planned Parenthood when EC first became available without a prescription. It was such a sense of hope and relief; that eliminating barriers would be helpful to the people we serve. But sometimes, even when we eliminate barriers, there are other barriers, hidden barriers, that we hadn't even thought about. But they're real. Until I saw Lynne's neighbors witness her challenging interaction with the pharmacist, I had no idea how many barriers there still were.

At sixteen, becoming a mom isn't easy for anyone, and while it wasn't going to be easy for Misty, she appeared to have a lot more going for her than many pregnant teens I'd worked with. Topping the list were her parents. Mom not only agreed to let Misty continue to live at home, she even agreed to babysit daily while Misty finished high school. And she had a car that runs and willingly drove Misty to her doctor appointments. Dad had a full time job, and they were willing to continue paying for groceries and all the other household expenses, plus the additional expenses of the baby as long as Misty stayed in school. I wished every teen mom I had known had had such a support system.

They welcomed me into their home for post-partum contraceptive planning. Misty knew almost nothing about birth control when we started, yet we neared the end of our first visit with a plan and next steps for obtaining an effective method. It was all going well, and I was hopeful. As I prepared to close the visit, I showed them a stack of brochures, letting them select which ones to take.

"And this one's about breastfeeding. Is that something you've considered?" I asked, after she had accepted a small stack of other brochures related to pregnancy.

"Nah," Misty replied.

"Do you mind if I ask you why?"

"I dunno, it's just..." and after a pause she added, "...gross."

"Well, if the thought of it seems gross to you, I can see why you wouldn't want to do it. But you've got several months to decide; you might want to think about it. Has anyone discussed it with you?"

"Yeah, the nurse told me I should. So did the WIC lady," she said, sounding annoyed.

I was glad they had. I was part of a local group that was working to increase the percentage of moms who breastfeed and the duration of breastfeeding, and we had all been urged to bring up the subject during pregnancy. We had been told that the more different people who encourage it, the more likely we were to reach that goal. And that bringing it up prior to the birth gave expectant moms time to consider it, educate themselves, and get over some of the misconceptions about it.

"Did they say why they were recommending it?"

She shrugged.

"I dunno, they said it's good I guess."

"May I ask what you think?" I asked, turning to mom. Misty seemed to really look up to her mom, so I thought a thumbs-up from mom might help.

"It's up to her. I know everyone pushes it these days, but it's gross." She paused and added, "But it's up to her."

Turning to Misty I said, "Well, I totally agree: it's your choice." And while I had wished that mom would encourage it, I was thankful that at least mom respected her daughter's right to make her own health decisions. "This brochure tells a lot about it, so you might want to read it," I added.

"Yeah, they really push it these days. They weren't so bad when I had my kids," mom added.

"Well, if it seems like it's being "pushed," it's probably because they've done a lot of studies, and they've learned that there are a lot of benefits to both the mother's health and the baby's health if new moms breastfeed."

"Yeah, they all try to push it!" mom said, sounding angry that I hadn't dropped the subject; that I was persisting. "But you listen to me," mom continued, speaking to Misty in an increasingly stern, defensive tone, pointing her finger right into Misty's face in a scolding motion, "Vivian's allowed to tell you to, the WIC lady's allowed to tell you to, the nurse is: they're all allowed to tell you. But they're not allowed to make you! When you have your baby, when you're in that frickin' hospital, they can tell you anything. But they cannot make you. That is just gross, and you have your rights!"

Within the culture of poverty, the culture outside the formal education system, there is a culture of mistrust. It's a mistrust of "the system." Within institutions like the school, the Department of Social Services, or the hospital, the professionals who I see as "service providers" are often seen as "the enemy," as the ones who are trying "to keep you down," as a force working against you, defining your role as a defensive one.

While I was glad that the uncooperative attitude about doctors and hospitals didn't look like it was going to prevent Misty from accessing and using effective contraception, it underscored for me how much attitude and attitudinal barriers affect my clients' use of the health care system. And I found myself wondering whether my clients' attitudes differ because they're treated differently or whether they're treated differently because of their attitudes. But it's like wondering which came first: the chicken or the egg.

Like in Lily's case. She knew she needed her birth control shot and her annual appointment when I visited her, but she didn't want to call to schedule it; she said she'd just show up at her doctor's office and wait. Knowing that her doctor operates on a tight schedule, I suggested she call first to find out when they could take her; otherwise, I figured, she'd be turned away or face a very long wait, further alienating her.

"Nah, I'll just go. They'll take me or they won't," she said.

"But if you call first and schedule it, they'll reserve the appointment time for you; you probably won't have to wait as long."

"Nah, I'll just go."

"How come you don't want to call first?"

"I hate calling; I'll just go."

"How come you hate calling?"

" 'Cuz that lady's a bitch."

"The lady who answers the phone?"

"Yeah, I hate her. She's got such an attitude."

"But don't you still have to talk to her when you get there?"

"Yeah, I guess."

"But if she's got an attitude, wouldn't it be better if you had an appointment, so she's expecting you? I mean, if you show up without an appointment, and throw her off schedule, wouldn't she have a worse attitude?"

"I don't know; she's always got an attitude. It don't matter, I just don't want to talk to her."

"Is that the only reason you don't want to call?"

"Yeah."

I offered to telephone and schedule the appointment for her, and she jumped at the chance, producing the phone number at lightning speed, saying, "That would be great, actually. 'Cause then I probably wouldn't have to wait as long. Yeah, if I don't have to talk to her."

So I called.

"Dr. Grey's office, this is Miranda."

"Hi, my name is Vivian Peters; I'm an educator from Planned Parenthood. I'm with a client who's a patient of Dr. Grey's and she needs her annual exam and her Depo shot. She's not sure exactly when her shot is due. Would it be possible for you to look that up and schedule her appointment?"

"Certainly," she answered, sounding friendly and helpful, as I'd expect any receptionist to sound. "I'll look it up. What's her date of birth?"

"March 30, 1990."

"And her name?" she added, still sounding professional.

"Lily Foster."

"Lily Foster?!" She repeated, sounding suddenly angry and horrified, immediately abandoning her previous, professional tone.

"Yes. Can you tell me when her shot is due?"

"One second," she snapped, and after a pause to look it up, she continued in a disgusted tone, "It's due on Nov 22. And she needs her annual, too."

"OK, could we schedule that appointment?"

"Well!" she said, and pausing between words she added, "Let. Me. Tell. You. Something." As she continued, her tone became downright nasty.

"Every time she shows up here, she's either late, or she has all those damn kids with her in the waiting room, or she just shows up without an appointment acting like it's our fault that she has to wait when she didn't even have the decency to call!"

"Wow, I can understand that that must be so frustrating to you. And yes, I'll confirm with her that it's important to show up on time. And just so you know, she recently moved into the village, so now she can walk to your office; transportation will no longer be a problem," I said, trying to remain professional and possibly help soften the attitude when Lily did show up, adding, "I hope you'll understand, it was hard for her when she lived farther away; she didn't have a phone and her car wasn't reliable, so there was no way for her to contact you when she couldn't make it. So could we schedule that appointment please?"

"Ugh," she moaned, and then after a pause, she snarled, "Well, OK, I'll schedule it. But I'll tell you right now, I can't keep making appointments for people who don't show up."

It sounded like it was going to take a lot more than my suggestion that Lily might be turning over a new leaf to soften this woman's attitude.

We scheduled the appointment, and I made sure Lily wrote it on her calendar. But the entire interaction taught me so much about how differently my clients and I are treated; I have made so many medical appointments for myself over my lifetime, in different towns, in different offices, through different receptionists, but I had never heard such a nasty attitude before. I could understand why Lily hadn't wanted to pick up the phone, and I could understand how that contributed to the snowballing negative relationship she had with her doctor's office staff. It renewed my respect for every person among us like Lily, or Misty and her mom when they do access services. I can't even imagine what they feel like when they go to the doctor's, but I can see that they have to overcome barriers that don't even exist for so many among us.

J oyce wasn't overly optimistic but sounded hopeful, or maybe it was desperate, as she stood giving me background information on a new referral: a twenty-year-old mother of three named Michelle who thinks she may be pregnant. Joyce was Michelle's caseworker from a Social Service agency, and hoped I could help.

"Vivian, I don't get it. I mean, I get it that she wants to have sex; I don't fault her for that." And leaning closer so the other caseworkers in her office didn't hear, she continued softly.

"Even though she's single; honestly, when I was fifteen, I was having sex. But I went on the pill; I'm still on it. It's been ten years. I mean, I'd love to have a baby; I'd love it more than anything. My husband and I talk about it. But I mean even for us, we finished college, we both have good jobs, we have insurance and everything, but I'm still not feeling ready. But her? Look at her! She's not married, she didn't even finish high school, all three of her kids have different fathers, she can't even support the kids she's got, she didn't even want them—she told me that!—and yet now she's telling me she might be pregnant? What is her problem? Why doesn't she just go on the pill?!"

By then, she stood very close to me, almost whispering in my ear. Standing so close, closer than normal, I could see how flawless her blonde hair looked: not a grey one in the bunch. The whites of her eyes shined bright: no little red lines. And as her expression changed between smiles and frowns, her skin creased, but the creases disappeared immediately without leaving a trace, as young skin does: so elastic, so fresh. Standing so close, she must have similarly noticed my grey hairs, the little creases in my aging skin, probably just like her mother's.

Her question was one of such innocence: "Why doesn't she just go on the pill?"

From her lips, it sounded rhetorical, the way she posed it. But to my ears, it was anything but rhetorical. It was an important, valid question. One I certainly couldn't answer before I met with Michelle. But one for which I could guess a hundred possible answers.

It reminded me of so many other confusing and derogatory comments I've heard about people in poverty, in my own experience and through the media, saying that "those people" who have so many babies they can't afford must really want them. But those accusations imply an assumption of a worldview that I believe should not be assumed. A worldview that says, "My life is something I create," instead of, "My life is what happens to me." That is not the worldview I see in the homes I visit, and from the little bit I had just heard about Michelle, it wasn't the worldview I expected to find in her home.

It was Joyce's use of the word, "just" that set my mind whirling. "Just." It implied so much. "Just" go on the pill, like it is a single action. So easy. So simple. So doable. For many people, it is. For Joyce it was. But for Michelle, and most of my clients before and since, it isn't. I wondered if I might have asked the same question in such a rhetorical tone when I was that age.

It made me realize how old I've become. Time slips by; suddenly years have passed. Then decades. We get these moments when it's right in our face, that jolting realization that we're not young anymore. Those moments can be unsettling.

And it doesn't just happen at work. I had just had another one of those moments recently. For years, I've loved taking my vacation during the middle of the winter, and going to a hot beach. But something's changed. Friendly strangers on tropical beaches used to stop me to try to sell me marijuana, now they try to sell me retirement property.

What happened; where did those years go? Do I look that different?

Mark Twain wrote, "Wrinkles should merely indicate where smiles have been."[14] Many of mine do. But many of them also don't. Looking at Joyce's youthful face, I felt suddenly proud of every grey hair, of each little wrinkle: like I had earned every one. Like each one represented a person I had tried to help; a story I had listened to that had deepened my understanding of the complexity of the problems people face. And while there was no way I could know what Michelle's problem was, what I did know that Joyce didn't know is that there are hundreds of important things that could have gone wrong. For success over time, every single one of them has to go right. And preventing each one of them from going wrong isn't as easy for some among us as it is for the rest of us; the obstacles can be very different.

Only one thing had gone wrong for Mandy after six years of effectively using contraception. Sometimes it's an emergency, like her partner's father's death that suddenly throws a well-made plan off track, or a sick babysitter the day of an important medical appointment. Sometimes it's a lack of comfort phoning for appointments, or fear of the complicated intake forms for people with literacy problems. And even when those women push themselves to overcome those fears and go to a medical provider for effective contraception, after filling out those difficult intake forms filled with words they know are important but can't understand, and after stripping naked and donning a paper gown, they sit there feeling stupider by the minute before the doctor even says "Hello." That doesn't give them the necessary solid grounding that Joyce or you or I might have if we were sitting in that same place.

The human body is so well designed to become pregnant, and for many people, whether the barriers to successfully taking charge of their fertility are attitudinal, logistical, intellectual, financial (real or perceived), or interpersonal, they are there. And their impact can be profound.

I remember in my college Introduction to Cultural Anthropology class, we read about cultures in remote jungles across the oceans; bold anthropologists lived among primitive peoples and wrote about their experiences, shedding light on our own experiences through the contrast. I now know that that college classroom, like many college classrooms in rural, central, New York State, was within a half hour drive of people living in rural poverty, like the families I've been meeting in my outreach work. Within a thirty-minute drive of almost any of those colleges there are homes like Michelle's that could provide anthropology students "cultures" to study that would probably teach them almost as much about their own cultures and about the world and the society we live in as a trip to a remote jungle halfway around the world. While most of us expect people in the jungle who use arrows with poison darts to be very different from ourselves, with different values and assumptions motivating their behavior, many among us don't expect such differences right within our communities.

But they're there.

And these differences have everything to do with how we approach the whole subject of family planning, from how we build relationships and how we behave sexually to how we see our reproductive capacity and how we relate to the medical establishment. I believe that it is within the subtleties of those differences that the answers to the questions lie about why certain subcultures of our population have such disproportionately higher incidences of unintended pregnancy.

And not only are certain subcultures experiencing more unintended pregnancy; it's worse than that. The consequences of an unintended pregnancy are extremely different for individuals in different subgroups. Many of the people I've known in my personal adult life—close friends and colleagues—people I know well enough to discuss private matters with, have confided in me that one or more of their pregnancies were unintended.

But it's not the same.

When an educated, professional, employed couple find themselves with an infant that they didn't intend or plan to conceive, yes, they face new challenges, and yes compromises and changes are made, but it doesn't devastate their lives. When someone in deep poverty, or a teen without a support system, or someone with extreme cognitive limitations or someone in a violent relationship or with a substance addiction experiences an unintended pregnancy, it's completely different; the impact of a baby born into a household that's already in chaos can be devastating. Perhaps we should be measuring a separate category of unintended pregnancy: unprepared pregnancy. That's what I see in the lives of so many of the clients I serve.

Yet over and over, I see the difference that timely, effective intervention can make, and Albert Einstein's words keep coming back to me; that imagination is more important than knowledge. Imagination fills me with hope; it is so easy for me to imagine a world in which everyone who struggles with these fundamental issues has a knowledgeable, safe, affirming person to talk with in a comfortable setting, in a timely fashion, to level the playing field in preventing unintended pregnancy.

THOSE QUIET BOYFRIENDS

"Boys are beyond the range of anybody's sure
understanding, at least when they are between
the ages of 18 months and 90 years."

–*James Thurber*[15]

Jordan appeared in my office doorway after school. Alone. Looking terrified. Frantically talking a mile a minute; so fast that it was hard to follow. Ex-boyfriends who have admitted that they were only visiting me at their girlfriend's mother's insistence, like Jordan had, usually don't show up unannounced a year later. So I was intrigued when I saw him there, and struck by the unmistakable urgency in his tone.

"I really have to talk to you, it's about my new girlfriend. She's in ninth grade. She's never had sex but like she really wants to and like she's really been wanting to bad and like I mean I want to too but like I told her I am so scared that she'll get pregnant and she told me to use a condom, but like, didn't you say that's not enough? When Naomi's mother made us come here after all that stuff happened I wasn't really listening—I'm sorry—but didn't you say something about that it was great that her mom was involved but that if we knew anyone who couldn't talk with their mother that they could still talk to you? 'Cause that's what I told my girlfriend but she says that's 'cause Naomi was eighteen and she's not eighteen—do you have to be eighteen to get birth control? She was scared that if I told you her name you'd call her mother, but didn't you say anybody can talk to you? Or do they have to be eighteen? That's why Lillian my new girlfriend like she didn't even want me to talk to you and that's why I kinda feel really bad coming here behind her back because I really don't want to lie to her or anything; I mean, I'm not like that! But I'm just so scared because she keeps pushing and it's like it's been like really hard to say "no" but I really don't want her to get pregnant. I mean, I'm going to college and if I got her pregnant it would ruin like everything and like I really love her and everything but I'm just like sooo scared."

Partway through his rant I had signaled that he was welcome to come in and sit down and I closed the door. I couldn't get a word in; I didn't try. I simply let him go on; he asked me so many questions but then immediately continued without waiting for me to answer any of them. Finally, once he had gotten it all out there, he stopped. Perhaps to rest. Or maybe to listen.

"Wow, Jordan. I'm really glad you came in. I get it that this is really challenging. But I have to say, I'm proud of you for your initiative and your discipline; I hope you're proud of yourself. It's great that you want to be so honest with your girlfriend, and get her the correct information."

"Yeah, I really do!"

"These are all important concerns. Let me try to answer as many of your questions as I can."

"OK, thanks," he said, seeming to suddenly realize that he had asked so many questions without stopping for answers.

"You're absolutely right that anyone of any age can talk to me and also get birth control. And it's all confidential."

"That's what I thought!"

"And yes, you're right that your entire plan about going to college could get turned upside down if you get Lillian pregnant. Remember, it only takes one sperm cell to fertilize an egg. If you want, you could bring her in so the three of us could talk together. And if she wants to involve her mom we can talk about how to do that, too. But it sounds like the first step is for you to bring her in. If you assure her that there's no age limit and that it's confidential, do you think she'd come in?"

He did. He brought her in, participated as we discussed method choices, and waited patiently as I responded to all her questions about what to expect at her first pelvic exam, about why it's important. I had the nurse practitioner come in to introduce herself and to encourage Lillian to come for an appointment before becoming sexually active. She gradually relaxed, and after clearly stating that she wasn't ready to raise a child, agreed to have a medical appointment. She did go on an effective method, they stayed together past his graduation, and he graduated without ever having gotten anyone pregnant.

Conversations between teens like Jordan and his new partner take place at times and in spaces that no sexual health educator could access; he does our job when we're off duty, which is when so many of the choices about sexual behavior are being made. Those quiet boyfriends can be so important and helpful. If the male is committed to preventing a pregnancy he can often prove to be more effective communicating with a teen girl than any educator.

It underscored everything I had learned about the importance of male involvement in teen pregnancy prevention efforts: programs that effectively reach males get more bang for their buck. While most reproductive health messages have been traditionally targeted at females, reaching the males is so important. The teen boys are going to be adult men someday; helping them plan their own futures is as important as helping girls plan theirs. And even though the males themselves can't get pregnant, teen girls can't get pregnant without a male partner. When we successfully reach males, they can be an enormous support reaching their female partners, like Jordan was.

Relationships have their own dynamics: their own language, their own decision-making patterns. Frequently, in teen couples, the younger partner looks to the older partner for guidance, and with heterosexual teen couples that's often the male. For better or for worse, males often have more than fifty percent of the influence on couples' decisions. It makes sense for pregnancy prevention programs to reach out to males; if the male is informed, if he cares, if he learns to set his own goals and use his voice with his female partner, he can be a huge support in the prevention effort. He can make the difference.

And males are totally capable of and interested in addressing these issues. They have as many concerns as females, but they have different roles. Males often tend to see their role as simply using condoms. Once they learn that the most effective methods are hormonal methods, which are only available to females, their gut instinct is often to give up and leave it to her. But each time I stress that they can have an *influence,* they rise to the opportunity. They genuinely want to, they just often lack the language; a little encouragement goes a long way.

One by one, over the years, guys proved to me that by reaching them, I was reaching their female partners.

Like the time the sixteen-year-old girl came to my drop-in, alone, hesitantly knocking softly on my door asking, "Are you Vivian?"

"Yes, come in, welcome to Planned Parenthood," I replied, hoping a gentle smile would soften her tight stance.

"I need to go on birth control. I heard you could tell me how to get it," she said as she plopped down on my couch. She intrigued me; girls alone aren't usually so direct in the first two sentences.

"Yes, you came to the right place. I'm an educator here."

"Yeah, I know. My boyfriend told me to come talk to you."

"He did?"

"Yeah, 'cuz like, we almost had sex but he said I should come here first."

"For birth control?"

"Yeah."

"You mean he wants you to go on birth control before having sex?"

"Yeah."

"Is that what *you* want?"

"I dunno, I guess."

"What do you mean?"

"Huh?"

"Well, you said he wants you to go on birth control before you have sex. But do you want to have sex? Having sex is a big decision. I really respect that you talked about this with your boyfriend. I just want to make sure you're doing what *you* want; that nobody's pressuring you."

"Oh, no, I want to have sex; I wanted to have sex last weekend! He's not pressuring me to have sex; he just said I have to go on birth control first. So that's what I wanna do."

"Did you want to have sex without birth control?"

"Not really, I had a condom. But he said they could break and stuff. He said it's not enough."

"Have either of you ever had sex before?"

"He has, but I haven't. He's a lot older; he's like twenty-three."

"Oh, wow, that is a lot older. That brings up a lot of other issues, too, including legal issues."

"I know. He said that's parta' why he wants me on birth control."

"What do you mean?"

" 'Cuz like he said I'm too young, 'cuz I'm sixteen. But I told him I wanna do it. But he said if I got pregnant they could make him go to jail."

"He's right. What do you think of that?"

"I don't want him to go to jail! He said it could be rape 'cuz I'm not seventeen, so I can't get pregnant."

"Besides the jail thing, have you thought about how you'd feel about pregnancy?"

"Oh, I don't wanna get pregnant!"

"Well, did you think the condom would be enough protection?"

"I dunno, I guess. I mean, I just figured it was better than nothing."

"Well, you're certainly right about that. But did you think about getting more protection, or was that just his idea?"

"Well, he said it, but I thought you haveta be seventeen to get birth control. He said you don't."

"He's right; there used to be age limits. But not any more. Now you can get birth control regardless of your age, with or without a parent."

We talked more; I showed her the choices of hormonal methods, I walked her through what to expect at her initial appointment, she said she wanted an appointment so I brought her downstairs to the clinic and we scheduled it. She was very appreciative of the whole thing; she really wanted to go on birth control. Before leaving, we got back to the boyfriend piece.

"I'm glad you came here today. It sounds like you're at an important crossroads in your life right now. If you do have sex, whether or not you become pregnant at sixteen is huge. It affects everything. I'm so glad you're taking charge of this before it's a problem. I'm glad actually that your boyfriend suggested you come here. Do you think you would have come here if he hadn't brought it up?"

"I mean, like, if I had known I might have, but I thought I couldn't 'till I'm seventeen or something."

"Well, I'm glad he knew, as this is really important for your future; for both your futures."

"That's what he always says. He says, 'Ya gotta think about the future.' "

"I'm so glad you two talk about this stuff; some couples don't even talk about it."

"Oh, we talk about it all the time. He says he really cares about me."

"Well, I have to say, I'm impressed with both of you; I'm impressed that he saw it as a sign of caring, to send you up to see me, and that you listened to him and accepted what he said."

She went on to tell me a little more about their relationship. They only see each other on weekends, as he lives a good half hour away. She named the town, and it was one I know well. She said that he had quit high school, gotten his GED, that he tells her he loves her, and that someday he might want to be a dad but that he's not ready yet. And that he wouldn't want to get her pregnant until he was really ready to be a good dad, not like the way his own dad was. His dad was never there; he just grew up with his mom.

I was impressed and quite surprised that a male who had dropped out of school living in what I knew to be a little hamlet of poverty was so proactive, articulate, and focused on the importance of preventing pregnancy and of the male role. It was the exact opposite of what I would have expected, knowing what I knew of the demographics.

Then she explained that he used to live in Springfield, and she casually mentioned his name. That's when it all made sense to me: he had gone to Springfield High School, and before he dropped out, he had come to my weekly drop-in many times. It had been clear to me from the start that he had so many of the classic "risk factors," so I had made an extra effort to engage him. He had accepted my invitation to join our steering committee; I knew it was probably more for the free pizza than the interest in serving his community, but I had hoped that the lure of the pizza would result in some learning, the way it had for a lot of teens that first came for the food. It had. He had ended up really enjoying our weekly meetings; he had been present for so many conversations that my colleague and I had facilitated with the group. Conversations about teen pregnancy, about the importance of teens thinking about their future, about the reasons why some teens get pregnant while others wait, about Planned Parenthood services, about misinformation that is prevalent among teens and how to reach out to them to correct it, about birth control methods, about communication within relationships, about the male role; he had been part of a group for several years that seriously discussed the challenge of reaching teens and helping them set and reach goals.

When he dropped out, I never saw him again; the other kids in the group told me he had left the area. He had. But until he sent this lovely sixteen-year-old girl-friend up to see me, I had no idea how much all those conversations had enabled him to step up to the plate, to initiate important conversations with his own girl-friend. Conversations that lead to measurable behavior change. They didn't have sex until she was on a hormonal method and had a condom. And it was all because of *his* initiative.

And other boys from those groups demonstrated the importance of the male role to me. Like Keith. Keith was actually ahead of Planned Parenthood in his thinking about the male role. He had also served for several years on our teen steering committee, so he too had participated in many conversations about the male role.

Emergency Contraception, or "the morning after pill" had gotten FDA approval during those years, and at that time it was only available by prescription. Keith had been present when I had explained that, and when I had explained that girls could get them at Planned Parenthood.

One evening a year later he stopped in to see me. He was in a panic.

"Vee, remember those pills you said girls can take *after* sex?"

"Yeah, you mean Emergency Contraception, EC?"

"Yeah. Didn't you say Planned Parenthood has them now?"

"Yes, we do."

"Oh, whew! I need some right now, can you give them to me?" he asked with urgency.

Today they're available over the counter, but back then they weren't, so I had to explain that he couldn't get them. "Well, they're only available by prescription, so the person who is going to actually take them has to come in. They're only available to females," I said.

"No, no, no, Vee," he said trying to correct me, "I know I don't take them, but they're for my girlfriend. I'm getting them for her."

"Wow, I'm really glad you're making such an effort, but she has to come in," I replied.

"No, no, no, she can't," he explained. "She's got soccer practice right now. By the time it lets out, you'll be closed. I have to pick them up for her."

If she had already been a patient, and if they had been prescribed for her, she may have been able to give him a note to pick them up. But since she had never been in, that wasn't an option; she'd have to come in herself. I tried to explain that to him.

"She has to see someone from our medical staff, so they can write her a prescription. Then they can give her the pills. I can't give them out; I'm an educator. Prescriptions have to be written by medical providers. I can get her an emergency appointment if she can come in tonight; the clinic is open 'till 8:00," I offered.

"Well then can you get me an appointment? She can't come in; she has to take the bus home from practice. If you can get me in, I can bring her the pills before she gets on the bus."

"But we're not allowed to do that. She has to see the practitioner," I tried again to explain.

"What are you talking about? That's ridiculous!" he exclaimed. "It's my girlfriend. I had sex with her; if she got pregnant that would be my kid! There's no way I'm ready to be a dad!"

Eventually, EC did become available without prescription to males and females ages seventeen and older, and some EC is now available to males and females of any age; the laws are continually changing,[16] eliminating barriers like the one Keith faced. So if this incident had been a few years later, the FDA regulations would have accommodated his needs. As much as it broke my heart to see him so distressed, it was affirming to see how effective our own efforts at reaching males had been. He completely internalized the responsibility of his role and was willing to step up to the plate, to do his fair share in trying to prevent pregnancy even after a mishap; he couldn't even imagine that Planned Parenthood didn't have a provision to allow him, as a male teen, to take initiative in preventing pregnancy in his girlfriend's body after unprotected sex. He saw the issues as "ours," not "hers." Society wasn't ready to welcome his effort yet; he was a young man ahead of his time.

"I have a question," Lucas said as he stood in my doorway. He entered my office and sat awkwardly on the couch, adding apologetically, "I mean it's not really a question. I mean, like, I mean, it's not like a *question* question. I mean it's kinda stupid." He kept squirming, stammering and stuttering, but he looked so intense, like he really wanted to ask me something. His friend Mark sat patiently at his side, saying nothing.

"Well," I replied, "whatever your question is, I'm glad you came here with it—" and I wanted to underscore that all questions are confidential, that there are no stupid questions, and that the reason we had created the teen drop-in was so teens could ask *any* question. But he interrupted saying, "Yeah, Mark said I should come talk to you."

Mark added, "He asked me but like I didn't know what to say so I told him to come here."

I had never met Lucas before, and I had only met Mark once, when he came just to quickly pick up condoms; we had never really talked much. I was curious about what the question was, but it was almost painful to watch Lucas struggling like that. I wanted to help him relax a little, but there were no words that I could think of adding that would be more encouraging than to simply sit back looking calm, patient, and highly interested. So I just raised my eyebrows a bit and waited; he seemed so self-conscious yet so determined.

"I mean, it isn't like a question like about stuff. I mean, it's just something I've been wondering about a lot lately."

After spinning his wheels some more, he wound down, paused, and finally leaned forward and spilled his question.

"Why does sex *feel* so good?"

There: he said it. Then he just sat back, almost holding his breath, looking vulnerable but open.

"Wow," I said. "I understand what you mean, that it's not an information type of question. But before I even try to address your question, I just have to say this: I don't think it's stupid at all! I think it's a great question!"

He immediately looked relaxed and began to breathe easier. I continued, "And you're absolutely right: it's not the kind of question that has a fact-based answer; even though I'm a professional, it's not the kind of question I can answer with authority. All I could really do is talk with you about it and maybe tell you what I think."

"Yeah, I know."

"But first, I'm intrigued that you've been thinking about this. I'm curious to know what you've been thinking so far. Would you be willing to share what you've thought; could we start from there?"

Now he looked eager to speak. "Well yeah, I've been thinking about it and that's the thing. I don't really know. The best I could think of is that like y'know how we always wear all this clothing?" It was the dead of winter; for months we had all been bundled up. "I was thinking maybe it's 'cuz we wear all these clothes all the time, so we get so used to it. So then, I mean, like, when you take them all off and the other person takes theirs off and like they see you and you see them, and like, there's all this skin and stuff, and it's like it's like it's like: finally"—and he paused, leaned back, arms spread, and with eyes towards the heavens he added—"ahhh," in a dreamy tone.

"Oh, wow, you *have* been thinking about this. That's an interesting theory. I think you might be on to something; I agree that the way we're clothed all the time makes being naked a huge contrast. And yeah, I think you're right, that contributes to something really fundamental about our sexuality." He looked like he appreciated a little affirmation.

"Maybe. That's what I thought."

"But I don't think that's all there is to it."

"Well, yeah, but that's all I could really think of."

"Because if we think about humans throughout history, and around the world, even today in more primitive cultures, and in hot climates where people hardly wear anything, I still think there's more to it; our sexual organs really are super-sensitive to the touch, I don't think it's only the visual thing."

"Yeah."

"I think if we consider not just people, but about all life on earth, anything that lives: animals, fish, insects, even plants; for life to sustain itself over time, over generations, life has to go on past the individual's life. From one generation to the next: reproduction is essential if any living species is going to survive. So for humans to survive, we have to reproduce. So in addition to the visual thing you were talking about, I think our bodies have evolved so our reproductive organs feel pleasurable to the touch; it's a way that ensures—" but before I could finish my sentence he broke in with a startled look of appreciation and understanding, saying, "Oh, if it didn't feel good, nobody would do it!"

We discussed it a little more.

When they left I thought about his tone as he had asked the question; the way it was almost an apologetic tone, as if he were implying, "I know we're not supposed to do it, I know we're supposed to wait 'till we're older; I know we're supposed to abstain: I get that," as though he had absorbed that message from adult society in general, but there was this one gnawing detail that didn't fit into the picture, that nobody had explained or even articulated, and that just didn't add up. The big, "…But."

Even though we had never anticipated conversations like that one when we opened the weekly teen drop-in, teens do have these unanticipated questions. And it was affirming to realize that we had successfully created a space and set a tone so that even a boy who had never met me could show up to discuss *any* question.

FATHER KNOWS BEST???

"It would be great if you could come over right away.
Tammy just got her period and when the egg
broke she thought she had worms."
*—Twelve-year-old Tammy's mother,
calling to request a rushed home visit*

I grew up in a child-centered home surrounded by adoring parents, sisters, and a grandmother; I was loved, treasured, and nurtured. We watched TV shows like *Leave It To Beaver* and *Father Knows Best*. Like many Americans, I have the image of an "ideal family" imprinted in my mind. When I hear people talk about "family values" I feel like I get it. They're talking about the way I was raised, and I have infinite gratitude for the upbringing I received; I truly wish we lived in a world in which every child was cherished and cared for the way I was.

But not all families have the same structure or the same values. Sometimes those differences are relatively minor, like different values about marriage. The girl who told me she hopes to have three kids but never wants to marry explained that it's because divorces are so expensive. "My aunt told me, no matter what, don't ever get married." Her aunt's first divorce had cost her the home and her second had cost her the car plus ten thousand dollars.

Other times those differences are more striking, making it exceptionally challenging for the kids to navigate their way through their teen years. As I visit my clients' homes, when I see some of the struggles the adults and children face, I see firsthand what happens when kids *don't* get the kind of nurturing I experienced in my own upbringing.

Father, it turns out, doesn't always know best.

Neither does mother.

If you ask me, the mom who needed to bring a clean urine sample to work didn't "know best" the morning she asked her thirteen-year-old daughter to pee in a cup for her. She angrily threatened that if she didn't have clean urine she'd lose her job and they'd lose their apartment. She implied that it would be her daughter's fault if the family all became homeless. That's a big ethical dilemma for a teen to face; it makes growing up a lot harder.

I wish everyone in America could see the homes I see. I think it would shed new light on the collective conversations about "family values"; about the relative role of family and the rest of society in raising the next generation. Especially as it relates to sexuality education.

Homes like Mary's. Since Mary was my client my primary attention was on her. She hadn't mentioned that her cousin Nicole would be visiting that day, so I was surprised that she wasn't home alone when I arrived. I had some very specific goals for our visit that day: to find out if she was still taking the birth control pills she had recently started; to find out if she had told her dad about going on the pill, as she had intended; and to find out if she was sexually active. But because of confidentiality, I couldn't be the one to bring any of that up with Nicole present. I knew nothing about their relationship or Mary's comfort level discussing these private issues with her cousin, so I simply sat with them as she suggested and let her take the lead.

Stories came out; though they were cousins, they agreed they felt more like sisters. Neither of them had a sister.

"Our family is so weird, our friends don't really understand us the way we understand each other." That told me a lot about Nicole; she, too, must have had a rough childhood. I didn't know the details about *why* Mary or Nicole had lived in foster homes, but I've dealt with enough kids in foster care to know that there have been some serious problems at home. Actually, some of the homes I've worked in that have been investigated and it's been determined that they're acceptable tell me even more: a lot has to go wrong for a kid to be removed from their home. Not just mom screaming, "I wish I never had you; you ruined my life!" or the dad who "never notices me unless I'm standing in front of the television." And usually it's not just one thing, there's a "case." But there's often a proverbial straw that breaks the camel's back.

Sometimes, when kids are removed from their parents' custody, it's related to sex. Then the caseworkers often tell me the story without me even asking. Like the time a twelve-year-old boy and his thirteen-year-old sister came home and walked in on their mom, almost naked, gleefully dancing a striptease on the dining room table as dad played with himself on the couch. I'm confident DSS wouldn't have cared about the color of her garters or the way her rolls of fat poured over her lace thong if, like most couples who enjoy that kind of thing, they were in private. And DSS probably wouldn't have even known about it except for the fact that the whole thing was being videoed and broadcast live over the Internet. Including the astonished looks on the kids' faces as they walked in. That was it, and that really sped up the case.

Or the girl who walked in on her stepfather who gets off on prancing around in adult diapers. Again, not mine to judge, but it was the privacy thing that lost that mom her daughter.

And then there are all the more typical ones; documentation of sexual abuse by an adult who lives in the home, mom's boyfriend being the most frequent offender. Long stories. Cops. Investigations. Lawyers. Denials. Jail sentences. I see that a lot; families struggle.

But when it's not of a sexual nature, the caseworkers don't usually say, and I never ask, but I can safely assume the kid has had some pretty big bumps in the road. That was the case with Mary.

I was relieved that Mary spoke frankly and comfortably in Nicole's presence, as I had driven an hour to get to this visit, and I didn't want the frustration of being unable to discuss some important issues. Mary was open about her pills with Nicole, and we were able to have a productive visit; she had some important questions, listened to my answers, and definitely left me with the feeling that she was on the road to success as far as preventing pregnancy was concerned.

And she told us about the conversation she had had with her dad when she told him she went on the pill. It had gone well. Nicole was envious.

"I wish I could talk to my dad about stuff," she said.

"Have you ever tried?" I asked.

"Oh yeah, we're like really close but he's in jail and I'm hardly ever allowed to visit." With no prompting from me, she went into the next room and quickly reappeared holding a three ring binder she eagerly showed me.

"I love my dad. I miss him so much. I made this album..." and she showed me page after page, some of photos of the two of them, some of just her dad, a few letters, and numerous newspaper clippings. Each one was carefully, neatly, perfectly cut out of the newspaper and taped to a page of loose-leaf paper. The contrast was sharp; she had clearly put such loving care into the presentation, yet the content of each article was so distressing. "Man charged with sexually abusing a minor in Lincolnville," and other headlines and articles following his last decade of arrests, charges, pleas, and trials.

It was eye-opening for me; here this girl had internalized the message from society and her family to value the ties of family, and she wanted to more than anything. She had put such effort into collecting every mention of him in the local papers, and had so lovingly collected and saved and treasured every mention of his name, the way a parent might save articles about a child's accomplishments.

Yet nothing had been "accomplished." It was all things that people aren't supposed to do that she was collecting. Sexual abuse, drug possession, drug sales. Misdemeanors, felonies, trials, sentences. I didn't know how to deal with it; on the one hand, we all want to be proud of our families. Part of me wanted to tell her about thicker card stock paper and permanent inks and adhesives, so she'd get longer lasting results from her efforts, as I'd have offered to anyone trying to create a lasting family album. But I let it go. And despite the sordid content of her tales, I was glad she felt so proud of herself and so comfortable in my presence to share that.

So many social problems are cyclical, generational within families, and it's so hard to break cycles. Not just teen parenting, other cycles, too: alcoholism, domestic violence, chronic unemployment, criminal activity, dropping out of school, poverty. Children grow up watching their parents and so frequently repeat the patterns of the lives they witnessed and experienced in childhood; there is comfort in familiarity, even when the familiar is unpleasant. Breaking any one of those cycles for any one individual can be such a struggle; circles have no beginning and no end. For outsiders who want to be helpful, it's hard to find a place where there's an opportunity to successfully intervene, to create a new pattern.

But the more I see, the more I read, the more I think and the more I learn, the more it confirms my firm belief that effective intervention *before* the conception of an unwanted pregnancy is the most efficient, effective way to create the potential for people to improve the quality of their own lives and the lives of their future offspring. That's the hope that's in the forefront of my mind when I work with individuals and families. And that's the message of hope I give the caseworkers and professionals when I train them about the services I offer: that we can work with people among us who are struggling, and that it will enable them to make a profound difference in their own lives and in their families' lives.

I think about the issue of social injustice, about how unfair it is that people like me are simply lucky enough to be born into a stable, loving home while others struggle from day one in cycles of turmoil. And every time we pull together with a teen like Mary and help her get to age twenty without her first pregnancy, I feel some of those seemingly unbreakable cycles breaking.

At fifteen, Pam had been appropriately referred for my services, partly because she was the younger sibling of a teen parent, partly because she was living in poverty, and also because she was not doing well in school. Those are three "risk factors" for becoming a teen parent herself. I was glad that her caseworker had correctly identified that and referred her to me.

Our first meeting was at her kitchen table, and she was babysitting her sister's son Jesse, who was crawling around. We were facing each other and Jesse crawled behind Pam, out of her field of vision. But I could see him going straight towards the dog dishes on the floor. I was concerned that Pam was so intent on the story she was telling me that she wasn't noticing. I try to never interrupt people, but for the baby's safety I did.

"Excuse me for interrupting, but I think the baby's going to eat the dog food," I said softly. I thought she might feel ashamed for not watching closer, and she did get a horrified look when she heard the phrase, "dog food." She immediately start-ed to jump up. But after turning and seeing the situation with her own eyes, she sat back down and looked at me like I was nuts, correcting me, with disappointment that I could think something so horrific would happen in her home, explaining, "No, he's not! He's just drinking the water. He always does."

This story stayed in my mind for over ten years, quietly undisturbed, until I attended a meeting with representatives from several other agencies collabo-rating on a project to increase the percentage of moms who breastfeed and the duration of breastfeeding. In a conversation about the importance of home-based education, one colleague shared a story about a nurse on a home visit in a nearby county who saw an infant crawl over to the family dog and drink the dog's breast milk. Suddenly, I felt like my girl who let the infant drink the dog's water out of a bowl was an easy client. I guess it's all relative.

At eighteen, there are probably a lot of girls who still live at home but fantasize about running away, or start planning their move, the way Natalia did. My guess is that they often unknowingly take for granted all that their parent(s) provide: a home, food, clothing, transportation, spend-ing money. So when Natalia told me she had had it and was going to move out on her own, "no matter what," I thought I should give her a reality check.

"How come you wanna move out?" I asked.

"I can't stand my mom!"

"Sounds like you're in a tough spot."

"I am."

"I know it can be hard living with a parent as you're becoming an adult yourself. But still, there's a lot your mom provides for you now. If you move out, have you thought about what you're giving up?"

"Yeah, I've thought about it a lot. I mean, my mom pays the rent and eve-rything; I don't really have no place else to go! That's why I didn't move out before. I've thought about it for a long time. I always wished I had somewhere to go. Somewhere else; any place. But I don't. That's why I stayed till now. And plus my mom is saving up to go visit her sister in Montana, and she said if I go with her maybe we could swing by my friend's house in Florida on the way home 'cause she was like my best friend and she moved there. But hon-estly, that was kinda keeping me home but I don't think she's ever gonna be able to save up enough gas money, and anyway, now…I've just had it. I don't care what I gotta do. I don't care if I gotta live on the street or something. I just ain't goin' back there!"

"You sound really fed up." I said without pointing out that coming from New York you don't "swing by" Florida on the way home from Montana; I had a feeling neither of them had gotten as far as looking at a map but I let that go, adding, "Do you want to tell me what's going on at home?"

"On Saturday night, I came home from work; it was late 'cause I had to close the restaurant. And I walked into our apartment, and there was my mom, drunk again; I mean, I'm used to her being drunk when I come home late, but I mean, this time, like, I mean, I knew she was gonna be at the bar, but she had brought this guy home with her, and like, there they were, they were both drunk, and they were having sex right there in the hall. I mean, like, that is so gross. I mean I just so don't need to be seeing that!"

"No! Wow, you really don't! I can't even imagine what that must have felt like for you."

"I mean, you can't. Like, it would have been really bad whoever he was, just walking in on your mom having sex, I mean…that's weird. Like, why couldn't they at least have gone into her room and shut the door or something. I mean, like, the hall? And then they must have heard my key in the lock 'cause when I opened the door they just kind of stopped and looked up at me and like it was just so weird 'cause like it took me a minute to even realize what was going on. And like, I"—she paused—"I know him. And he looked so surprised and he said something and she said, "That's my daughter," and then I realized they were both drunk and I just left and I didn't say nothin', I went to my friend's house and her mom was really nice, I didn't tell her all about what happened, I just said, like, can I stay over and I must have looked really freaked out and her mom let me sleep on the couch, but like, tonight, I don't even know where I'm gonna go. But I ain't goin' home, that's for sure. My mom just makes me sick. I mean, I know she's always hangin' out at the bar, and she always just like brings home some guy, and like, I hate it but I try to mind my own business 'n stuff, but I mean: that guy?"

Clearly, Natalia knew the guy; they had met. I don't know what had happened, but clearly something had transpired between them previously, as he was shocked that the woman he went home with from the bar that night turned out to be Natalia's mom. Clearly, he wouldn't have had sex with her in the hall had he known that she had a daughter, specifically Natalia, who was scheduled to come home right when she did.

If Natalia had been fifteen telling me or any other professional in New York State this story, it would have led to a "hotline" call. But at eighteen Natalia is not a child; her mom no longer has a legal responsibility to provide a home in compliance with basic standards.

In our society, at eighteen, Natalia's on her own.

Three teen girls plopped comfortably on my couch during our weekly "teen drop-in." I didn't recognize any of them. After a welcome and introductions I asked them what brought them in today.

"I want them to go on birth control," the one in the middle said. She only looked a year or two older than the others, but she acted much older.

"And do either of you want to go on a birth control method?" I asked them.

"Yeah," they both said, in unison. It turned out that those two were sisters.

We got talking about "the usual"; clarifying myths about how pregnancy happens, articulating goals about not wanting to become pregnant, discussing the different methods available, discussing the benefits of using both a hormonal method and a barrier method, etc. Then I started asking about family support and communication.

"Who knows you're here today; anyone at home?" I asked. That's when they clarified that the one in the middle, who was two years older than the older of the two sisters, is already on a method, and that it was her and her partner—who is their father!—that suggested that the sisters go on birth control.

So here's this girl who is all of eighteen, dating the father of two girls who are only two and three years younger than her, acting "motherly."

Suddenly, it made sense why she had been acting almost maternal to them: leading them up the steps of Planned Parenthood, introducing them to me, telling me that they need birth control. I had had so many experiences prior to that one of talking with teen sisters and their mother, or stepmother, or dad's girlfriend. But I had never experienced that dynamic with only two years separating the generations. Fortunately I didn't miss a beat and they all got what they needed.

But afterwards, at the end of the night, when I went to list all my visits from the day for the detailed records I have to submit to the state health department, I got flustered. I'm required to list how many "teen visits" I have (teens alone—without parents) and how many "family visits" I have (teen with parent). Once again, those forms with boxes that probably seem so clear to the person in Albany who created them posed a challenge to me; was that a "teens" visit or a "family" visit? I was stuck.

I wanted to do it right; I'm a detail person. I struggle over details even when I know they don't matter.

While I felt confident that I had helped them overcome communication barriers, as I had so many "families," it felt very strange to count an eighteen-year-old as a "parent" to a fifteen- and sixteen-year-old. But it also didn't feel right to list them as simply three "teens" as I did regularly, every time three teen friends came to see me.

I've heard that the devil is in the details; I've also heard that God is in the details. I think both may be true. I decided to leave the form until the next morning, hoping that a good night's sleep would clarify my dilemma.

It didn't.

"I need to schedule her depo shot, and it has to be today," I told Marla, our medical receptionist in Springfield. I handed her a slip of paper with Paula's name and date of birth.

She pulled up Paula's name on her computer and gave me that fed up look. I knew she was about to say, "Vee, this is ridiculous; she is eighteen! She's been on the shot for two years. She knows she needs it every twelve weeks. She's been coming here for years. It was one thing, when she was fourteen and she used to pull this, but she's eighteen! When is she going to grow up and realize that we can't always drop everything for her? I'm sick of this bullshit. We're too busy today; I've got patients double-booked already! She has got to learn to call ahead...."

I don't remember how many of those words actually crossed her lips, versus how many of them I just knew she was about to say, but I knew that's where she was heading, and I didn't have time to listen to it. None of us did; this was before our clinic had switched to electronic medical records, and Paula's chart would have to be faxed from our main clinic, setting staff behind in two busy clinics. So I dashed over to Marla and simply extracted a few of what I considered to be the most important details from the half hour rant I had just listened to upstairs in my office. I was thankful that she was willing to listen as I whispered softer and faster than I've ever spoken, right into her ear.

"Marla, when Paula's father was released from prison two months ago, the first thing he did was take her out of her grandmother's custody and into his home, against her will. Her grandmother didn't fight it, and Paula was devastated. And when she told her dad and her stepmom that she needed her shot; that she gets it at Planned Parenthood they said, 'You're not going to Planned Parenthood: only whores and sluts go there!' And the stepmother insisted, 'You're going to my doctor.' And Paula said she loves Planned Parenthood but they insisted and she finally agreed, 'Fine, I'll go anywhere but I need an appointment,' and stepmom kept saying, 'I'll do it, I'll do it,' but never did. So on Tuesday when she turned eighteen and was legally allowed to leave dad's home, she came back to Springfield to her grandma's but they don't have a phone so she just walked in now, crying—" and I was interrupted by the image of Paula coming down the stairs; after crying, she had gone to freshen up her red eyes in the restroom while I tried to pull some strings for her to get into the clinic. I didn't want to make her self-conscious, and I hoped Marla had gotten enough of an earful to change her attitude.

She had.

As I straightened my back and walked back out into the public area where I belonged, Paula came over and was greeted by Marla's warmest smile, and her patient words, "Hi Paula. Vivian tells me you need your shot today. We're really busy," and then scrunching her nose and leaning forward in the friendliest possible way, with a gentle smile she said, "Gimmie a sec. I'll go out back and see what I can do." And somehow, within the hour, the chart was faxed, there was an empty exam room, and Paula got her shot.

On time.

A disheartened mom phoned; maybe I can be helpful, I hoped.

She was concerned about her oldest daughter, Nora. Puberty was happening. "Oh, we're fine talking about all that. It's the way she talks that I'm worried about. It's like she's so disrespectful."

In the background I could hear the younger siblings playing, and occasionally interrupting. She interrupted herself, and in a gentle tone addressed the little girl: "Mommy's on the phone, Sweetie. Wait till I'm done." She returned to me, complaining more about Nora, and again the little one bugged her. Sounding a bit frustrated, she reminded her, "I said I'm on the phone. Wait 'till I hang up." And after mom complained a little more about how Nora yells and shouts instead of talking, the younger one kept interrupting, and each time mom's voice sounded harsher. "I said: wait till I get off the phone, damn it!" and then "Shut up!"

Finally she digressed to an earsplitting scream, "I am on the God damn phone! Will you show some fucking respect?!"

She continued her story, complaining about Nora's outbursts of anger, her cursing and shouting, unable to imagine why.

P at had welcomed me into her home and her life, and especially into her daughter Margaret's life. Having been a teen mom herself, Pat had high hopes for Margaret. Over a period of several months, I met with them together and separately and the three of us did well; to Pat's delight, Margaret went on a hormonal method of birth control before becoming a teen mom. First the pill, then the Depo shot, which has to be injected every twelve weeks. I monitored it carefully, and Margaret was good about keeping her appointments. But one day, she didn't show up for her appointment to get her shot. I was concerned.

I phoned to find out why, and got their answering machine. Pat's voice started out sweet on the recording.

"Hi, it's Pat. We're not here to take your call. When you hear the tone, you can leave a message." As she went on, her voice sounded louder and tighter: stressed.

"But I'll tell ya right now, we won't ever hear it. We left. And we ain't comin' back. Ever!"

And then sounding livid, she continued, shouting, "And if ya wanna know why you can ask those fuck-faces at DSS!"

And then the beep.

I didn't leave a message.

I don't know if Margaret ever got her shot.

"I forgot to tell you: when you get to Patricia's house, don't get out of your car unless you see dad and he sees you, or unless you see that the dogs are tied up. One of them bites. Just honk your horn and if dad doesn't come out, leave. My boss insisted I call you right back and that you promise you won't get out of the car. They're going out there today and dealing with that. The dogs will probably be taken away but we don't know what'll happen by the time you go…"

I promised. I was thankful for the caseworker's warning.

At age thirteen, Patricia was wearing extremely provocative clothes to school, making sexual comments in public, and reportedly using sexual innuendo in many conversations. The school complained to dad, he mentioned the concern to the caseworker, and she invited me in.

Arriving at the home, I pulled into the driveway, tooted my horn, and as I sat waiting, I couldn't help notice the bumper sticker on dad's dilapidated old car, in a wild crooked font declaring, "If you think sex ain't dirty then you ain't doin' it right!"

So dad's driving around in this car, his daughter is reading it, and everyone else is wondering why the girl is "acting too sexy."

And sexuality education is supposed to be only taught at home?

Father knows best???

And moms concern me, too. One mom told her teenage daughter to try the pill, saying, "I never knew nothin' about it, but Kurt told me his wife really likes it and that I should try it. So I did, and it's great." Kurt was mom's boyfriend; her idea of helping her daughter grow up was to share the birth control "tip" she got from her current lover's current wife.

And then there's Patience's mom. She called me in a panic, saying, "I think Patience is pregnant with twins! Can you come over today?"

I had worked with them for months and helped her get her daughter to go on the patch; Patience had been adamant that she didn't want to get pregnant. So I arrived, expecting Patience to be concerned. She wasn't.

"I ain't pregnant!" she insisted.

"Are you still using the patch?" I asked.

"Yes!" she snapped back, sounding annoyed about being bothered.

"Have you changed it each week, like we talked about?"

"Yes, of course! For three weeks in a row, just like you said; like the nurse said. I don't wanna get pregnant!"

"And then do you go one week without a patch?"

"Yes!"

"And have you been getting your periods?"

"Yes!"

"When was your last period?"

"I'm having it right now!"

"So I'm a little confused; it sounds like you're doing everything right. What makes you think you might be pregnant?"

"I know I ain't pregnant. It's just her!" she said, nodding at her mom, annoyed, frustrated, adding, "She's just nuts!"

So I asked Patience's mom, "Listening to Patience's description, does it sound to you like she's doing something wrong, the way she explains it?"

"No, I mean, no, not that stuff; not with the patches."

"It sounds to you like she's using them correctly?"

"Oh yeah, she's good about that."

"And you knew that?"

"Oh yeah, she's always really good about that kind of thing."

"So how come you called me sounding so concerned? What makes you think she might be pregnant?"

" 'Cuz I read her crystals and it said she's pregnant with twins. And I mean, she's too young; she can't handle twins…"

Grandparents aren't perfect, either. Grandma was sitting by the living room window when I arrived at a teen mom's apartment. It was a cold, windy winter day. She had cracked the window open a little to blow the smoke from her cigarette outside. But the baby was sleeping right across the room, and a lot of the smoke was blowing back inside.

"A baby's lungs are so much more sensitive than ours," I said, trying to gently approach the subject of smoking indoors around a newborn infant.

"I know, that's why I never smoke around her. I always come over here and open the window."

She genuinely didn't see that the open window provided almost no benefit, that the room was still completely smoky.

Another one of my girls confided in her grandma that her mom wouldn't let her go on birth control until she was sixteen. At fifteen, she really didn't want to get pregnant, and since her dad had taken his life by sniffing propane, mom was her only parent. Grandma sympathized and told her to pour soda in her vagina to prevent pregnancy, "It worked for me," until mom allowed birth control.

And then there was the grandfather who was raising his grandson in their old run-down farmhouse on the end of a long dirt road. It was just the two of them. He called me out to help him talk to his grandson about growing up. When I arrived, he told his grandson that he was glad to have a woman there to talk to him about sexuality. "Women know what to say. I don't really know what to say." And turning to me he added, "It's hard for kids growing up these days. It's harder for him than it was for me."

"What do you think makes it harder for teens today?" I asked.

"Well, 'cuz like, for him, he's gotta learn so much about *dating* and every-thing. I think it's harder; it's more complicated. When I was his age, I went in the navy. So like we just hired prostitutes and that was it. I mean, ya know, ya need the release. But like for him, he can't do that. It's gonna be a lot harder."

It reminded me of Groucho Marx when he said, "I remember the first time I had sex—I kept the receipt."[17] But Groucho was saying it as a comedi-an, not as a parent-figure.

One of the first things we did when we received funding to reduce teen pregnancy in Springfield was to start a weekly girls group at the local Boys & Girls Club. Our researchers had surveyed the community, and locals always named the club as a great asset to the teens, yet it was usually also named as a problem: not enough supervision, kids smoking outside, and fighting or making out in the stairwells. Also, it was attracting way more boys than girls. Reasons for this were identified: the staff was all male, most of the activities were sports, and girls didn't feel interested, affirmed, welcomed, and/or safe there. Teens with parents who kept a watchful eye frequently weren't allowed to hang out there, while the ones with no discipline were, lead-ing to more division within the community.

So we used part of our grant money to hire a part-time woman to work there, and a colleague and I started a weekly girls' group at the club. Over the years our girls did different things, always "youth led"; the girls would decide what they wanted to do and we would facilitate to the best of our ability.

We opened the meeting each week with "Sharing Time"; girls took turns speaking. We had a "magic wand" that the speaker held and passed when her turn was over. The timekeeper of the day gave the speaker a ten second warn-ing, and then announced when the time was up. When it was one girl's turn to speak, it was everyone else's turn to listen in silence. The girls eagerly imple-mented guidelines: The speaker could speak for the agreed upon amount of time, usually two or three minutes per participant. No talking about anyone else. And no talking outside the group about anything that you heard during sharing time. Nobody ever had to share; everyone always had the right to pass.

Trust grew over time. The hardest part for all the girls was the silent listen-ing, but they gradually, eventually mastered it and it became habit. Girls got to the point where they treasured the sharing time so much that they went through their weeks making mental notes, occasionally even written ones when something special happened, so they'd remember to share it. We be-came like a family, listening and being supportive. After sharing time was over, we had more informal conversations over a snack, and the laughter probably connected us as much as anything. But during sharing time, each girl knew that for three minutes, she'd be listened to. About anything. Any-thing she chose. Without interruption. That was huge. It was so simple, yet so affirming. It was so popular with the first group that we tried it again, and it quickly became a tradition with each new group, every year.

It was amazing to me how much really significant content they each brought out in just three minutes. Stories about dads who aren't there for them; one dad who tried to get the dead grandpa's money, dads who they haven't seen or heard from in years, one dad on the west coast who doesn't call. "He says it's 'cuz he always works but he's off Sundays and he just watches movies."

One girl shared how her parents are both alcoholic and go out drinking every night. She wished they'd stay home sometimes, so she and her mom could hang out. She went on about how lonely it is, how she usually hates it when they come home drunk. "But sometimes they do really funny things, like my mom, one time she got drunk and fell asleep in the sink."

There was a girl who was growing up in a relatively structured, functional home who complained for almost her entire time about her parents' rules. But towards the end she changed her tone, and said, "I mean I know it's 'cause they care." I loved that she got to hear herself go from complaining to that conclusion all on her own, in just three minutes, with no input from anyone.

There were stories about relatives driving each other nuts, stepparents who give two huge bags of Christmas gifts to their biological kids and nothing or one small gift to them. Name-calling, insults at home. A brother who has a kid but never sees it.

But I think what I loved most was the tone; even though their stories tugged at my heartstrings, there was a resilience, a hope, a seriousness, and a sense of connectedness and *wanting* to be connected that is priceless.

After those meetings, I reflect on their young faces, on their often chilling stories, and I wonder about their futures. I can imagine each of these teen girls in my mind's eye in ten years; right now I can so easily imagine how each one of them could go either way. They're all bright enough to become like many of the successful professionals we all know. Or they can become like the adults in my caseload with hardened faces: with five kids and no plans, money or hope. They're at that perfect age for intervention, as they're so open to think, communicate, laugh, connect and question. And I ponder the significance of our attempts at intervention; whether or not they graduate from high school without becoming a parent will be one of the biggest factors determining so much about the rest of their futures. It's a variable that can facilitate or derail all their other dreams. Days when I get to facilitate those teen groups, hear their stories, witness their resilience, and help them find strength from the process of sharing their stories fill me with hope.

When one of the girls shared that she was going to drop out of school, saying, "It's just bullshit; I don't need no diploma. My mom's doin' fine without one," the other girls encouraged her. I let them speak with their own voices, and in the following weeks I genuinely believe that as I quoted her friends' words back to her during our private meetings those words had more clout than any I added on my own. And the connectedness helped her stay in school. As she once said, "I woke up and I was gonna tell my mom I was sick and stay home, but then I remembered group is today, so I just got dressed and went." And she stayed in school and graduated, without a pregnancy.

Other girls came back years later and told me how important it had been to them growing up, to have that time. I was so thankful to have had the opportunity to introduce them to this notion of creating a trusting group of people who meets regularly and shares conversations in ways that affirm each individual.

When I was growing up, it happened in our home: we called it dinner. It happened every night. We didn't have a "talking wand" and we didn't have silent listening. On the contrary, like in many large, close-knit families, several people were usually talking at once; it was lively. But we were all sharing our lives with each other. From that regular check-in we supported each other, we nurtured each other; we all grew. So many kids grow up without that support system in their families today, without family dinner and the nurturing conversations it can inspire; without the sounds of serious family conversations alternating with family laughter and expressions of love forming a solid foundation for the start of their own life journey. It was an honor to me to give that parallel experience to so many of the girls who grew through our groups over the years. Especially to those who had single parents, often working two jobs, wanting so much for their kids to thrive, but unable to be home in those critical after-school and evening hours for that daily nurturing.

Memories. Images. The glimpses I've had of family life in the homes I've visited and the stories I've heard linger in my mind, posing questions nobody seems to answer. Questions about the role of family. And questions about society's responsibility, especially when it comes to sexuality education, and to whose responsibility it is to help these struggling teens through their teen years.

It's so easy to say that sexual health education belongs at home. It does. But it's also important to remember that "home" means different things to different people. Anyone can be a parent; anyone can start a family and become the "head of household." And sometimes, that can raise concerns about what the kid is learning.

Like the dad who was wearing the T shirt that had a 4 by 4 grid, each box showing a silhouette of a naked woman from the waist up, with different shaped breasts, each labeled with a "cute" caption; headlights, knockers, pointers, beach balls, Yo-Yos....as his four-year-old daughter played with her toys. Is he really the best person to teach her about gender roles and sexuality as she grows up?

Or the boy who came into my office right before his road test.

"Are you nervous?" I asked.

"Hell, no, I can drive fine. I been driving since I was eleven."

"What do you mean, how could you have been driving at eleven?" I asked.

"My dad taught me. 'Cause when they'd go to their friends' drinking on the weekends, they'd get too drunk to drive home, so he taught me."

"When you were eleven?"

Seeing my look of confusion and concern, he anticipated my next question and answered it without being asked.

"Hell, Vee, we live out on a dirt road. Waaay out in the boonies. Ain't no cops up there, 'specially on the weekends. I always got us home safe."

That's "home" to him.

And "home" to another girl I worked with was where she learned to do cocaine. When she got busted with it at school and they asked her where she had gotten it, she explained: from her dad. Apparently she had watched all the fun that he and his buddies had at their coke parties, and got curious. He let her have some to try. Just a few times before she got busted and he got put in jail. But still, even though she ended up in a foster home, that is what "home" had been to her.

Some people say that sexuality education should be provided exclusively at home. That puts the entire responsibility on parents. But as a society we have no mechanism to ensure that all parents have accurate information, with heads and hearts that are positioned to see their kids safely through their teen years, and schedules allowing them the shared time needed to give their kids the loving guidance and support that enable teens to thrive. And many of them don't. Depriving kids of vital information simply because their parents don't have it is completely unfair to many young people, especially to those who are most vulnerable.

For the girl who goes home to headlines about her father molesting children and selling drugs, for the girl who comes home from work to find her mother drunk, having sex in the hall with a guy she met in a bar, for the boy whose grandfather longs for the days when teen boys could simply hire prostitutes, for the girl whose mom assesses pregnancy risk by reading crystals, for the boy who comes home to an empty house because his mom works two jobs and only sees him on weekends, do we, as a society, really want sexuality education to be handled exclusively at home? Don't these kids deserve more?

When father doesn't know best, personally, I think the rest of us can pull together to do better.

WHEN BABY'S FIRST WORD IS "BULLSHIT"

"Teenage pregnancy may be the single greatest
threat to America's social fabric."
*–Joycelyn Elders, M.D., former Surgeon
General of the United States of America*[18]

In 2004 there were 422,043 teens that gave birth in America; one of them was Sarah.[19]

When Kyle and Sarah first learned she was pregnant, Kyle's mom was shocked, but agreed that she didn't want her grandchild to be homeless; she let Sarah move in with them when her own mom threw her out. She was particularly relieved when their caseworker told them about my program and offered to bring me over for a home visit. Sarah and Kyle had never even thought about birth control when we met. So we had to start at the beginning. Over the course of our continued visits, they set the goal of not becoming pregnant again, learned about methods, choose one, discussed it with each other and their doctor, had the baby, got the method as planned, started it, and went back for her checkups as needed; regarding my issues, they represented the epitome of success.

Sarah had had a hard life and being a teen mom wasn't going to make it any easier, but she was truly thankful for my support and for Kyle's mom's support. Even after Kyle got sent to jail, his mom allowed her to stay in their home with the baby. Sarah decided to continue her birth control anyway, so that she'd be protected when he got out.

But while Kyle was in jail, she formed an intimate relationship with his brother. That kind of thing probably isn't so uncommon with teens in general: conflicting affection for siblings. Especially when they're living under the same roof.

But throwing a baby into the equation really changes things.

The caseworker and I had both experienced so many teen moms who consider it a "benchmark" in relationships when their baby calls their new boyfriend "dad." But this baby's mother's new boyfriend was dad's brother. What would this child call him if they stayed together, we wondered, "Uncle Dad"?

It takes time to grow up, to learn to develop healthy, mature relationships. I wish Sarah could have really had that time: time to date, time to simply be a teenager. Time to prepare herself for the job of being a parent instead of simply becoming one. This is the theme I see over and over with teen parents: they're unprepared.

That unpreparedness plays out in different ways with different teen parents.

Like with Stacy. The caseworker who referred her said, "She's a very passive seventeen-year-old mother with a much older partner. She quit school and moved in with him during the pregnancy. He refuses to wear condoms, and she told me she believes that birth control causes cancer. Now the baby is three months old; for all I know, she could be pregnant again already. And if she's not, she's certainly at high risk."

I went to Stacy's home, and after a brief, friendly introduction I started asking her some very general questions about how she felt about being a mom and about the prospect of having another child. I wanted to hear her articulate a goal before making any assumptions; maybe she wanted a large family, and maybe the fact that she still hadn't graduated from high school was more of a concern to me than to her. I knew enough to know not to make those assumptions.

"How would you feel about another pregnancy in the near future?" I asked.

"Ugh! That would be the worst! Especially not in the summer," she replied. And nodding towards her infant that she was carrying on her hip she continued, "Last year, she ruined my whole summer!"

Similarly, when Shirley told me she didn't want any more kids, and I asked if her partner agreed, she snapped right back, "Him? Are you kidding? He didn't even want her!" nodding to refer to the infant she was bouncing in her arms.

Both of these young moms spoke openly about these situations in front of the infants they were referring to. Their assumption was clearly that the infants in their arms don't yet understand language, which is true.

But words and the meaning of words are only one aspect of communication. The conversations triggered other concerns for me; the tension in the tone of voice, in their hands, the tone of blame in Stacy's voice, blaming her baby for ruining her summer before she was even born.

It was such a sharp contrast to so many of the conversations I've had with women in my private life as they held their new babies; women who spoke of the gratitude, the miracle of the pregnancy, the birth.

And it was such a sharp contrast to my own life experience. In my earliest memories I can still remember my own mother's loving hands as she held me as a baby. And later, I remember how her firm grip felt when she held my hand as she guided me across the street in the Bronx, teaching me to wait for the light, to cross safely in the crosswalk. That hand that always left me feeling safe and loved. It was the same hand I had recently held as my mother exhaled, and the hospice nurse confirmed that that breath was her last. I was glad I got to return the favor, of letting the touch of our hands leave her feeling loved and safe.

Hands are important. Mothers' and baby's hands communicate a lot; in infancy, the stage is set for that lifelong relationship. Contemplating how tense these new moms' hands were as they held their babies tugged at my heartstrings. While I knew Stacy's baby couldn't understand, literally, "Mom resents me for ruining the summer she was sixteen," and Shirley's baby couldn't understand, "Daddy wished I was never born," the feeling was already there, the stage was already set.

During Mackenzie's pregnancy, we had worked on a reproductive life plan. But she was a tricky kid to work with: a funny combination of strong-willed, determined, skeptical, and angry. And intellectually, she was quite limited and clearly lacked the skills to make and keep a reproductive life plan without help. I hoped I could provide it. Fortunately, she always seemed to like me, or at least not to mind me. Yet the way she spoke about other adult professionals in her life—her probation officer, her DSS caseworker, her teachers and the administrators in her school—made it very clear to me that she generally saw adults as enemies, not as resources. I sensed I'd get nowhere with her if she ever saw me as someone who was trying to tell her what to do or how to live her life, as an authority figure. I needed her to only see me as a resource, as someone on her team.

She didn't have a phone, so I couldn't schedule a home visit, to see the baby, to follow up about the plan. So I simply rang her doorbell a few weeks after her due date.

"Is this an OK time for a visit?" I asked hesitantly as she opened the door.

"Sure," she replied. That was her word, but her tone was flat, detached. And her look matched her tone.

I entered her apartment, and saw her beautiful baby sleeping in a crib in the living room. Tiptoeing over for a somewhat closer look, I whispered, "He's beautiful; congratulations!"

She had already seated herself back on the sofa, facing the TV, watching Jeopardy, and she ignored me.

It felt peculiar to have a new mom not respond to a compliment regarding a new baby. I just stood there for a moment, taking in the scene. On the one hand, I was there with a focus and a goal: I wanted to know whether she still wanted to prevent another pregnancy, and if so, to learn whether she had gotten the shot before discharge, as planned. And if there was a problem, to help her identify and overcome it, to help keep her plan moving forward. But on the other hand, I was there for her, not for me. The body language suggested that she had absolutely no interest in meeting with me.

Yet she had let me in.

I didn't want to be directive in any way against her wishes, but I wanted to make myself available, and to be available at her pace. I knew she knew why I was there, yet she just sat there watching TV. "Perhaps I should leave? She doesn't appear interested," I thought to myself. "Or maybe she's tired, or overwhelmed, or experiencing postpartum depression. Or maybe I interrupted her favorite show and she doesn't want to say that."

Well, I decided, she said I could visit, so I'll give it a try, and I'll let her lead; my gut told me that if I tried to lead a conversation in any direction, she'd resist for the sake of resisting.

So I simply sat at the other end of the couch, and watched TV with her. I don't have a TV; I hadn't watched Jeopardy since I was a kid, lying on the couch, home from school, sick. Daytime television shows are often on in the background when I do home visits. I'm used to that. But usually, they're just providing background noise; nobody is actually watching them. This was unusual.

My mind raced with thoughts. "I have so much work to do! I don't have time to watch TV; if she doesn't want a visit, why didn't she just say so?"

But I just watched with her in silence. There was a digital clock displaying the time right below the screen. Good, I thought. I can watch the time without being obvious, looking at my watch. I made a mental note of the time and said to myself, "I'll give it ten minutes. I'll use that time to decide what to do if she doesn't bring anything up." I was leaning towards one quick question, like simply asking, "Is there anything you want to discuss?" or maybe even a little bolder, a little more directive, like, "Did you get the shot?" but I was afraid that might be too directive. Anyway, I had ten minutes to decide. Plenty of time.

So I just watched Jeopardy with her, and tried to get into it. I learned that a person who is afraid to ride in cars is amaxophobic. I already knew that the fish that leap into the air and glide, that don't flap their pectoral fins are flying fish. I was feeling antsy, but I forced myself to sit still and watch. Stay calm.

When the clock showed that we had sat for four minutes she turned her head for the first time and simply looked at me. I was hopeful, but I kept watching. Then she looked back at the TV. Bummer!

"Hmm," I wondered, "what should I do?" All the things I needed to be doing haunted me. Other visits. My monthly report. Overdue phone calls, emails that needed replies.

I couldn't figure out what she wanted.

I wanted to either have a significant visit or leave.

Alex Trebek wanted a dictionary word with three W's. It's a Native American get-together.

I tried to focus. Three W's? That was hard.

"Powwow."

Of course! I should have guessed.

Half a minute later she looked at me again and said, "I think I wanna go on that shot thing." I was thrilled that she brought it up; that I didn't have to. But sitting right next to her, next to her detached demeanor, I sensed it was important to match her pace: not to overreact, not to reveal my enthusiasm. So I kept watching for a bit and then said softly, "Oh, yeah? How come?" still watching the screen.

" 'Cause I don't want another kid right away."

We continued to speak slowly, softly, with long pauses, but I knew that in fact we were off and running. By the end of the visit she had articulated reasons for not wanting another pregnancy, confirmed that she wanted the shot, and we had scheduled an appointment, transportation, and childcare. I sensed that none of that would have successfully happened if I hadn't waited for her lead.

It's so often like that with "problem" youth. Teens who have been "in the system," those who have had so many mandated services, often get to a point where they feel powerless. So many services that supposedly exist to "serve" high-risk teens don't have a design that puts the teen in the driver's seat; it's often yet another adult telling a teen what to do rather than empowering them. By simply giving them the clear message, "You are in control. You get to decide if we talk, what we talk about; it's for you," they often turn their attitude 180 degrees within minutes. It's always nice to see.

Those 4½ minutes were well invested, I thought as I left. And since I'm not amaxophobic, I drove to my next visit.

As I did, the roads got snowier. But I couldn't cancel. I hadn't seen Terri since her baby was born. She had dropped out of school shortly after learning she was pregnant, and she and her boyfriend had just moved into their own apartment. There was new housing for individuals receiving Supplemental Security Income (SSI), and they had qualified. She had so many learning issues; she could barely read and write. But either her boyfriend or her mom had helped her with the paperwork, and here they were.

Her first apartment.

A new apartment.

Home.

A baby.

A whole new life. I looked forward to seeing how she was adjusting.

But as I raised my knuckles to knock on her door, the note that was taped there stopped me in my tracks, haunting me. In large, hand scrawled, black magic marker letters she had written:

Sign on sixteen-year-old mother's apartment door

I paused before knocking; my yoga teacher had recently ended a class saying, "Now take your practice off your mats." I knew that the inner strength, calm, and focus we had worked on was what I'd need now. Pondering that note, in the time it takes to breathe one long, slow, deep breath, I felt the paradoxical pulls in opposite directions.

On the one hand, she's a new mother with a baby in her first apartment, everything starting clean and new. She's determined to keep it that way. She's willing to be assertive now, to instruct people, to demand that they do their part; if they're entering her home, to keep it clean. A parent protecting a child and a home: it was impressive.

But on the other hand, there was that ever present concern about her limitations. The thought of a person who can only spell one out of four words correctly in the phrase "Take off your shoes" trying to raise a child in today's world was chilling. That's 25%; my heart ached.

It was a Tuesday, around 2 P.M. While all the other sixteen-year-old girls in town were in school furthering their education, Terri was home caring for her daughter. Already light years behind them academically, all the girls who could have correctly spelled "Take off your shoes" were in school, broadening the educational gap I read about between teen moms and adult moms. I knocked, she answered; I went in and took off my shoes, leaving them on the mat she had provided by the doorway.

At the end of the day, driving home, the roads were downright icy. "I should have left early," I thought. Despite how slowly I drove, I completely lost control of my car, and it spun 180 degrees into the oncoming lane. I have no idea why I was so lucky, that nobody was coming from the other direction. I had always thought I'd panic in that situation, but a mysterious, quiet peace came over me as I righted my car and drove home.

Although the teen pregnancy rates have gone down in the U.S., it's frequently the teens in the most challenging situations that are becoming parents. No matter how many times I go into their homes, contemplating the fate of their babies is chilling. And while I don't like to find myself in the oncoming lane of traffic, facing the wrong direction and totally out of control on an icy road, I certainly do appreciate the opportunity to try to have an impact on these teens.

When Sherry told people she was pregnant, the news spread like wildfire, and the panic spread faster. Any 10th grader announcing a pregnancy is a concern, especially when they are as developmentally delayed as Sherry, but people's concerns about her cognitive limitations were exceeded by their concerns about how she'd behave as a mother: Sherry was generally pretty quiet and mellow, but enough adults in her school and community had witnessed her unpredictable violent outbursts that they genuinely feared for the baby's safety.

One prominent professional quickly arranged a private meeting with me.

"Vivian, Sherry's pregnant. You need to make her an appointment to get an abortion. She's completely unqualified to be a mother."

I was a little confused; Sherry had told me she was carrying to term and had expressed absolutely no interest in terminating her pregnancy.

"Did she tell you she wants one?" I asked just to be sure she wasn't giving different people different messages.

"No. She said she's having a baby. She has no idea what she's doing. You've got to get her to have an abortion."

I, too, was deeply concerned about her ability to be a parent, but having already worked for Planned Parenthood for years I knew immediately, with certainty, that it is *never* my right or my job to attempt to influence anyone's decision regarding their pregnancy options. Aside from the fact that doing so would cost me my job, it was against my personal beliefs, so dealing with this man was a no-brainer.

"I don't do that," I simply explained. And I responded to his blank stare by simply elaborating in a calm tone, "Sherry has the right, as any woman has, to make her own choice. And she has made it."

"That's ridiculous!" he snapped back fiercely. "You can't give her this choice; she isn't capable of understanding what it all even means. She just needs someone to give her an appointment card and say, 'Here, your abortion is Tuesday at 1:00. We'll pick you up at noon. You have to do it. You're the only one who can. The school can't, DSS can't, and her family won't. People expect you to: you're Planned Parenthood. Why not? Your supporters would thank you. Your opponents already hate you; they're not going to hate you any more."

I was shocked, but still wanted to remain respectful, so I simply repeated, "We don't do that. If people think we do, they're mistaken."

He added, "But she's so violent. She threw a desk across the classroom in school. This baby is going to be one of those babies that gets thrown through a trailer window and we hear about it on the six o'clock news! It's irresponsible of us to let her carry to term, knowing she's incapable of comprehending the magnitude of what she'd be doing. We must act."

I ended the conversation by saying that my opportunity to act, to influence Sherry's decisions had ended when she became pregnant. He hated it.

Although I had never witnessed her violence first hand, I had witnessed her limitations for years. I had met her when she was in middle school, when a professional referred her for private education with me, to ensure that she understood how pregnancy happens and to establish a relationship with her; to build comfort between us so she'd come to me as a resource when necessary. For quite a while, I was successful.

The first time I met her I had gone over some basic facts about the male and female reproductive systems, and information about how pregnancy happens. She knew about sexual intercourse; "That's what my brother and his girlfriend do." My reply had included the word "private" and she corrected me: "They do it all the time on the bed, and I'm sittin' there watchin' T.V."

So much for private.

She stated she had never done it and didn't want to, and over the years I kept in infrequent but regular contact with her.

But when she started having sex, I worked with her closely; she clearly stated she did not want a pregnancy, and by then she appeared to understand the connections between sex, pregnancy, and childbirth. And when I explained that there are birth control methods that can help reduce the chance of pregnancy she was interested. But she had a lot of trouble with the complexities of making and carrying out a plan to prevent pregnancy. I quickly got her to enlist the help of her mother, but it seemed as though her mother was only a little more skilled than she was at navigating the health care system. I had suggested she talk with her mom about going to her doctor or coming to Planned Parenthood for birth control, and one day her mother literally dropped her off at Planned Parenthood at 4:45 and said, "Go in there and get birth control pills and I'll pick you up at 5:00."

It astonished me that her mom, an adult, wouldn't know that in order to get prescription medicine a person needs an appointment, time, and the ability to fill in the stack of intake forms and health history that Planned Parenthood requires. Sherry could barely write her name, let alone read the important questions her practitioner would need answered, about her family health history and her own. So we used the fifteen minutes to schedule an appointment for another day, and I urged her to bring her mom in to help her with the forms. We also gave her blank forms to take home in case that would be more helpful.

Somehow, we got her on a method, and for several years I monitored her use carefully, frequently checking to see if she remembered that it was to help reduce the chance of pregnancy, and she did. So as everyone else was freaking out about the pregnancy, I was simultaneously celebrating what felt like a major accomplishment. We had gotten her to age sixteen without a pregnancy. Still, I was deeply concerned about her pregnancy, and horrified at the thought of how limited and possibly violent she might be as a mother.

Later in her pregnancy, Sherry dropped out of school, but I kept visiting her at home. When the baby was a few months old I remember asking her, "How's it going for you, being a mom?" She was calm as she replied, "I like it. It's going pretty well. It's like, before I had Rosie, I didn't really like have a life. Now I have a life."

It's funny sometimes, her wisdom. It's so simple: she has a life.

I wish we had more to offer to the Sherry's of the world. Being a parent is one way to have a life, but there are others. Most of the girls who were in Sherry's class were in school at that moment, day by day making progress towards their dreams. Most of them will not become parents while they are in high school. They wouldn't want to; they have dreams, goals, skills to master, books to read, parties to attend, and friendships to nourish. Having a baby would interrupt all that; they wouldn't get to have a life.

For Sherry, I realized, it interrupted almost nothing. She was never going to be a great student and on some level she may have sensed, and maybe accurately, that that whole school thing was leading her nowhere.

A few months later I was parked way across town, sitting in my car getting caught up on writing some notes. I looked up at one point and I noticed Sherry down the block, going up a flimsy old staircase onto the porch of an old house, and entering the front door. She was carrying the baby, wrapped appropriately in blankets to keep out the howling winter winds. She didn't see me, parked a few houses away. I had ascended that same staircase and been in that house fairly recently, visiting another referral: a boy who needed some education about puberty. I had gotten chatting with the boy's grandmother, who was lying in the bed in the living room. She knew it would soon be her deathbed. She had spoken to me frankly of her illness, and of the gratitude she has for each day she has, "Especially when my granddaughter comes over with her baby."

Until I saw Sherry walking in that door, I had no idea that they were part of the same extended family, or that Sherry's baby was the center of this dying woman's joy. And while Sherry must have known that her feeble attempts at being a student were getting her nowhere, she may also have known that she could bring her aging grandmother joy, simply by becoming a mom herself.

I got a bit choked up.

And I thought to myself, Sherry was right. Indeed, now she has a life.

andy came dashing around the corner, ran down the hall, toddling from side to side as toddlers do, and stopped suddenly at Tabatha's side, burying his face in her leg. Then he looked up at me with his enormous, brilliant blue eyes, still holding his face close to his mom's thigh, where he could bury it again in a heartbeat if he needed a little extra security.

I knew from experience that if I give a toddler a little special attention in the beginning of a home visit, there tend to be fewer interruptions afterwards. So I paused slightly, bent my knees so I was closer to eye level, smiled at the boy, and speaking softly I said, "Hi, my name is Vivian. What's your name?"

We stood there in the hallway, right inside the entrance to their apartment. He stared at me as I spoke, but as I looked to him for a reply he buried his face in his mom's leg again. Then he looked up at her, and reaching his arms up, he said, "Mama, mama!" in that tone that babies use, that says, "I only have one word, and it's just the one I need!" She lifted him into her arms and he stared at me again with those beautiful, bulging eyeballs.

"Do you want to tell me your name?" I asked again, softly.

He stared at me for a split second, and buried his face, this time in his mom's chest as she held him.

"His name's Randy," she said. "But he can't say it yet."

"That's OK. It's nice to meet you, Randy," I added in a gentle tone, trying to be comforting. And then I told his mom, "He's beautiful. Those eyes are amazing!"

"Thanks," she said with a tender smile, looking relaxed, as though she appreciated that I was willing to interrupt our conversation briefly as Randy discovered the strangers who had appeared in his apartment. I was with my newest colleague, Sylvia, a thirty-year-old educator who had just joined our team. "Shadowing" home visits is part of her training, and I was glad that Tabatha had agreed to let me bring her along.

As Randy relaxed in his mother's arms, Tabatha and I resumed our conversation. We had been talking about why her request for an IUD had recently been denied by her nurse practitioner.

"She said I had this infection. It keeps coming back. She said I can't get the IUD until it's cleared up. And even then, she said I might not be able to get it. She wants to wait a few months to make sure it doesn't come back again; it keeps coming back."

"Did she give you medicine?"

"Yeah. Well, she gave me a prescription, but I filled it."

"Did she say when to come back?"

"Yeah, she said I should make an appointment two weeks after I finish the medicine. I have three days left on it."

"Shit!" Randy said, seemingly out of nowhere. I almost couldn't believe my ears, but he enunciated the "T" so clearly that it was unmistakable. I felt a bit embarrassed for his mom, but I didn't think it was my position to tell him not to use that word. I paused to allow her the opportunity to address it with him, but she didn't acknowledge it, so I figured I'd mind my own business and get on with the visit. The last thing I wanted to do was call attention to it. So I ignored Randy's word and continued.

"Do you know what the medicine is?"

"Yeah, it's an antibiotic. And I know, I know, it might make the pills not work so good. So we gotta use condoms."

"Have you been using them?" I asked.

"Yeah. We hate 'em, but we use 'em. We gotta." She said.

"I know what you mean, they can be a pain to use, but hey, they sure do help! I have some with me, would you like me to leave you some?"

"Sure, I guess so. I mean, we have some, but it wouldn't hurt to have extras."

I took some condoms out of my pack and gave them to her.

"Thanks," she said, and went into the bedroom and put them in the bedside drawer. I was glad to see that she had an easy-to-reach spot for them and that she was organized enough to put them away immediately; it gave me a little hope. I knew that it was going to be tough for them, having to wait for a long-acting, effective method. She came back into the hallway and I picked up where we had left off.

"So you're on the pill now. Other than the problem about the antibiotic, how's the pill for you?"

"It's OK."

"How are you doing with remembering it every day?"

"Pretty good, but that's the part that scares me. I'm so afraid that I'll forget it and get pregnant; that totally freaks me out. I wish I could get that IUD so I wouldn't have to worry about it. The nurse said I should get the shot, 'cause I told her I was scared I'd forget the pill."

"It's true that you only need the shot every twelve weeks, it's not something you have to remember every day. If you can't get the IUD, is the shot something you want to consider?"

She scrunched up her nose as she replied, "I dunno. I get so scared of needles, I'm just, like, I dunno. I mean, I know, it'd be over so fast, I was thinking maybe I should do it, I dunno."

"Well, it's your choice," I said, and added, "Is there anything else you want to know about the shot?"

"Nah, she gave me this thing about it, I read it. I'm just like scared of the needle part. She showed me the needle. It's not as big as the one I had these other shots with. She said it doesn't hurt as much, so I don't know. I'm thinking about it."

"Did she discuss side effects with you?"

"She said you could quit getting your period. That's tempting. But she also said you could get more bleeding. That'd be a pain."

"It's true; bleeding patterns usually change on the shot. You might find you don't bleed at all, or you might have longer periods or bleeding between periods. We can't say for sure what'll happen to any individual person on the shot, but definitely, unpredictable bleeding is common. About half the women who go on the shot stop having periods after six months."

"That would be awesome."

"Well, think about it. It's highly effective. But it also sounds like you're doing pretty well on the pill. It's really up to you."

"I know. I just really don't wanna get pregnant again right away. That's why I'm tempted." I could understand why she didn't want to get pregnant again right away. We had discussed it at length during my first visit with her. She had just gotten a job at a convenience store within walking distance, she and her boyfriend had just gotten this apartment, she was working on her GED; she was really trying, but life was hard. I knew she just had a few minutes before having to leave for work, and it was a new job, so I figured I'd better wrap up and leave.

"Well, you don't have to decide anything right this minute. I know you have to get to work soon so we'll take off and let you get going. You can think about it all and let me know if I can be helpful. Meanwhile, it sounds like—"

"Bullshit!" interrupted Randy.

Again the clear "T"; the perfect pronunciation.

Again, I paused slightly for mom to address it. Again, she let it go.

I continued, ignoring Randy's vulgarity. "It sounds like you've really done a lot to prevent pregnancy and to take care of your health. I hope you're proud of yourself." I closed the visit quickly, Sylvia thanked Tabatha for letting her join us, and we left. Carefully holding the wobbly handrail on the poorly lit, grimy stairwell we walked back downstairs and outside, back onto Main Street in Greenville, and got in my car.

I drove a few blocks away and parked. I wanted to take a little time to make sure Sylvia was seeing what she needed to see, learning what she needed to learn. She was. We had spent time before the visit stopping at homes of clients I've worked with. I didn't have any other scheduled visits because the two I had scheduled had both cancelled last minute, so before going to Tabatha's we had spent time stopping at various homes of people I know, unannounced. I was devastated each time nobody answered; I wanted it to be an important learning day for Sylvia, I wanted her to see a lot. We had tried eight clients, all within the village, but not a single one was home. But before stopping at each home, I had given Sylvia a brief overview of the client; how long I had been working with them, where they had been when we met, where they were headed with long-term goals, and what my goal was for this visit. At each empty house, I knocked on the door and often peeked in the window part of the door. I had Sylvia look in, too. She saw the homes, the clutter, the dirt, and the obvious lack of organizational systems in the homes.

Until I found a day when nobody was home, I never realized how much training potential there is in viewing empty homes! The buildings spoke volumes that I had never heard, since I'm always so much more focused on the people inside them. But when you look in the window and see a half of a case of boxes of instant macaroni and cheese on the floor next to the pile of dirty clothes, surrounded by kitty litter, gun parts, and some batteries and empty milk jugs, or the kitchen table that would take an hour to clear because there are so many mountains of clutter on it, or the new crib that is partially assembled on the pregnant woman's porch, catching some of the rain through the leaks in the porch roof, with a broken bicycle on top of it, and new boxes of diapers awaiting the new baby, covered with bags of trash; things that are being discarded completely mixed in with important new items, until I saw the chaos without the people in it, I never realized how much the empty homes could teach a new educator about the lives our clients lead.

Sylvia got it. She asked good questions, about how "typical" or "atypical" that visit with Tabatha was. I explained that when it comes to the likelihood of success, Tabatha was a lot more responsible than many of the teen moms I meet. Sylvia listened with concern as I articulated a list of impressive points about this particular case; that Tabatha had made and kept her own medical appointments, had made a plan to get a highly effective IUD, listened carefully to the practitioner's reasons for delaying it, and made an interim plan. She got an effective method, used it, communicated with her practitioner and partner well, read the information her doctor gave her, had an appropriate place to store her pills and condoms, could find them when she needed them, lived within walking distance of Planned Parenthood. She understood that the antibiotics she was taking might impact the effectiveness of her pills. And even more basically, she understood that sex leads to pregnancy and that a person can choose to try to take control of their fertility. And she really was taking action to prevent a pregnancy. But while it was a lot more than many teen moms I've worked with have done, still, her journey wasn't going to be easy, even if she could successfully avoid another pregnancy right away.

Sylvia agreed with all the signs of hope I outlined, and she was also able to completely understand that even if this case was successful, even if Randy didn't have a little baby brother or sister before he went to Head Start or kindergarten or even third grade, a baby who says three words during a visit, two of which are swear words, is going to have a tough time. It was clear that a baby with a simple, two-syllable name who can say, "bullshit" before he can say his own name is probably not being raised in the most child-centered, nurturing home. Sylvia really understood how telling this glimpse into this woman's life and this little boy's life were. About both the importance of the success of preventing the next pregnancy, and the ongoing significance of the fact that this girl had become pregnant before she was fully ready.

Sylvia went on, "When I was in high school, I came to Greenville all the time, 'cause I did gymnastics, and we played with them. I had friends here. It's so weird; I've probably driven down Main Street a hundred times. But I never even noticed that there were apartments above the stores. It's like you don't even see them. And even if I had noticed them from the road, until you go up those stairs and see how gross the whole place is, you wouldn't know. And all the streets we went on today, I've been in so many homes on those same streets, but those rows of big old Victorian homes, driving by they don't look that different, some have been fixed up and maintained so nicely, but when you stop and look, a few of them have been divided into little apartments. All the ones I had gone in, to meet with girls who did gymnastics, they were all really nice. But, I mean, I get it: you have to have money to do gymnastics. These little apartments are all full of people who couldn't afford gymnastics; I never met them. It's weird, it's like they're right there to see, but they're hidden."

"Camouflaged," I said, correcting her. "We can see them, they're not hidden, but we somehow look right at them and don't see them."

She agreed.

I was glad Sylvia had gotten to see it: a worthwhile day after all. I drove her back to the office, where we had left her car. Pulling into the Planned Parenthood driveway, we had to cross through the line of protesters that was marching up and down the street, with their signs claiming that we were baby killers. I was used to them, and although we had warned Sylvia that facing them would become a routine part of life if she accepted the job, I just wished she wouldn't have to see them today. Fortunately, she didn't seem too disturbed by their predictable presence. I was glad Owen wasn't there; he's the only one who regularly shouts at me. Most of the others aren't as threatening.

I dropped her off at her car so we could each go home in our different directions. I didn't have it in me to listen to the news, so I switched the radio to my favorite oldies station and they had just started playing Bruce Springsteen singing The River. I love him. The reception was terrific. I blasted it. I was in heaven: great music after an intense day. The perfect way to unwind, to let go. But as I listened to that voice I love, he sang, "...Then I got Mary pregnant and man that was all she wrote ~ and for my nineteenth birthday I got a union card and a wedding coat ~ We went down to the courthouse and the judge put it all to rest ~ No wedding day smiles no walk down the aisle ~ No flowers no wedding dress..." and I realized, here's this fantastic song, and it's all about a man's dreams that didn't come true, thrown off by an unintended pregnancy when he was a teenager. The beauty of Bruce's voice and of the music touched my heart. But the realization of how real, how tragic, and how totally unnecessary it all was, broke it.

So much for letting go.

"Thirty years ago, we got a lot more calls from pregnant teens and their concerned family members; the numbers have gone down nationally and our calls reflect that," Eileen told me when she heard my stories about the pregnant teens and teen moms I work with. She had been in this work for thirty years, so she saw trends that I couldn't see. "Back then, we'd get a lot of calls from people in a panic when they first learned about the pregnancy. But then the vast majority settled down; families pull together, they make the most of a tough situation. They cope. But there would be those few and far between calls that absolutely tugged at our heartstrings; the teens who totally lacked the basic skills and support systems they'd need. The difference is that now, that's almost all the calls we get. It's fewer in total number, but each one is the highest need one. The girls who can read and write and think; the girls who have a future, have absorbed the prevention messages and one way or another they're protecting themselves. It's the ones who are so desperate that we're missing."

Her words were sobering. I knew she was right; looking at even the bigger trend, in the 1950s it was common for Americans to have their first child as a teen. But now, teen parenting is not the social norm; the vast majority of teens I work with who do become parents are the neediest girls. The pregnant girl with anorexia, the fifteen-year-old who was concerned that if DSS found out her adult boyfriend's identity, the freedom he was finally enjoying after serving time for his three felonies would be short lived. The drug users, the ones who can't read, the one in her ninth month who hadn't even thought about what she was going to name her baby. The ones with no dreams or hopes for their own future; with no serious interests, no skills they're in a process of mastering, no goals. And of course, the ones who are cutting themselves and those that have to go to the emergency room for their hands after they punch the walls.

They are the ones we're not reaching with our prevention messages. Sometimes I have to pinch myself, to contemplate the reality that I'm deliberately working with the neediest teens in our community. Even when it feels like preventing teen pregnancy is an insurmountable task, I need to remember that the vast, overwhelming majority of teens do reach their 20th birthday without having been involved in a pregnancy. That the vast majority of teens do have the skills, goals and support systems necessary to successfully navigate their way through their teen years without a baby in tow. We need a way to replicate the success that the majority enjoys for the underserved minority. Until then, teens like the ones I work with remain at high risk all across our nation.

And their babies are suffering. When I'm visiting the teen parents, I'm focused on them. It's only after I leave; when I'm alone, when I'm driving, or in the evening reflecting back on the day over a quiet glass of wine, that I allow myself to think about these babies, the one who drinks water out of the dog dish, or the one who learns to say "bullshit" before he learns to say his own name. The one whose mother was feeding him orange soda out of a can, oblivious to both the negative impacts of the sugar and the danger of the sharp edge of the can. The baby who appeared to be holding a toy, but it turned out to be a razor. What will happen as they grow up? Who will be there for them?

In today's world, babies born to teen parents often face a tough road ahead right from the start; they are more likely to be born prematurely and at low birth weight. Later, they are more likely to be abused or neglected, more likely to live in poverty, and less likely to receive a high school diploma. And they cost taxpayers a lot more money than babies born to older parents, often needing expensive services later in life; they are more likely to need extra support in school and to end up in foster homes and prisons.[20,21] So even if we discount the quality of life issues, the simple economics of the situation is clear: the benefits of effective prevention efforts are extremely cost effective.

After several years of working with many of the neediest teen moms in my county, I received a letter from my agency's Board of Directors. It was to recognize, congratulate, and thank me for the fact that for the second year in a row our county had zero repeat births among girls age fifteen to seventeen, while the upstate average rate was 18.5%. They attributed that to the work that I was doing in collaboration with Sophie, a worker from one other local program.

While I was thankful for the recognition, the letter concerned me.

"Yes, I've had some successes with the teen moms I've been working with," I told my boss, Eileen. "But the way this letter connects the birthrate to my work makes me a little uneasy. I mean, these girls are tough, and despite my best efforts many of them could end up pregnant. If I accept thanks when it works out, does that mean I'll get the blame when it doesn't? And also, when you look at the numbers, there were over thirty new teen moms in that age group. I only worked with a fraction of them. I mean: I literally never even met the vast majority of these girls. I feel like the Board is giving me credit for something I didn't do."

"Absolutely not," she assured me. "Relax. They're simply acknowledging what you're doing. And look at it this way. How many teen moms do you think you worked with last year?"

"Probably only between five and ten."

"OK, so think about this. Some teen moms have support systems; parents, partners, friends, relatives who can help them set goals and learn what they need to learn to prevent repeat births before they're ready. Look at those five to ten girls you've worked with. Do they have that?"

"Absolutely not!" I insisted without hesitation.

"And that's the point. When we're talking about secondary prevention, we have to focus on the girls who don't have those supports. They're the ones who need that intense one-on-one intervention, all that handholding you and Sophie provide. Whenever you tell me about the referrals you get, it is so clear that you're getting the neediest girls. That's what we hired you to do—to be connected in the community with professionals who reach the neediest girls and refer them to you—and you're doing it."

"The school nurses and caseworkers don't call you every time a teen becomes a parent; most of those teens will make it on their own. They call you when it's the girl who doesn't have those skills and supports, and you and Sophie provide it. Communities that want to bring down their repeat teen birth rates don't need the kind of expensive, intensive services you and Sophie provide for *every* teen parent, just for the highest risk ones. And what makes those programs so easy, in a bizarre way, is that those girls are so easy to identify. It just takes effective networking and educating the professionals who interact with teen moms about how to identify these teens and how to refer them in an affirming way, so they'll take advantage of the support you can offer, and that's exactly what you do."

Looking at it from that perspective, she was right, and I became thankful for the letter. And my grandmother's simple words, "An ounce of prevention is worth a pound of cure," echoed in my mind. When we help a fragile individual prevent a pregnancy, it's a triple win. First, by not having to deal with a pregnancy, birth, and raising a child they're unprepared to handle, that individual and her partner have the time and energy needed to focus on the other challenges they face without the additional challenge and stress of raising a child. Second, for the child; if the potential parents wait until they've resolved some of the other challenges they face before becoming pregnant, that child will have the benefits of a stable home that would have otherwise been lacking. And third, for the community; when a person becomes a parent before they're ready, it brings so many extra costs to society.

With teens in particular, each time we can get one to graduate from high school before becoming a parent, that triple win is underscored even more. Even for the girl who grows up in the worst case scenario; exposed to violence, abuse, neglect, alcoholism, inconsistent care including foster or institutional placements, if we can support that same girl, helping her get from puberty to twenty before her first pregnancy, we've opened countless other doors for her. Even for her, with all her challenges, those vital, irreplaceable developmental years will provide her with the time she needs to prepare for the challenges and joys of parenting, and will benefit her future children in countless ways.

That's something I've always known in my gut, but Amanda and Tiffany were the two girls who shifted that certainty from a quiet feeling in my gut to a new career calling, years before I joined Planned Parenthood.

WAVES OF LAUGHTER

*"There is no such thing as a baby; there is
a baby and someone."*
—Donald Winnicott[22]

You've waited long enough, dear reader, for the story behind that important phone call from Amanda that left me sobbing in Paul's arms; that inspired me to change careers.

When I first met Amanda, she was a girl in a tough spot. Her mom was single, living with her boyfriend on and off, and their drug and unemployment problems left them lacking the energy and focus a girl with special needs demanded, but they were all she had.

I had agreed to serve as a mentor through a volunteer organization. We met regularly from the time she was eight until she was fourteen. By then she had sprouted this gorgeous body of a woman, despite the fact that she could barely read or take care of herself or her things. Puberty doesn't wait. At fourteen she still behaved like the scattered little girl I had met a few years prior; she still enjoyed visiting my home, and eagerly continued our rituals like baking brownies or going for a walk together. She seemed completely unaware of the new messages her changing body now sent out to the world. She was dazzled by the attention a nineteen-year-old guy now paid to her.

I remember the summer day when I first realized I needed help with her; I went to pick her up and she came eagerly bounding out to my car, proudly wearing the "art project" she had just made with her church group. It was a tight fitting sleeveless white T-shirt, on which she had used their fabric paints to write in large letters, "I love Mario" across the chest. But her protruding breasts made it almost impossible to read the words.

She had clearly done the decorating on a flat table, where the lettering, surrounded by the carefully drawn hearts and rainbows probably had a genuine look of innocence. But I was guessing that the church women who had so generously volunteered their time that morning never saw Amanda's shirt on her, where it looked completely different. None of them had broached the subject of how Mario, age nineteen, might feel or react seeing her in that shirt. Nobody had checked in with her to see if she was prepared for how that scene might transpire. She looked sexy. Very sexy. She was fourteen, very naïve, and was about to greet a nineteen-year-old boy wearing this braless, skin-tight invitation to her body with so little self-awareness about the messages the "look" was sending. I was concerned.

Proud of herself, she asked me what I thought. Not being a parent myself, and being a professional craftsperson with almost no contact with teenagers, I had absolutely no prior experience that prepared me. I just decided to wing it.

"I really like the design you did and I'm so glad you went to the church group and participated." I started. That part was easy. She smiled, appreciating the approval.

"How are things going with you and Mario?"

"Great!" she replied, beaming.

Hesitantly, I continued. "But honestly, I have to tell you, I'm concerned. About what might happen when Mario sees it. I remember when I was around your age; I had an older boyfriend, too. Most of the time it was fine. But sometimes I remember it was confusing. When we were alone together. Usually it was no problem, but I can remember sometimes he started kind of playing with the buttons on my shirt. And I remember feeling torn; part of me wanted—" but before I could finish my sentence she chimed right in, eagerly, "Oh, I know what you mean. Paul used to do that all the time. But Mario would never do that; he's a gentleman. He respects me. That's why I stopped calling Paul. That's why I like Mario."

Dealing with her in that shirt jolted me; while her question had prompted a conversation, I could see that she needed serious guidance regarding her sexuality, and I knew that I needed help with what I felt was coming.

It had been so much simpler when our visits had involved helping her memorize the capitals of each state, or figuring out how to disguise a math lesson by trying to double our brownie recipe together. Or going out for pizza and a movie. But now I couldn't look to Boise, Topeka, multiplication tables, or pepperoni for help. Now I was in a new and important place with her, and I felt unprepared.

I had a vague memory of an ad for Planned Parenthood in the local newspaper saying they offered counseling, so I wondered if they could help me. I called, expecting some bureaucratic run-around about insurance I didn't have, and an offer for an appointment in a few weeks. Instead, after a brief "phone tag," they put me through to a woman named Eileen Jackson, the Director of Education. Little did I know that years later that stranger would become my mentor, not to mention my boss. I was immediately struck and impressed with her kindness, patience and skill as she asked me questions and then listened to me struggle and stammer. My voice kept cracking; I was so concerned that I could barely hold it together. She acknowledged the stress in my voice, but presented it back to me as my strength, not as the weakness I was shamefully labeling it in my own mind. She dropped whatever she had been doing, giving me her undivided attention, acting like the concerns of a total stranger on the telephone were the most important thing in the world.

"I can hear the deep concern in your voice as you talk about her. For most of the young teens we see who get pregnant, there's usually *not* an adult in their everyday life who really cares about them enough to make a difficult call like this one, and who's willing and available to support them in the entire process of learning about their bodies, about pregnancy, and about how to prevent pregnancy." She spoke so comfortably about how teens need support from adults who love them: to make healthy decisions, to select effective methods of contraception and use them correctly in a timely fashion. And she affirmed that from everything I was saying, it sounded like I was right on target with my concerns.

She confirmed that local girls Amanda's age do show up pregnant at the clinic, and she recited a list of "risk factors" for teen pregnancy: poor academic achievement, few friends, socially isolated, older partner—Amanda had all but the last one, "the lack of a supportive adult in their everyday life." Eileen identified that it was me, and how much I cared, that might actually be the one variable that made the difference for this one girl. She quoted research on teen pregnancy at a time when I wasn't even aware that teen pregnancy was a "subject" that is researched.

"You're raising a lot of concerns on a lot of levels, and it sounds like it feels overwhelming. It may be more manageable to address each one separately."

Quickly and skillfully she divided my intertwined tale into separate categories: legal questions about teen access to contraception, interpersonal concerns about how to communicate with Amanda and about how to effectively involve her mom, practical concerns about getting her transportation to Planned Parenthood for an education session, logistical concerns about how to pay for the clinic visit that this all might lead to. And with each category she helped me establish a goal and a next step. She made it so easy, so manageable.

We ended the conversation with a fine plan, which I immediately began to implement. To this day, I firmly believe that the intervention plan we designed together on the phone would have been effective, but things were falling apart for Amanda at home, and she called to tell me she was going to move to Kentucky suddenly, to live with her aunt.

My gut told me that if Amanda hadn't started having sex yet, there was a good chance she was going to soon. And that without help, she didn't have the skills necessary to read, learn, and access services to protect herself from pregnancy. I had invested so much time, energy and love in my relationship with her, and I felt like it would all be for nothing if she had a baby while she was still so unprepared.

Contemplating her move, I wondered if there would be an adult there who she felt comfortable with, someone she could trust and confide in, someone who would listen to her, care, and watch over her. Someone who would intervene and get her to a doctor—or at least a drugstore—before it was too late. I didn't know if that person existed in or near her aunt's home; it felt like that person was essential if she was going to succeed. And I knew I wouldn't be able to fill that role from such a distance.

"Write to me!" she had demanded before hanging up. This was before email, when people used to write postcards and letters. And when out-of-state phone calls were expensive.

"I will," I replied.

"Promise?"

"I promise. Will you write back?"

"Of course!"

Her first letter came quickly as promised, giving me her new address. I knew how challenging it was for her simply to write; I had been coaching her for around six years. So I understood the lack of details in the letter and just gave thanks for the address, and the, "I love you" and "I miss you," she had boldly scrawled. I wrote back immediately as promised, and after several weeks she wrote again. I always answered immediately. Her responses were slow in coming, especially at first. But it surprised me a few months later when they came more frequently; I had expected her to get more focused on her friends and everything in her immediate surroundings than an out-of-state former mentor who was old enough to be her mother. Yet her letters kept coming. Each time, I nervously opened them, wondering if there would be mention of a boy. Or a pregnancy. Another letter; neither. Another; neither. Maybe I was wrong! The thought thrilled me.

October came, and I used my letter to remind her how much fun we had had making Halloween costumes together, like the year we were paper flowers and it snowed on us and people answered her "Trick-or-Treat" with big smiles, eyeing the damp colored paper saying, "Just like a real flower, wilting in the snow." I closed by asking her what she was going to be for Halloween.

Her reply came; a much longer letter than usual. Despite her lack of basic writing skills, I was able to piece together most of the story, and phoned her to clarify the rest.

That was the phone call I told you about earlier, the one that left me sobbing in Paul's loving arms.

She had stayed home from school with a bad stomach ache, resting in bed, alone in the house. When it got really bad she had called 911, and shortly before the EMTs arrived, as she sat on the toilet thinking she had the worst gas ever, she gave birth to a little boy, all the while wondering what could possibly be happening that would hurt so much.

She never knew she was pregnant. She had gone to gym in school every day; nobody noticed. Neither did anyone else in the house.

"We knew I was gaining weight, but my aunt is pregnant, and like at night we always sit watching TV and she's always eating chips and stuff and I eat it with her and I figured I was just getting fat from that."

She closed her letter saying, "So I guess for Halloween you could say I'm going to be a new mother."

She didn't Trick-or-Treat that year.

She held her baby as she listened to everyone arguing, in shock, about this new baby and who would raise it. She said she enjoyed holding him, "He's so perfect," but feared letting go, as she knew she'd have to. It explained why her letters had become more frequent, and why they hadn't mentioned a pregnancy.

In the weeks following, she agreed with the adults in her family who decided that it would be best for the baby to be raised by the out-of-state brother. He'd allow her to visit from time to time. She did what she felt was best for her son and herself; she let the brother raise the boy. A painful choice, but she did the best she could with it.

We saw her a few times in the years that followed; brief visits when she returned to see her mom. She even came up once and went fishing again with Paul, like old times. He was the one who pointed out to me that her childhood smile was gone. Even when she smiled. Her face had become hardened; that hardened look I've now come to know so well from my clients.

She was different.

There was no going back.

Several years later, I called Planned Parenthood again. This time it was about Tiffany, another teen I was volunteering with, and Eileen and I planned another intervention.

"I can't believe you think I would do that!" Tiffany had exclaimed, insulted and outraged whenever I tried to bring up the subject of sexuality. Yet the conversations I overheard and the crumpled up notes she left lying around suggested otherwise. She had clearly been raised to believe that having sex is bad, and that admitting it is even worse. I didn't want to judge her, accuse her, put her on the defense, or rush her, but I did want to make sure she knew how to protect herself.

So after encouraging her to wait, I added, "There are so many things I don't know. I don't know if you've ever had sex, when you'll have sex, who you'll have sex with; it's all so private. There's only one thing I know with certainty."

And that had her attention.

"I'm certain that when you do have sex, I won't be in the room with you!"

"That's for shit-sure, Vee!" she replied, giggling.

"So it's my responsibility now, while I am in the room with you, to be sure that you know everything you'll need to know to keep yourself healthy and safe when the time comes. I'm struggling because on the one hand I want to be respectful of your privacy. I don't want to ask you questions that are none of my business, but on the other hand it is my responsibility to make sure you're prepared. So many girls end up pregnant when they didn't mean to, before they're fully ready to become mothers. It can throw their whole futures off track. I believe in you so much. You can have such a bright future ahead of you. I don't want anything to stop you."

"I ain't gonna do nuthin', you don't hafta worry!" she said, defensively.

I said, "Listen, if I'm worrying needlessly, so be it; I'd rather be too careful than not careful enough. You're growing up, and I really care about what happens to you. As you go through your teen years, sexuality is an important subject, whether you have sex or not. It's a big part of life. And it can help to talk to an adult. I really hope I'll be able to make you comfortable, so you'll be able to talk to me if you want. But I also have to say that the most important thing is that you have someone, even if it isn't me. So I have an idea."

"Yeah?"

"I want you to go talk with this woman at Planned Parenthood. Her name is Eileen. You can talk to her about anything you want. Just check her out. Anything you talk to her about is confidential; she's not allowed to tell me anything. When you come out I'm just going to ask you one question. It'll be, 'If there was ever anything you needed to talk about, and for any reason you didn't feel like talking with me about it, would you be able to talk to her?' If you answer 'yes,' great. I'll bring you back to see her any time you want. If you answer 'no,' then my job is to keep looking until I find someone you are comfortable with. OK?"

She agreed.

For about an hour, I sat in the waiting area, unsuccessfully trying to concentrate on the book I was reading, while she spoke with Eileen in an office down the hall. The distance was enough to provide the necessary confidentiality; I couldn't hear a word. But I was close enough so that on about five occasions during the hour long visit, I heard waves of laughter flow down the hall to my chair; it warmed my heart.

Every time I had tried to discuss sexuality with her, it had been challenging and strained. It had never occurred to either of us to have the kind of joyful, laughter filled conversation that we had about so many other things.

This model of starting out by setting a relaxed, lighthearted, affirming, comfortable tone with a teenager before talking about sexuality has served me ever since. This time our intervention worked, and this second girl, Tiffany, a teen with as many "issues" as the first, ended up graduating from high school without a pregnancy. I stood stunned at her high school graduation when her mom came with a new boyfriend and introduced us saying, "This is Vivian, the woman who raised my daughter." Her daughter was the first one in generations to get a high school diploma. Her mom, older sister, and just about every female in her circle had a baby during high school.

While the other issues in her life were not all solved by simply getting a diploma without a pregnancy, and while I knew that her life would still be a struggle on many levels, the contrast of the outcomes in these two girls lives were mind-boggling to me. Their stories were so different, yet with all the combined problems their young lives faced—learning difficulties, domestic violence, substance abuse, lack of friends, frequent homelessness—I believed that no one achievement would have a more long lasting impact on their entire life journey than graduating from high school without becoming a parent.

It was this experience, of having been personally, directly involved in two attempts at intervening with teens regarding pregnancy prevention—one failed and one successful—that made me realize my own potential for making a world of difference in the lives of young people by addressing this one issue. It motivated me to learn more about Planned Parenthood and to want to join the organization and work directly with Eileen as my mentor.

Fifteen years later, I know that I have become that voice on the phone or that comforting face during an important visit like Eileen was for me. On so many occasions, I have been the one to introduce the roar of laughter that set the stage for comfortable learning about these vital life issues. On so many others, I have been the one to help a parent untangle what felt like an infinite web of intertwined stories to come up with a clear and specific plan to actually help the teen who was driving them to despair. And with some, either I wasn't there or I was there but my efforts failed, leaving an infant to grow up in one of these fragile households with a parent who wasn't ready for the enormity of the task of parenting. And for fifteen years, every experience I've had of working with teens—both the successes and the failures—has underscored the importance of successfully intervening regarding this one variable.

A professor at a nearby state university invited Eileen to her Adolescent Psychology class when they were studying adolescent pregnancy. Most of the students at the university are from the greater New York City area which is only a four-hour car ride away, but light years away culturally from our rural area. Most of them went to high school in New York City or its surrounding areas of Long Island and suburban Westchester County.

Eileen started with an activity in which she placed the names of various countries on large cards and had the students try to line them up in the order of teen pregnancy and birth rates. Some knew that the U.S. has the highest rates in the industrialized world; many did not know that our teen birth rate was almost ten times higher than Switzerland's, or that it was more than triple those of Japan, the Netherlands, Italy, France, and Greece.[23] And that the sexual activity of U.S. teens isn't that different, but their contraceptive use is.[24]

Then, after a little discussion, she divided them into small groups and instructed them: "Imagine that you are given unlimited funding to reduce teen pregnancy in America today. How would you spend the money? Put your heads together; brainstorm, discuss it, and list your ideas on newsprint. In the end we'll compare."

She had explained to me her two reasons for doing this.

First, it would show them that even with money, it's not simple. Usually groups quickly identify free condoms and easy access to hormonal contraception, but then they have to look at the question, "Is that all?" and they realize that that alone won't do it. They have to figure out how to empower teens to identify that they're going to have sex before it happens, to motivate them to want to prevent early parenting; they have to look at the complex processes involved in trying to influence these private decisions through public policy. Even with unlimited funds, they quickly realize, it's a daunting task.

Secondly, they're young, they're fresh. Since being a teen was so much more recent for them than it was for us, they may understand today's teens in ways that we don't; maybe they'll come up with some good ideas that we can use!

When they finished, free condoms and birth control came quickly towards the top of each group's list, as expected. Some also had items like free transportation to clinics, PSAs about teen pregnancy, and some had considered youth development activities; more things for teens to do after school, like music, drama, arts, and sports programs.

On the last group's list there was an item that said, "Have an adult in schools to help teens." Eileen asked the group to elaborate and they all turned to the one girl who had suggested it.

"In my high school there was this teen pregnancy prevention thing and there was this lady who came to school once a week. In the beginning, she just went into each class and explained that it's important to graduate before you get pregnant and that kids could talk to her and that it's private. It was all just really positive. I didn't really know her; I never needed to 'cause I talked with my mom. But a lot of kids went to her. It was no big deal and nobody would know your business. I mean everyone knew she could help you get birth control, but kids talked to her about a lot of stuff. She was just really friendly and easy to talk to."

"That sounds interesting," Eileen replied. "What do the rest of you think of that idea?"

"We all thought that would help a lot," replied one of the students in her group. "That's why we put it on our list."

"And what do the rest of you think," Eileen asked, looking to the other groups. Simultaneous replies came from all around the room.

"That's a great idea."

"That would make a huge difference."

"I wish we had had that when I was in high school!"

"Me, too!"

It seemed unanimous.

"Did any of you have someone like that in your high school?" Eileen asked.

None but the one girl had, and nobody else in the other groups had even thought of it.

The lone girl who had suggested it was shocked. "I can't believe you guys didn't have that!" she exclaimed. "I didn't think it was anything special, I mean, in our school. It just seemed so normal. I mean, let's face it: a lot of teens don't have someone at home to talk to. That's the most obvious thing! I mean, where did kids go in your school?" she asked the other students.

Some mentioned their local Planned Parenthood, some said moms or friends or friends' moms, but most, with shrugs, agreed that it was a huge unmet need.

Eileen continued, "That sounds like a unique program you had in your high school." Thinking it must have been some expensive, progressive, private school, she added, "Do you mind if I ask where you went to school?"

"Oh, I just grew up an hour from here in this little town called Springfield." None of the other students had heard of Springfield.

"Springfield! Are you talking about Vivian?" Eileen asked.

"Oh my God," the girl replied, stunned. "You know Vee?"

"Know her? I trained her! I'm her boss! That's part of our local program."

There it was: an entire university class brainstorming how to effectively reduce adolescent pregnancy, with students from such varied high school districts, including both impoverished and very wealthy neighborhoods, and yet not a single one had had a friendly, trusted adult in their school or community that teens could just go to, to learn to manage their fertility within the context of their unfolding futures.

"Why isn't that in every school?" they wondered.

So did we.

I still don't get why. Why are we, as a society, not training adults all throughout this country to deal effectively with teens about something this important? Most communities don't have adult professionals who are trained in that role. The teens have the needs and the interest; it's the adults that are hesitant.

Why? Do people not perceive it to be a problem? Do people hearing my stories think it's only a problem in rural America, in little "hick towns" full of "hillbillies"? It's not. Many urban areas have even higher teen pregnancy rates. Areas of New York City have rates that are double and triple those in the areas I serve, and the U.S. average is around double that of our area.

Is it a question of cost? Do we not have it because it's too expensive? I don't think so. The money is there; it's being spent, but it's being wasted: between 1996 and 2010, congress funneled a total of over one and a half billion taxpayer dollars into abstinence-only-until-marriage programs[25] (yes, that's billion, not million). In order to get the money, local programs had to comply with the federal government's criteria for the programs.[26] Like every Planned Parenthood educator I've ever met, I am all in favor of teaching about abstinence and supporting it by teaching things like self-awareness, decision making and refusal skills. But while sexuality education needs to start there, it can't end there. If it does, it isn't helpful.

A former colleague phoned me; she was baffled. She had gotten a call inviting her to apply for a new job. The 25% pay increase was tempting with her son about to start college.

"But Vee, as she explained the job, it got a little weird. She said I'd have to tell kids that sex is only OK between a married man and woman. She read me this thing from the federal regulations; it said the program has to teach that, 'A mutually faithful monogamous relationship in the context of marriage is the expected standard of sexual activity.'[27] So I'm thinking: that's weird. I mean, single parents are raising a lot of the kids in school; what message is that giving them about their parents? And what message is it giving about same-sex relationships? And then she told me that I'd have to agree to never talk about birth control methods, except to say their failure rates, to stress that they don't always work. Even to parents, even in private. If I so much as gave someone a card or brochure or a website, or told them where to look in the phone book, I'd be misusing federal funds. I've never heard of federal money being paid specifically to withhold accurate information! So I asked her, 'Is this for real? Who does that? Who would go to parents and teens that want accurate information and withhold it?' And she said, 'That's the problem, that's why I'm calling you.' Vee, they advertised the position in the newspaper and every single candidate who came in for an interview just talked on and on about their own religion, mostly about their personal relationship with Jesus. They didn't even realize you don't talk like that in a public school, where there are kids from diverse backgrounds. Those were the only people who expressed interest in the job. That's why she called me, inviting me to apply; she knows me and she remembered that my programs were really good. But Vee, is this for real?"

It was. It was what had been frustrating to all of us at Planned Parenthood for so long. The money that could be spent on effective programs was being spent instead on ineffective and harmful programs. It was painful to see the waste in the face of such need.

> **"ABSTINENCE-ONLY POLICIES VIOLATE THE HUMAN RIGHTS OF ADOLESCENTS BECAUSE THEY WITHHOLD POTENTIALLY LIFE-SAVING INFORMATION ON HIV AND OTHER SEXUALLY TRANSMITTED INFECTIONS."**
> *–Excerpt from review of literature on medical accuracy, program effectiveness, and ethical concerns related to abstinence-only policies for adolescent sexuality education, published in 2007*

"I ain't never gonna have sex again," Sabrina had said with confidence, within five minutes of meeting me.

"It was the stupidest thing I ever done; I ain't never doin' it again."

She took a deep drag from her cigarette and blew the smoke out of the side of her mouth, considerate not to blow it in my direction before continuing.

"I'm the type that learns from makin' a mistake. I ain't gonna make the same mistake twice!"

At sixteen, in her fourth month of pregnancy, Sabrina was single. Socially a loner, she was confident she wouldn't have another boyfriend or have sex again for years, if ever.

Taylor, her DSS caseworker, had her doubts. It was those doubts that had inspired Taylor to refer Sabrina to me for education about how to successfully prevent a second pregnancy right away. I was glad Taylor had given me the referral so early in the pregnancy.

Sabrina didn't want to think about birth control, and I didn't blame her. Her boyfriend had dumped her several weeks ago; she was single, pregnant, and uninterested in sex. She had bigger things on her mind. She was preparing to become a mom. In fact, birth control was probably the last thing she was interested in thinking about, with the possible exception of tobacco cessation during pregnancy.

But she had agreed to meet with me. She agreed to a lot of services to please Taylor; that was a major priority for Sabrina. She knew Taylor was there to ensure that the baby was safe. And she probably understood that there were a lot of things that Taylor was concerned about, that she was monitoring, that would determine whether Sabrina got to keep her baby or whether it got taken away and placed in a foster home.

The razor blade Sabrina had taken to her wrists numerous times before becoming pregnant was one. Another was the weight she had lost early in the pregnancy, during critical fetal development. Another was the physical safety of the home, and Sabrina was really making an effort; according to Taylor, the smoky air I smelled represented a huge improvement to the indoor air quality now that the litter box was being cleaned regularly.

It turned out that the weight she had lost during her first trimester was deliberate; when she first learned she was pregnant, she had starved herself, thinking that that would help ensure a smaller baby and therefore an easier delivery. It wasn't until she told her dad she was pregnant and the doctor noted the weight loss that they asked her mental health worker to address it. That's who had figured out what was happening; she referred Sabrina to a nutritionist who explained the importance of nutrition during the first trimester and set the record straight about health risks associated with low birth weight babies. Sabrina's eating habits immediately improved and her weight came back, but it left a lot of people with their fingers crossed, hoping that it hadn't caused any irreversible damage.

I had been warned during my training not to use the phrase, "low birth-weight baby" assuming pregnant women will be concerned: many women hear that term and figure low weight is smaller, and that a smaller baby will make labor easier; they think it's something to strive for, not prevent. But Sabrina was the first real person I actually saw who had had that misconception, and who had acted on it.

Sabrina was trying; she really was. She was going to her scheduled mental health visits and meeting as assigned with her home tutor. She cooked with the nutritionist from Cornell's home education program who also taught her about safe food handling and budgeting to use limited food dollars wisely.

I met with Sabrina in her home several times during the pregnancy and after her baby was born. She came up with a plan that she was OK with and that also pleased Taylor; she would use abstinence as her main method and go on birth control pills as a backup. I easily accepted both her ambivalence and her plan. And shortly after the baby was born, I closed her case. It made sense: I really believed she was abstaining, she had the pills and didn't mind taking them, she lived walking distance from the clinic, she wasn't very interested in continuing to meet with me, and she and Taylor both knew they could call me if they felt that either the abstinence or the use of pills needed to be reexamined.

But I reflected on her a lot, on this sixteen-year-old mother in a little town in America.

I reflected on the service providers I had run into during my own visits to her home, and the others she had told me about. From prenatal and infant care to home tutors during pregnancy and her mental health worker, each service provider offered something that would benefit the girl and the infant. I knew many of them; I knew many of the programs they represented. All of the programs, without exception, could show hard data to demonstrate that the money spent on the service provider actually represented a savings to society: it costs less to provide *all* those services combined than it would cost to keep the baby in a foster home. And it costs less for any one of those services than it would cost to pick up the pieces if the service wasn't there. From a purely economic perspective, each one of these services to such a needy sixteen-year-old mother is clearly, measurably, cost effective.

But what isn't cost effective is having this sixteen-year-old girl pregnant in the first place.

Any time we try to pick up the pieces, to support struggling teens after they become parents instead of before they're pregnant, it's so much harder, and more expensive. Not to mention heartbreaking. Sophie, a professional I know who works with teen parents summed it up well: "My program is supposed to show outcomes; that I help these young moms get jobs. I'm all for that. When I work with one of these girls, I'm supposed to go to her house and enroll her in a job training program, and explain that she can make $25 an hour if she learns to operate a bulldozer…but I get there and she doesn't have enough diapers to make it through the afternoon and she has no cash or transportation to get to the store. And even if I could get her to agree to enroll in the program, there's no way for her to get to the class every day; she has no ride and nobody to watch her kid. I mean, I'm supposed to show outcomes?"

When I think about Sabrina and add up all the costs that society pays for all these special programs and service workers to try to help her and her baby get life off to a decent start, the numbers of dollars are staggering. We pay these costs, you and me: taxpayers. I'm not complaining about them. With Sabrina pregnant, I'm honored to pay my share of the cost. I want Sabrina's baby to have the best start possible. What bothers me is not that we provide those services when they're needed. What bothers me is the fact that they're needed.

Sabrina never wanted to be pregnant. That pregnancy could have been prevented.

It's not her fault that her mom was dead or that her dad who was struggling to raise her hadn't really talked frankly with her about her sexuality or about birth control when she suddenly became involved with a boy. And it wasn't her fault that her school or community hadn't provided her with an adult to talk with about these issues before she became pregnant.

As I drove home from my last visit with her I reflected back to the meetings I had had in her school three years prior. The school nurse, emotionally exhausted from being the first one girls went to in tears when they were concerned that they might be pregnant, had tried hard to get permission for me to meet with students in her school, for preventive education and support like I offered in Springfield. Productive meetings with administrators left us all feeling hopeful that the services would be welcomed. Everything was moving forward until one woman on the school board became vocal. She didn't want Planned Parenthood to have any presence in the school. She believed that teaching high school students about effective contraceptive methods was the same as "promoting" sinful, premarital sex. I met with her, and explained that according to the Youth Risk Behavior Survey, conducted by the CDC, almost half the high school students in our county have had intercourse.

"We believe that their health is important, too, and we don't want to abandon them or their health needs."

Despite hard evidence that abstinence-only education is ineffective, she was a strong proponent of it. She spearheaded an effort to keep us out of the school.

It worked.

I never met with students in her school.

So I never met with Sabrina.

Not until she was pregnant, and being tutored at home. So I never had the opportunity to teach her about protecting herself from pregnancy until it was time to learn about postpartum contraceptive planning. And even then, only at home.

I think about the consequences to Sabrina and her baby and their community from her having become pregnant long before she was ready to be a parent, long before she could take care of herself. And it hurts. I wish that I, or someone, could have been there for her sooner. The way I had been there for so many girls in Springfield, for years. Girls with as many "risk factors," girls who struggled as much as Sabrina. I had worked with so many of them, week after week, for years, and I had successfully helped many graduate without a pregnancy. But not Sabrina.

I reflect back on those meetings with her school officials, long before a sperm cell reached Sabrina's egg cell. They generally supported the nurse's request. But they're also busy people. In a way, I can't blame them for caving in to the angry phone calls that woman's phone tree had set in motion, demanding that Planned Parenthood not be allowed in the school. As administrators, they're responsible to the citizens of their community.

But studies routinely show that the overwhelming majority of parents want accurate information about both abstinence and contraception available in high schools.[28] Over and over in Springfield, I hear parents tell me how thankful they are that I was there for them and for the teens they love and nurture. Yet the parents who support our work, the parents who see it as vital, aren't focusing on this when it isn't an issue for them. They may have never even heard about the nurse's request to have me in the school, about the meetings with the officials, about the angry school board member.

Teen sexuality is a complicated topic, and it is one that many adults don't even like to think about. Preventing teen pregnancy and STDs is a tough job. But it can be done. They do it in Europe; they do it better than us in every country in the industrialized world. I've studied the models, I know what works; lots of people do. But in this country, if somebody like me tries to address it in schools, the people who are opposed use their well organized tactics to stop it.

I often wonder what would happen if the parents and community members who want these issues addressed effectively in schools became as vocal as those who don't. Every time another study comes out that demonstrates that comprehensive sexuality education is effective, and every time new data is released that shows the teen pregnancy rates in communities, I wonder what would happen if school administrators' phones rang with parents quoting the study and asking, "What are you doing about that?" My guess is that more schools would offer services like the ones I provide if they believed that parents wanted it.

Some people are concerned that this kind of intervention is intrusive into family life. But when parents who grew up with silence around the subject of reproductive life planning are introduced to caring ways to support their teen, I almost never see anything but gratitude. Extreme gratitude. Like what Tammy's mom expressed the day we met.

She asked lots of questions about the work I do in the Springfield High School, and after I explained all the parameters and policies she said, with an incredulous tone, "That's fantastic! And the school knows you do this? I mean, this is all on the up and up; they let you?"

"Oh, yes; they don't know the private details of what I talk about with anyone, but they know I only do it with parental consent, and they know the full range of our services."

"That is so fantastic! Honestly, I've thought about this stuff. I mean, Tammy's only in eighth grade, but I think about her going into high school, and it's kinda scary. I went to that school; they didn't have anything like this back then. And I've thought back on that so much. It's like you said: the decisions teens make about sex are some of the most important decisions they make about anything. I mean, when I went to school, I am not kidding, three of my friends had babies while we were there. And they all dropped out. Honestly, when I look at how hard their lives are, so much of it stems back to that. And I've often thought: isn't school supposed to prepare you for life? I mean, isn't that why we have school? And I've always thought how odd it is that the whole time we were there, nobody ever said anything about it. I mean, girls were getting pregnant, and it was just like...," and after a pause she shrugged her shoulders and said, casually, "Oh well," mimicking an administrator who was suddenly abandoning a former student, now another teen mom who dropped out. "A few of them went back and finished school later, most of them just dropped out, but I just can't understand: how could it be that nobody ever talked about it. When, really, nothing mattered more. Wow, things have changed. I mean I really hope Tammy will talk to me about this stuff if she needs to talk to someone, but I'm so glad she'll have you, if she ever feels she can't come to me. And not just Tammy: all her friends, and all the other kids. I'm so glad that the school is finally addressing this."

I was glad, too. Other parents haven't started out being as supportive as Tammy's mom, but once they learn the details, gratitude prevails. Moms like Ray Larson's mom.

"Hi, my name is Vivian. May I please speak with Mrs. Larson?"

"Speaking," the voice replied.

"Oh, hi, you don't know me, but I met your daughter Ray in the Springfield High School today and she gave me your number. I'm from ABC Springfield; have you heard of it?"

"Hmm, I don't think so. I don't remember Ray saying anything about this."

"Oh no, she wouldn't have; I just met her today and told her about it. I'd like to talk with you because Ray expressed an interest in meeting with me. I always like to involve parents when I can, plus I need parental permission to meet with students in school. Do you have a few minutes right now so I could tell you about the project, and about my role in it, or could I make an appointment to talk with you some other time?"

"Now is fine, what's this about?" She sounded a little concerned, or maybe just confused.

"The ABC stands for A Better Community. ABC Springfield is a community based teen pregnancy prevention program here in Springfield. It's a collaborative effort involving a number of local youth-serving agencies that are trying to work together to ensure that all our teens set goals for their futures and that they postpone pregnancy until they're fully ready to become parents. One of the partners is the school district and one is our local Planned Parenthood. I'm an educator there. The goals—"

"Oh my goodness!" she interrupted, gasping. "Is there a problem with Ray?"

"No, not at all. This project is totally about prevention. We got the grant here in Springfield because we had such a high rate of teen pregnancy; the health department funds it. The idea—"

"Is she at risk? Did something happen in school?" she interrupted again.

"No. Please, let me assure you, everything is fine; Ray didn't do anything involving any trouble in school," I added in a calm tone.

"Oh, thank goodness! Ray is a good girl. We've always raised her to be respectable! I can't even imagine her being involved in something like this. I mean I know she has a boyfriend, but we are very clear with her about our expectations. We expect her to be respectable!"

"I'm so glad to hear that. And I have to admit, even though I've only met your daughter once, today, I'm not surprised to hear that from you; she seems like a lovely person. And I'm glad to hear that you're clear with her about your values and expectations. We know that teens do much better if they have families that talk about these issues. It's so important."

"Oh, absolutely; we're very clear with her about our expectations. We always have been," she added defensively. She clearly sounded like a professional, and like a parent who never gets calls regarding problems or concerns about their kid. And it reminded me; calling a parent when there isn't a problem is something parents don't expect. I could relate to her concern.

"So anyway," I continued, "The goals of the project are set by the health department. We got the grant to collaborate with the school and other local agencies to try to reach the goals. There's a lot we are already doing in the community; did you, by any chance, see our display at the school's open house last month?"

"No, I was there, but I don't remember seeing anything about it."

"Oh, I was there that night. Our display was in the cafeteria with the other community groups. We're coordinating with a lot of agencies in the community to try to expand youth development opportunities; most of our programs involve working with groups of youth, but part of the project involves me working with individuals. I met so many parents that night and spread the word so much about our work."

"Oh, I'm sorry I missed it."

"That's OK, I was just asking because we had a whole display, and if you had seen it, it would help make sense; we had pictures and information about the projects we do, and explanations about why we do it. You sound concerned that I'm calling, like it indicates a problem. I can see where it would feel like that if you hadn't heard about the project already. But I hope you'll feel differently if I just explain a little more about the project, OK?"

"OK."

"OK, thanks. So, the goals that the health department sets are very important and very specific. One of them is to increase the number of teens who abstain from sexual activity: to promote abstinence. Another is to promote timely access to effective contraception among teens that do become sexually active. Other goals include promoting family communication about these important issues, reducing sexually transmitted diseases, and increasing community awareness of the issue of teen pregnancy. I mean, some people aren't aware of the importance of looking at the issue of teen pregnancy prevention beyond the parts about sexual health; it's really so much more. It's about creating a community that enables teens to feel connected, and to set goals for their futures and reach them. I'd be glad to tell you as much or as little as you want to know about what we're doing, but I don't want to talk your ear off. I mainly phoned today to talk about the services I could offer to Ray, and to find out if it's something you support."

"What does any of this have to do with Ray?"

"Maybe nothing, maybe something; I don't know. I just met her today. She was having lunch with a friend who forgot she had an appointment to talk with me. So when she remembered, she brought Ray to my office. And I explained to her that I can do that once or twice but if she wants to do it more regularly I'd need parental consent, so she gave me your number so I could explain the whole thing to you."

"Hmmm."

"The idea behind meeting with students one-on-one or in small groups is that these are important issues and they are also private issues. By offering students accurate information and encouraging them to set and reach personal goals, we hope to really make a difference in bringing the teen pregnancy rate down. I meet with students and let them set the agenda; we can discuss anything related to setting life goals and postponing parenting until they're fully ready."

"But we've always told Ray to be respectable!"

"Good for you. Respect is so important."

"Absolutely!" she replied. I wanted her to elaborate; while I agree that respect is a vital component of healthy relationships, I'm also aware that the word can imply different things to different people. I wanted to know what it meant to her.

"And when it comes to sexuality, may I ask what you mean by behaving respectfully?"

"I mean, we've taught her to respect herself and her boyfriend. Both."

"Well, that's great. Really, as a sexual health educator, it's my job to make sure people I educate have accurate information. But with teens, it's so important for parents to talk with them about values."

"Yes! Always! We always tell her to behave respectfully."

"And when you are talking about within the context of an intimate relationship between teens, do you have a clear sense of the role of that respect relative to sexual activity?" I asked.

"What do you mean?"

"I mean, within your family, does the term 'self respect' imply specific behavior, like abstinence?"

Here she was a little hesitant. After a slight pause she added, "Well, um, yes, I guess so."

"Well, I certainly agree that there are many important reasons for teens to abstain from sexual activity; it's the only way they can be certain not to be involved in a pregnancy or an STD, not to mention a broken heart. It takes a lot of emotional maturity to deal with the consequences of intense relationships. But I also believe that if and when they decide to become sexually active it isn't necessarily a lack of respect; I believe some young people respect themselves and their partners and do have sex. But they're so young; even if they have respect for themselves and their partners, if they get into intimate sexual relationships there's so much they need to know, so they don't throw their futures off track. My role is to be available to help them figure out how to protect themselves and their partners."

"But why would you meet with Ray? Is she at risk?" she asked, still sounding very concerned, as Ray had said she would.

"Honestly, there's no way I can know that right now, knowing so little about her. That's not why I'm calling. I mean, granted, there are risk factors, red flags that we watch for that place some teens at higher risk than others. Based on what you've told me, it doesn't sound like she has them. But we don't like to look at it simply from the perspective of labeling certain teens 'at risk' and others 'not at risk'. We believe that since all young people are growing up, over time, at some point in life everyone is at some risk. Everyone needs accurate information. We're trying to remove that stigma: to normalize the need for accurate information. We want to be available to as many teens and families as we can be, whether it's for a single contact or ongoing support."

"I see," she said, still sounding concerned, but interested, and opening the door to let me continue.

"The agreement we have with the school is that I can meet in private with any students, with a few conditions. First, it's voluntary, so I only meet with students if they want to meet with me, and only during their study halls or lunch periods. I don't take students out of any classes, even electives. Only free periods. And since I work in the school but I don't work for the school, we get parental consent. So I'm wondering if you'd be willing to sign the consent form, to allow me to meet with her in school."

"Well, yes, I suppose so, as long as you'd promise to notify me immediately if she has sex."

"I'm glad you brought that up; that's a really important point. Actually, I couldn't do that. Here's the thing. We always encourage teens to discuss these issues with their parents, but the bottom line is that it is the teen, and not me, that sets the pace in that regard. You can choose whether or not to give me permission to meet with your daughter, but I want to be very careful not to misrepresent what I would or wouldn't do, and these details are very important. Teens do come to me when they've had sex. When that happens, I take what we call a two-pronged approach. One thing I do is I discuss family involvement. The other thing I do is I ask them if they want to get pregnant, and if they don't, I encourage them to access effective contraceptive methods quickly. Teens are allowed to access those medical services with or without a parent; we encourage parental involvement, but we don't require it."

"Oh, heavens, I'd certainly allow her to get birth control if she had sex, but I just mean I'd want to know about it."

"I'm so glad to hear that. For whatever it's worth, there's a good chance that won't even become an issue while she's in high school; the latest studies show that less than half of all high school students have had sex,[29] and students from homes where their parents talk about their values and expectations the way you do are less likely to engage in sexual activity at a young age. But still, if or when she does have sex, if it's before she's fully ready to be a mom herself, I'm glad to hear that you'd encourage her to protect herself with an effective method."

"Oh, definitely."

"And as far as my role is concerned, when parents have given me a clear sense of where they stand on these issues the way you have, it makes it easier for me to encourage their teens to bring it up at home. But I need to be clear: if you allow me to talk with Ray in school, if she ever tells me she's having sex, I'd encourage her to talk to you, but if she refused—and some teens do— I wouldn't delay helping her access medical services and I wouldn't abandon her. My guess, from everything you've told me, is that if she did tell me that, she'd have already told you, or she'd agree to immediately. But I need to stress that that would be her choice. If that happened, and she told me she didn't want to discuss it with you, if you'd want me to refuse to make her a medical appointment or if you'd want me to stop meeting with her, then please don't sign that form now."

"Hmmm. I'll have to think about that."

"Yes, please do. Take your time; I know this is a lot to take in all at once. I mean: this is your daughter! I'm not expecting an answer right away. It's really important that we're in agreement on that from the start, as that's an important part of our intervention. We know that there are teens who are comfortable going to their parents, and that's great. But if teens come to me first and they want my help accessing these important services, as part of my job, I can't refuse them or make it conditional on parental notification. I can't abandon them at that important time. New York State used to require parental permission for reproductive health, but they stopped. The State now allows minors to access certain services without parental involvement. They changed the laws; they reduced barriers for the teens."

"Actually, as I think about it and listen to you, this makes sense. I mean I really hope she will wait. And I certainly hope that if she doesn't, she'll come to me. But no, no, I would never want her to put herself at risk just because she didn't feel she could come to me. Actually, that sounds really good; I'm glad she'd have someone who could help her."

"I'm glad to hear you say that. And if that did happen, I'd be there for her with accurate information. And I'd encourage her to go to you. So many teens turn to their friends, even when their parents want them to have accurate information and to protect themselves. And it is amazing how much misinformation is still out there. But like I said, think about it; take your time."

"Actually, no, I don't need to. I mean: I really hope she'd come to me, but if she couldn't, I wouldn't want you or anyone to abandon her. Yeah, I'll sign that consent. I'm really glad you called."

Before our conversation, if Mrs. Larson had been asked, "Should schools provide assistance to teens that want help accessing effective contraception without notifying parents?" she'd have probably answered, "No." But when given the opportunity to have her own daughter talk to a professional in private, putting sexuality in the context of pregnancy prevention and reaching life goals, when faced with the question, "Should the professional abandon your teen and/or withhold medical services if your teen refuses to talk to you about it?" she chose "No."

These issues are complicated. They aren't always black and white; there are lots of shades of grey. Americans seem to want everything to fit into a sound bite. Parents want what's best for their teens, but it's often hard to simplify all these complex nuances.

In communities, all across the nation, teens are becoming pregnant, yet few professionals and parents are having timely, targeted, personalized conversations together like the ones I get to have with the parents I serve; like the one I had with Mrs. Larson. Conversations in which it's clear that the bottom line is that the parent makes the "rules," but the professional offers voluntary supportive intervention, and the parent accepts it with gratitude. Conversations in which teen pregnancy prevention is discussed in the context of being important in reaching life goals, in which the parent hears that they are the most important, central figure, but that there are professionals available for extra support.

Perhaps if parents and professionals had more conversations like this, we could bring our teen pregnancy rate down.

It took about ten minutes.

Please Don't Bite the Nurse

"I want to get a tubal litigation."
—Woman who wanted a tubal ligation,
but didn't know how to pronounce it.

Like so many of the old, Victorian homes in upstate New York, Samantha's home had a grand front entrance. And like so many, it looked as if it hadn't been used in decades. I imagined that the last person who actually used that front door was a woman in a hoop skirt, or someone going out to saddle the horses for a ride into town, prior to cars. The firm grass warned me to ignore that entrance; a well-worn path invited me instead to walk on the side, through the narrow passageway between her house and her neighbor's, to the rear kitchen door. Samantha had just returned home from grocery shopping when I knocked unexpectedly at her door. She was understanding about the fact that I showed up without calling first; her phone had been disconnected. She was busy putting away groceries, but recognized me from my recent presentation at her job-training program, and welcomed me in.

I had facilitated a lively question and answer game. One multiple-choice question was: "Of the women who die from cervical cancer each year, what percentage of them had never been tested for it? 10%, 25%, or almost 50%?" The correct answer is 'almost 50%.' Her group got it wrong, as has every group I've asked. I explained that Pap smears test for pre-cancerous cells in the cervix, and that if caught early and managed properly these lives can almost always be saved; apparently I reached her.

At the end of the program, she had cornered me, and told me that she was really concerned about what I had said about cervical cancer. She had whispered about her stage 3, about how she's been so scared, about how Ursula, the Planned Parenthood nurse practitioner, had sent her letters and used to call all the time, "It's really important that you come in…" and had quit calling. I felt confident that Ursula's calls had quit right around the time Samantha's phone got disconnected, so I was glad Samantha requested my home visit.

She shared bits of her history with me; she had been going to Planned Parenthood, but when she became pregnant with her son, her OBGYN at the hospital told her she should delay her colposcopy until after giving birth. Now, she said, she was completely confused; in the year since her son was born, "I couldn't figure out who to call: Planned Parenthood because they had told me to come back for the colposcopy, or the hospital because they did the last Pap." So, not knowing whom to call she simply hadn't called anyone. I easily found the patience to get her to realize that it didn't matter which one she called, it just mattered that she called. If she called one and they couldn't help her, they'd tell her to call the other. She agreed to call right then, with me there. But before lending her my cellphone, I checked to see if she needed anything else. We hadn't discussed anything except her abnormal Pap, so I wanted to assess whether she had addressed family planning and whether that was a concern.

"So you said you have two kids. Have you thought about if you want any more?"

"Oh, God, that's the last thing I want! But I'm all set; I'm on the shot." And, sounding happy, relaxed, and proud, she added, "At least I don't have to worry about that!"

"Good for you, you've chosen a highly effective method. When are you due for your next one?"

"In April."

"What date?"

"Oh, just sometime in April. I got the last one in January and it's good for three months."

A few more questions and answers confirmed that she was unaware that the shot is highly effective for precisely twelve weeks, that pregnancy is a risk in the thirteenth week, and that after that the risk is so high that most providers won't even give another injection for fear of interfering with a potential pregnancy. As I explained that, she looked shocked and horrified. Dashing over to her calendar, she confirmed that her last shot had been on Jan. 7. Looking on my twelve-week chart, I confirmed that her next one was due on April 1. It was already April 5, three days before the end of her thirteenth week; she was at risk already. She was so appreciative of that information.

"I just figured I needed it in April, I didn't realize it was due this week—if you hadn't stopped by tonight I wouldn't even have been thinking about it— I've got so much else on my mind. Thank you so much; I'll definitely get it tomorrow, first thing."

And she did; using my cell phone, she called the clinic. She had finished putting away all the groceries and was making supper. She stirred the spaghetti sauce a bit too hard while she waited on hold, frustrated, chatting nervously. Her eyes said more than her words as she thought out loud about the horror that another pregnancy would bring. With no prompting from me, simply contemplating pregnancy risk led her to babble quickly about how much she loved her two children, how much she wanted to keep them safe, how much she didn't want DSS to ever take them away again, how much she was committed to being the best mom she could be. Another pregnancy, she feared, with all the hormonal changes pregnancy brings, all the energy the pregnancy and infant would take away from her two kids, could be the card in her house of cards that would make all the others tumble.

Our follow-up visit later confirmed that she went to her appointment, was not pregnant, and that the nurse had answered all the questions I had encouraged her to ask. Unlike so many of the clients I've tried to support, she was easy: she had a goal, a partner with the same goal, a method she liked, good communication skills, a doctor, insurance, a working vehicle, and a job that allowed her to take time off for a doctor's appointment. It was truly an honor to provide support to her.

Even just knowing the little bits that she shared with me, I felt really good about the intervention I had provided; helping her take charge of both preventing an unwanted pregnancy and moving forward with her overdue colposcopy.

That feeling was reinforced when I later learned that the kids had been removed because the little girl told her teacher, "Last night when mommy and daddy were fighting mommy yelled to me, 'Bring me the knife, bring me the knife!' and I didn't know what to do." DSS quickly snatched up both the girl and her baby brother, and Samantha's downward spiral didn't bottom out and begin to improve until after she had to be restrained in the psych ward for biting a nurse.

When I learned all that, I asked her if they had discussed her contraceptive method choice at discharge.

"No," she told me, "I wish they had."

They had reviewed all her other medications before discharge, but the subject of contraception or reproductive life planning had not been discussed. "They didn't say anything. Now that you mention it, I should have brought it up." Beating herself up for the close call, she continued. "Honestly, I can remember, I was wondering about it in the back of my mind, I know it's really stupid, but all I could think of was, 'Get me the hell out of this place; I just wanna go home and see my kids.'"

She had incorrectly assumed that the precise timing of her next shot was irrelevant. I assured her she was not stupid, that it was completely understandable that she didn't choose to linger there asking more questions when they told her she could leave; that it's completely understandable that she was focused solely on reuniting with her two children.

I started my car to go home and the radio came on: Terry Gross with Fresh Air. Perfect! Hearing her familiar voice when I'm out on these back roads felt like having an old friend in the car. Anticipating her probing questions with one of her remarkable guests promised to be the perfect antidote to the visit I had just had. Perfect timing. But as I rounded the first hill, the radio waves got a lot of static.

"I'll leave it for a couple of minutes," I thought, hoping it would get clear again as I went up the hill I was approaching. But as I got up the hill, without touching the dial on my radio, her voice was replaced by a man's voice.

"Is this her guest?" I wondered at first. For several miles, I could barely hear a word, but Terry's voice and this man's voice each came on and then vanished into the static as I drove around hills. Finally I realized it wasn't her guest; her voice totally faded and the man's voice became loud and clear. It was a radio preacher telling me that my soul would be saved if I sent him money. I fiddled with the manual dial, trying in vain to hear Fresh Air. But our local National Public Radio didn't have a strong enough signal. Like many areas of the U.S., the religious fundamentalists' station had a spot on the dial close to NPR and with a stronger signal. This was not the distraction I needed.

I turned off the radio, pledging to myself to raise my contribution to NPR, and promptly got lost in my thoughts. As I drove, questions kept popping into my mind, uninvited. How could a young mother of two, in the peak years of her reproductive life, whose children have been removed from her care because of her violent outbursts, who has herself been temporarily removed from society and restrained, be released home to a male partner with no discussion of her goals regarding childbearing, no mention of her fertility, no offer to review whether she had a method and/or questions or concerns about it? It was beyond my comprehension. And what puzzled me even more is that I don't think her case is the exception; I believe it's the norm. I've heard of numerous other cases of women being released from different types of residential settings with nobody asking some basic questions, having conversations like the one I had with her. "How would you feel about another pregnancy at this time in your life?" "Are you in a relationship where this is a concern to you?" And offering support at setting up a reproductive life plan. Or at the very least, referring them to someone who could. And connecting them with any medical services needed if they don't want a pregnancy.

Pulling in my driveway, taking in the beauty of the thawing pond, trying to welcome spring's arrival despite the April snow, I treasured the thought that whatever changes tomorrow brings, today, and for the next 84 times this magnificent earth spins on its axis since Samantha's shot, it is very unlikely that a fertilized egg will implant in her uterus, and I played a little part in that. I felt the entire universe thanking me.

And that night I got to I give myself "pillow points"; when my head hit the pillow at night, in those quiet, restful moments before I drifted off into sleep, I felt like I had helped level the playing field a little for one more person in the next generation, as generations before had for me. And it felt good.

A few months later I was driving right by her house, so I decided to stop in, simply to check that her plan was still working, and to make sure that she had gotten that colposcopy. As I walked that same path along the side of her home, to the rear entrance, I noticed a hole in the window. It was the size of a fist, at the height of a fist. Nobody was home. There was no towel or blanket stuffed in the hole to keep out the cold autumn air. No plywood or cardboard covering it. Just free and open to the breeze. I paused, thinking about a fist going through that window.

I thought about how differently I'd have described it if I had seen that hole at one of my friends' houses. "It was around the same size as a tennis ball." I'd have rung the bell expecting a story about a group of kids playing, an adult turning their back for a split second: a pitch too fast, a toss too high. Then I wondered, was I being judgmental to picture a fist here?

No.

The angle was wrong; the neighbor's house was too close: a ball wouldn't have gone that way. And anyway, even if I was wrong about that, a child's ball gone astray on a brisk autumn day would leave adults scurrying to improvise a temporary solution. Cardboard. Duct tape. Plastic. Something. But here, nothing. A violent outburst, a home fled. I paused, alone at the scene, praying that whatever had transpired hadn't left anyone physically hurt; that children hadn't witnessed it, and that wherever they all were, they were safe. And as sorry as I was that the violence still wasn't under control, I gave thanks that whatever had transpired hadn't involved a pregnancy. I knew she would need time, and probably help, to stop the violence. But at least she had time; she wasn't pregnant.

I think about clients like Samantha. Their needs are so vast and my ability to intervene is so limited. But when I learn, "Samantha showed up for her Depo shot," I believe that despite all the limitations, these opportunities I'm blessed with really are significant.

The women lined up against the side of the hall in their blaze orange jumpsuits and matching canvas shoes before entering the classroom, like they do each month when we come to the county jail. I look for familiar faces, especially young moms; it concerns me about who is raising their kids when they're locked up. Like the twenty-two-year-old I had recognized last month. Her twin babies were healthy, and she had begged for a tubal. She argued that with four kids including twins, she knew she'd never want another. And that she really needed the meds her mental health worker prescribed after her suicide attempts; she was terrified of quitting her meds if she got pregnant again. But her doctor refused the tubal because she was so young. Life can be so hard; it's hard to believe that by age twenty-two so many things could have already gone so wrong for her.

She had never used anything except condoms and desperately wanted something effective, so I had been surprised when she wasn't home for the visit we had scheduled to discuss other methods, and when she didn't return my calls. Then, when I saw her in jail, her long silence suddenly made sense. I prefer when they're strangers, when I don't know their history, when I don't know who's lonely for them. Fortunately, I didn't know anyone this time.

We were trying one new activity: this one about relationships. The worksheets we distributed had five category columns. "Thumbs up" (Essential), "Yeah" (good but not required), "Whatever" (neutral), "Yuk" (rather not) and "No way, Jose" (forbidden: deal breakers). We read a list of descriptive words and phrases describing potential partners and the participants could list each one in whichever column worked for them. We explained that it's subjective; there are no right or wrong answers, it could be different for everyone.

Once they had all the descriptions in their columns, we invited dialogue, and we got plenty of it: about what qualities are important in a partner, in a relationship. About how we choose partners and how we then decide what we're willing to work on versus what's a dead end.

Then we gave them an opportunity to reflect back on past relationships. "When you look back over actual relationships you've been in, have you always chosen people with all the 'thumbs-up' qualities and none of the 'No way, Jose's'?" We facilitated a lively conversation about the process.

Finally, we asked them for feedback about the activity. One woman said, "This was actually really eye-opening. I mean, in the whole first part, when you were reading off all the words and we were putting them in the columns, honestly, it was so easy it seemed stupid. Like obviously, 'Treats me with respect,' 'Has a steady job,' 'Fun to be with' and 'A good listener' are essential, and obviously things like, 'Can't control anger,' 'Hits me,' 'Lazy,' 'Steals' and 'Drinks too much,' are deal breakers. But then, when I actually thought about the last relationship I was in, well, he didn't hardly have any of the qualities I listed as essential. And he had a lot of the qualities that I called deal breakers! So: why did I stay with him for so long? And then I got thinking about relationships I was in before, and it's the same thing. I never thought about it that way. Why did I choose these people?"

The perfect question.

Another woman chimed in, "I had the same thought; it was like a no-brainer listing the qualities, but why did I get involved with all these assholes? Ya know what it is? It's all the stuff like 'Handsome,' 'Buys me drinks,' 'Flirts with me,' 'Looks sexy,' 'Tells me I'm pretty,'—all the stuff that I put under, 'Whatever' that I thought I don't care about. But that's actually why I was drawn in to these jerks. I mean, like the last guy, it was obvious from day one that he didn't have any of the qualities I put on my 'essential' list. So why did I even give him the time of day?"

They all had something to add. "I swear, it's weird, honestly, I'm not kidding, it would be good to carry this list around with me when I get out, and when I meet a guy and I'm even thinking about going out with him, go down the list and say, 'Check... check... check... check... check,' 'cause if I had done that I wouldn't have gotten half way through the list and I'd have said, 'Uh-oh, he's so not for me.' God, think of the agony I could have saved myself!"

"No kidding. Can I keep this list?"

As required by the jail, we had taken care not to have staples or paper clips, and the guard let them keep the paper.

We affirmed that it's common when people meet to be influenced by first impressions, that there can be mysterious attractions, but that it's not always based on what we know we want or need. We affirmed that when two people meet and start to get to know each other, it's good to give the relationship time, to let these things play out, to figure out who we're dealing with before getting overly involved; to use our heads.

Behavior change is hard. Habits are hard to change. But the first step is seeing what needs to change and making a plan for change. I'll never know what happened in their relationships when they got out, but it felt good to have given them that opportunity for some serious self-reflection.

We always include the basic information about Planned Parenthood medical services when we do our monthly jail programs, and we included them that day. We explain that reproductive health care is an important part of overall health care, that pregnancies can be planned and prevented until the time is right, that our medical services are free or affordable to everyone, and about where our medical centers are and how to access them.

Invariably, once we establish ourselves as being there to help them set and reach personal goals when they get out, we get questions that reveal basic misinformation about pregnancy, birth control, and sexually transmitted diseases. This happens in both the male and female programs; the guys who asked my male colleague whether spreading earwax on their penises before intercourse would reduce their risk of contracting STDs weren't kidding.

"**M**ay I speak to Sandy?"

"This is me."

"Oh, hi Sandy, this is Vivian. I'm an educator from Planned Parenthood. Do you remember filling out a form at DSS, requesting the Reproductive Life Planning Service?"

"Oh, God, I filled out so many forms there, I dunno, but I remember something about Planned Parenthood. I go there."

"Well, your application has been approved. That means you qualify for free education services, and I'm the educator who provides the service. So I'm calling to see if you'd like to set up a time to meet."

"Oh, God, I've been meaning to call Planned Parenthood. I really need more pills; I only have three left!"

"Oh wow, do you have a prescription for more?"

"No!" she said with a tone of urgency, and she told a long tale. Her parole officer calls her at 9:00 every morning, after she takes her pill, and reviews her list of daily obligations: appointments with Drug & Alcohol, Mental Health, DSS, Job Training, etc. One missed appointment will put her back in jail. So by the time she gets off the phone with him, she forgets about the pills, focusing on her mandated appointments; five months in jail was enough.

"I've been meaning to call; I feel so stupid!"

"Well, listen, I didn't call you today to make you feel stupid."

We scheduled a home visit in fifteen minutes.

"Can you bring me pills?"

"Well, no, I'm an educator, not a doctor or nurse, so I can't give prescriptions. But I might be able to help you get them on time. I can't promise; all I can promise is that I'll try."

When I arrived at her home, she welcomed me, holding the pack with three lonely pills left, and a look of deep concern on her face. She filled me in on some of the details of her past: she had gotten her pills from our local Planned Parenthood and had been doing great on them, taking one every day. At twenty-one, she had been pregnant once; an abortion a year ago, which served as a real wake-up call, followed immediately by the pill start. She was diligent about remembering her pills, and when she was put in jail she asked if she could bring them but it wasn't allowed. So when she was discharged she still had one and a half packs. She and her boyfriend were equally determined to avoid pregnancy; he was already struggling to meet his child support payments. She was paralyzed about calling Planned Parenthood; she knew she needed an annual exam but couldn't commit to a date and time for fear that it would interfere with her parole officer's mandated appointments.

Sounding defeated, she added, "I don't know what I'm gonna do."

I tried addressing the helpless tone first.

"Listen, you sound really concerned. And I get that. I may be able to help you, but first, I just want to point out that you have a lot going for you that makes you very likely to be successful. You know your goal: you don't want a pregnancy. You've talked with your partner and he agrees. You have a method—the pill—and you like it. You have insurance. You have a doctor you're comfortable talking with. You live within a fifteen minute drive of the clinic, and you have transportation. And you have a phone. That's a lot that you have working in your favor! The only thing you need is more pills, and you need them fast. That's a barrier, but compared to a lot of what I'm used to, it's relatively minor."

"Wow, when you put it that way, oh God, yeah, I definitely know what I want."

"OK, so listen, let me break this down and see if it helps. If we call Planned Parenthood, you could schedule your annual exam, and if something comes up you could call back to change it. And based on what you just told me, there's a good chance that you might be able to pick up an 'emergency pack' within the next three days, to hold you over until your exam. That would be a medical decision that the practitioner will have to make; I can't promise, but we could try. How does that sound to you?"

"Oh, wow, yeah, that would be great. That would be amazing, actually!"

"So do you want to call right now while I'm here?"

She looked troubled and welcomed my offer to call for her. "You'll know what to say; I wouldn't know how to explain all that stuff."

So I called.

"Planned Parenthood; this is Vanessa."

"Hi Vanessa, it's Vivian. I'm on a home visit, and I need to schedule an annual exam for an established patient." We scheduled an annual in two weeks. "Thanks, Vanessa. Also, she's only got three pills left. Is there any way she could stop in and pick up one emergency pack to hold her over until her annual."

Vanessa came back after checking her chart, sounding concerned. "She should have run out months ago...."

With Sandy's permission I explained that the gap was due to incarceration. Vanessa agreed to check with the practitioner and as long as there were no problems Sandy could stop in today after her mental health appointment at 2:00.

"Perfect."

I hung up, left her some condoms, and wrote out an appointment card for her annual. "Thank you so much for doing that. This was so helpful. I mean, just, like, the way you said it all. The way you said that whole thing about how I need my exam but then also about that whole 'emergency pack' thing, like, I never woulda known like how to say all that. It sounded so easy the way you made it sound, I just couldn'ta explained it like that. Like, I can call and just say, 'I need to make an appointment,' or something like that. But not like all that!"

Hearing her words, I understood exactly what she meant. She lacked the "simple" or "obvious" skill of being able to navigate her own way through the intricacies of the health care system, even though the receptionist was helpful and friendly, even though she knew what she wanted and was familiar with the clinic. And she lacked the confidence to try.

I tried to encourage her before I left, "Listen, if you ever don't think you know what to say just feel free to call Planned Parenthood anytime and just tell her what you want. If you had just called and said, "I want more pills" her questions would have led you to tell her everything I told her. You don't have to be able to lead the conversation the way I did, you'd just need to tell her what you want and then answer her questions. You would totally be able to do that. The most important thing is to pick up the phone." Yet I knew that her feeling of inadequacy went pretty deep, and that it would still be challenging for her.

The whole interaction made me wonder about our "rehabilitation" system. Here was a woman who was absolutely clear that she didn't desire a pregnancy, completely unprepared for the daunting task of becoming a parent until she rebuilt her own life, on the pill when she became incarcerated, and the only relevant thing she reported that the jail did was to forbid her from bringing her pills with her. No mention during the discharge process about how to resume them or how to get more; no mention of the fact that resuming after several months off would leave her at high risk during the first month; no support whatsoever.

Unfortunately, that's typical.

"Rehabilitation?"

A few days after Shelly gave birth to her perfect little boy the nurse entered her hospital room, and preparing for discharge, offered her birth control. Shelly later told me that she fought back tears as she declined the offer. According to her side of the story, the nurse then asked if she's still with the baby's father, and she stuttered and stammered not knowing exactly how to answer the question, "And I said something really stupid like, 'Not really but kinda sorta.'" The nurse rolled her eyes and said in an impatient, annoyed tone, "It happened once, it'll happen again," implying that Shelly should take a method, that she'd need one.

What Shelly couldn't summon herself to explain to the nurse, what she didn't want to dwell on at that moment as she was holding her son and treasuring the miracle that he was alive in her arms, was the circumstance that had brought her to that moment; "I just didn't want to dwell on the negative."

The father of the baby had been her first love. She had been somewhat of a loner, not a lot of friends, never so much as a kiss from a boy. Richard was different. He noticed her. He was kind to her. He told her he loved her. He was extremely patient with her; "not until you're absolutely sure you're ready." Spontaneously they made love just two or three times and she got pregnant.

They did have the opportunity to tell both families about the pregnancy right before he was suddenly killed in an accident.

I found it understandable that she had declined the nurse's offer of birth control.

I found it understandable that an experienced nurse in a maternity ward of a local hospital would be frustrated with yet another seventeen-year-old mother denying the likelihood of future sexual involvement.

I found it understandable that Shelly didn't want to discuss the accident, the death, or the loss with a nurse she barely knew as she held her brand new baby in her arms.

And I found myself overwhelmed with gratitude for that moment, as I so often do in this job; gratitude that this particular moment exists, and that I am the person who gets to live it. She was so clearly relieved to tell me her story, so unselfconscious about the tears that flowed gently down her cheeks as she contemplated her future with this baby with a dead father. The entire visit was less than an hour. I said so little; mostly, I just listened.

I left her with a plan, a realistic plan. The nurse or someone in the hospital could have, too, but in this girl's case, she wouldn't have even been able to consider a plan without first sharing her story.

Storytelling can be so empowering.

It was for Whitney, too.

As we sat in her living room, she explained that she hadn't had a pelvic exam since her daughter's birth, and her daughter was twelve when we met. For twelve years she procrastinated making the appointment she knew she needed, despite the fact that her periods were so heavy that she used literally cartons of tampons and pads every month. She kept cases on hand, piled up in the garage. Recently her daughter came home from school where she had puberty education, asking, "Mom, they said in school that tampons and pads should be changed every few hours. They said if we need to change it more than once an hour for more than a day each month, something might be wrong and we should ask a doctor. How come you have so many?"

Whitney knew she had a medical problem, but didn't muster the strength she needed to make the appointment until we spoke, on the heels of her daughter's innocent question. I simply let her tell me her story; I listened and nodded as she explained that on the day of her daughter's birth there was an emergency.

"I didn't know what was going on. First they were delivering the baby and then all of a sudden the doctor got all weird and uptight and pushed these buttons and all these guys in those white uniforms came in pushing carts with all these machines and stuff. And they were all so intense, and then I passed out. And when I came to I had my daughter and it turned out everything was OK but I lost so much blood that they said I almost died right there on the table. Now, when I so much as *think* about going back to one of those tables, I can't even…I can't even…I can't even think about it."

It was a challenging story to hear; she was clearly upset as she spoke about her memory of that day. It would have been challenging under any circumstances; I had already become skilled at quickly tuning out all the physical clutter, at not wondering about all the prescription bottles that were scattered randomly around the living room, some empty and some partially full, right next to the box of Cap'n Crunch Cereal that was spilling all over, between the overflowing ashtrays and her boyfriend's gun parts. But sitting in her living room with the caged birds screeching so loud made it even harder. I kept having to lean closer to simply hear her soft words.

"Wow. You went through a lot. I can see why you don't even want to think about going back," I said as the birds kept screeching. Somehow she could hear me over their calls. Please don't ask me how; it was deafening. I guess she's just used to it.

"I really don't. Thank you."

"Of course. I mean I can see why you're stuck. It sounds like on the one hand, you've got totally valid reasons to shudder at the thought of going back, I mean, after what you went through. It sounds like it was so frightening."

"It was; it was the most frightening thing I ever experienced."

"Wow." I paused before adding, "But I can also see why you're tempted; why you're thinking about it now. I mean, if your periods are as heavy as you're making it sound, there may well be something seriously wrong, and in all likelihood it's something that can be addressed and hopefully healed if you do go. That's what it sounds like to me. Is that what it feels like to you?"

"Yes, exactly. Like maybe if I go they could help me."

"Yes. There's a very good chance they could. But it's a choice; it's a trade off. Only you can decide if the possible pay-off is worth putting yourself through this now; only you can decide if you're ready."

We talked a little more, and finally she said she was ready. I told her some strategies she could use to make it all easier, to get through the day of the appointment. Bring a friend. Focus on your breathing.

By simply listening and not pushing or forcing, but making it clear that accessing helpful medical services was still a choice she could make, she agreed. And I later confirmed that she went to that appointment and also had the follow-up surgery she needed.

It wasn't rocket science.

But for twelve years nobody beat me to it.

Setting matters, comfort matters. Entering her comfort zone and listening to her turned out to be life altering. The birds intimidated me, but they didn't intimidate her. The clutter tempted me to distraction but I overcame it easily; to her it was home. Home is where we're comfortable. She's probably as uncomfortable on the unfamiliar soil of a spotless medical setting as any of the medical staff would be in her home. But by putting myself there I was able to form the human bridge she was otherwise lacking.

 SNAPSHOT

SHE'S "NOT SEXUALLY ACTIVE"!

NURSE: I'M A LITTLE CONFUSED. YOU WROTE HERE THAT THE REASON FOR YOUR APPOINTMENT TODAY IS TO GET BIRTH CONTROL. IS THAT CORRECT?

PATIENT: YEAH.

NURSE: BUT I SEE YOU ALSO WROTE THAT YOU'RE NOT SEXUALLY ACTIVE. IS THAT CORRECT?

PATIENT: YEAH.

NURSE: OK, SO MAY I ASK YOU: HOW COME YOU WANT BIRTH CONTROL IF YOU'RE NOT SEXUALLY ACTIVE?

PATIENT: 'CAUSE I DON'T WANNA GET PREGNANT.

NURSE: BUT ARE YOU SEXUALLY ACTIVE?

PATIENT: NO, NOT ANYMORE. I USED TO BE, BUT NOW I JUST LIE THERE. BUT HE'S ACTIVE, AND I REALLY DON'T WANNA GET PREGNANT!

Sharon was still fighting to get custody of her two-year-old son when her daughter was born. She had miscarried twice in between. After the second miscarriage, the nurse in the Emergency Room had told her not to get pregnant again for six months, to let her body heal. But she became pregnant a little over a month later, and none of her three attempts at suicide during that pregnancy were successful. So there she was, at age eighteen, holding her new daughter when I met her.

I asked a bit about the experience in the ER, and she told me that while they had told her "not to get pregnant," there had been no mention of *how* to not get pregnant, no questions about whether she had or wanted a method, no offer of condoms or a follow-up appointment or referral to discuss or access other birth control methods. Not even instruction to abstain, to give her body time to heal.

Even in a modern American hospital setting, it wasn't discussed or offered, even to a teen who was clearly fertile, who would clearly have medical reasons to avoid a pregnancy and psychological reasons to postpone parenting, and who was clearly not already on a method.

The avoidance of the subject is not unusual, even in such extreme situations. Similarly, when her daughter was born, the doctor told her to abstain until her six-week checkup, and that they'd discuss birth control then. Like many people, Sharon didn't make it to her six-week checkup on time, and didn't abstain. Fortunately she did use condoms and wasn't pregnant when we met.

"I'm really glad you're here," was Vicki's greeting: my favorite greeting.

She was expecting me; her caseworker had explained that I could help her learn to successfully space her pregnancies.

I started by just getting her talking about her life: her experiences, goals, and her concerns about planning her family. She was eager to talk.

"We always said we wanted either two or three kids. When we found out I was pregnant with our first son, it was, like, the happiest day of our lives. But this one, I mean, like, I know we'll really love her and everything, I mean, like, we really wanted another, but when I found out I was pregnant again it was just, like, oh my God, we never wanted it to happen this soon. I mean, we were hoping to wait 'till Sean was four or five years old. Instead, he was eight months old when I found out I was pregnant! I just can't believe I'm gonna have two in diapers at the same time. I don't know how we're gonna manage. I mean, like, I know we'll manage, it's just like...so soon," she added, as she held her bulging mid-section.

She went on a bit more, and after we had clearly established that she wanted an effective, reversible method of birth control following her upcoming daughter's birth, I wanted to learn about her history with contraceptive methods; which she had tried, how they had been for her.

"Have you ever used any methods before?"

"Mostly just condoms. But that's how I got pregnant with her." she said, pointing to her swelling uterus. "And they're such a pain. But I really don't want to get pregnant for like a long time. I need something better."

"Are condoms the only method you've used?"

"Mostly. Once I tried the shot."

"How'd you like that?" I asked.

"Oh, God, the shot? I loved it. It was great. They gave it to me right in the hospital when my son was born. I didn't get my period the whole three months. I loved that part. And plus, they said it was like 99% effective. It was great; I was so relaxed."

So if she loved it so much, and didn't desire a pregnancy, I wondered why she quit it. Unusual. So I asked.

"No, I didn't quit it. It ran out; it's only good for three months. That was the only thing I didn't like about it." And with a dreamy, longing, look she added, "I wish they made one that lasted like three years instead of three months!"

"Well," I asked, "How come you didn't go back for another one?"

She looked completely baffled. "I didn't need to go back for anything."

"But if you didn't want to get pregnant, and you knew the shot was wearing off, how come you didn't get your second shot?"

"What do you mean?" She was utterly confused.

When I explained that the shot can offer continuous protection for several years by getting another injection every twelve weeks, and that doctors expect their patients to schedule follow-up appointments just for the next shot, and that her insurance would cover the cost with no co-pay, she looked absolutely stunned, and her words matched her expression.

"You're shittin' me!" she said. "You mean even if I don't have to go there for something else? You mean just so I won't get pregnant?"

It was beyond her comprehension that medical facilities would provide visits exclusively for contraceptive needs; she couldn't even imagine that. She asked me to repeat myself several times, as if she wouldn't allow herself to believe what she had heard.

It always fascinates me when I realize the assumptions people make; she assumed that wanting effective contraception which enabled her to enjoy a healthy sex life with little risk of pregnancy was not a medical need. By then, I had learned not to assume anything about what her doctor did or did not say; what a medical provider says and what a patient hears and remembers are not always in synch. He had clearly explained that the shot provided effective protection for twelve weeks. She got that. He may have assumed she'd know to return for the next one, or he may have said to return. But she had such a deep sense of that not being a "medical need" that even if he had said it, without elaborating, she missed it.

I often think about errors like these. And I find myself wondering how they can be prevented. When it comes to patients getting birth control methods from medical establishments, I imagine the addition of a person in medical facilities trained in the "Teach-Back Technique"; at the end of the visit, the provider asks the patient to state in their own words answers to specific questions, designed to identify potential future problems before they occur, and avoid them.

If Vicki's provider, or a trained person on his staff had asked questions like, "How long will the shot protect you for?" she'd have said, "12 weeks."

If he had then asked, "What will you do then?" she probably would have said something like, "Try to use condoms," and the problem would have been identified and then easily corrected. But most medical establishments are either too busy to take that time or don't identify this as a need.

Change can be difficult, and when it comes to institutions changing policies it can be extremely difficult; I understand that. But I bet that if we could add up all the unintended pregnancies that happen which could have been prevented by that kind of troubleshooting, all these over-stressed medical establishments would suddenly have more time. It might be, as they say, "Longer in the short run, but shorter in the long run."

I hold an image: it's a medical provider and a patient in an exam room. Two people. Just two. Let's call them Person #1: the patient, and Person #2: the medical provider. They spend a bit of time together; there's an interaction. Then they both leave, and each goes on their separate way.

When it's a patient who doesn't desire pregnancy, and a provider who is trained and willing to dispense contraception, there's a lot at stake. A lot has to happen during that visit. And for any meaningful success to occur over an extended period of time, a lot has to happen after the visit, too.

During the visit, a lot rests on both of them.

After the visit, and until the next time the patient contacts the provider, it all rests on the patient: Person #1. And that is where the "failure" so often happens: with Person #1, after the interaction. And I think about that, that scene. It happens over and over in America today, probably in every county of every state in this country, every day. Two by two, behind closed doors in an exam room. Person #1 wanting to avoid pregnancy, Person #2 providing a method and support, and within a year, Person #1 is facing one of those 50% of all pregnancies that are unintended, despite the fact that most of the methods that Person #2 provided access to are over 97% effective.

I think about those two people; about what brought them together, about what will determine the success or failure of reaching the goal, and of how they've both been prepared for the interaction. Thousands of dollars, years of study have gone into preparing Person #2 for this interaction, whether it's a doctor, a nurse practitioner, a nurse; whatever. There are guidelines, protocols, regulations, laws, and countless systems in place to prepare, support and monitor this person.

But what about Person #1? Who teaches Person #1 how to, "be a patient"? Sometimes, mom did. Sometimes, dad did. Sometimes, "common sense"; they simply figure it out.

Frequently, at least in my caseload, nobody did. And that shows; it's a huge problem.

There are a whole series of expectations and assumptions that individuals need to know and follow to be a successful Person #1. As a society, we've invested so much in preparing Person #2, yet we routinely invest almost nothing in preparing Person #1. But that is where the breakdown almost always happens; around half the women who experience unintended pregnancies in the U.S. each year used a birth control method during the month they got pregnant.[30] Something isn't working, even when women try.

I reflect on the people I've helped become effective Person #1s; the list goes on, seemingly endlessly. The girl who threw out her pills because her friend said they make you fat, and she told me this while drinking a can of soda. The woman who didn't understand that the Depo shot her doctor said is, "good for twelve weeks" can be administered *every* twelve weeks for continuous protection. The girl who threw out her birth control patches because they irritated her skin. The countless women who didn't return to a clinic for their method because they learned their insurance had expired and didn't know how to advocate for the free services they were entitled to. The obese woman who confided in me that she'd never go back to the gynecologist, saying, "He called me Obeast!" She had always been called names like "fatty" in school. She didn't realize that "obese" is a medical term; she thought he was calling her a beast.

And then there are the women who experienced side effects like changes in their menstrual cycles (which are common with hormonal methods), became concerned, and simply quit their methods. The ones who heard scary stories about their method: stories saying it leads to infertility or cancer. Those who told me they saw a lawyer's ad on TV repeatedly, offering women an 800 number to call if they're on the patch and they've had a stroke, figuring that means it causes strokes. The ones who misunderstood basic instructions about method use; what to do if they forget a pill, how often to change a patch, and simply guessed or quit their methods rather than exercising their right to simply phone their Person #2. Or who make a minor mistake like skipping one pill, think they may be pregnant, discontinue use to wait for their period because they "don't want to hurt the baby," and become pregnant while waiting for that period. The ones who hear part of the instructions and remember details but miss the big picture, like hearing, "You'll get your period during your patch-free week," and incorrectly figuring they have to wait until their period ends to put on the next patch. The ones who don't keep an organized calendar: who lack a system for remembering when they need an appointment or when they've scheduled it.

And of course all the teens who simply hadn't matured enough to maintain ongoing focus on the importance of actually using their methods, like the girl who finally showed up for her first pelvic exam, got her method, and three weeks later still hadn't started it.

"How come?" I asked.

"They gave me a bag. I don't know where it is; I must have left it in Julie's car."

Each of these people was leaving themselves at risk unnecessarily, because they didn't have what it takes to follow all the way through to success, or to advocate for oneself, even when that "advocacy" is as seemingly simple as phoning the doctor's office and asking a question, or reading the handout the doctor or pharmacist had given them.

To some people that's not "simple."

One at a time, I work with individuals, helping them identify and overcome barriers to accessing medical services. It may sound simple and unnecessary; if you can do it, it is simple and unnecessary. It may sound like "common sense," but to people who didn't grow up exposed to it, it's anything but "common." If nobody ever modeled to someone how to be Person #1, it can be overwhelming.

An enormous part of my job is to work with individuals, and in the case of teens, with small groups or families, to empower them to become effective users of the medical system; effective Person #1s. Increasingly, the way I've been dealing with teens who want prescription methods has been to invest more time in the very beginning discussing what it takes for successful contraception over time; how it's a joint effort between the teen and the medical provider, and articulating what the teen's role and the provider's roles are in that process.

Once the teen has decided to try a method, even before they have their first appointment, I find myself saying things like, "If you want to be successful it can help to see yourself and the practitioner as partners, as a team. You each have a different role. Your job is to use your method, pay attention to how well you use it, pay attention to your body, consider how you feel about the method, and communicate all that clearly to the practitioner. Her job is to know all the stuff about the methods, to listen to you, and then to talk with you to figure out together what to do. She can't do her job if you don't do yours. You need to make an appointment, show up, and tell her what's going on in order for her to be helpful." And I give some examples, like, "If you tell her, 'I love my pills; I want more,' or 'I'm having trouble remembering to take them everyday,' or 'I've been spotting a lot and I don't like it,' then she'll listen to you and go from there, according to what you've said. She gives a lot of people pills and patches and shots and different methods. Some of the people love the first method they try, but many don't. She has no way of knowing how they are for you unless you come back and tell her." For teens that access services without an adult at home guiding them, I find that that kind of hand-holding and the accompanying follow-up monitoring are as important in reaching success as all the information about the methods.

And an enormous part of my job when I do professional trainings is to help other professionals in our community identify this as an important concern; repeatedly, I encounter professionals who have no prior understanding of the challenges many people face regarding establishing reproductive life plans and reaching their goals. So I start with raising awareness, and then develop skills and strategies to address it. While it's effective, I'm aware that I'm just one person in one community, and I'm confident that this dynamic is not only happening in my community.

"How many kids do you have?" I asked Wendy. She was one of the clients I met the very first year on my job. I bet there are women like Wendy in many communities.

"Four," she replied.

"How old are they?"

"Russell's seven, Vince is six." She was going to go on with the ages but interrupted herself to explain, "They have a different father. Now I'm with Tony and we got Scott, he's one and a half, and Tara. She's four months. And Tony's got a boy and a girl but they live with their mom." She was holding Tara in her arms, lovingly rocking her gently as she slept.

"Have you thought about how many kids you want to ever have, total?" I continued.

"Want?" she asked, with a look of disbelief coming over her face, like she didn't "get" the question: who would "want" kids?

"Like, do you hope to have more?"

"Shit. I don't hope to have any more! I didn't hope to have her, ya know, it just, like, happened."

"And what about Tony? Have you talked with him about it? Does he want more?"

"Are you shittin' me? Tony? He didn't even want her!" she answered, pointing down to Tara with her chin, with the same tone of disbelief. Like what guy would want a kid.

"When I realized I was pregnant, he wanted me to get an abortion," she went on, for emphasis, "but I told him, 'I ain't killin' my kid!' But no, he didn't want her. He definitely don't want no more. I mean, I didn't wanna be pregnant either, but like, hey, the test don't lie; I was pregnant. I wouldn't murder no kid. If he wanted to leave, he could leave. At first he said he was going to, and I was like, whatever. I mean if he's gonna split he's gonna split, but I ain't killin' my kid. That's my kid! Actually, I thought he might leave, he was so mad at first. But ya know, he kinda got used to it."

After a long pause the tension that had mounted melted, and she added sweetly, "Now he loves her," looking down at her daughter, smiling.

"So it sounds like you both totally agree that you don't want another pregnancy anytime soon. Can I ask: are you doing anything to try to prevent another pregnancy?"

"Yeah, we got some condoms," she replied, and added, "but shit, I really ought to get some birth control. I just hate it is the thing."

"When you say birth control, are you referring to the pill?"

"Yeah," she replied, with this look like she couldn't believe I work for Planned Parenthood and don't know what birth control is. She didn't realize there were other methods.

"So you've used the pill before; can you tell me a little about that? What do you hate about it?"

"I went on it after Vince was born, 'cuz like, I had gotten pregnant with him right after I had Russell, and the doctor told me to go on it and I was like, OK, I'll try."

"And what was that like?"

"I kept forgettin' to take them and then I'd like take two or something but like then I'd forget again and I was always, like, shit, I'm gonna frickin' get pregnant on these things. And that's when I was with Bill. He wouldn't use condoms. So it was like so scary all the time, 'cuz I always was thinkin' I might be pregnant. But then he left and so I wasn't with nobody so like I just quit 'em."

"So you had trouble remembering them. Was that it, or was there something else you didn't like about them; did you have any side effects or anything?"

"Oh, no. They didn't bother me. I just thought, shit, I'm gonna get pregnant on them. But I'm thinking I should really go back on them, 'cuz now, like I really don't wanna get pregnant."

"Well, you're absolutely right in thinking that the pill has to be taken at the same time every day to be effective."

"Yeah, that's what I'm worried about."

"Well, there are a lot of other methods, too. Have you heard of any others?"

"I heard there's some shot thing, I was thinking that might be better, 'cuz then I wouldn't haveta remember every day."

"Yup, there's a shot, and there are other reversible methods. There are also permanent methods. Do you think you guys want something reversible or permanent?"

"Permanent?"

"Yeah, like for people who don't ever want more kids. There are surgical procedures we can get when we're certain we don't ever want more kids. There's a vasectomy for men or a tubal ligation for women."

She rolled her eyes. "Yeah, I heard of that thing for men, but he'd never do that. He'd never let nobody cut his nuts off. But what's that thing you said for women?"

"Well, first let me explain, they wouldn't cut his nuts off! I'd be glad to show you and him what they would do if you're interested. It's a simple out-patient procedure, and honestly, it's much simpler than the tubal for women."

"He wouldn't do nufin'. But what's that tubal thing?"

"They can cut the fallopian tubes," I said, and with her permission I pulled out my model of the female reproductive organs, reviewed the basics, and showed her where they cut the tubes.

"And then you can have sex and you don't get pregnant?" She looked shocked.

"Oh, well, I can't say it's impossible, but the tubal is more effective than any of the reversible methods."

She looked at the model. She had appeared to completely understand all the information I had given her, but continued with a tone of disbelief, like this was too good to be true.

"But the thing is, Vivian," she said, and paused slightly, looking concerned but unsure of how to put her concern into words. Then she continued, leaning towards me, whispering, "The thing is, with Tony, I mean, with Tony, like, I mean, like, we really go at it."

"As is your right," I said, trying to help her build comfort in my presence; hoping to normalize that sexual activity is part of life, as is wanting effective protection from pregnancy.

"I mean, so then, would that really work?"

"That's what I meant when I said it's more effective than any of the reversible methods," I said, and again showed her the chart illustrating relative effectiveness of methods and explained it a bit.

"Where would I have to go to get that done; can you get that done in this country?" she asked.

She meant the United States.

Now I was the one who was stunned.

"Yes; absolutely. You could go back to the same hospital where you had Tara, or there are other doctors who could do it nearby."

"You're shittin' me!" she insisted. "Dr. Matteson who delivered my baby, he could do that? Right in Fairview?" It was a half hour from her home.

"Oh, yes, definitely. Did you like him? Would you want to go back to him for that?"

"Oh my God! I can't believe you could get that done right in Fairview. That's amazing!" And after a pause, she added, "How much does it cost?"

"Well, you'd have to check with his office, but all the major health insurances pay for it."

"I ain't got no insurance, I got Medicaid."

"Medicaid *is* insurance. Medicaid pays for it."

"You're shittin' me!" she said again.

During the rest of the visit, I answered a few more questions about the tubal and I left her with brochures about tubal ligations, vasectomies, and an overview of all the methods to read. But I knew her questions had been answered. I explained that she'd have to have two appointments. At the first one they'd talk with her and do some tests, make sure she's healthy, make sure she understands that it's permanent, and have her sign forms for Medicaid. It could take up to thirty days for Medicaid to process the request, and then her doctor could perform the procedure. She was shocked and delighted by the statistics about how common and effective tubal ligations are.

She declined my offer to call with her to schedule her appointment, wanting to wait to read the brochure and discuss it with Tony first. But she was a person who called her doctor and scheduled appointments without a problem, so I wasn't concerned. She was thrilled, armed with this new possibility of a tubal ligation. She did, in fact, read the information, talk to Tony, and schedule her pre-tubal consultation as planned. We had one more home visit between her first and second appointments. I was curious to see if she still sounded eager as the date drew nearer.

She did. In fact, as I asked her about what her doctor had said, she went into great detail, and it all sounded accurate to me, as though she had listened carefully and retained everything. And I noted her use of the word "incision," a word I had not yet used with her; it was when she explained to me what he had said about the small incision that I was convinced she was going to go through with the procedure.

Many people who first hear about permanent and long-acting methods are eager, based on the thought of not having to mess with methods anymore. But as they think about the reality of anesthetics and incisions, it's another story. Not with Wendy. I could tell by the way she spoke that she had already considered the downside and upside of the procedure with a solid reality check, and the upside easily won.

I was right. She later confirmed on the phone that she got her tubal ligation as scheduled. It was the first time I had ever helped someone through the process of voluntary sterilization. I hung up and took a deep breath.

A few months later, I did my last follow-up visit to Wendy's, just to close her case and make sure she wasn't having any problems. I also wanted to remind her how important her annual gynecological exams were, still. We chatted a bit. I asked her how she felt about having had the procedure.

"I can't thank you enough; I can't tell you how glad I am I did this. I mean, I knew I was gonna be glad, but I never imagined how different I would feel."

"What do you mean? What's different from what you expected?" I asked.

"I mean, I figured it would help with sex, that sex would be better, that I'd be able to finally relax, not having to worry about getting pregnant every time he touches me. But I never realized how nervous I always was; I don't mean just in bed, I mean, like, in life. Just hanging out. Like in the grocery store the other day, I was in the tampon aisle, and I always used to kinda pause and think, 'Do I really need these? 'Cuz if I'm pregnant I ain't gonna need 'em and I don't wanna waste the money.' But now I'm just like, 'Yup, throw 'em in the cart, I'm gonna need 'em. I ain't pregnant, and I ain't gonna be!' And even when I'm doin' stuff like the dishes, and my mind wanders. There used to be so many times during the day that I'd be wondering if I could be pregnant. Now that I know I'm not, I'm realizing how much I used to be worried about it even when I wasn't pregnant, just from not knowing. This is the best thing. I can finally put my energy into my kids, like I want to."

I knew that her two older kids had been removed from her custody by DSS shortly after she and Tony got together, and I knew how desperately she didn't want that to ever happen again, now that she had them back. And I understood that it would take a lot of energy; I was glad she'd be able to focus it where she wanted.

Here was a woman who had given birth to four babies in a modern hospital in America and agreed with her partner that they didn't want any more, and had never once had a serious conversation with a professional explaining the ease and availability of permanent sterilization.

As I sat in my office completing my paperwork, listing her as another closed case, with the reason "Complete," I had the same paradoxical feeling that I've had with so many of my clients. On the one hand, a deep sense of gratitude that my path had crossed hers, that I had just created a memory to cherish. I had helped someone make a profound positive change in her life that would benefit her, her partner, her kids, and her community for the rest of her fertile years and beyond, literally decades.

But at the same time, I had the troubling feeling of disbelief that after four hospital births nobody had beaten me to it. It wouldn't have bothered me so much if I believed that she was the exception to the rule, but experience later taught me that she's probably not. There had been numerous opportunities for professionals in medical settings to effectively address these issues with Wendy before I ever learned her name.

Opportunities missed.

Lots of them.

When I think about how different our society would be if more of those opportunities were captured, either within the institutions by existing staff that serve people like Wendy in other capacities, or by specially trained sexual health educators, it is astounding to me.

During my first years on the job, I quickly learned that my position, which involved working one on one with individuals to support them in making a reproductive life plan, was unique. When I was sent to trainings and conferences, I was eager to meet people in other counties or other states who do similar work, to share stories, to brainstorm about how to best address the challenges we face: to learn from them. But for the most part, there simply weren't any. Almost all the other sexual health educators I met provided group programs. Few, if any, had provisions that enabled them to provide ongoing support services to targeted individuals. As a society, why don't we take advantage of every opportunity we have to help individuals establish reproductive life plans, to help them set goals and identify and overcome barriers to reaching them?

I once had the chance to ask about that when I attended a professional training. I sat in a packed university auditorium, filled with human service professionals from a huge region of central New York State. We had all gathered for a presentation by a speaker from an award winning model program in New York City that served parents with developmental disabilities who lived in their own homes, raising their own kids. The program had outreach workers who regularly provided home-based education and support on a host of issues in an effort to enable these struggling families to remain intact: to prevent foster placement. The presenter proudly shared success stories that illustrated the chilling challenges clients faced, the support the worker provided, and the resulting improved outcomes.

After a thorough assessment that takes many hours over several visits, they provide targeted, individualized support based on needs. The case studies showed a wide array of successes, striking differences in the "before" and "after," demonstrating the results of effective intervention. Teaching budgeting to families who were spending money on getting their hair done when they hadn't paid the electric bill. Teaching parents that kids benefit from toys and providing activities for kids. Breaking down tasks like taking a shower into manageable steps: go into the bathroom, take off your clothes, turn on the water.... Teaching parents how to cook some basic meals: a can of soup, a simple sandwich. They had a lot to be proud of; these were fragile families, parents at high risk of losing custody of the kids they loved if they couldn't master some fundamental life skills, and it was working. They deserved their place in the spotlight.

But I had concerns. These clients were already parents, and during several of the presenter's case studies, clients became pregnant during the year the intervention was happening. One was a client with five kids who was in crisis with her fiancé. All were struggling simply to keep the kids they already had from being removed from their custody. Yet in their 4-8-session assessment, in which they asked the parents about an enormous range of life skills, experiences, goals, health, and family history, the speaker never mentioned whether they asked anything about their goals regarding their fertility. That puzzled me; I've routinely gotten women who had never considered family planning to consider whether they wanted kids, and if they didn't, I've helped them learn about methods, then make a medical appointment, and then get and use a method in fewer than eight visits, even women with as many limitations as the ones we were hearing about.

So during the question and answer portion, I asked, just to check, whether, during their detailed assessment, they ask the parents if they hope to have more kids, and whether they have access to related medical services. "No," the presenter answered, "not unless they bring it up." She added something about respecting the client's privacy, and about not wanting to "push the issue." I wanted to talk with her about that at length, to explain how helpful it can be to individuals to simply ask them their goals and then offer support without invading privacy or "pushing" an agenda on them, other than the agenda of helping them reach their own goals. But there wasn't time; there were hands raised all over the room, questions about other aspects of the great work they were doing, and so I let it go.

But it still haunts me.

Sexuality is private, and respecting privacy is important; I get that part.

And human sexuality is an enormous subject with a lot of "issues"; I get that, too. The messages we all grow up with, the messages that influence our sense of self and ultimately our sexual behavior and our thoughts and feelings about it are complicated. They come from so many sources; our parents, our families, schools, society, religions, the media. Our sexual identity has so many components: our sense of intimacy, our sensuality, our gender identity, and our sexual values. And there are religious, mystical, magical aspects to our sexuality.

But we don't have to deal with all the private enormity of individuals' sexual identity to be helpful. Our sexual health and our capacity to reproduce is only one small part of our entire sexual identity; I don't mean to imply it's the only part. But it's a vital one, and when professionals learn to isolate it and help those among us who are unable to successfully manage it without assistance, the results benefit everyone.

So while I get it that sexuality is complex and private, I also want to point out the flip side of that coin: becoming a parent is *not* altogether private. A baby isn't just a part of its parents' life and world; it is a part of our society. We're all connected. As a society, I believe it is irresponsible of us not to help the neediest people in the most fragile families successfully address their reproductive health goals. And certainly, parents who have such developmental deficits that they can't read to their kids, those who need assistance taking a shower or preparing a can of soup are heads of fragile households. And if they're so open to support with so many other issues from these well trained, caring professionals who find respectful ways of dealing with all these other challenges, why not assume they'd be open to help at successfully spacing their pregnancies and limiting their family sizes if they want to?

Why not ask, and offer support to those who say they'd find it helpful? Why is that considered "pushing the issue"?

When we look at the disparities in the unintended pregnancy rates in our nation, especially the high rates among young women in poverty who lack formal education, and when we ponder how to bring those rates down, it can help to ask, "Who are these women?" and "How and where can we effectively reach them?" One obvious answer is that we can try to support them in institutions and through programs that they already access.

Some already try. Some maternity wards of hospitals address family planning at discharge. But based on what I've seen among my own clients, and based on the high rates of unintended pregnancy among the neediest women in our society even following hospital births, I am certain we'd benefit from offering much more support there. The subject isn't addressed in enough detail, and the staff needs much more specialized training.

When I have provided professional trainings for discharge nurses in maternity wards of local hospitals I have found nurses who literally had never even seen some FDA approved methods. That's despite the facts that the method had been around for years, the nurse had worked in that department for years, and the hospital had a discharge policy that stated that that nurse was responsible for teaching all new moms about birth control options before discharge, after giving birth. And these are the relatively effective hospitals in this regard; these are ones that are willing to address contraception in the first place: doctors and nurses in Catholic hospitals aren't even allowed to do that, and in many areas, including large sections of the county I serve, they're the only hospitals that women have access to. Apparently the separation of church and state doesn't protect women's rights to access medical services that a powerful church doesn't want to provide.

And other institutions like mental health institutions, crisis centers, drug and alcohol rehabilitation centers, jails, and prisons could effectively provide desperately needed support in reproductive life planning. So could ongoing job training programs and education programs for people who need assistance with life skills, whether it's in residential facilities or homes.

Yes, they'd need to revisit their policies, including their discharge policies. And yes, the workers would need special training in how to address family planning in an affirming, non-threatening, non-judgmental, non-directive, helpful way. Yes, they'd need some basic information about contraception and health care and referral information for local providers. And some skill-building about how to help individuals identify and overcome barriers as they try to reach their goals. But there are people like me who could provide that important training; I do it in my community all the time. And it's effective: even among human service workers in my own community, even when I just go in and do brief trainings, I correct so much misinformation that's out there, and I see immediate changes in attitude that lead to more effective work afterwards.

I've had participants who proudly say in the beginning, "I always ask my clients if they're on birth control: that's so important!" But after listening to some of my stories about how the women I've served take offense hearing that question, they say, "Wow, I never even thought about it like that," and they quickly learn to open the dialogue by asking about life goals instead, only moving to contraception after a client expresses a desire to avoid pregnancy.

And I've seen human service workers who genuinely wanted to be helpful and benefitted so much from the lists of simple questions I provided to help clients set goals and then help monitor their specific method use to avoid the most common mistakes.

Trainings like those could be happening for staff in health and human services all over our nation. Yes, that would involve extra costs. But really, how much? It might seem expensive until one compares it to the costs of not providing that training. There are vulnerable families among us who don't desire pregnancy and who don't want their kids to be placed in foster homes. Even if we disregard the moral imperative to help them, the measurable financial costs of helping them successfully prevent untimely pregnancies would be so much less than the costs of providing foster homes when their kids get taken away. Wouldn't it be worth it?

As a society, it's our choice. Will we help people manage their fertility, or keep providing jails and foster homes and so many other services?

So many institutions and programs have professionals who have regular, ongoing opportunities to help some of the most vulnerable members of our society who are at highest risk for unplanned pregnancies; with proper training, they could help them set and reach reproductive health goals. Yet routinely and systematically these opportunities are missed; almost none of them even address the issue. Failure to take advantage of these opportunities has an enormous impact on many of the people who struggle most in our society, and on the entire society that ends up "supporting" them in countless ways.

And while I'm concerned about the impact of these missed opportunities within our society, I'm also aware of how very fortunate Americans are compared to so many people around the globe.

I once had the opportunity to see that first hand, when my experience in Springfield qualified me to participate in an exchange program, connecting people from my county with groups of Mayan Indian women in Chiapas, Mexico. As I think about how far we still have to go as a community, as a nation, and as a world, I ponder whether sharing some of my own stories from those exchanges could help.

I'm optimistic enough to believe it could.

Think Globally, Act Globally

"No woman is completely free unless she is wholly capable of controlling her fertility and...no baby receives its full birthright unless it is born gleefully wanted by its parents."

—Alan F. Guttmacher[31]

"It's taken generations of political struggles to get where we are today in America. Over a hundred years ago, it was illegal to even distribute written information about contraception. Gradually, birth control methods became available to many Americans. It really changes things for people; our lives today are so different from our grandparents' lives because of it. It enables us to think about our childbearing potential within the context of other issues in our lives," I said, and paused to allow Zoey, our first translator, to translate my words into Spanish, and then the next translator to translate into the Mayan women's local dialect.

Eileen and I were in Chiapas, Mexico, as part of Planned Parenthood Federation of America's Global Partners Program. The Mayan women listened with interest; our histories are so different, as is our present situation.

"Now," I continued, "many Americans prefer to get an education and have a career underway before they have their first child, and many families find that if they wait, they're better prepared emotionally and financially for the joys and the challenges of having a family. Also, many people decide to limit their family size; birth control makes those choices possible for people. But even with all the progress we've made in the last hundred years, we still have a long way to go," I said, and explained that for women in poverty and those without formal education there are still often barriers to accessing health care.

What completely fascinated them was the notion that many Americans voluntarily limit their family size; they could hardly imagine that, and we discussed it at some length. Then they wanted to know how people voluntarily prevent pregnancy.

"Is it a pill, or a shot, or a plant that you use? There is a plant here that some people say prevents pregnancy, but everyone who tried it says it doesn't work."

The phrase "Think Globally, Act Locally" had always inspired me; now was my chance to broaden my reach.

"Think Globally, Act Globally," I thought as we showed them samples of modern contraceptive methods. I felt honored to be even one tiny part of the changing global picture as we watched them carefully examine and marvel over "common" methods like packs of pills that they had never seen, and as we talked about their use and significance together.

When we showed them the IUD, one of the women immediately asked, "Is it true that if you have a baby in the hospital they put that inside you automatically?"

Wow. That was tricky, and it was eye-opening to me; I had shown so many individual women and groups of women IUDs at home, and I had fielded so many questions about IUDs, but never that one.

They approached the whole subject of contraception from the opposite perspective: in the U.S., I'm used to women who want IUDs and have trouble getting them. Here, the Mayan women were afraid of medical settings because they didn't trust the government or the doctors; they feared unwanted IUD insertions.

"In the U.S., that is against the law. And in our community we never heard of that happening, but we have heard stories of that happening here in Chiapas," I replied. We had already had a meeting with a local OBGYN who had explained what she sees with IUDs.

"About once a month I remove an IUD from a woman who didn't know she had one; the women come to me for some other reason, like irregular bleeding or cramps. So I do an exam. And if I see an IUD I ask, 'how long have you had your IUD?' and if they answer, 'what IUD?' or, 'what's that?' I explain, and if it's something they don't want, I offer to remove it immediately. Invariably, it is in the uterus of a woman who delivered her last baby in a hospital."

So I knew to choose my words carefully; Chiapas is not New York.

But nothing underlined the differences in our perspectives more than when I got to the part about permanent sterilization. The Mayans are considered an underclass, an unwanted subculture, and the social tension regularly plays into their concern that there's a broad interest in eliminating them. So involuntary sterilization was a primary concern, and their only reference point for the conversation about sterilization.

Even though it was illegal to perform sterilization on a man or woman without consent forms signed, we heard stories about Mayans who had gone to the hospital for something else, like to deliver a baby when a home birth got complicated, and never became pregnant again. Investigations were underway in local hospitals, where hospital officials allegedly produced consent forms with official "signatures" for sterilizations that had been performed on numerous Mayans who didn't speak Spanish and rely on thumbprints for signatures. While they agreed their thumbprint was authentic, they claimed they hadn't been told that the procedure they were consenting to was sterilization. The doctors and nurses all spoke Spanish, and Mayan woman generally didn't trust the hospital translators. Probably with good reason. This was one of the violations being investigated by the man who was on our flight from an international human rights organization; I was glad he was there.

And the violations we heard about weren't limited to medical settings; at a shelter for victims of domestic violence we listened as Willow, an American in Chiapas, told us about more private violations of human rights that were happening routinely within homes.

"Before I worked here in Chiapas, I worked in a similar shelter for victims of domestic violence in a major city in the U.S., where women came to us all the time. After awhile, we got used to 'the usual': black eyes, bruises, cuts, broken bones. I mean, it's always hard to witness, but every now and then, maybe one in ten, it would be women who were beaten almost to death. I mean, really; internal bleeding, damaged organs, absolutely unbelievable abuse. The kind of abuse that you wouldn't even understand if it were happening by enemies in a war, but it was happening right in homes, between people who supposedly love each other. I mean, unbelievable. But here in Chiapas, it's almost the opposite; maybe one in ten does *not* have such horrible wounds."

"Why don't the women come in sooner?" we asked. "Don't they know about the shelter?"

"That's not the problem," she explained. "The women know the shelter is here, but if they come simply because they have some scratches or black eyes or broken bones, then what? Once their wounds are attended to, they'll have to leave: they'll have to go home; they have no place else. And if their husband finds out they came to the shelter for help and that someone outside the home knows of the violence, he'll beat her even worse."

It was hard for us to hear, it was hard for her to describe.

It happens every day.

"More than anything, we want to see American women who live in poverty," Xiomara had requested, when the group from Chiapas visited us in the U.S. as the next part of the exchange. "Yolanda and I want to meet real women, women who struggle like us; we'd love to go to some homes, to see them where they live. Not just clinics and hospitals with professionals; regular people."

So I took them to Val's.

Walking up the old wooden steps to knock on Val's trailer door felt paradoxically familiar and new to me, the day I had the Mayan women with me. The boards that bounced trampoline-like below my feet had always seemed so flimsy, such a sign of deferred maintenance. But today I saw them as such a sign of wealth, of the opulence of American life, as I remembered driving up the steep mountain roads of Chiapas, and the countless people we had seen walking, carrying bundles of wood on their heads. It's an ever-present sight there. Mostly it would be used as firewood; it was their only source of fuel for cooking. The homes we had visited all simply had dirt floors, so they didn't have steps, wooden or otherwise. But I knew that nobody who had to haul the materials for miles uphill on their head would ever build steps that were four feet wide, even if they ever did need steps. I imagined the waste of that extra length of wood was puzzling to my guests. But we didn't discuss it; I simply knocked on the door and Val welcomed us.

She appeared interested as soon as she saw her guests. At 5' 4", Val had never thought of herself as tall, yet she towered above them. She quickly took in their long, dark braids with traditional colorful ribbons braided in, their dark skin, hair, and eyes, the traditional embroidered outfits they wore, outfits they had made, as generations before them had made. It was strange to see the way Val was so fascinated by Xiomara's wardrobe; I knew that what excited Xiomara the most about her own clothing that day was the fact that, for the first time in her life, she had bought a pair of sneakers that morning. She had gotten them at our local Wal-Mart; it had been her wildest dream, come true. She was wearing them, and had been beaming about them all morning.

Val had thoughtfully prepared by moving the piles of laundry from the couch to the table to make room for all of us to sit. The trailer was wide enough so she had chairs facing the couch, so we could easily sit in a comfortable, intimate circle. The television softly provided background noise. Val always had it on, even though she usually ignored it. To our guests it was an unexpected focal point.

"In our whole village, everyone is so poor," Xiomara opened through our translator. "We have to work so hard just to have enough food for our children. When somebody is sick, there's no money for the doctor, and even if there was, there's no money for medicine. Life is so hard; every day is a struggle. Here in America, it looks to us like life is so easy, like there is no struggle. We struggle all the time. Some of the people in this project told us that there are people in America whose lives are a struggle; we're not sure if we believe it. We want to know what it is really like in America, and if anybody here understands our struggles, or has struggles like we do."

"Oh, I know exactly what you mean," Val replied. "When you watch TV, it makes it look like life is just fun and easy. Like everyone's rich. That's not real. I mean, maybe for some people it's like that. But no, definitely not for everyone. Not for people like me. You came to the right place; my life is a struggle just like yours is."

"Would you be willing to tell us about your struggle?"

"Sure," Val agreed, but looked a little unsure where to start, so Xiomara encouraged her.

"Just tell us about your life. Your family. What you do. A typical day. What your husband does."

"OK, well, um," Val started hesitantly. But as she went on, she gained confidence.

"I live here with my husband and our four kids, and I'm pregnant with our fifth. My husband works out of his van at a job outside New York City, so he's gone all week and only comes home on the weekend. So it's just me here all week with the kids. The two older ones go to school, so I have to get them up and fed and dressed on time for the bus every day. Then I have to stay home alone with the little ones all day by myself. I have to constantly watch over them, changing diapers and everything, plus I have to do all the chores, ya know, the cleaning, the laundry, grocery shopping, cooking, bathing the kids, helping the older ones with schoolwork. And like if I'm sick or something, there's nobody here to help. Like with this pregnancy; early on, when I had morning sickness, there was nobody but me. I had to get them up no matter how sick I felt. And anytime I need anything, if I have to go to the store, it's so isolated out here, even though it's just about a fifteen-minute drive into town, I gotta take the kids, so I gotta put them in their snowsuits, in their car seats, and take them with me everywhere. I never get a minute to myself. It's a struggle every day."

She paused to allow the double translation, from English to Spanish to their local dialect. Even before the translated words reached their ears, Xiomara and Yolanda's eyes were glued to Val, eagerly anticipating every word. The body language suggested that they had hit the jackpot. They were about to hear about how some Americans really do live in poverty; about their struggle. But as they listened to the final translation they looked confused and started chatting in their dialect.

The translation came back, first by Rosa, from their dialect into Spanish, then by Zoey, from Spanish to English. "They appreciate what you are saying, but they are puzzled. They are waiting to hear: what is the struggle?"

Val repeated some of the tasks, this time with a little more detail, pointing to the enormous piles of laundry awaiting the machine at one end and awaiting folding at the other. Then she pointed to the kitchen and bathroom she had to clean, the funky old vacuum cleaner that wasn't strong enough for the old, stained shag carpeting. After hearing the translation, the question came back, with its innocence underscored. "They understand what you are saying, but they don't understand: what is the struggle? Could they ask you some questions?"

"Sure."

"They are looking for why you say you struggle. Where they live, during the dry season, they have to haul all their water very far. They want to know if you have a season when you have to haul your water."

"No; our seasons are different, not so much wet and dry, it's more hot and cold. In the winter it gets very cold, and we have to shovel snow. But we almost always have running water. I mean, not always; once in a while the pipes freeze and we have to buy bottled water."

They kept fishing for the struggle; the translator kept coming back with questions.

"While you're pregnant, is there a doctor nearby you can go to?"

"Well, I go to my prenatal visits close by, but I'll have to go about forty-five minutes away to the hospital when it's time to deliver."

"What happens at the prenatal visits?"

She showed them the most recent of the three ultrasound prints that were hanging on her refrigerator door. It was a routine ultrasound, not a problem pregnancy. They had never heard of "routine" ultrasounds. In their village, if someone was suspected of having a very serious abnormality, they might be able to go three hours away to the hospital for an ultrasound, but that almost never happened. There were no ultrasound machines in their village.

"If your children get sick, is there a doctor who you could take them to?"

There is.

"If they need medicine, is it available?"

"Yeah."

"Where would you get it?"

"At the drugstore in town."

"Could you pay for it?"

"Yeah."

"How?"

"I have Medicaid. It covers most things, but once in awhile I have to use my own money to pay for the medicine."

"Where do you get the money?"

"My husband works."

"He gives you the money?" they asked in a tone of disbelief, and went on to elaborate, for clarity, "If you need clothing or food, for yourself or the children, does your husband give you some of his money?"

He does. They were absolutely astounded; they had never even imagined such a thing. They started chatting a mile a minute in their dialect, clearly puzzled.

As they chatted, we heard a scratching on the door and Val got up and let the dog in. He ignored us and sat in his favorite corner, chewing on his toy. The women heard the chewing and stopped chatting, distracted by the dog.

"What is in his mouth?"

"His toy," Val replied.

"What do you mean?"

"It's his chew toy."

"Did you make it?"

"No." Val answered, confused.

"Where did it come from?"

"I got it for him in the store."

"What was it made for; what is it really?"

"What do you mean? It's a chew toy," Val replied, not understanding why they were wasting precious time making the translators translate a conversation about a stupid dog toy.

"You mean they sell toys for dogs?"

Zoey was more than a translator; she was an interpreter. Having grown up in Europe, in a modern city, and then having lived among the Mayan women, she understood how to explain their confusion to Val. So she explained that they had never heard of such a thing. In their village most of the children don't even have any toys. They invent games out of little sticks and pebbles they find. So the concept of purchasing a dog toy was a luxury beyond their wildest dreams.

"They look at your laundry, but they have never seen so many clothes in one home," she continued after the distraction about the dog's toy. "Most of the women in their village have at least six to eight children, so your family seems very small to them. They all just have a few clothes and they all wash them together in the river. So they were speculating about why you say you struggle; that's what all their talk is. They are very puzzled; they were saying maybe if you can afford so many clothes, and you have a washing machine, you have to spend more time washing them. And maybe if you have a beautiful home like this with carpets, it takes a lot of time to clean it. They all live in shacks with dirt floors, so they never thought about the fact that it would take time, if you have all these nice things, to keep them clean. But they are still having trouble understanding why you say you struggle."

The women persisted with their questions, and every answer brought them farther, rather than closer, to understanding why Val said her life is a struggle. Finally, by the end, Val said that maybe she really is lucky; maybe she has a lot more than she ever realized.

I had a feeling that the next time Val presented her Medicaid card at her doctor's office and got a "routine" ultrasound or got her sick child treated, she'd experience a sense of gratitude she had never felt. And it led me to think that Bill and Melinda Gates' foundation money that had led to the plane tickets for these women, enabling us all to sit and talk was money well spent. In their efforts to make the world a better place, I was glad they had factored in the importance of having people from different countries get to simply sit and talk; to share their own life stories, to see both how similar and how different we all are.

Reflecting back on that visit, I realized that I had witnessed an important shift in Val's perspective, from being focused on how she struggles to being focused on how much she has to be thankful for. Although her circumstance didn't change at all, her perspective shifted 180 degrees. As Americans, rich or poor, we do have so much to be thankful for.

"Recently, a Mayan woman came to me for an abortion," the doctor told us. He was putting a lot on the line, sharing his story with us. It was 2002 in Chiapas; abortion was illegal. "It took her three days to walk from her village in the hills to my clinic here in town. On day two of the walk her shoes wore out, so when she arrived barefoot the next morning her feet were cut up and bleeding. So before discussing the abortion, of course I cleaned and attended to the cuts on her feet. Then, working through a translator, I briefly explained the abortion procedure and asked if she had any questions."

She only had one: "Will my husband be able to find out I was here?"

"He beat her regularly, but for this: he'd kill her."

This is the desperation that is commonplace for so many women in the world. Despite how sobering it was to hear his tales, we were thankful that he was so willing to share them with us. Like the women we had met in the safe house, he truly wanted to. They're busy every day, working. Working hard. Working hard because they care, because they want to make someone else's struggle a little easier. That's why he was willing to take the risk of admitting to us, as foreigners, that he was engaged in performing illegal abortions; they all wanted us to know what they're experiencing, what they routinely see. And they want help; they want the world to know and to care about what they see.

Someday I should really write a book, I thought.

In the U.S., women who want abortions face challenges, too, but the challenges are different. I wanted to see for myself what a typical day is like in an abortion clinic in the U.S.

Once, I got to do exactly that.

Every day in the U.S., thousands of people walk through the entrance doors into abortion

✔ **FACT**

BY AGE 45, MORE THAN HALF OF AMERICAN WOMEN WILL HAVE EXPERIENCED AN UNINTENDED PREGNANCY, AND 3 IN 10 WILL HAVE HAD AN ABORTION.

clinics. They generally fall into one of three categories: employees who work there, patients who come to terminate a pregnancy with those who are supporting them, and a few random service providers. In 2007 I entered one as an anomaly: I lacked the familiarity of the daily routine that employees had. I had the freshness of a new patient; like them, I had to use GPS to find the clinic, but I lacked the emotional attachment that they and their caregivers had. And while I had the objective detachment of an outsider, I was not removed from the fundamental context of the place like those who come to deliver packages, fix the copier or clean the floors. As a Planned Parenthood educator, I was simply there to watch, listen and learn; it was part of my ongoing training. This, combined with the many hours I've spent listening to people talk about their experiences regarding sexuality, contraception, pregnancy, and accessing reproductive health services gave me a unique perspective.

As I entered the clinic, having been in the car for over an hour, I was relieved to find a restroom literally inside the entrance door, before I had to go in and announce myself to the receptionist. Being aware of the history of abortion clinic bombings, it surprised me that anyone off the street could enter the restroom. I was also surprised that I didn't see any security cameras, I didn't have to be buzzed into the waiting room, and there was no sign of protesters.

The waiting room had several people, scattered in pairs or small intimate groups. The receptionist sat behind glass that enabled her to pass paperwork through and be easily heard, but without the big open space that ours at Planned Parenthood has; nobody could reach in to touch her.

I wondered if it was bulletproof.

She buzzed me in and Tina, the director, welcomed me and showed me around. The somber looks in the waiting room paired with the affirming ambiance of the clinic. The space seemed to "expect" the mood, and to honor and support it. The recovery area had comfortable recliners separated by small tables with neatly arranged tempting plates of cookies. Nobody goes there for the cookies, but there they were; a silent reminder to each patient that somebody cares.

The procedure room was similar to our exam rooms at Planned Parenthood but much smaller. The exam table had stirrups sporting colorful handmade knitted covers, to ensure warm feet. The lighted panel of the ceiling had a sky and cloud design that you'd see if you were lying on the table: a soothing ambiance.

The counseling room had two comfortable matching chairs with a quiet flowery print and a plate of worry stones on the coffee table. Affirming and inspiring phrases on plaques and posters were sprinkled in very appropriate places: a calm, safe space.

I got to shadow two counseling sessions, and Tina took time to process with me after each one, ensuring that her guest understood the significance of what had transpired.

The first was a young woman who was a "frequent flyer," there for her third abortion. She had three young kids and was overwhelmed. Her attempts to effectively use birth control often failed; her most recent failed attempt was when she had gone to her local Planned Parenthood requesting the Mirena IUD and was told they no longer have it. She got pills instead, and her sonogram indicated that she probably got pregnant after one week on the pill. She didn't remember the nurse saying anything about using a backup method during the first cycle. When I hear things like that I've learned to assume nothing. I don't assume that the nurse said it and the patient missed it, or that the nurse forgot to say it. But whether those vital instructions weren't said, weren't heard, or weren't followed was past; there she sat, pregnant.

The other was a sixteen-year-old who was facing her first pregnancy. She was quieter, gave shorter answers, and asked few questions. Each counseling session felt simply like a comfortable talk, yet an awful lot of education and assessment was happening. Logistics were all thoroughly covered; the procedure was fully explained, anticipatory counseling about how the drugs and procedure would make the patient feel and what the rest of the day would be like. The support system was discussed: family, partner, friends, self. Who knows, who is with you here today, who will be with you when you get home? Feelings were discussed, motivations and pressures were assessed. Even the quiet sixteen-year-old left no doubt that she was there because she wanted to end this pregnancy, not because someone else was pressuring her to terminate. I could tell that Tina was skillfully getting both women to talk about what brought them in, so she could listen to their stories in their own words, to be certain of that. Both made it very clear that they had thought this through a lot and freely chose to be there.

Birth control was discussed for the future; a plan was discussed but it was clear to me—and Tina later confirmed—that while women might make a plan about birth control that day, birth control is a big subject and it would be impossible to adequately address it at this time. The focus is on today's procedure, not tomorrow's pregnancy risk, which is appropriate to the many needs of the day.

But it doesn't bode well for the future.

After the counseling sessions, we ran into another counselor who told us that her patient had decided fifteen minutes into her session to go home and have her twins. She had known she was pregnant with twins before driving over two hours to the clinic that morning. Everyone on staff was completely at peace with that, thankful that the counseling session had given her the quiet, thoughtful space where she could sort out everything that was going on and make the best decision for herself.

When Dr. Nelson came out of the procedure room from her last patient and went to look for her next patient, the counselor explained that she had changed her mind and gone home to have her twins. At first, Dr. Nelson's face quickly showed a bit of joy for the mother-to-be, then changed to a slightly saddened expression. "Oh, I'm *so* sorry I wasn't out here to see her and wish her well. I just missed her."

I can't remember ever seeing a "business" with less concern felt or expressed for "losing business" or "customers." It was clear that nobody had "an agenda" regarding the outcome of any potential patient's visit, other than the agenda of making certain that each woman was fully aware of the decision she was facing and making what she believed was the best choice.

Afterwards, I got to see the pathology room. I saw two clear rectangular glass trays, about the size of the smallest Pyrex one I use at home to bake drumsticks. Each had water plus the contents from a uterus: the lining of the uterus and "the pregnancy" which had been removed. Everything floated in the tray awaiting the pathologist's careful examination.

The first one was at six weeks, and the pathologist had a lot of trouble getting me to be able to distinguish the lining of the uterus from the pregnancy pieces, despite how obvious it was to her well trained, experienced eye. To me, it all looked like little pieces of a sea sponge. Nothing I could recognize as the potential beginning of human life had I not been told.

The second one was at twelve weeks, and that was quite a different story; visually, a lot changes from six to twelve weeks. She used her pointy tool to show me recognizable body parts: arms with hands and legs with feet and toes, which appeared detailed and undistorted, as opposed to the head and eyes, which looked relatively rough. They were all camouflaged among pieces of the uterine lining, which looked like what gets flushed down the toilet each month that one of our eggs isn't fertilized. The skin surprised me: it was clear, exactly like the textbook photos. I had thought they did some kind of X-ray thing to photograph embryos; I never really realized you could actually see through the skin even though it's there. At that stage, the skin looks like plastic wrap, but not shiny. On the arms I could actually see through the skin to a complex web of what looked like tiny threads: maybe veins, bones, or muscles. It was all so small; had it been intact, the entire embryo would have been shorter than my pinky finger.

My shadowing experience was almost finished; the little break room was quickly filling with plates of food and some gifts and cards. It turned out I was shadowing on Suzanne's birthday, and they had all organized a potluck lunch to celebrate it. She's a nurse who, like many of the staff, has worked there for over twenty years. I was invited to stay for lunch and I accepted their kind offer. I always feel "right" in an undersized room that overflows with women and food; perhaps it's because I grew up with three sisters, a mom, and a grandma who lived with us, in an apartment with a tiny kitchen. I got chatting with some of the staff over lunch; they were fascinated by the work I do in my nearby county, doing home-based education, much of which is aimed at preventing unintended pregnancy among women in poverty. They were so deeply understanding of the need for this kind of service, and genuinely appreciative of the effort I make and some of the success stories I shared.

Of course, when my efforts are successful they don't see anything, as these become the women who don't need abortions. I loved how we could sit and eat lunch together and talk about my work which, when successful, eliminates the need for much of their work, and we could all be fine with that.

Like me, the staff has been working and advocating for years to keep abortion legal and safe, and we'll all continue to. But also like me, they'd love to see the number of abortions take a nosedive due to a lack of need for abortions, due to a huge reduction in the number of unwanted pregnancies.

The two pregnant women I had observed with Tina wanted abortions and got them. The fact that abortions are safe and legal here was probably the last thing on their minds; I don't know if either of them would have labeled themselves "pro-choice," and during their struggle to get through this crucial day I have no way to know whether either of them paused to give thanks for the thousands of people who have worked so hard to keep that possibility legal and safe in the U.S. today. I don't know if the older one had ever voted, or if the younger one ever would.

They both looked so young to me; I realize in reflection that they probably weren't even born when we were debating the Supreme Court's recent Roe v. Wade decision in my high school government class. I doubt they thought at all about the politics of abortion law.

There's a good chance they weren't political; they just didn't want to be pregnant.

But they were.

As they waited to put their feet into those stirrups with the soft, warm, hand knitted covers to keep them comfy, I remembered the stories of the woman in Mexico whose feet needed bandages before her abortion, and I gave thanks to all those who have worked so hard to make abortion legal and safe in America.

I ponder these pregnancies, and our reactions to them.

Biologically, when a human egg is fertilized, one of two things usually happens. Around half the time, the egg passes through the uterus and is shed the same way unfertilized eggs are shed, unbeknownst to the woman. The other half of the time the fertilized egg implants in the wall of the uterus.

At that time, according to the medical and legal definition, the woman is pregnant.

If she doesn't want to be pregnant, what she does next gets everyone's attention. Everyone seems to have something to say: she should do this or she should do that.

As a society, we're obsessed with arguing about what happens after fertilization, after implantation, what to do about unintended pregnancy, what to do about abortion. We spend millions of dollars supporting politicians who promise to sway the laws one way or the other about how we'll deal with unintended pregnancy after it begins.

But what about before? What few Americans want to acknowledge or discuss is the fact that about two weeks before that egg was fertilized, whoever she was, she wasn't pregnant. Back up the tape: in every unintended pregnancy, there's always a before. There are the months, weeks, days, hours, and moments before the egg was fertilized, before the clothes came off, before the touching started, the kissing, the talking, the flirting. It's a process; it's not always the same, but there's always a before. And that's where we can make a huge difference. But our collective focus is disproportionately magnified onto the abortion issue, instead of on helping prevent unintended pregnancy.

I think about those moments, those most private of moments between two people, right before unintended pregnancies happen. I'm well aware of how much I am not a part of those moments among strangers, how outsiders don't access that space. So I've wrestled with the question, "How can one person make a difference in one community, with something that is fundamentally so private?" and it's made me realize that that's totally possible: we don't have to access a space to influence it.

The vision I carry in my own community is that during those private moments, each person involved will have the learning skills, communication skills and access to resources they need to prevent an unwanted pregnancy, and that if they don't, they'll have someone to turn to. I am not naïve enough to think that I can know or impact each couple on my own; that they'd all know me and turn to me. But I realized early on that I don't have to. I just need to be connected with the people they do turn to. The school nurses, the DSS caseworkers, the human service professionals, the local doctors, and, of course the teenagers. And I need to make it easy and rewarding for them to turn to me.

While I haven't succeeded 100%, I know I've made a huge difference in the community I serve. Throughout our nation, for every girl or woman who faces an unintended pregnancy, and for every boy or man who was involved in that pregnancy, there was an opportunity for someone, somewhere in their lives, to have a caring, supportive, helpful, even loving dialogue to help prepare them for what they were getting into; to help them figure out how to get that darn little egg about two inches farther through her Fallopian tube without running into a single sperm cell. An opportunity missed.

Like that mother of three who had the abortion that morning, the one who got pregnant after being on the pill for one week. She, like 59% of the women who obtain abortions, already had kids.[32] She had given birth in hospitals, she had gone to a clinic for birth control; she had been in contact with so many health care providers. Even just shadowing the conversation she had with Tina, in which she made it clear that she had never wanted that pregnancy and now wanted it over, I could so easily imagine the conversation that I wished I, or someone, had had with her before she became pregnant. I could hear it so clearly in my mind's ear.

"How many kids do you have?" I'd have started with after a little chitchat.

"Three," she'd have answered.

"Have you thought about whether you want any more?" I'd have continued.

"Maybe someday, but definitely not right away," she'd have replied.

"Are you in a relationship now?"

"Yeah, I live with my boyfriend."

"Have you discussed it with him?"

"Uh huh."

"Does he agree?"

"Oh yeah, definitely."

"Do you have a doctor you're comfortable discussing these issues with?"

"Yeah, I go to Planned Parenthood."

"And are you doing anything to prevent pregnancy?"

"Yeah, I'm on birth control."

"May I ask what you're on?"

"The pill."

"When did you get your pills?"

"Last week. I wanted the Mirena, but they didn't have it anymore, so I just got pills."

Here I'd have paused a bit and explored the availability of IUDs, in case she still wanted to get it, to help her figure out how to get one and to identify and plan the next step. Then we'd have gotten back to the conversation about the pills for immediate protection.

"When did they say to take the first one?"

"She said to start Sunday, so I did."

"How long did they say you need to take them before they're fully effective?"

"What do you mean?"

"I mean, do you remember what the nurse said about when they'll protect you from pregnancy; that it takes awhile before they really work on their own? Did she say anything about using condoms or some other 'backup method' during your first package of pills?"

And right there: bingo. She'd have had a confused look, or she'd have said "No." I'd have found it. It probably would have taken me fifteen minutes. If she wasn't clear regarding her pill instructions, I'd have asked her to show me the papers that her doctor had given her. If she didn't have them, we'd have called together, and the receptionist would have put us through to a nurse who would have told her to use a backup method, and depending on her cycle would have told her for how long. I'd have offered her condoms and spermicides, I'd have assessed whether she needed Plan B, I'd have gotten her to tell me in her own words how she was going to protect herself until the pills provided protection, I'd have listened carefully to her words for any mistakes and corrected them and it all would have worked out; she'd never have had to learn Tina's name. I've walked that road or similar roads so many times that I could do that visit in my sleep.

She'd have been an easy case if she had been in my caseload, much easier than most of the clients I've successfully helped; she was motivated, her partner agreed, she had transportation, insurance, no misconceptions about the safety of her method, willingness to admit she's a sexual being with life goals and willingness to discuss it with a stranger who's in a position to be helpful. She could read and write. She understood cause and effect and wanted to take an active role in preventing pregnancy. She was capable of staying focused in an important conversation, remaining on topic.

To me, she exemplified the unmet need for supportive intervention.

There were a million things she'd rather have done that day than have an abortion. The only reason she was having an abortion was that she was pregnant; if we could have supported her just a tiny bit more in preventing that pregnancy, her whole story would have been different. As Tina says, the human body is relentless in its drive to reproduce. I think the reason that woman stayed in my mind so much is that I know, personally, I could have and would have loved to have met her unmet need.

But she lived in a county like most counties in America: a county that doesn't have an educator available to provide these individualized services, home-

 SNAPSHOT

"WOULD YOU PUT YOUR TWO-YEAR-OLD IN A BLENDER?"

–LOCAL DOCTOR'S REPLY TO A HOMELESS WOMAN'S QUESTION, "WHERE COULD I GET AN ABORTION?" WHEN HE TOLD HER SHE'S PREGNANT. SHE WAS LIVING WITH HER TWO-YEAR-OLD IN A LOCAL SHELTER FOR BATTERED WOMEN AFTER HER HUSBAND BEAT HER.

based or otherwise. A county that has lots of adults willing to label and judge her for having an abortion, but almost nothing in place outside her doctors' doors to support her in trying to prevent a pregnancy. A county in which teens regularly interact with countless adults between the first time they have intercourse and the first time they access medical services for contraception, with none of those adults taking advantage of the opportunity to reach out a supportive hand, helping them navigate their way to a future in which they don't become pregnant until they are ready to parent. It made me so thankful for the opportunities I've had to prevent so many other women, young and old, from ever having to take the drive I took that day, to sit in those flowery chairs as their feet awaited those stirrups. It made me so grateful that Planned Parenthood exists; it underlined my belief in the vitality of our mission. It seemed so obvious to me that prevention of unwanted pregnancy is the best way to address the abortion debate, and it got me thinking about that whole debate in our country today, and wondering about the people who protest our Planned Parenthood clinics.

I once had the opportunity to meet one of our protesters; it was unexpected, and eye opening to both of us, I think.

I had gotten a call from a woman named Sue, who was a "professional mom" to a twenty-year-old named Tracy through a program that enables developmentally delayed adults to live in homes in our community. Tracy had been living in her home for several years, and it was working out very well. But on the phone, Sue made it clear that the comfort she enjoys around most subjects with Tracy disappears when it comes to the subject of sexuality, so she was calling me for help. She accepted my offer of a home visit, and a little time on the phone enabled me to get some goals and concerns from Sue, so I'd be prepared.

Sue had three big concerns she wanted me to address. First, it was time for Tracy to have her first pelvic exam, and Sue didn't know how to explain what to expect. That one would be easy for me. Second, Tracy was sweet and gentle and liked to make people happy. While those were generally qualities that Sue judged to be strengths, in the realm of romantic relationships Sue was concerned that Tracy needed some guidance on saying "no", what we in the field call "refusal skills." I had some nice role-play activities that I'd bring; I was thankful for the advance notice. And third, although Tracy was generally very well chaperoned and had only recently experienced her first kiss, Sue was concerned that the whole subject of contraception was going to be a challenge when the time came. Although she had no idea when that time would be, the thought of Tracy becoming pregnant terrified Sue; Tracy had none of the most basic skills that are essential for effective parenting, so Sue wanted me to get that dialogue started. Perfect, I thought. All three sounded appropriate, important, and well within my comfort zone.

As expected, Tracy was as sweet as sugar when I arrived for our visit. Although she had trouble reading, learning, and remembering, it was clear from "Hello" that Tracy, with her child-like demeanor, was a person who wanted to please others. We spent a good hour talking, and a number of times during the visit I could feel Sue's relief that the issues she had struggled with and stressed over were being addressed comfortably and effectively. It felt good to see Sue's relief; she cared deeply about Tracy, and clearly she had been stuck. We did several "role-play" pretend situations, and the activity gave Sue the openings she needed for the dialogues she wanted to have with Tracy. After I shared imaginary scenarios with Tracy, asking her how she might respond, Sue listened to Tracy's responses and comfortably interjected important, caring feedback. At those points I simply sat back and treasured the moments. I knew that together we had opened precisely the conversations that Sue had wanted to have with Tracy but had been unable to initiate, and I knew those conversations would continue after our visit, and that Sue was now prepared.

By the end of the visit, Tracy had learned about what to expect at a gynecologist appointment and had agreed to go. She genuinely seemed to accept that a couple of minutes of awkwardness would be important to her long-term health, and she was willing. Sue suggested that it would be best if Tracy's reproductive health needs were addressed by someone other than her primary care provider and asked if I would schedule an initial appointment for Tracy at our Planned Parenthood clinic. When I hung up the phone, handing Sue the appointment card I said, "We're located at 54 Maple Street here in Springfield. Do you know where that is?" I knew it was only a ten-minute walk from their home.

Suddenly Sue lost her confident, relaxed composure; she hesitated, blushed and finally stammered, saying, "Uh, um, um, y-y-yeah, I know where the clinic is." I thought maybe the mention of our clinic stirred up some personal memories and I didn't want to pry. She continued anyway, apparently feeling like she owed me an explanation for her peculiar demeanor. "Um, see, uh, the thing is, I went there once, so I definitely know where you're located. I was one of the protesters there across the street the day you had that big opening."

One of the protesters? Inviting me into her home? Accepting my services at helping her communicate with her daughter about sexuality and relationships and decision-making and accessing reproductive health care after protesting the fact that we were in town? I was surprised to hear it; it sounded like such a mismatch.

I had been to that grand opening; the village mayor and our CEO had cut the bright blue ribbon as the TV cameras panned back and forth from them, their speeches, and our supporters to the protesters across the street. I had seen all the protesters, I had been thankful that they weren't violent. I had read their letters to the editor of the local newspaper, and I was aware that I was one of the unwelcome "sexperts" they referred to; I had accepted the fact that they'd rather we weren't in town. But my colleagues and I were passionate about what we considered to be the important services we had to offer, and we knew there were many people in the community who would agree.

So I hadn't lost any sleep over the protesters; I'm so used to them. In fact, the ones at some of our other clinic sites are much worse, where they hold signs about God and scream hatefully at me calling me a baby killer as I walk from my car to the door. I simply hadn't expected any of them to ever call me and invite me into their home a few years down the road. But we don't discriminate based on political beliefs. So while I was startled at first, unexpectedly finding myself in the peculiar situation of actually sitting face-to-face with one of our protesters, I calmed that unsettled feeling quickly. It was clearly an opportunity to soften what sometimes feels like an impenetrable wall with support and kindness. I was fine about providing the services I had provided to Sue and Tracy.

> "BE KIND WHENEVER POSSIBLE. IT IS ALWAYS POSSIBLE."
> –DALAI LAMA

"Well, if you protested our coming to Springfield that day, I hope you're glad we're here now; I hope this visit was helpful," I said. It was the only thing I could think of saying.

"Oh, heavens, it was very helpful!" she responded with conviction. "Actually, I just went there, 'cause, well, my friend asked me to. She's against abortion. I mean, I kinda am, too. Like, I wouldn't have one. But really, I was just protesting to call attention to abortion. I mean, like, I know you guys do a lot of really important work. I wasn't protesting that. I just want people to think."

"We do, too!" I said. "We believe that our reproductive health is really important and also private. We try to eliminate barriers for everyone, so people who need reproductive health services can get them. We work to eliminate the need for abortions by reducing unintended pregnancy. But we're completely pro-choice; that means that if someone is pregnant, we believe it should be that person, not the government, who decides what she's going to do."

"Oh, that's totally what I believe, too. I mean, I think there are waaay too many abortions. But when my friend Yvonne got pregnant she told me about it and she made me promise not to tell anyone. I was the only person she told. I'm not kidding; she didn't even tell her husband! Really, that probably sounds awful to you but, no kidding, if you knew her and if you knew him, she couldn't tell him. With all his drinking and everything, and I mean they already had two kids and she called me and like she begged me to come with her to

Albany to get her abortion and I went. I mean, I don't believe in it, I just went for her, you know what I mean? To comfort her."

"Oh, yeah? I think I know what you mean. Do you mean you wish there weren't so many abortions, but that if someone finds themselves in a situation like your friend did, you want them to have the legal right to choose an abortion?"

"Yeah, that's right; exactly."

Hmmm. So what did it mean, when she was one of the people you saw on TV protesting Planned Parenthood? Your guess is as good as mine; based on her actions, protesting our clinic, she'd appear "anti-abortion," "anti-Planned Parenthood." Based on her words, clearly articulating that she wants women to have the legal right to choose abortion, she's "pro-choice." My guess is that she's a bit of both; she's "anti-abortion" meaning she doesn't like the concept of abortion, but she's pro-choice in that she wants the Yvonnes in our country to have legal access to safe abortion procedures if and when they're needed.

And she was one of our protesters.

Sitting together in her home, speaking with her, listening to her, it all felt paradoxical. On the one hand, it felt normal, like a normal home visit, like what I do every day: try to help people communicate effectively about sexuality within families. Seeing all the good she was doing for the world by providing this supportive home to Tracy felt normal; it felt like I belonged there. But learning that she had been one of our protesters, it seemed like I should feel like a "fish out of water." Yet I didn't; I felt fine. While I didn't respect her action of protesting our clinic, I respected and appreciated her efforts with Tracy and I could tell that both the respect and appreciation were mutual: we were both thankful that the other person was alive and doing what they were doing.

Learning that she had protested our clinic's presence, and knowing how passionately I believed in the work it represented, I figured we must disagree on some fundamental ideas. I believe that when people disagree it is helpful for each of us to try to understand the other's side. So I try to understand our protester's positions. I saw this visit as an opportunity to fine-tune my thinking on the whole pro/anti-choice movement.

I think a lot of people like to polarize the two camps, and the media certainly does, but I also think there are a lot of people like Sue; people who'd say they're "against abortion," who protest simply to call attention to the fact that they wish there were fewer abortions, but would drop everything to hold the hand of a hurting friend who for one of a million reasons finds herself in a medical facility ending a pregnancy. Or who would bend over backwards to help a young woman like Tracy learn about the wonders of human reproduction. And people like me, who moan at the sight of those protesters but are willing to put politics aside to proactively help prepare a needy young woman to navigate the challenges of her emerging sexual identity.

I doubt that Sue considered the fact that her action of protesting one of our clinics could potentially advance the future of defunding or closing them down; that was not the statement she was trying to make. Like many people who protest Planned Parenthood clinics or abortion clinics, she simply wanted to call attention to abortion; she wanted to publicly show that she wishes there would not be so many abortions. But she hadn't thought through all the steps of what would happen if abortion were outlawed.

It was what I call "partial thinking."

When it comes to attitudes about abortion, that partial thinking is not uncommon; a video on YouTube from 2007 shows protesters in Libertyville who were asked if they believed abortion should be legal or illegal. They all answered illegal. But when asked what the punishment should be for women who have abortions if it ever actually becomes illegal—which it could—the vast majority of them said they had never thought of that, despite the fact that they had been actively protesting to make it illegal for years. When it was pointed out to them that breaking other laws results in penalties like jail time, they had no practical answers. They were simply protesting because they don't want abortions to be happening.

Our protesters often call themselves "pro-life," and even respectable media sources refer to them with that title, but to me, that's not appropriate. Language is important; if we're going to use labels for groups of people, the label should refer to what differentiates the groups, so they should be called "anti-choice." What differentiates "pro-choice" from "anti-choice" is simply how we answer the question "Who decides?" when there is an unwanted pregnancy. Pro-choice people like me believe that women should have the legal right to decide; that it should be the individual's choice. Anti-choice people believe that abortion should be outlawed: that the government, not the pregnant woman, should get to decide. In my mind, that is the single, defining, vital difference that separates us.

Sometimes it concerns me that pro-choice groups overreact to their frustration with the anti-choice movement by minimizing the significance of abortion. It's vital that we make abortion safe, legal, and readily available, and that we remove the stigma that is so often associated with it, but it's also important to acknowledge that abortion is a Big Deal. Unlike many other safe, common surgical procedures, it brings a unique set of moral questions, and to deny the existence of those questions is to undermine our cause. Removing a fertilized egg from a uterus invites different ethical considerations than removing an impacted wisdom tooth or a cancerous mole. There is an element beyond our understanding: we can call it Nature, call it Mystery, call it Life, call it God, call it anything we please, but it is important to acknowledge that when we discuss abortion we are discussing meddling with something we don't usually meddle with. That doesn't mean it's wrong or bad, just that it's important; that we're on uncommon territory, and that that unfamiliar ground should be addressed thoughtfully. And to say that abortion should be readily accessible worldwide is not to say that we don't value life, mystery, nature, or God.

I care about life, too, and it is precisely my concern for life that brought me to this job in the first place and keeps me here every day. And it is what makes me want to shift the focus in the abortion debate; to reset the true north of our collective moral compass. If we really care about life and we want to make a difference, to work for the greater good, we must prioritize our tasks. We need to start with a broader, more global perspective, and the first priority should be ensuring that every child born on earth simply has enough food and safe drinking water to get through the day. And maybe add vaccines for things like malaria and preventable childhood diseases, or inexpensive cures to common deadly illnesses like diarrhea.

But we are living in a world in which almost six million children under the age of five die per year, and more than half of those early deaths are due to conditions that could be prevented or treated with access to simple, affordable interventions.[33] That's over 16,000 per day, or roughly one every five seconds. Plus, over 800 women in our world die every day due to complications from pregnancy and childbirth.[34] Yet people in the developed parts of the world rarely discuss that, and certainly, our protesters never bring it up.

That's the reality of the world we're living in today.

In my attempt to understand our protester's positions, I know that having a moral compass can motivate us to speak up, act, and change policies about what happens in the lives of strangers; I care about strangers, too. But I fail to understand priorities that motivate people to be more concerned and vocal about the fate of a fertilized egg in the uterus of a woman who isn't prepared to parent than about the hungry, dying child in the arms of a stranger; a stranger who wants that child to live more than anything. I can't help but think that moral compass is seriously flawed.

When the protesters are outside our clinic in Springfield, there are usually eight of them, once a week, during lunch. I see them outside my office, chanting and praying, delicately and lovingly handling their rosaries, holding signs that claim to value the sanctity of life. And I think to myself: if those eight people in this one tiny village can all spare one hour each to remind the world that life is sacred, then what about the lives of the families I visit all day. What about Sherry? And her baby? Aren't they sacred? What about Sabrina?

During the single hour that those eight protesters chant in Springfield each week, hundreds of children die of preventable diseases, thirty-three women die in childbirth around the world, and closer to home a host of teen moms right within our little village are staying home, caring for their babies as their own dreams of a high school diploma drift further out of reach, ushering them and their families into poverty. If only those eight people would demonstrate the sanctity of life by volunteering to babysit for Sherry's sacred baby for an hour each, instead of volunteering to protest our clinic, then maybe Sherry could go to school. Maybe she could learn to spell "Take off your shoes." Then their work would be doing something positive, or "pro" life. But the notion that making abortion illegal will bring life affirming changes to society is entirely unrealistic, and such a "positive" name is misleading and deceptive.

The facts are there for us to see. Throughout history and around the world today, in countries that outlaw abortion, the number of abortions doesn't go down.[35] They simply go to different places. Instead of happening in specialized medical facilities like the one I visited, they happen in unsafe settings; instead of being performed by doctors who meet medical standards, they're performed by unlicensed amateurs. The safety of the procedure shifts radically from one of the most common, safest medical procedures a woman can undergo to a very dangerous one; one in which many women die unnecessarily.[36]

> **"WHEN ABORTION IS MADE LEGAL, SAFE, AND EASILY ACCESSIBLE, WOMEN'S HEALTH RAPIDLY IMPROVES. BY CONTRAST, WOMEN'S HEALTH DETERIORATES WHEN ACCESS TO SAFE ABORTION IS MADE MORE DIFFICULT OR ILLEGAL."**
> *–WORLD HEALTH ORGANIZATION*

On the other hand, in countries that make reproductive life planning possible, there are fewer abortions because there are fewer unintended pregnancies.

Facts are important, and should inform our thinking and our actions. Yet routinely, politicians who say they'll work to make abortion illegal—despite the fact that that wouldn't reduce the number of abortions—are not only taken seriously, they also receive huge donations. And individuals who say they want to see the number of abortions go down spend time protesting abortion clinics and the very health centers that make family planning available; the very places where people are actually, effectively reducing the number of unintended pregnancies.

That ability for Sue, a protester at an abortion clinic, and me to sit and put our heads and hearts together to help Tracy made me wonder, as I've wondered so many times, if there is a way that more people in our society could pull together and stop being so focused on the adversarial qualities of the pro and anti-choice movements, and instead work together to help the people around the world and right in our communities who struggle the most, the way Sue and I were trying to help Tracy.

If we could successfully reduce unintended pregnancies nationally and globally, the abortion rates would drop, pleasing everyone. The two go hand in hand. I believe we could do that if we focus on finding ways to ensure that all individuals can establish reproductive life plans and then successfully reach their goals. This could happen if we shift the primary focus of our national dialogue from "What should our laws be regarding abortion?" to "How can we eliminate unintended pregnancy?"

In the small town of Springfield, teen pregnancy rates, like the rates in most of the U.S., are so much higher than in the rest of the developed world. And the U.S. unintended pregnancy rates among adults in poverty are also needlessly, disproportionately high. It doesn't have to be like that; those rates could be brought down. There are successful programs around the world and here in the U.S. Intervention works! I've seen it work in Springfield.

And Springfield is a small town in a large world. Women in Springfield have relatively minor obstacles; unlike women around the globe, almost all the women in my caseload have had potential access to the essential health care that makes childbearing relatively safe. In fifteen years, the number of my clients who died in childbirth was zero, and the number of them who lost a baby during the birthing experience was one. But around the world, women who lack access to modern medical care routinely become pregnant when they don't want to and routinely die from pregnancy related problems. In Half the Sky: Turning Oppression into Opportunity for Women Worldwide, Nicholas D. Kristof and Sheryl WuDunn point out that the number of women in the world who die during labor every day would fill five jumbo jet liners.[37] They elaborate, explaining that there is one maternal death every minute, and that some 99% of those are in poor countries.[38] This is a global tragedy and it is completely unnecessary and disgraceful.

And the World Health Organization points out the benefits of ensuring access to family planning services. Yet "An estimated 225 million women in developing countries would like to delay or stop childbearing but are not using any method of contraception."[39] The opportunity to use effective contraception is not yet available to everyone.

I believe we can change that. After all, the estimated cost of meeting all the unmet needs for contraception in the developing world today is $9.4 billion dollars annually. That sounds like a lot of money. But please don't try to tell me we can't afford it; Americans spend significantly more than that every year on sugary soft drinks.

To achieve these kinds of changes I believe we'd benefit from collectively rethinking the way we talk about sex and reproductive health.

Sex is such a fundamental, important aspect of human life. And it is a hot topic for getting people's attention; as Americans, we are obsessed with talking about it. Especially about politicians' and celebrities' sex scandals. Yet when it comes to having real, helpful, productive conversations about sexual health, so many people find themselves tongue-tied. From the privacy of lovers between the sheets, to stammering parents, to our local school boards and the halls of Congress, we still haven't figured out how to talk about it. That failure has led to the current situation. Real and important issues of sexual health are not being effectively addressed; unintended pregnancies and sexually transmitted diseases are far too common. This is detrimental to individuals and costly to society. It doesn't have to be like that; it isn't like that in other nations.

I hope Einstein was right, that imagination is more important than knowledge; I can so easily imagine these things changing. After all, it used to be that nobody spoke seriously about sex in public. Dr. Ruth opened important communication doors, getting people comfortable speaking seriously, publicly, about some of the private aspects of sexuality, like sexual pleasure, sexual problems, and sexual health. But on a community level and on a national level, it's time to take the next step: bringing conversations about successful reproductive life planning into the mainstream. If we could build public comfort speaking out about this within communities, if we could get people motivated to create the systemic changes in our society that would level the playing field, we'd be closer to creating a society in which all individuals could become successful regarding reproductive life planning.

I hope things will continue to change and during my more optimistic moments I think they are changing.

The media has the potential to become a positive force, and changing technology may bring us solutions to problems more quickly. A study of the impact of MTV's series *16 and Pregnant* found that the teen birth rate declined significantly by regular viewers of the show and that there were more searches and tweets with the words "birth control" and "abortion" by regular viewers.[40] Since the teen abortion rate also fell, the impact of the show appears to be a reduction in teen pregnancy as opposed to greater use of abortion. The fact that there are people who made that show and researchers who figured out ways to measure its impact gives me hope. So does the reality of how quickly technology has changed; when I was hired in 1996, nobody in my organization, including our CEO, even had a smart phone or a computer in their office. The encouraging fact is that we went so quickly from there to where researchers are counting computer searches as a way to gather vital data.

Melinda Gates spoke beautifully about the importance of opening a dialogue about family planning during her bold speech in 2012. And she pointed out that "...One of the simplest and most transformative things we can do is to give everybody access to birth control methods...there's a global movement waiting to happen and ready to get behind this totally uncontroversial idea."[41] And by prioritizing this and promising to invest money in this effort, her foundation could truly change our nation and the world.

And right here in the U.S., there are numerous helpful organizations such as the Sexuality Information and Education Council of the United States (SIECUS), Power to Decide (formerly The National Campaign to Prevent Teen and Unintended Pregnancy), Guttmacher Institute, and American Sexual Health Association (ASHA). They give us information and the vital, helpful tools we need, and they're the click of a mouse away. Now, as a society, from parents to communities to schools and institutions to the media and policy makers, I hope more among us will click our mouses in their directions and utilize these readily available tools.

In 2006 the CDC identified a list of recommendations to improve preconception health and health care. Item #1 was "Each woman, man and couple should be encouraged to have a reproductive life plan."[42] My first reaction was to roll my eyes and say, simply and sarcastically, "Like, duh." It seemed so obvious to me. After all, I had been helping people do that for a decade. But then I realized how significant that was. I worked for Planned Parenthood and many would label my thinking "radical," but the CDC is not perceived to be the hotbed of radical thought. The fact that they were calling attention to this vital issue gave me hope. Their list went on to include important points like the necessity of increasing public awareness, and of health professionals providing risk assessment, education and health promotion counseling to all women of childbearing age as part of primary care visits. That's significant because using primary care visits puts reproductive life planning and reproductive health care into the mainstream, normalizing it. For me, trying and hoping to move things forward, it helps to focus on gratitude. So I give thanks for the progress that's been made, from the days when the Comstock laws made it illegal to even distribute printed information about contraception, to the present, when the CDC is making recommendations like these.

Everyone would benefit from reducing unwanted pregnancies. And we have the means to reduce them. If we could all hold that thought in the forefront of our minds, we could find some common ground and work together on the local, national and global levels. I'm confident we'd all agree that there's plenty to be done: rather than dividing humankind, I hope we'll choose to serve it.

AFTERWORD

It's Friday night. Finally. I was in the high school all day, meeting with students, one at a time. Listening to their stories, trying not to let their carelessness about missed pills, unplanned sex, and forgotten medical appointments take the wind out of my sails after a long week. Our hill was icy; I fishtailed all the way up, praying I wouldn't get stuck and have to walk home, alone in the dark, in the snow, as I have many times. I was just too whipped.

I made it. Relieved, exhausted, I hadn't realized how tightly I was clenching my muscles until they immediately relaxed as I walked in the door and the warmth of the woodstove welcomed me. Paul always has the fire going so it's nice and warm and cozy when I get home; I'm spoiled. And thankful that he teaches sixth grade, so he always gets home first. He was already poking at the hot coals, adding more wood.

Usually, when I get home, I need to tell him a couple of stories about my day, to shift gears, to unwind. Usually, I'm wired. Not tonight: tonight I'm too exhausted to talk, or even to think. And usually, he's quiet when I get home. But not tonight: he told me about his day.

"A girl I had in sixth grade two years ago came to the school today to show everyone her new baby. She's been out for a few weeks. She plans to come back as a student soon; this was just a quick visit. The baby was so perfect and she was all smiles, but I got thinking: here's a girl who couldn't make change of a dollar two years ago, already a mother. How is she possibly going to raise this baby? What hope is there for this child? Who will help her? This will be so hard. I mean, she's a really nice girl, and I know she'll try real hard and everything, but she has no idea what she's in for. Her parents could barely raise her, and here she is at fourteen, she can barely read, she's only in eighth grade! I mean I know the school will do everything it can, but still, for everyone, this is huge. And after she left I got thinking about you and about your work." He paused a little, and kind of tilted his head as he asked, "Is that what you do? Work with girls like her to set goals? Help them figure out how to wait longer?"

"That's exactly what I do," I answered, a bit confused that he'd even ask that after all the years of listening to stories of my day over dinner.

"So I got wondering," he continued, "do you think it's safe to say that you get even one girl a year who's like her to wait?"

"Way more than one!" I answered with confidence, almost laughing at the thought of working all year and only impacting one girl.

"That's so great. That's what I kind of thought you do. But when I saw that little baby today it really hit me: even if you just get one a year to wait, it's so worth all your effort. And even the money. What they pay you in a year; it will take more money from society just to help with this one baby. This is so important; I'm so glad you do that," he said.

And he gave me a big hug.

Paul's hugs are always comforting, but that one was even more comforting than most.

ACKNOWLEDGEMENTS

To all my friends, family, and colleagues whose eyes sparkled whenever I told them stories about my day, saying, "You should write a book!" please know: it took me awhile, but I was listening to you. Thank you!

Special mention to Hudi Podolsky for encouraging me to write, and then to keep writing, and then, finally, to stop writing. And heartfelt thanks to Shayne Schneider, Roe DiBona, and Marvin Beck who always encouraged me to do my best, and who always asked me the perfect, challenging questions to make me think harder. Thanks to Tamar Roman, Lorrie Paul and Jan Eisner for helpful feedback and encouragement on various stages of the manuscript. Thanks to Ginnah Howard and Valerie Haynes for their guidance about the publishing process. Thank you to Kim McDougall at Castelane Inc. for creating the book cover. And thanks to Jeanne Roussel of Write One Plus for her feedback, care and patience in editing and formatting the book.

This book is based primarily on the fifteen years I spent providing Outreach Education Services for my local Planned Parenthood affiliate, and I offer my thanks to the countless individuals who made that work possible. In a continuing effort to protect the privacy of the people in the stories, I am not naming any of the professionals that I worked with. But I offer sincere thanks to all the people who were part of my education team and encouraged me. Also, thanks to all the medical staff and reception staff who welcomed and supported my clients and partnered with me in helping them, and to all the administrative staff who made our work possible. And our funding sources included Title X, The New York State Department of Health, our local Departments of Social Services, and private donors; I'm thankful to all of them, and to The Bill and Melinda Gates Foundation for funding most of the Chiapas exchange work.

In addition to the people who worked with me within Planned Parenthood, I want to thank everyone from the other local health and human service agencies and schools who partnered with us. In particular, I thank those who envisioned, created and supported the unique home-based education services program long before I entered the field, and all the professionals who gave me referrals and partnered with me in serving our clients.

To all the people I based these stories on, who spoke with me and trusted me with extremely private aspects of their lives: thank you for your trust. Many among you are or were struggling when our paths crossed; I hope that each of you joins me in my belief and my hope that sharing some parts of our conversations and some aspects of your stories may lead to changes that brighten the futures and lessen the struggles that you and others face in the future.

And infinite thanks to my husband and best friend Paul, who supported me before, during, and after every day on this job, and who somehow found patience to accept all the things I wouldn't do because I was too busy writing, and to love me anyway.

Book Group Discussion Questions

"Keep your thoughts positive because your thoughts become your words.

Keep your words positive because your words become your behavior.

Keep your behavior positive because your behavior becomes your habits.

Keep your habits positive because your habits become your values.

Keep your values positive because your values become your destiny."

—*Mahatma Gandhi*[43]

Author's Note to Book Groups

It is my hope that this book will be discussed by groups, and that those conversations will help lead our society towards a day when every child is wanted and loved, and when no child is conceived until their parents are ready. I am deeply thankful to any individuals and groups who join me in examining these issues and pursuing that vision. My hope is that conversations will be lively, interesting, thoughtful, and productive. But even more importantly, I hope that they will do no harm.

Even for groups that have discussed many books and many issues, please remember that the subject of sexuality poses unique challenges. Some of the stories may lead readers to reexamine and want to discuss their own private experiences, including their sexual experiences, their sexual health history, and their experiences of learning about sexuality and sexual health. While this may be helpful, please consider beforehand the potential negative consequences of sharing.

Words, once spoken, can't be taken back, and there are valid reasons why some private aspects of our lives are generally kept private. So before discussing the book, groups are encouraged to consider guidelines that minimize reliance on personal disclosure. At the very least, I recommend that groups agree that there will be no disclosure of anything that reveals private information about anyone who is not present. For example, disclosing that you experienced an unintended pregnancy is disclosing information about your partner, and possibly about your child. And while discussing conversations you've had with your children or teens might be tempting to move a dialogue forward, it could also disclose information about them which they would not want shared.

Discussion Questions

My Grandmother's Douche Bag

- Brenda was only twelve years old when the author suggested she consider her childbearing capacity relative to her life dreams. Do you think it's common for an adult to encourage a young teen to think of their future in that manner? Why or why not? Do you think it's helpful? Harmful? Discuss.

- Andrea thought she might have become pregnant by a boyfriend who had $500.00, and that that would mean she'd "never have to worry about money" because he was rich. Do you think it is common for teens that are old enough to become pregnant to be so naïve?

- Within this chapter, people were vulnerable regarding becoming pregnant when they didn't want to, for a wide variety of reasons. Did any of them surprise you?

Forty-Three Minutes

- What did you think of the messages that Vivian and her colleague presented to the entire school, identifying themselves as being available to support teens in the goal of graduating without a pregnancy or STD? Do you think it is appropriate for adults in a school to bring this up? Did your school have that where you grew up?

- Darcy thought that the puddle in the bed after sex was a sign that she's infertile; why do you think she used this magical thinking instead of rational thinking? How do young people learn to rely on scientific thinking, and how can adults support that process? Can you remember a time when someone or some experience helped you learn to think rationally?

- When Ellen was unsure about how to correctly use her pills, instead of calling her doctor's office she asked a friend. The friend gave her advice that was based on misinformation. Do you think this is a common dynamic among teens in general?

- What did you think about the dialogues with the students? Did any stand out to you as being especially important, unimportant, or surprising? Do you think the teens benefitted from them? Can you think of a better way to address these varied needs?
- Do you think it is appropriate for someone other than a parent to have these conversations with teens? Why or why not?
- On the broadest level, all the dialogues Vivian had with the teens were about how to graduate without a pregnancy or STD, but within that framework, the conversations took extremely different directions. Do you agree with Vivian's assertion that addressing teens' needs for education and support should be individualized, catered to the specific teens' timely needs as they are in this chapter?

Clueless

- When Holly was so ashamed of herself for having unprotected sex, Vivian shifted the focus to praise her for admitting it and for taking immediate action in trying to get EC. Do you think it was an appropriate response? Why or why not?
- Do you think it's a helpful idea to have a weekly teen drop-in, where teens can get accurate information about sexual health from a trained professional? Do you think many communities have that? Why or why not?
- Stories in this chapter point to teen sexual behavior that is sometimes unplanned and in times and places that adults wouldn't consider appropriate. These are individual stories of individual teens in one community; do you think these behaviors are typical among teens in other communities, too? Do these behaviors impact their risk of pregnancy?
- Many of the teens in this chapter were sexually active yet they had rudimentary understanding of their reproductive systems and of correct use of contraception. Do you think this is common?
- Whose responsibility is it to ensure that teens have the information and skills they need to prevent pregnancy until they are ready to become parents?

She Wanted Miracles

- Do you agree with the author's assertion that babies and young children are generally encouraged by their parents, yet teens building intimate relationships are not? Why?
- The author suggested that fear and anger may be barriers to effective family communication regarding sexuality. Do you agree? Can you think of other reasons?
- In your community, if a parent wanted to improve their skills at com-

municating with their teen about these issues, are there resources?

- The author suggested that it's healthy for parents to encourage babies to explore their own genitals the same way they encourage them to explore other body parts, and to similarly teach them the correct names. Do you agree? Do you think it matters? Do you think most parents do this? Discuss.

- When talking with teenagers, the author suggested that there are valid reasons not to discuss some private aspects of sexuality and that removing the dialogue about sex from the dialogue about life goals and contraception can be helpful in parent/teen conversations. She also suggested that parents might benefit from shifting their own role, focusing primarily on their listening skills. What do you think of each of these suggestions?

- What did you think about Harry's mom, Judith, insisting that Harry demonstrate that he could walk into a store to buy condoms as a condition to using her car to drive his girlfriend to and from the dance?

Drunk Enough

- What do you think about the idea of sentencing white-collar criminals to work and live on minimum wage instead of sentencing them to jail or prison? Discuss.

- People in this chapter faced a variety of barriers in their attempts to prevent pregnancy. Did any of them surprise you?

- The difference between a proactive and reactive mindset was explored in this chapter. Where do you think people get these two different mindsets?

- When the caseworker asked, "Why doesn't she just go on the pill?" making it sound easy, the author claimed that for some people it's very difficult. Do you think those difficulties were exaggerated or do you agree that it was a valid claim?

Those Quiet Boyfriends

- Did any of the dialogues with young males surprise you?

- Several male teens in this chapter showed initiative in starting conversations with their female partners about preventing pregnancy. Do you think that's typical? Why or why not?

Father Knows Best???

- Were you surprised by any of the stories of family life in this chapter?

- Do you think there are teens in your community growing up in homes like those described?

- If a teen grows up in a home without parents who can provide the information and support the teen needs regarding sexuality and sexual health, whose responsibility do you think it is to provide that information, support and guidance?
- Regarding helping people break generational cycles such as teen parenting, poverty, and others, the author stated she believes that "Effective intervention *before* the conception of an unwanted pregnancy is the most efficient, effective way to create the potential for people to improve the quality of their own lives and the lives of their future offspring." Discuss.

When Baby's First Word Is "Bullshit"

- What was your response to the teen parents that were described in this chapter? Did anything surprise you?
- Becoming a mother gave Sherry a purpose to her life. Is there something else we, as a society, should or could do for girls who are not successful in school to "have a life"? Whose responsibility is it to give girls like her "a life"?
- Why do you think the prevention efforts haven't reached the teens that are least prepared to parent? What do you think would be effective ways to reach them?

Waves of Laughter

- What variables can have a greater impact on a teen's future than whether or not that teen becomes a parent?
- What did you think of the dialogue in which Vivian tried to convince Tiffany to meet with a professional sexual health educator even though Tiffany insisted she wouldn't have sex?
- Do you think there's value in having the kind of one-on-one education and support services available to teens in school and/or in the community that are outlined in this chapter? Most schools do not have an adult in that role. Why do you think that is?
- Do you know if there is anyone in that role in the high school in your community today? If not, what would happen if there were? Would it help the teens? The families? Would the community support it? Would it make a difference in the teen pregnancy rate? What, if any, problems might it create or solve?
- Do you agree that school administrators are more influenced by the vocal minority of parents who are opposed to comprehensive sexuality education in schools than the majority who favor it? Discuss.

Please Don't Bite the Nurse

- Sandy wanted more birth control pills but lacked the "simple" skills needed to get more pills in a hurry. Do you agree that this lack of skills—the essential skills needed to access the medical system—leaves some individuals more vulnerable to unintended pregnancy?

- Individuals in this chapter lacked some of the skills that are necessary to "be a patient." Did any of these stories make you think differently about what those skills are; skills that many among us take for granted? Who taught you to "be a patient"? Whose responsibility is it to teach those skills? Whose fault is it if adults lack those skills?

- Did it surprise you to learn that individuals in facilities including jails and psychiatric institutions are often discharged without a conversation about reproductive life planning? Do you think it would be appropriate or helpful if these issues were addressed? What would it take to change that? Discuss.

Think Globally, Act Globally

- Do you think it is more appropriate to label groups that work to make abortion illegal "anti-choice" or "pro-life"? Does it matter? Does the label we use affect anything?

- Who should get to decide what a group is called?

- The author suggests that we should shift the emphasis from a national dialogue regarding abortion to a national dialogue about trying to reduce the unintended pregnancy rate. What do you think about doing that? Is it a realistic idea? What might it solve? What problems might it create? Discuss.

- Did any of the information about global health surprise you? As Americans, what role (if any) do you think we should be taking to improve these outcomes? Do you think there are ways that individuals in your community can make a difference?

Afterword

- Looking back on the entire book, do you think that having read it might lead to you doing anything differently on either a personal level, professional level, or as a community member? Discuss.

- What struck you most about the book? What, if any, important messages did it have?

- Is there anything else that you want to discuss about this book?

CHAPTER NOTES

Forward

Regarding the number of school buses needed:

According to The National Center For Health Statistics, in 2009 there were approximately 717,000 pregnancies to women younger than age 20.[44]

According to information from the National Academy of Sciences, the U.S. Department of Transportation and the school transportation industry, the average school bus transports 54 student passengers.[45]

Arithmetic: 717,000 (female) + 717,000 (male) = 1,534,000 (number of teens who would ride the buses), divided by 54 = 28,740.7 buses.

My Grandmother's Douche Bag

Regarding Title X:

In the U.S., Title X is the only federal grant program dedicated solely to providing individuals with comprehensive family planning and related preventive health services. It was enacted in 1970. The U.S. Department of Health and Human Services' Office of Population Affairs (OPA) oversees the Title X program. OPA funds a network of 4,200 family planning centers. Services are provided through state, county, and local health departments, community health centers, Planned Parenthood centers, and hospital-based, school-based, faith-based, and other private nonprofits. In 2011, Title X-funded centers served approximately five million clients. Title X family planning centers help to avert an estimated one million unintended pregnancies.[46]

Forty-Three Minutes

Regarding the Fact box, see source.[47]

Regarding the failure rate of male condoms and the likelihood that they will break or fall off and that this would lead to infection:

The failure rate of male condoms with "perfect use" is only 2%, and with "typical use" it is 18%.[48]

Only about 1.5% of condoms break or slip off the penis.[49]

Regarding the likelihood that this would lead to infection, the author read numerous scientific studies regarding condom use in an attempt to document the likeliness of that happening, but none even mentioned it as a possibility.

Regarding the effectiveness of the federally funded Abstinence-only approach to sexuality education:

The Waxman Report evaluated programs which used the federal money and found that over 80% of the abstinence-only curricula used by over two thirds of SPRANS (Special Projects of Regional and National Significance) grantees in 2003 contained false, misleading, or distorted information about reproductive health, including false information about the effectiveness of contraceptives.

For the full report, go to: http://www.apha.org/apha/PDFs/HIV/The_ Waxman_Report.pdf (accessed January 16, 2016).

For more detailed information about the Federal Funding for Abstinence-Only-Until-Marriage Programs see: A History of Federal Funding for Abstinence-Only-Until-Marriage Programs from the Sexuality Information and Education Council of the United States (SIECUS) website: http://www.siecus.org/index.cfm? fuseaction=page.viewPage&pageID=1340&nodeID=1 (accessed January 16, 2016).

For Dedicated Federal Abstinence-Only-Until-Marriage Funding By Year (1982-2010) go to: http://www.nomoremoney.org/index.cfm?fuseaction=page.viewPage& pageID=1004&nodeID=5&stopRedirect=1.

See also: chapter notes (below) under "Waves of Laughter."

She Wanted Miracles

Regarding parent-child communication about sex:

"Research suggests that parents can play a critical role in their children's' decisions about sex. In fact, teens report that their parents influence their decisions about sex more than their friends, the media, or their siblings…Moreover, a majority of teens agree that it would be easier for them to postpone sexual activity and avoid teen pregnancy if they were able to have more open, honest conversations about these topics with their parents…It is important to note that while conversations about sex are helpful for teens, the overall quality of parent child relationships are even more critical for helping teens make positive decisions. Close parent-child relationships—not just discussions about sex—help protect adolescents from risky sexual behavior such as early and unprotected intercourse."[8] For more information, see source.

Regarding the components of human sexuality:

See Advocates for Youth, Circles of Sexuality, http://www.advocates foryouth.org/storage/advfy/documents/circles.pdf.

Regarding the effectiveness of latex condoms in preventing the transmission of HIV:

The following information is from the Centers for Disease Control and Prevention (CDC) Condom Effectiveness - Fact Sheet for Public Health Personnel:

"…The body of research on the effectiveness of latex condoms in preventing sexual transmission of HIV is both comprehensive and conclusive. The ability of latex condoms to prevent transmission of HIV has been scientifically established in "real-life" studies of sexually active couples as well as in laboratory studies…Laboratory studies have demonstrated that latex condoms provide an essentially impermeable barrier to particles the size of HIV. Epidemiologic studies that are conducted in real-life settings, where one partner is infected with HIV and the other partner is not, demonstrate that the consistent use of latex condoms provides a high degree of protection."[50]

Regarding the recent declines in teen pregnancy in the U.S.

"Improvements in contraceptive use have led to a drop in the risk of pregnancy among U.S. adolescents aged 15–19—and these changes also appear to be driving the recent declines in teen pregnancy rates, abortion rates and birthrates. A new analysis titled *Understanding the Decline in Adolescent Fertility in the United States, 2007–2012*, by Dr. Laura Lindberg and colleagues, estimated that improved contraceptive use accounted for the entire 28% decline in teen pregnancy risk between 2007 and 2012. The authors found significant increases in teens' use of any contraceptive method, use of multiple methods and use of highly effective methods, as well as a decline in contraceptive nonuse."

" 'There was no significant change in adolescent sexual activity during this time period,' says lead author Dr. Lindberg. 'Rather, our new data suggest that recent declines in teens' risk of pregnancy—and in their pregnancy rates—are driven by increased contraceptive use.' "[51]

Regarding the quotation from the CDC, see source.[52]

Regarding the quotation from Melinda Gates, see source.[53]

Regarding the Internet search, a Google search on August 3, 2017, for "naked people having sex" provided 10,600,000 results in 0.62 seconds.

Drunk Enough

Regarding the quotation by Bryan Stevenson, see source.[54]

Regarding the quote attributed to Eleanor Roosevelt:

The webpage http://thinkexist.com/quotation/it_takes_as_much_energy_to_wish_as_it_does_to/186924.html (accessed February 16 2015) attributes it to her. The author has unsuccessfully attempted to locate the source; according to the webpage http://www.barrypopik.com/index.php/new_york_city/entry/it_takes_as_much_energy_to_wish it has been credited to her but it is not clear if she ever said it or who originated it.

Those Quiet Boyfriends

Regarding the availability of EC by prescription and over the counter (OTC):

Plan B was approved by the FDA as a prescription drug in May, 1999. In April, 2009 the FDA announced that it may be sold OTC to women and men aged 17 and older. In the U.S. today, progestin-only EC is available on the shelf without age restrictions to women and men. Plan B one-Step, Take Action, Next Choice One-Dose, My Way or other generics can often be found in the family planning aisle. For more information about EC—including links to availability in specific locations—and for detailed history of the changing laws see source.[16] The website is operated by the Office of Population Research at Princeton University and by the Association of Reproductive Health Professionals and has no connection with any pharmaceutical companies or for-profit organization.

When Baby's First Word is "Bullshit"

The Jeopardy questions referred to are from the show aired March 11, 2003: http://www.j-archive.com/showgame.php?game_id=2804.

Waves of Laughter

Regarding teen pregnancy rates within New York State by county:

The New York State Department of Health website provides vital statistics at: https://www.health.ny.gov/statistics/vital_statistics/2012/ table30.htm (accessed October 14, 2016).

Regarding the U.S. government funded Abstinence-Only education programs:

See chapter notes (above) under the heading Forty-Three Minutes. In addition, below are excerpts from a review of the literature.

The purpose of the review was "To review recent literature on medical accuracy, program effectiveness, and ethical concerns related to abstinence-only policies for adolescent sexuality education." Findings included "The federal government invests over 175 million dollars annually in 'abstinence-only-until-marriage' programs. These programs are required to withhold information on contraception and condom use, except for information on failure rates. Abstinence-only curricula have been found to contain scientifically inaccurate information, distorting data on topics such as condom efficacy, and promote gender stereotypes. An independent evaluation of the federal program, several systematic reviews, and cohort data from population-based surveys find little evidence of efficacy and evidence of possible harm. In contrast, comprehensive sexuality education programs have been found to help teens delay initiation of intercourse and reduce sexual risk behaviors. Abstinence-only policies violate the human rights of adolescents because they withhold potentially life-saving information on HIV and other sexually transmitted infections."

In summary, the authors stated, "Federal support of abstinence-only as an approach to adolescent sexuality education is of much concern due to medical inaccuracies, lack of effectiveness, and the withholding and distorting of health information."[55]

Regarding the quotation from the review of the literature related to abstinence-only education, see source.[55]

Regarding public support of comprehensive sex education that includes messages about abstinence *and* provides young people with information about contraception for the prevention of teen pregnancy, HIV/AIDS, and other STIs, in addition to the majority of parents supporting it, leading public health and medical professional organizations support it. These include: American Medical Association, American Academy of Pediatrics, American Psychological Association, American College of Obstetricians and Gynecologists, The Institute of Medicine, Society of Adolescent Medicine, American Nurses Association, and the American Public Health Association.[56]

Please Don't Bite the Nurse

For more information for professionals about the "Teach Back" technique, go to: *In Other Words...Confirming Understanding With the Teach-Back Technique,* by Helen Osborne, M.Ed., OTR/L, President of Health Literacy Consulting: http://healthliteracy.com/2007/11/20/teach-back/.

Think Globally, Act Globally

Regarding the quotation about the percent of women who will have an abortion by age 45, see source.[57]

Regarding the quotation from the Dalai Lama, see source.[58]

Regarding the global unmet need for family planning, according to the World Health Organization:

"Promotion of family planning—and ensuring access to preferred contraceptive methods for women and couples—is essential to securing the well-being and autonomy of women, while supporting the health and development of communities."[39]

Regarding the quote from the World Health Organization about the safety of abortion relative to its legality, the quote was taken from the WHO website Journal Paper *Unsafe Abortion: The Preventable Pandemic* by David A Grimes, Janie Benson, Susheela Singh, Mariana Romero, Bela Ganatra, Friday E Okonofua, Iqbal H Shah. It is identified there as a pre-print copy of a paper published in the journal *The Lancet Sexual and Reproductive Health Series,* October 2006.

Regarding access to abortion services in the U.S.:

The number of U.S. abortion providers declined 3% between 2011 and 2014, and the number of clinics providing abortion services declined 6%. Ninety percent of all U.S. counties lacked an abortion clinic in 2014; 39% of women live in those counties.

The number of states considered hostile to abortion skyrocketed between 2000 and 2016. In 2000, 13 states were considered hostile to abortion rights. By 2016, the number of hostile states increased to 27.

More than half of U.S. women of reproductive age live in states that are hostile to abortion rights.[32]

Regarding the Annual Expenditures needed to meet contraceptive needs compared with sugary soft drinks:

According to The Alan Guttmacher Institute, if all unmet need for modern contraception were satisfied, unintended pregnancies would drop by 70%, from 74 million to 22 million per year; and unsafe abortions would decline by 74%, from 20 million to 5.1 million. Meeting all women's needs for modern contraception in the developing world would cost $9.4 billion annually, an increase of $5.3 billion.[59]

Americans spend $14.3 billion annually on sugary soft drinks.[60]

To view the video of the protesters, go to: YouTube, Libertyville Abortion Demonstration.

Recommended Resources

The following resources are recommended by the author. She does this as an individual sharing personal preferences, not as a representative of any agency or group. She is not responsible for the accuracy or content of information contained in these sites.

For parents and mentors who want additional information about teen sexuality and family communication, the following organizations' websites may be helpful:

- Power to Decide (formerly the National Campaign to Prevent Teen and Unplanned Pregnancy):
  https://powertodecide.org/
  https://powertodecide.org/what-we-do/information/resource-library/ten-tips-for-parents.

- Advocates For Youth, Parents' Sex Ed Center:
  http://www.advocatesforyouth.org/parents-sex-ed-center-home.

- American Sexual Health Association, Inc.:
  http://www.iwannaknow.org/teens/index.html.

- Centers For Disease Control and Prevention, Teen Pregnancy-Reproductive Health-Parent and Guardian Resources:
  http://www.cdc.gov/teenpregnancy/parents.htm.

- Planned Parenthood Federation of America Inc., Tools for Parents:
  http://www.plannedparenthood.org/parents.

- American Academy of Pediatrics: http://www.healthy children.org/English/ages-stages/teen/dating-sex/Pages/default.aspx.

- The Mayo Clinic: http://www.mayoclinic.org/healthy-lifestyle/sexual-health/in-depth/sex-education/art-20044034.

For teen-friendly, accurate information about sexuality and reproductive health, try these websites:

- Bedsider: https://bedsider.org.

- Sex, Etc: http://sexetc.org.

- Planned Parenthood: https://www.plannedparenthood.org.

- Go Ask Alice! From Columbia University, New York City: http://www.goaskalice.columbia.edu.

For help talking about abortion:

- Abortion Conversation Project, Inc.: http://www.abortionconversation.com.

For information about reproductive justice:

- Religious Coalition for Reproductive Choice: http://rcrc.org.

For information regarding U.S. and worldwide statistics related to a wide range of subjects regarding reproductive health, the following organizations are recommended:

- The World Health Organization: http://www.who.int/en/.

- The Alan Guttmacher Institute: https://www.guttmacher.org.

For ongoing, evidence-based news, analysis, commentary, and investigative reporting on issues of sexual and reproductive health, rights, and justice:

- Rewire: https://rewire.news.

For more information regarding sexual orientation, the following organizations are recommended:

- GLSEN, Inc., The Gay, Lesbian & Straight Education Network. http://www.glsen.org/.

- PFLAG, Parents, Families and Friends of Lesbians and Gays, Inc. http://community.pflag.org/Page.aspx?pid=194&srcid=-2.

For more information regarding U.S. teens' sexual activity, contraception, and pregnancy, note that The Alan Guttmacher Institute updates their fact sheets regularly. For the most current information, see:

- Fact Sheet: American Teens' Sexual and Reproductive Health, The Alan Guttmacher Institute: https://www.guttmacher.org/sites/default/files/factsheet/fb-atsrh.pdf.

For more information regarding the Positive Youth Development model for engaging youth in creating communities in which youth postpone parenting until they are prepared, the following are resources:

- Principles of Youth Development, ACT for Youth Center of Excellence: http://www.actforyouth.net/youth_development/development/.

- Guiding Principles for Sexual Health Education for Young People, New York State Department of Health: http://planaheadnewyork.com/publications/0206/guiding_principles.htm.

- Youth Development: Strengthening Prevention Strategies by Susan Pagliaro and Kent Klindera, Advocates for Youth, Revised edition, August 2001: http://www.advocatesforyouth.org/storage/advfy/documents/ythdevelop.pdf.

For information regarding sexuality education:

- The Sexuality Information and Education Council of the United States (SIECUS): SIECUS.org.

For anyone who wants to advocate for comprehensive sexuality education programs, SIECUS's community action kit provides a helpful tool: http://www.communityactionkit.org/index.cfm?pageid=885.

For more information about Emergency Contraception (EC), including the changing laws regarding over the counter sales: The Emergency Contraception Website and associated Hotline (1-888-NOT-2-LATE) operated by the Office of Population Research at Princeton University and by the Association of Reproductive Health Professionals: http://ec.princeton.edu/ndex.htm.

SOURCES

1 U.S. Department of Health and Human Services, Office of Population Affairs, *Title X Family Planning* (accessed October 15, 2017), http://www.hhs.gov/opa/title-x-family-planning/index.html.

2 William D. Mosher, Jo Jones, and Joyce C. Abma, "Intended and Unintended Births in the United States: 1982–2010*," National Health Statistics Reports*, no. 55 (Hyattsville, MD: National Center for Health Statistics, July 2012) (accessed August 3, 2017), http://www.cdc.gov/nchs/data/nhsr/nhsr055.pdf.

3 BrainyQuote (accessed August 3, 2017), http://www.brainyquote.com/quotes/quotes/m/mahatmagan150724.html.

4 "Teen Pregnancy Rates Declined In Many Countries Between The Mid-1990s and 2011," (Washington, DC: Guttmacher Institute, January 2015) (accessed August 3, 2017), https://www.guttmacher.org/news-release/2015/teen-pregnancy-rates-declined-many-countries-between-mid-1990s-and-2011.

5 Saturday Night Live, Season 5, 1979 (disc 5 Netflix).

6 P. J. O'Rourke, (accessed August 3, 2017), goodreads.com.

7 *Parent-Child Communication: Promoting Sexually Healthy Youth* (Washington, DC: Advocates For Youth, 2008)*,* (accessed August 3, 2017), http://www.advocatesforyouth.org/the-facts-parent-child-communication.

8 Katherine Suellentrop, *Science Says #25: Parent-Child Communication about Sex and Related Topics* (Washington, DC: The National Campaign to Prevent Teen and Unplanned Pregnancy, May 2006), (accessed August 3, 2017), https://thenationalcampaign.org/resource/science-says-25.

9 "Fact sheet: American Teens' Sexual and Reproductive Health," (Washington, DC: Guttmacher Institute, September 2016), (accessed August 3, 2017), https://www.guttmacher.org/sites/default/files/factsheet/fb-atsrh.pdf.

10 Martin Luther King Jr., "Letter from Birmingham Jail," (accessed August 4, 2017), https://www.goodreads.com/work/quotes/197294-letter-from-birmingham-jail.

11 Barbara Ehrenreich, *Nickel and Dimed: On (Not) Getting By in America* (New York: Holt, 2008), pp. 223–226.

12 U.S. Census Bureau, "Census 2000 Summary File 3, Matrices P37 and PCT25" (accessed September 28, 2016), http://factfinder.census.gov/faces/tableservices/jsf/pages/productview.xhtml?src=CF.

13 *KWIC Indicator: Children Receiving Free or Reduced-price School Lunch—Public Schools,* (New York State Council on Children & Families, Kids' Well-being Indicators Clearinghouse) (accessed August 3, 2017), http://www.nyskwic.org/get_data/indicator_profile.cfm?subIndicatorID=52.

14 Mark Twain, *Following the Equator: A Journey Around the World,* vol. 2 (New York: Harper and Brothers, 1897), p. 173.

15 Goodreads, goodreads.com/quotes/tag/boys?page=2.

[16] "History of Plan B OTC," *The Emergency Contraception Website* (Princeton, NJ: Office of Population Research, 2017) (accessed August 3, 2017), http://ec.princeton.edu/pills/planbhistory.html.

[17] Brainyquote; http://www.brainyquote.com/quotes/authors/g/groucho_marx_2.html #p1CfSfrsgieqd64u.99.

[18] Joycelyn Elders and David Chanoff, *From Sharecropper's Daughter to Surgeon General of the United States of America* (New York: William Morrow and Company, 1996), p. 337.

[19] Joyce A. Martin et al., *Births: Final data for 2004* (Hyattsville, MD: National Center for Health Statistics. 2006) (accessed September 29, 2016), http://www.cdc.gov/nchs/data/nvsr/nvsr52/nvsr52_10.pdf.

[20] *Briefly: Effective Planning for Child Welfare Leaders to Help Prevent Teen Pregnancy*, (Washington, DC: The National Campaign to Prevent Teen and Unplanned Pregnancy, 2010) (accessed August 3, 2017), http://thenationalcampaign.org/resource/briefly-effective-planning-child-welfare-leaders-help-prevent-teen-pregnancy.

[21] *Why it Matters: Teen Pregnancy and Overall Child Well-being,* (Washington, DC: The National Campaign to Prevent Teen Pregnancy, 2007) (accessed August 3, 2017), http://thenationalcampaign.org/resource/why-it-matters-teen-pregnancy-and-overall-child-wellbeing.

[22] Donald Winnicott, *The Family and Individual Development* (New York: Basic Books, 1966).

[23] *Teen Birth Rates: How Does the United States Compare?* (Washington, DC: The National Campaign to Prevent Teen and Unplanned Pregnancy, 2014) (accessed August 3, 2017), https://thenationalcampaign.org/resource/fast-facts-how-does-united-states-compare.

[24] "Fact Sheet: American Teens' Sexual and Reproductive Health," (Washington, DC, Guttmacher Institute, September, 2016) (accessed August 3, 2017), https://www.guttmacher.org/sites/default/files/factsheet/fb-atsrh.pdf.

[25] *A History of Federal Funding for Abstinence-Only-Until-Marriage Programs,* (Sexuality Information and Education Council of the United States; 2010) (accessed August 3, 2017), http://www.siecus.org/index.cfm?fuseaction=page.viewPage& pageID=1340&nodeID=1.

[26] Ibid.

[27] Ibid.

[28] "Fact Sheet: On Our Side: Public Support for Comprehensive Sexuality Education," (NY and Washington, DC: SIECUS, 2010) (accessed August 3, 2017), http://www.siecus.org/index.cfm?fuseaction=Page.ViewPage&PageID=1197.

[29] "Sexual Risk Behaviors among U.S. High School Students, Trends from the National Risk Behavior Survey," (Atlanta, GA: Centers for Disease Control and Prevention, July 2014) (accessed June 12, 2017), https://www.cdc.gov/nchhstp/newsroom/docs/factsheets/yrbs-fact-sheet-final-508.pdf.

[30] L. B. Finer and S. K. Henshaw, *Disparities in Rates of Unintended Pregnancy In the United States, 1994 and 2001, Perspectives on Sexual and Reproductive Health, 2006,* vol. 38, no. 2, June 2006, pp. 90–96 (accessed October 12, 2016), http://onlinelibrary.wiley.com/doi/10.1363/3809006/epdf.

[31] "About Alan F. Guttmacher," (Washington, DC: Guttmacher Institute), (accessed August 3, 2017), https://www.guttmacher.org/who-was-alan-guttmacher.

32 "Fact Sheet: Induced Abortion in the United States," (Washington, DC: Guttmacher Institute, January 2017) (accessed August 3, 2017), https://www.gutt macher.org/fact-sheet/induced-abortion-united-states.

33 "Children: Reducing Mortality, Fact Sheet N⁰-178," (World Health Organization, updated September 2016) (accessed August 3, 2017), http://www.who.int/ mediacentre/factsheets/fs178/en/#.

34 "Global Health Observatory (GHO) Data, Maternal and Reproductive Health," (World Health Organization, 2017) (accessed August 3, 2017), http://www.who.int/ gho/maternal_health/en/.

35 "Restrictive Laws Do Not Stop Women From Having Abortions," (Washington, DC: Guttmacher Institute Infographic, May 2016) (accessed August 3, 2017), https://www.guttmacher.org/infographic/2016/restrictive-laws-do-not-stop-women-having-abortions.

36 "Fact Sheet: Preventing unsafe abortion," (World Health Organization, updated 2017), (accessed August 3, 2017), http://www.who.int/mediacentre/factsheets/fs388/en/.

37 Nicholas D. Kristof and Sheryl WuDunn, *Half The Sky: Turning Oppression into Opportunity for Women Worldwide,* (New York: Vintage Books, 2009), p. 98.

38 Ibid.

39 "Family Planning Fact Sheet no 351," (World Health Organization, updated May 2015) (accessed August 4, 2017), http://www.who.int/mediacentre/factsheets/fs351/en/.

40 Melissa S. Kearney and Phillip B. Levine, *Media Influences on Social Outcomes: The Impact of MTV's 16 and Pregnant on Teen Childbearing,* (Cambridge, MA: National Bureau of Economic Research, January 2014) (accessed October 15, 2016), http://www.nber.org/papers/w19795.

41 *Let's put birth control back on the agenda/Melinda Gates,* (YouTube, April 2012) (accessed February 17, 2015), https://www.youtube.com/watch?v=2BOTS9GAjc4.

42 Kay Johnson, MPH, et al., *Recommendations to Improve Preconception Health and Health Care --- United States, A Report of the CDC/ATSDR Preconception Care Work Group and the Select Panel on Preconception Care,* (Atlanta, GA: Centers for Disease Control and Prevention, April 2006) (accessed October 15, 2016), http://www.cdc.gov/mmwr/preview/mmwrhtml/rr5506a1.htm.

43 Mahatma Gandhi, *Notable Quotes* (accessed October 21, 2016), http://www.notable-quotes.com/g/gandhi_mahatma.html.

44 Sally C. Curtin, et al., "Pregnancy Rates for U.S. Women Continue to Drop," NCHS Data Brief #136, (Atlanta, GA: Centers for Disease Control and Prevention, December 2013) (accessed October 12, 2016), http://www.cdc.gov/nchs/data/data briefs/db136.pdf.

45 *Safe Routes to School National Partnership,* (Oakland, CA: 2015) (accessed August 3, 2017), http://saferoutespartnership.org/sites/default/files/pdf/school_bus_ cuts_national_stats_FINAL.pdf.

46 *Title X Family Planning,* (Washington, DC: U.S. Department of Health and Human Services, Office of Population Affairs, May 2014) (accessed September 16, 2016), http://www.hhs.gov/opa/title-x-family-planning/index.html.

47 *Unintended Pregnancy in the United States* (Washington, DC: Guttmacher Institute, September 2016) (accessed August 3, 2017), https://www.guttmacher.org/fact-sheet/unintended-pregnancy-united-states.

[48] Robert A. Hatcher, MD, MPH, et al., *Contraceptive Technology,* 20th revised edition, (NY: Ardent Media, Inc., 2011), p. 50.

[49] Ibid., p. 784.

[50] "Condoms and STDs - Fact Sheet for Public Health Personnel," (Atlanta, GA: Centers for Disease Control and Prevention) (accessed August 5, 2017), https://www.cdc.gov/condomeffectiveness/docs/condoms_and_stds.pdf.

[51] "Declines in Teen Pregnancy Risk Entirely Driven by Improved Contraceptive Use," (Washington, DC: Guttmacher Institute, August 2016) (accessed August 5, 2017), https://www.guttmacher.org/news-release/2016/declines-teen-pregnancy-risk-entirely-driven-improved-contraceptive-use.

[52] *Condom Effectiveness* (Atantla, GA: Centers for Disease Control and Prevention), (accessed August 3, 2017), http://www.cdc.gov/condomeffectiveness.

[53] *Condom Efficacy and Use* (Washington, DC: Advocates for Youth), (accessed August 3, 2017), http://www.advocatesforyouth.org/condom-efficacy-and-use-home.

[54] Bryan Stevenson, *Just Mercy,* (NY: Spiegel & Graw, 2015), p. 18.

[55] M. A. Ott and J. S. Santelli, *Abstract from article from Current Opinion in Obstetrics & Gynecology* (PubMed.gov, US National Library of Medicine, National Institutes of Health 2007, Oct; 19(5): pp. 446-52) (accessed September 15, 2016), http://www.ncbi.nlm.nih.gov/pubmed/17885460.

[56] "What the Research Says... Comprehensive Sex Education SIECUS Fact Sheet," (Sexuality Information and Education Council of the United States, October 2009) (accessed October 12, 2016), http://www.siecus.org/_data/global/images/What%20the%20Research%20Says-CSE-1.pdf.

[57] "Fact Sheet: Unintended Pregnancy in the United States," (Washington, DC: Guttmacher Institute, September, 2016) (accessed August 3, 2017), http://www.guttmacher.org/pubs/FB-Unintended-Pregnancy-US.html.

[58] Brainyquote; accessed February 16, 2015, http://www.brainyquote.com/quotes/quotes/d/dalailama378036.html.

[59] "Fact Sheet: Adding It Up: Investing in Sexual and Reproductive Health," (Washington, DC: Guttmacher Institute, December 2014) (accessed September 16, 2016), https://www.guttmacher.org/pubs/FB-AddingItUp2014.html.

[60] "Rethink your drink," (Kaiser Permanente, Reviewed April 2016) (accessed September 28, 2016), https://healthy.kaiserpermanente.org/health/care/!ut/p/c4/FcpBDoMgEEDRs3iAyYhWsO6wyhVaupuQCZIIGkL0-mr-7uXjH-8SHcFTCVuiFX9oHafCeTg5-KXg91n2TD4S2rSBI7fwY5RLcCuj1bJpjWleIE3_BiHmGsZJS_go1YlajVpOM-4x9qeuqgt3zERA/.

ABOUT THE AUTHOR

Vivian Peters worked as an Outreach Educator for her local Planned Parenthood in a remote, rural area of New York State where poverty was prevalent and where teen parenting and large families were the norm.

Prior to becoming a sexual health educator, she was a designer/craftsperson working with clay. She and her husband worked as partners, and for twenty years they sold their work to hundreds of galleries in almost every state in the U.S. including Alaska and Hawaii, and in the Virgin Islands and Japan.

During those years, she volunteered as a mentor to several girls: some graduated without becoming a parent and one did not. When she saw the impact of the presence or absence of effective intervention—talking effectively with individual teens about sex and birth control in a timely fashion—it was so striking to her that it motivated her to change careers.

For fifteen years, she worked with individual teens and adults through two unique community partnerships at her local Planned Parenthood. She became passionate about trying to change the way we talk (and don't talk!) about sex. She believes in the power of storytelling; the impact of the interventions she provided was so striking to her that it motivated her to write this book.

She holds a Bachelor of Arts Degree from Kirkland College and a Master of Fine Arts Degree from Rochester Institute of Technology's School for American Crafts.

She can be contacted at <u>Vivian@VivianPetersOops.com</u>.

Note: To protect the identity of the people she served, all names are fictitious, including the author's pen name Vivian Peters.

Made in the USA
Columbia, SC
28 June 2018